ROBOT MANIPULATORS: MATHEMATICS, PROGRAMMING, AND CONTROL

The MIT Press Series in Artificial Intelligence

Artificial Intelligence: An MIT Perspective, Volume I: Expert Problem Solving, Natural Language Understanding, Intelligent Computer Coaches, Representation and Learning edited by Patrick Henry Winston and Richard Henry Brown, 1979

Artificial Intelligence: An MIT Perspective, Volume II: Understanding Vision, Manipulation, Computer Design, Symbol Manipulation edited by Patrick Henry Winston and Richard Henry Brown, 1979

NETL: A System for Representing and Using Real-World Knowledge by Scott Fahlman, 1979

The Interpretation of Visual Motion by Shimon Ullman, 1979

A Theory of Syntactic Recognition for Natural Language by Mitchell P. Marcus, 1980

Turtle Geometry: The Computer as a Medium for Exploring Mathematics by Harold Abelson and Andrea diSessa, 1981

From Images to Surfaces: A Computational Study of the Human Early Visual System by William Eric Leifur Grimson, 1981

Robot Manipulators: Mathematics, Programming and Control by Richard P. Paul, 1981

ROBOT MANIPULATORS: MATHEMATICS, PROGRAMMING, AND CONTROL

The Computer Control of Robot Manipulators

Richard P. Paul

The MIT Press
Cambridge, Massachusetts and London, England

PUBLISHER'S NOTE

This format is intended to reduce the cost of publishing certain works in book form and to shorten the gap between editorial preparation and final publication. The time and expense of detailed editing and composition in print have been avoided by photographing the text of this book directly from the author's computer printout.

Fourth printing, December 1982
Third printing, August 1982
Second printing, April 1982

Printed in the United States of America.

Library of Congress Cataloging in Publication Data

Paul, Richard P.
Robot manipulators.

(The MIT Press series in artificial intelligence)
Bibliography: p.
Includes index.
1. Robots, Industrial. 2. Manipulators (Mechanism) I. Title. II. Series.
TS191.8.P38 629.8'92 81-13689
ISBN 0-262-16082-X AACR2

CONTENTS

Preface ix

Introduction 1

Chapter 1
Homogeneous Transformations 9

Chapter 2
Kinematic Equations 41

Chapter 3
Solving Kinematic Equations 65

Chapter 4
Differential Relationships 85

Chapter 5
Motion Trajectories 119

Chapter 6
Dynamics 157

Chapter 7
Control 197

Chapter 8
Static Forces 217

Chapter 9
Compliance 231

Chapter 10
Programming 245

Index 273

SERIES FOREWORD

Artificial intelligence is the study of intelligence using the ideas and methods of computation. Unfortunately, a definition of intelligence seems impossible at the moment because intelligence appears to be an amalgam of so many information-processing and information-representation abilities.

Of course psychology, philosophy, linguistics, and related disciplines offer various perspectives and methodologies for studying intelligence. For the most part, however, the theories proposed in these fields are too incomplete and too vaguely stated to be realized in computational terms. Something more is needed, even though valuable ideas, relationships, and constraints can be gleaned from traditional studies of what are, after all, impressive existence proofs that intelligence is in fact possible.

Artificial intelligence offers a new perspective and a new methodology. Its central goal is to make computers intelligent, both to make them more useful and to understand the principles that make intelligence possible. That intelligent computers will be extremely useful is obvious. The more profound point is that artificial intelligence aims to understand intelligence using the ideas and methods of computation, thus offering a radically new and different basis for theory formation. Most of the people doing artificial intelligence believe that these theories will apply to any intelligent information processor, whether biological or solid state.

There are side effects that deserve attention, too. Any program that will successfully model even a small part of intelligence will be inherently massive and complex. Consequently, artificial intelligence continually confronts the limits of computer science technology. The problems encountered have been hard enough and interesting enough to seduce artificial intelligence people into working on them with enthusiasm. It is natural, then, that there has been a steady flow of ideas from artificial intelligence to computer science, and the flow shows no sign of abating.

The purpose of this MIT Press Series in Artificial Intelligence is to provide people in many areas, both professionals and students, with timely, detailed information about what is happening on the frontiers in research centers all over the world.

Patrick Henry Winston
Mike Brady

PREFACE

This book on robot manipulators brings together theories from a number of fields: computer graphics, kinematics, dynamics, control, and programming. The book is written in the style of a text and has been used to teach robotics to graduate and undergraduate students in engineering and computer science. The field of robotics is new and interdisciplinary, with an almost constant flow of theories into robotics from many areas. This book presents only one theory in each area. These theories are selected because they can be brought together to provide a working and consistent approach to the overall problem of robot manipulator control. Most of the material in the book is at the level of trigonometry but is conceptually new and different. The chapter on dynamics assumes that the student is prepared to accept the Lagrangian formulation of dynamics. The chapter on control makes use of the Laplace transformation, and the final chapter on programming assumes a knowledge of PASCAL.

This work represents ten years experience in robotics; most of the material presented has been experimentally tested and verified and is in use today running robot manipulators. Some material clarifies past systems or simplifies and extends earlier theories. All the theory is developed with a digital computer implementation in mind. Computing speed, roundoff, and memory requirements have guided the selection of many of the theoretical approaches. With the advent of VLSI, however, more computationally intensive approaches may be appropriate.

The book is based on course notes developed at Purdue University over the last four years and has been completed using the facilities of the Massachusetts Institute of Technology Artificial Intelligence Laboratory. The camera-ready copy was produced using Knuth's TEX system. Much of the theory presented in the book was developed at Stanford University Artificial Intelligence Laboratory, and the author wishes to thank John McCarthy and Jerome Feldman, who provided him with the possibility of performing the research. The author also wishes to thank Antal Bejczy, upon whose work the dynamics chapter is based, and Bruce Shimano, who has been part of the development of much of the theory. The support of Mike Brady and Eric Grimson made the final transition into print a pleasant experience. John Birk, Mike Brady, William Fisher, Tomas Lozano-Perez, Johnson Luh, William Perzley, and Bruce Shimano helped by reading parts of the manuscript and correcting many errors; the author is entirely responsible for any that remain. Mel Paul assisted with revisions and editorial changes.

This material is based partially upon research supported by the National Science Foundation under Grant Numbers APR77-14533, APR75-13074, and APR74-01390. Any opinions, findings, and conclusions or recommendations expressed in this publication are those of the author and do not necessarily reflect the views of the National Science Foundation.

ROBOT MANIPULATORS: MATHEMATICS, PROGRAMMING, AND CONTROL

INTRODUCTION

This book is about industrial robot manipulators, their programming and their interaction with sensors. We will cover robot manipulator programming and control in detail but will treat external sensors, such as vision, only in so far as they interact with the manipulator. In order to gain an overall understanding of the topics to be addressed in later chapters, let us first look at the origins of industrial robots and the problems that arose as their capabilities were extended.

The present day industrial robot had its origins in both the teleoperator and the numerically controlled machine tool. The teleoperator, or *telecheric*, is a device to allow an operator to perform a task at a distance. The numerically controlled machine tool shapes metal automatically, based on digitally encoded cutting data.

The teleoperator was developed during the second world war to handle radioactive materials [Goertz]. An operator was separated from a radioactive task by a concrete wall with one or more viewing ports through which the task could be observed. The teleoperator was to substitute for the operator's hands; it consisted of a pair of tongs on the inside (the slave), and two handles on the outside (the master). Both tongs and handles were connected together by six degree of freedom mechanisms to provide for the arbitrary positioning and orienting of the master and slave. The mechanism was provided to control the slave in order to replicate the motion of the master.

In 1947, the first servoed electric-powered teleoperator was developed. The slave was servo-controlled to follow the position of the master. No force information was available to the operator, and tasks requiring that parts be brought into contact were difficult to perform, even though the operator could view the task. Teleoperator tasks are well described by Goertz: "The general-purpose manipulator may be used for moving objects, moving levers or knobs, assembling parts, and manipulating wrenches. In all these operations the manipulator must come into physical contact with the object before the desired force and moment can be made on it. A collision occurs when the manipulator makes this contact. General-purpose manipulation consists essentially of a series of collisions with unwanted forces, the application of wanted forces, and the application of desired motions. The collision forces should be low, and any other unwanted forces should also be small." [Goertz]

In 1948, one year after the position-controlled teleoperator was introduced, a new teleoperator system was developed in which the force exerted by the tongs could be relayed to the operator by backdriving the master; the operator could once again feel what was going on.

In 1949, faced with the need to procure advanced aircraft whose parts were designed to be machined rather than riveted, the Air Force sponsored research in the development of a numerically controlled milling machine [Rosenberg]. This research was to combine sophisticated servo system expertise with the newly developing digital computer techniques. The pattern to be cut was stored in digital form on a punched tape and then a servo-controlled milling machine cut the metal. The MIT Radiation Laboratory demonstrated such a machine in 1953.

In the 1960's, George Devol demonstrated what was to become the first Unimate industrial robot [Engelberger], a device combining the articulated linkage of the teleoperator with the servoed axes of the numerically controlled milling machine. The industrial robot could be taught to perform any simple job by driving it by hand through the sequence of task positions, which were recorded in digital memory. Task execution consisted in replaying these positions by servoing the individual joint axes of the the robot. Task interaction was limited to opening and closing of the tongs or end effector, and to signaling external equipment or waiting for a synchronizing signal. The industrial robot was ideal for pick and place jobs such as unloading a diecasting machine. The part would appear in a precise position, defined with respect to the robot; it would be grasped, moved out of the die, and dropped on a conveyor. The success of the industrial robot, like the numerically controlled (NC) milling machine, relied on precise, repeatable digital servo loops. There was no interaction between the robot and its work. If the diecast machine were moved, the robot could in no way adapt to the new position, any more than an NC milling machine could successfully cut a part if the stock were arbitrarily relocated during cutting. If the diecasting machine were moved, the robot could, however, be retaught. The success of the industrial robot lay in its application to jobs in which task positions were absolutely defined, and in its reliability and positioning repeatability in lieu of adaptation.

Another development took place in MIT's Lincoln Laboratory in 1961 [Ernst]. A teleoperator slave arm, equipped with touch sensors, was connected to a computer. In this case, touch feedback from the tongs, not absolute position, guided the robot in the performance of the task. Although the absolute position of the hand in space could be obtained, this approach was not used, since humans do not perform the trigonometric calculations necessary to obtain a hand position. Instead, tasks were defined as a sequence of touch-defined states to be attained. The lack of any global idea of the position of objects limited this robot as much as the complete lack of task information limited the position-controlled industrial robot.

In 1963 Roberts [Roberts63] demonstrated the feasibility of processing a digitized halftone picture of a scene to obtain a mathematical description of the block-like objects which comprised the scene, expressing their location and orientation by homogeneous coordinate transformations [Roberts65]. This work was important for two reasons: it demonstrated that objects could be identified and located in a digitized halftone image, and it introduced homogeneous transformations as a suitable data structure for the description of the relative position and orientation between objects. If the relative position and orientation between objects is represented by homogeneous transformations, the operation of matrix multiplication of the transformations establishes the overall relationship between objects. In Chapter 1 we introduce homogeneous transformations, which we use throughout the book to describe both position and orientation between objects and between objects and the manipulator.

Touch feedback, because of its slow, groping nature, was dropped in favor of vision as an input mechanism. By 1967, a computer equipped with a television camera as an input mechanism could, in real time, identify objects and their location [Wichman]. The manipulator, stripped of its touch sensors, relied on position-servoed joint axes. Homogeneous transformations, however, expressed the position and orientation of the end effector in Cartesian coordinates, not as the angles between a series of unorthogonal manipulator joints. Pieper applied the theories of closed-link chains to obtain a solution to this problem, and the manipulator could then be commanded to move to Cartesian positions in the workspace [Pieper]. In Chapter 2 we develop the methods of obtaining the Cartesian coordinate position and orientation of the end effector for any manipulator, given the joint coordinates as input. The position and orientation are represented by a homogeneous transformation. In Chapter 3 we investigate the inverse problem of obtaining the joint coordinates for a manipulator given the Cartesian coordinate description of the end effector. This problem is difficult, requires intuition, and can be solved analytically for only a limited number of simple manipulators. Fortunately, most commercially available manipulators are of this form and are solvable (see Figures 3.2, 4.3, 6.2, and 9.1).

By 1970, a camera- and arm-equipped computer could play real-world games and the "instant insanity" puzzle was successfully solved at Stanford University [Feldman]. In this puzzle, four cubes with different colored faces must be stacked so that no identical colors appear on any side of the stack. At MIT, a block structure could be observed and copied. In Japan, research led to a hand-eye system which could assemble block structures when presented with an assembly drawing. The drawing was first viewed, the materials surveyed, and then the required structure built [Ejiri]. Potential applications of this research appeared to be in deep space probes and in factory automation. Corresponding to these goals, vision research was directed to the more difficult task of identifying castings and rocks, and manipulation research was directed to the assembly of objects.

The manipulator, working in relationship with a vision sensor, is frequently required to make small motions of accommodation. In Chapter 4 we consider the differential relationships between objects and the manipulator required to make these motions. When working in cluttered environments, such as described above, it is no longer sufficient to move the manipulator directly from position to position; the concept of trajectories was therefore developed. Chapter 5 develops a structural task description, in terms of homogeneous transformations, and then develops the theory for the two basic forms of motion trajectories, joint and Cartesian. With the introduction of trajectories, the simple point-to-point servos used to control manipulators were no longer adequate. Chapter 6 develops the dynamics of manipulators which forms the basis for the discussion of control in Chapter 7. The dynamics of manipulators is complicated: the main problem is to identify those terms which are important in controlling the manipulator. We employ Lagrangian mechanics to obtain the dynamics equations and then, based on the differential relationships developed in Chapter 4, simplify the resulting equations in order to obtain the key control equations in symbolic form. The chapter on control employs classical methods in an attempt to give the reader insight into the overall problem. The control of any particular manipulator is always a unique problem and general principles act only as a guide.

Although vision was excellent for locating parts relative to the manipulator, it was no of help in putting parts together. What was needed was force feedback, which, as described above, had been added to teleoperators only one year after the purely position-controlled system had been introduced. Inoue, in Japan, demonstrated a manipulator turning a crank [Inoue]. This was achieved by driving the appropriate manipulator joints at constant torque, in place of the usual position servo control of the joint axes. At Stanford University, Inoue's approach was developed into a system in which manipulator joints were automatically selected by the computer and force-servoed, rather than position-servoed, in response to instructions specifying directions of compliance in Cartesian coordinates [Paul72]. In Chapter 8 we investigate the relationships between forces and torques in various coordinate frames and manipulator joint torques. Chapter 9 is devoted to a discussion of providing compliance necessary in assembly by the method of matching joints to degrees of freedom [Shimano]. Using this approach, a language called WAVE was developed at Stanford University in which a task could be specified symbolically in Cartesian coordinates together with necessary force compliances and gripper commands [Paul77a]. In 1972, a water pump was assembled as a demonstration of this approach [Bolles]. The WAVE system was important in so far as it brought together for the first time force, touch, vision, and position feedback and related them to one another in a world model that represented data in terms of homogeneous transformations.

While these developments have been taking place in laboratories, the industrial robot industry has increasingly relied on the precise control of motion and has tried to improve the economics of the position-controlled robot by increasing its speed of operation. In order to extend the range of possible tasks of these robots, increasing attention must be given to the design of tools. The first computer-controlled industrial robot was developed by Cincinnati Milacron [Hohn]. This robot was able to interact with a moving conveyor whose position was sensed by a digital encoder. The computer was used to provide for the coordinate transformations between fixed and moving coordinates.

In Chapter 10 we discuss manipulator programming languages. Instead of developing a manipulator language, however, we embed the manipulator control in PASCAL in order to make distinct the essential manipulator aspects of programming. The computer and its programming language are essential parts of an industrial robot; they provide the logical, mathematical, and transformational interface between a small number of general purpose sensors and a general purpose actuator.

The computer-controlled industrial robot represents the first truly general purpose automation device. The industrial robot can be readily programmed to perform any number of jobs and will eliminate the need for high cost, custom designed automation equipment. It can provide for the automation of product assembly, and its low cost will make possible the automation of small batch production shops. Such industrial robots will have a major social effect in the future, as the simple, repetitive, assembly line jobs of today, whose ideal performance is characterized by our conception of a robot, not a human, will be eliminated.

References

Bolles, R. & Paul, R. P. The Use of Sensory Feedback in a Programmable Assembly System, The Stanford Artificial Intelligence Laboratory, Stanford University, AIM-220, Oct. 1973.

Ejiri, M., Uno, T., Yoda, H., et al. "A Prototype Intelligent Robot That Assembles Objects from Plane Drawings," *IEEE Trans. Computers* **C-21**, 2 (Feb. 1972), 199–207.

Engelberger, J. F. *Robotics in Practice* , IFS Publications Ltd., Kempston, England, 1980.

Ernst, H. A. A Computer-Operated Mechanical Hand, Sc.D. Thesis, Massachusetts Institute of Technology, 1961.

Feldman, J. et al. "The Use of Vision and Manipulation to Solve the Instant Insanity Puzzle," *Proc. Second Int'l Joint Conf. on Artificial Intelligence* , London, England, 1971, 359–364.

Goertz, R. C. "Manipulators Used for Handling Radioactive Materials," *Human Factors in Technology* , Chapter 27, edited by E. M. Bennett, McGraw-Hill, 1963.

Hohn, R. E. Application Flexibility of a Computer Controlled Industrial Robot, SME Technical Paper, MR 76-603, 1976.

Inoue, H. "Computer Controlled Bilateral Manipulator," *Bulletin of the Japanese Society of Mechanical Engineers* **14**, 69 (1971), 199–207.

Paul, R. P. Modeling, Trajectory Calculation and Servoing of a Computer Controlled Arm, Stanford Artificial Intelligence Laboratory, Stanford University, AIM 177, 1972.

Paul, R. P. "WAVE: A Model-Based Language for Manipulator Control," *The Industrial Robot* **4**, 1 (March 1977), 10–17.

Pieper, D. L. The Kinematics of Manipulators Under Computer Control, Stanford Artificial Intelligence Laboratory, Stanford University, AIM 72, 1968.

Roberts, L. G. Machine Perception of Three-Dimensional Solids, Lincoln Laboratory, Massachusetts Institute of Technology, Report No. 315, 1963.

Roberts, L. G. Homogeneous Matrix Representation and Manipulation of N-Dimensional Constructs, Lincoln Laboratory, Massachusetts Institute of Technology, Document No. MS1045, 1965.

Rosenberg, J. A History of Numerical Control 1949–1972: The Technical Development, Transfer to Industry, and Assimilation, U.S.C. Information Sciences Institute, Marina del Rey, California, Report No. ISI-RR-72-3, 1972.

Shimano, B. E. The Kinematic Design and Force Control of Computer Controlled Manipulators, Stanford Artificial Intelligence Laboratory, Stanford University, AIM 313, 1978.

Wichman, M. W. The Use of Optical Feedback in Computer Control of an Arm, Stanford Artificial Intelligence Laboratory, Stanford University, AIM 56, 1967.

CHAPTER 1

HOMOGENEOUS TRANSFORMATIONS

1.1 Introduction

The study of robot manipulation is concerned with the relationship between objects, and between objects and manipulators. In this chapter we will develop the representation necessary to describe these relationships. Similar problems of representation have already been solved in the field of computer graphics, where the relationship between objects must also be described. Homogeneous transformations are used in this field and in computer vision [Duda] [Roberts63] [Roberts65]. These transformations were employed by Denavit to describe linkages [Denavit] and are now used to describe manipulators [Pieper] [Paul72] [Paul77b].

We will first establish notation for vectors and planes and then introduce transformations on them. These transformations consist primarily of translation and rotation. We will then show that these transformations can also be considered as coordinate frames in which to represent objects, including the manipulator. The inverse transformation will then be introduced. A later section describes the general rotation transformation representing a rotation about a vector. An algorithm is then described to find the equivalent axis and angle of rotation represented by any given transformation. A brief section on stretching and scaling transforms is included together with a section on the perspective transformation. The chapter concludes with a section on transformation equations.

1.2 Notation

In describing the relationship between objects we will make use of point vectors, planes, and coordinate frames. Point vectors are denoted by lower case, bold face characters. Planes are denoted by script characters, and coordinate frames by upper case, bold face characters. For example:

vectors	$\mathbf{v}, \mathbf{x1}, \mathbf{x}$
planes	$\mathcal{P}, \mathcal{Q}$
coordinate frames	$\mathbf{I}, \mathbf{A}, \mathbf{CONV}$

We will use point vectors, planes, and coordinate frames as variables which have associated values. For example, a point vector has as value its three

Cartesian coordinate components.

If we wish to describe a point in space, which we will call p, with respect to a coordinate frame E, we will use a vector which we will call **v**. We will write this as

$$^{E}\mathbf{v}$$

The leading superscript describes the defining coordinate frame.

We might also wish to describe this same point, p, with respect to a different coordinate frame, for example H, using a vector **w** as

$$^{H}\mathbf{w}$$

v and **w** are two vectors which probably have different component values and $\mathbf{v} \neq \mathbf{w}$ even though both vectors describe the same point p. The case might also exist of a vector **a** describing a point 3 inches above any frame

$$^{F1}\mathbf{a} \qquad ^{F2}\mathbf{a}$$

In this case the vectors are identical but describe different points. Frequently, the defining frame will be obvious from the text and the superscripts will be left off. In many cases the name of the vector will be the same as the name of the object described, for example, the tip of a pin might be described by a vector **tip** with respect to a frame **BASE** as

$$^{BASE}\mathbf{tip}$$

If it were obvious from the text that we were describing the vector with respect to **BASE** then we might simply write

$$\mathbf{tip}$$

If we also wish to describe this point with respect to another coordinate frame say, **HAND**, then we must use another vector to describe this relationship, for example

$$^{HAND}\mathbf{tv}$$

$^{HAND}\mathbf{tv}$ and **tip** both describe the same feature but have different values. In order to refer to individual components of coordinate frames, point vectors, or planes, we add subscripts to indicate the particular component. For example, the vector $^{HAND}\mathbf{tv}$ has components $^{HAND}\mathbf{tv}_x$, $^{HAND}\mathbf{tv}_y$, $^{HAND}\mathbf{tv}_z$.

1.3 Vectors

The homogeneous coordinate representation of objects in n-space is an $(n+1)$-space entity such that a particular perspective projection recreates the n-space. This can also be viewed as the addition of an extra coordinate to each vector, a scale factor, such that the vector has the same meaning if each component, including the scale factor, is multiplied by a constant.

A point vector

$$\mathbf{v} = a\mathbf{i} + b\mathbf{j} + c\mathbf{k} \tag{1.1}$$

where **i**, **j**, and **k** are unit vectors along the x, y, and z coordinate axes, respectively, is represented in homogeneous coordinates as a column matrix

$$\mathbf{v} = \begin{bmatrix} x \\ y \\ z \\ w \end{bmatrix} \tag{1.2}$$

where

$$\begin{aligned} a &= x/w \\ b &= y/w \\ c &= z/w \end{aligned} \tag{1.3}$$

Thus the vector $3\mathbf{i} + 4\mathbf{j} + 5\mathbf{k}$ can be represented as $[3, 4, 5, 1]^{\mathrm{T}}$ or as $[6, 8, 10, 2]^{\mathrm{T}}$ or again as $[-30, -40, -50, -10]^{\mathrm{T}}$, etc. The superscript T indicates the transpose of the row vector into a column vector. The vector at the origin, the null vector, is represented as $[0, 0, 0, n]^{\mathrm{T}}$ where n is any non-zero scale factor. The vector $[0, 0, 0, 0]^{\mathrm{T}}$ is undefined. Vectors of the form $[a, b, c, 0]^{\mathrm{T}}$ represent vectors at infinity and are used to represent directions; the addition of any other finite vector does not change their value in any way.

We will also make use of the vector dot and cross products. Given two vectors

$$\begin{aligned} \mathbf{a} &= a_x\mathbf{i} + a_y\mathbf{j} + a_z\mathbf{k} \\ \mathbf{b} &= b_x\mathbf{i} + b_y\mathbf{j} + b_z\mathbf{k} \end{aligned} \tag{1.4}$$

we define the vector dot product, indicated by "·" as

$$\mathbf{a} \cdot \mathbf{b} = a_x b_x + a_y b_y + a_z b_z \tag{1.5}$$

The dot product of two vectors is a scalar. The cross product, indicated by a "×", is another vector perpendicular to the plane formed by the vectors of the product and is defined by

$$\mathbf{a} \times \mathbf{b} = (a_y b_z - a_z b_y)\mathbf{i} + (a_z b_x - a_x b_z)\mathbf{j} + (a_x b_y - a_y b_x)\mathbf{k} \tag{1.6}$$

This definition is easily remembered as the expansion of the determinant

$$\mathbf{a} \times \mathbf{b} = \begin{vmatrix} \mathbf{i} & \mathbf{j} & \mathbf{k} \\ a_x & a_y & a_z \\ b_x & b_y & b_z \end{vmatrix} \tag{1.7}$$

1.4 Planes

A plane is represented as a row matrix

$$\mathcal{P} = [a, b, c, d] \tag{1.8}$$

such that if a point v lies in a plane $\mathcal{P}$ the matrix product

$$\mathcal{P}\mathbf{v}\cdot = 0 \tag{1.9}$$

or in expanded form

$$xa + yb + zc + wd = 0 \tag{1.10}$$

If we define a constant

$$m = +\sqrt{a^2 + b^2 + c^2} \tag{1.11}$$

and divide Equation 1.10 by wm we obtain

$$\frac{x}{w}\frac{a}{m} + \frac{y}{w}\frac{b}{m} + \frac{z}{w}\frac{c}{m} = -\frac{d}{m} \tag{1.12}$$

The left hand side of Equation 1.12 is the vector dot product of two vectors $(x/w)\mathrm{i} + (y/w)\mathrm{j} + (z/w)\mathrm{k}$ and $(a/m)\mathrm{i} + (b/m)\mathrm{j} + (c/m)\mathrm{k}$ and represents the directed distance of the point $(x/w)\mathrm{i} + (y/w)\mathrm{j} + (z/w)\mathrm{k}$ along the vector $(a/m)\mathrm{i} + (b/m)\mathrm{j} + (c/m)\mathrm{k}$. The vector $(a/m)\mathrm{i} + (b/m)\mathrm{j} + (c/m)\mathrm{k}$ can be interpreted as the outward pointing normal of a plane situated a distance $-d/m$ from the origin in the direction of the normal. Thus a plane $\mathcal{P}$ parallel to the x, y plane, one unit along the z axis, is represented as

$$\mathcal{P} = [0, 0, 1, -1] \tag{1.13}$$

or as

$$\mathcal{P} = [0, 0, 2, -2] \tag{1.14}$$

or as

$$\mathcal{P} = [0, 0, -100, 100] \tag{1.15}$$

A point $\mathbf{v} = [10, 20, 1, 1]$ should lie in this plane

$$[0, 0, -100, 100]\begin{bmatrix} 10 \\ 20 \\ 1 \\ 1 \end{bmatrix} = 0 \tag{1.16}$$

or

$$\begin{bmatrix} 0 & 0 & 1 & -1 \end{bmatrix}\begin{bmatrix} -5 \\ -10 \\ -.5 \\ -.5 \end{bmatrix} = 0 \tag{1.17}$$

The point $\mathbf{v} = [0, 0, 2, 1]$ lies above the plane

$$[0, 0, 2, -2]\begin{bmatrix}0\\0\\2\\1\end{bmatrix} = 2 \tag{1.18}$$

and $\mathcal{P}\mathbf{v}$ is indeed positive, indicating that the point is outside the plane in the direction of the outward pointing normal. A point $\mathbf{v} = [0, 0, 0, 1]$ lies below the plane

$$\begin{bmatrix}0 & 0 & 1 & -1\end{bmatrix}\begin{bmatrix}0\\0\\0\\1\end{bmatrix} = -1 \tag{1.19}$$

The plane $[0, 0, 0, 0]$ is undefined.

1.5 Transformations

A transformation of the space $\mathbf{H}$ is a 4x4 matrix and can represent translation, rotation, stretching, and perspective transformations. Given a point $\mathbf{u}$, its transformation $\mathbf{v}$ is represented by the matrix product

$$\mathbf{v} = \mathbf{H}\mathbf{u} \tag{1.20}$$

The corresponding plane transformation $\mathcal{P}$ to $\mathcal{Q}$ is

$$\mathcal{Q} = \mathcal{P}\mathbf{H}^{-1} \tag{1.21}$$

as we require that the condition

$$\mathcal{Q}\mathbf{v} = \mathcal{P}\mathbf{u} \tag{1.22}$$

is invariant under all transformations. To verify this we substitute from Equations 1.20 and 1.21 into the left hand side of 1.22 and we obtain on the right hand side $\mathbf{H}^{-1}\mathbf{H}$ which is the identity matrix $\mathbf{I}$

$$\mathcal{P}\mathbf{H}^{-1}\mathbf{H}\mathbf{u} = \mathcal{P}\mathbf{u} \tag{1.23}$$

1.6 Translation Transformation

The transformation $\mathbf{H}$ corresponding to a translation by a vector $a\mathbf{i} + b\mathbf{j} + c\mathbf{k}$ is

$$\mathbf{H} = \mathrm{Trans}(a, b, c) = \begin{bmatrix}1 & 0 & 0 & a\\0 & 1 & 0 & b\\0 & 0 & 1 & c\\0 & 0 & 0 & 1\end{bmatrix} \tag{1.24}$$

Given a vector $\mathbf{u} = [x, y, z, w]^T$ the transformed vector $\mathbf{v}$ is given by

$$\mathbf{v} = \begin{bmatrix} 1 & 0 & 0 & a \\ 0 & 1 & 0 & b \\ 0 & 0 & 1 & c \\ 0 & 0 & 0 & 1 \end{bmatrix} \begin{bmatrix} x \\ y \\ z \\ w \end{bmatrix} \tag{1.25}$$

$$\mathbf{v} = \begin{bmatrix} x + aw \\ y + bw \\ z + cw \\ w \end{bmatrix} = \begin{bmatrix} x/w + a \\ y/w + b \\ x/w + c \\ 1 \end{bmatrix} \tag{1.26}$$

The translation may also be interpreted as the addition of the two vectors $(x/w)\mathbf{i} + (y/w)\mathbf{j} + (z/w)\mathbf{k}$ and $a\mathbf{i} + b\mathbf{j} + c\mathbf{k}$.

Every element of a transformation matrix may be multiplied by a non-zero constant without changing the transformation, in the same manner as points and planes. Consider the vector $2\mathbf{i} + 3\mathbf{j} + 2\mathbf{k}$ translated by, or added to $4\mathbf{i} - 3\mathbf{j} + 7\mathbf{k}$

$$\begin{bmatrix} 6 \\ 0 \\ 9 \\ 1 \end{bmatrix} = \begin{bmatrix} 1 & 0 & 0 & 4 \\ 0 & 1 & 0 & -3 \\ 0 & 0 & 1 & 7 \\ 0 & 0 & 0 & 1 \end{bmatrix} \begin{bmatrix} 2 \\ 3 \\ 2 \\ 1 \end{bmatrix} \tag{1.27}$$

If we multiply the transformation matrix elements by, say, -5 and the vector elements by 2, we obtain

$$\begin{bmatrix} -60 \\ 0 \\ -90 \\ -10 \end{bmatrix} = \begin{bmatrix} -5 & 0 & 0 & -20 \\ 0 & -5 & 0 & 15 \\ 0 & 0 & -5 & -35 \\ 0 & 0 & 0 & -5 \end{bmatrix} \begin{bmatrix} 4 \\ 6 \\ 4 \\ 2 \end{bmatrix} \tag{1.28}$$

which corresponds to the vector $[6, 0, 9, 1]^T$ as before. The point $[2, 3, 2, 1]^T$ lies in the plane $[1, 0, 0, -2]$

$$[1, 0, 0, -2] \begin{bmatrix} 2 \\ 3 \\ 2 \\ 1 \end{bmatrix} = 0 \tag{1.29}$$

The transformed point is, as we have already found, $[6, 0, 9, 1]^T$. We will now compute the transformed plane. The inverse of the transform is

$$\begin{bmatrix} 1 & 0 & 0 & -4 \\ 0 & 1 & 0 & 3 \\ 0 & 0 & 1 & -7 \\ 0 & 0 & 0 & 1 \end{bmatrix}$$

and the transformed plane

$$[1 \quad 0 \quad 0 \quad -6] = [1 \quad 0 \quad 0 \quad -2]\begin{bmatrix} 1 & 0 & 0 & -4 \\ 0 & 1 & 0 & 3 \\ 0 & 0 & 1 & -7 \\ 0 & 0 & 0 & 1 \end{bmatrix} \tag{1.30}$$

Once again the transformed point lies in the transformed plane

$$[1 \quad 0 \quad 0 \quad -6]\begin{bmatrix} 6 \\ 0 \\ 9 \\ 1 \end{bmatrix} = 0 \tag{1.31}$$

1.7 Rotation Transformations

The transformation corresponding to rotations about the x, y, or z axes by an angle θ are

$$\mathrm{Rot}(x, \theta) = \begin{bmatrix} 1 & 0 & 0 & 0 \\ 0 & \cos\theta & -\sin\theta & 0 \\ 0 & \sin\theta & \cos\theta & 0 \\ 0 & 0 & 0 & 1 \end{bmatrix} \tag{1.32}$$

$$\mathrm{Rot}(y, \theta) = \begin{bmatrix} \cos\theta & 0 & \sin\theta & 0 \\ 0 & 1 & 0 & 0 \\ -\sin\theta & 0 & \cos\theta & 0 \\ 0 & 0 & 0 & 1 \end{bmatrix} \tag{1.33}$$

$$\mathrm{Rot}(z, \theta) = \begin{bmatrix} \cos\theta & -\sin\theta & 0 & 0 \\ \sin\theta & \cos\theta & 0 & 0 \\ 0 & 0 & 1 & 0 \\ 0 & 0 & 0 & 1 \end{bmatrix} \tag{1.34}$$

Let us interpret these rotations by means of an example. Given a point $\mathbf{u} = 7\mathbf{i} + 3\mathbf{j} + 2\mathbf{k}$ what is the effect of rotating it 90° about the z axis to $\mathbf{v}$? The transform is obtained from Equation 1.34 with $\sin\theta = 1$ and $\cos\theta = 0$.

$$\begin{bmatrix} -3 \\ 7 \\ 2 \\ 1 \end{bmatrix} = \begin{bmatrix} 0 & -1 & 0 & 0 \\ 1 & 0 & 0 & 0 \\ 0 & 0 & 1 & 0 \\ 0 & 0 & 0 & 1 \end{bmatrix}\begin{bmatrix} 7 \\ 3 \\ 2 \\ 1 \end{bmatrix} \tag{1.35}$$

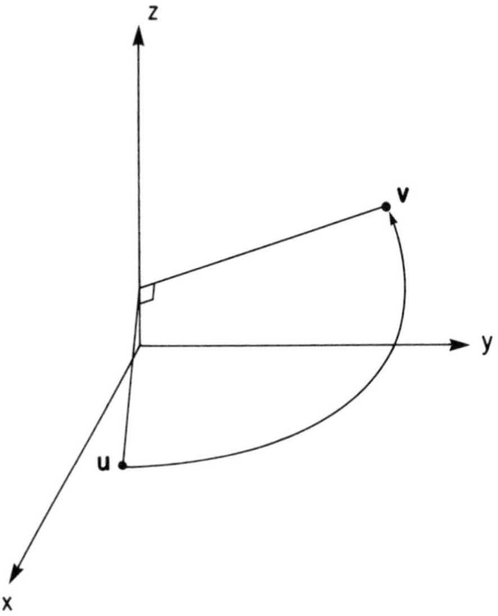

Figure 1.1. Rot(z, 90)

The initial and final points are shown in Figure 1.1. and it can be seen that the point has indeed been rotated 90° about the z axis. Let us now rotate **v** 90° about the y axis to **w**. The transform is obtained from Equation 1.33 and we have

$$\begin{bmatrix} 2 \\ 7 \\ 3 \\ 1 \end{bmatrix} = \begin{bmatrix} 0 & 0 & 1 & 0 \\ 0 & 1 & 0 & 0 \\ -1 & 0 & 0 & 0 \\ 0 & 0 & 0 & 1 \end{bmatrix} \begin{bmatrix} -3 \\ 7 \\ 2 \\ 1 \end{bmatrix} \tag{1.36}$$

This result is shown in Figure 1.2. If we combine these two rotations we have

$$\mathbf{v} = \mathrm{Rot}(z, 90)\mathbf{u} \tag{1.37}$$

and

$$\mathbf{w} = \mathrm{Rot}(y, 90)\mathbf{v} \tag{1.38}$$

Substituting for **v** from Equation 1.37 into Equation 1.38 we obtain

$$\mathbf{w} = \mathrm{Rot}(y, 90)\,\mathrm{Rot}(z, 90)\,\mathbf{u} \tag{1.39}$$

$$\mathrm{Rot}(y, 90)\,\mathrm{Rot}(z, 90) = \begin{bmatrix} 0 & 0 & 1 & 0 \\ 0 & 1 & 0 & 0 \\ -1 & 0 & 0 & 0 \\ 0 & 0 & 0 & 1 \end{bmatrix} \begin{bmatrix} 0 & -1 & 0 & 0 \\ 1 & 0 & 0 & 0 \\ 0 & 0 & 1 & 0 \\ 0 & 0 & 0 & 1 \end{bmatrix} \tag{1.40}$$

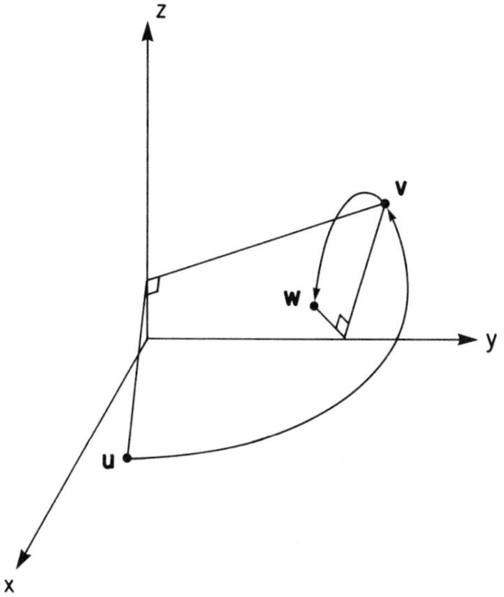

Figure 1.2. Rot(y, 90)

$$\text{Rot}(y, 90)\,\text{Rot}(z, 90) = \begin{bmatrix} 0 & 0 & 1 & 0 \\ 1 & 0 & 0 & 0 \\ 0 & 1 & 0 & 0 \\ 0 & 0 & 0 & 1 \end{bmatrix} \quad (1.41)$$

thus

$$\mathbf{w} = \begin{bmatrix} 2 \\ 7 \\ 3 \\ 1 \end{bmatrix} = \begin{bmatrix} 0 & 0 & 1 & 0 \\ 1 & 0 & 0 & 0 \\ 0 & 1 & 0 & 0 \\ 0 & 0 & 0 & 1 \end{bmatrix} \begin{bmatrix} 7 \\ 3 \\ 2 \\ 1 \end{bmatrix} \quad (1.42)$$

as we obtained before.

If we reverse the order of rotations and first rotate 90° about the y axis and then 90° about the z axis, we obtain a different position

$$\begin{aligned} \text{Rot}(z, 90)\,\text{Rot}(y, 90) &= \begin{bmatrix} 0 & -1 & 0 & 0 \\ 1 & 0 & 0 & 0 \\ 0 & 0 & 1 & 0 \\ 0 & 0 & 0 & 1 \end{bmatrix} \begin{bmatrix} 0 & 0 & 1 & 0 \\ 0 & 1 & 0 & 0 \\ -1 & 0 & 0 & 0 \\ 0 & 0 & 0 & 1 \end{bmatrix} \\ &= \begin{bmatrix} 0 & -1 & 0 & 0 \\ 0 & 0 & 1 & 0 \\ -1 & 0 & 0 & 0 \\ 0 & 0 & 0 & 1 \end{bmatrix} \end{aligned} \quad (1.43)$$

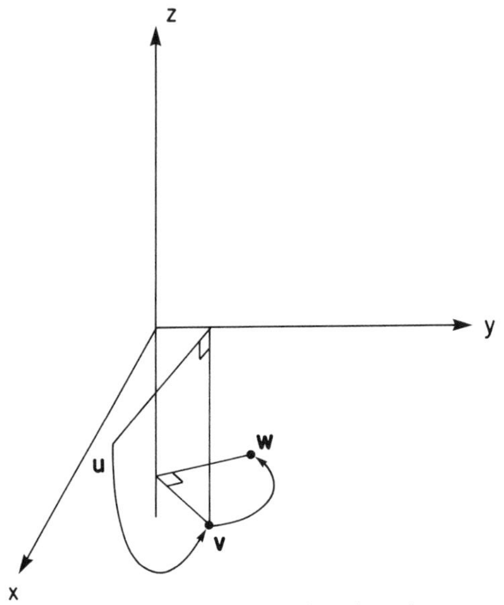

Figure 1.3. $\mathbf{Rot}(z, 90)\mathbf{Rot}(y, 90)$

and the point **u** transforms into **w** as

$$\begin{bmatrix} -3 \\ 2 \\ -7 \\ 1 \end{bmatrix} = \begin{bmatrix} 0 & -1 & 0 & 0 \\ 0 & 0 & 1 & 0 \\ -1 & 0 & 0 & 0 \\ 0 & 0 & 0 & 1 \end{bmatrix} \begin{bmatrix} 7 \\ 3 \\ 2 \\ 1 \end{bmatrix} \tag{1.44}$$

We should expect this, as matrix multiplication is noncommutative.

$$\mathbf{AB} \neq \mathbf{BA} \tag{1.45}$$

The results of this transformation are shown in Figure 1.3.

We will now combine the original rotation with a translation $4\mathbf{i} - 3\mathbf{j} + 7\mathbf{k}$. We obtain the translation from Equation 1.27 and the rotation from Equation 1.41. The matrix expression is

$$\mathbf{Trans}(4, -3, 7)\ \mathbf{Rot}(y, 90)\ \mathbf{Rot}(z, 90) = \begin{bmatrix} 1 & 0 & 0 & 4 \\ 0 & 1 & 0 & -3 \\ 0 & 0 & 1 & 7 \\ 0 & 0 & 0 & 1 \end{bmatrix} \begin{bmatrix} 0 & 0 & 1 & 0 \\ 1 & 0 & 0 & 0 \\ 0 & 1 & 0 & 0 \\ 0 & 0 & 0 & 1 \end{bmatrix}$$

$$= \begin{bmatrix} 0 & 0 & 1 & 4 \\ 1 & 0 & 0 & -3 \\ 0 & 1 & 0 & 7 \\ 0 & 0 & 0 & 1 \end{bmatrix} \tag{1.46}$$

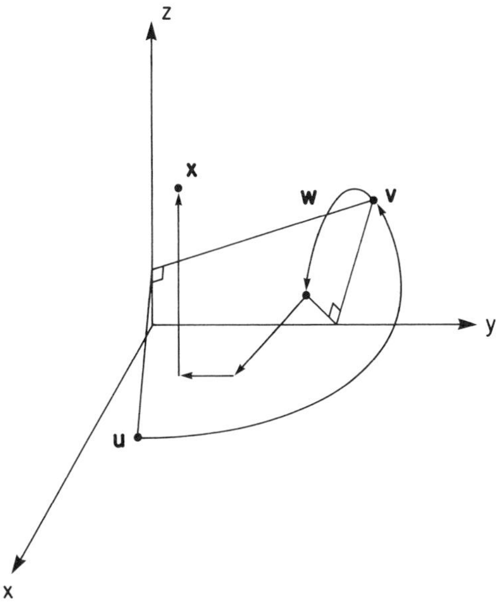

Figure 1.4. Trans(4, —3, 7)Rot(y, 90)Rot(z, 90)

and our point w = 7i + 3j + 2k transforms into x as

$$\begin{bmatrix} 6 \\ 4 \\ 10 \\ 1 \end{bmatrix} = \begin{bmatrix} 0 & 0 & 1 & 4 \\ 1 & 0 & 0 & -3 \\ 0 & 1 & 0 & 7 \\ 0 & 0 & 0 & 1 \end{bmatrix} \begin{bmatrix} 7 \\ 3 \\ 2 \\ 1 \end{bmatrix} \tag{1.47}$$

The result is shown in Figure 1.4.

1.8 Coordinate Frames

We can interpret the elements of the homogeneous transformation as four vectors describing a second coordinate frame. The vector $[0, 0, 0, 1]^T$ lies at the origin of the second coordinate frame. Its transformation corresponds to the right hand column of the transformation matrix. Consider the transform in Equation 1.47

$$\begin{bmatrix} 4 \\ -3 \\ 7 \\ 1 \end{bmatrix} = \begin{bmatrix} 0 & 0 & 1 & 4 \\ 1 & 0 & 0 & -3 \\ 0 & 1 & 0 & 7 \\ 0 & 0 & 0 & 1 \end{bmatrix} \begin{bmatrix} 0 \\ 0 \\ 0 \\ 1 \end{bmatrix} \tag{1.48}$$

The transform of the null vector is $[4, -3, 7, 1]^T$, the right hand column. If we transform vectors corresponding to unit vectors along the x, y, and z axes, we

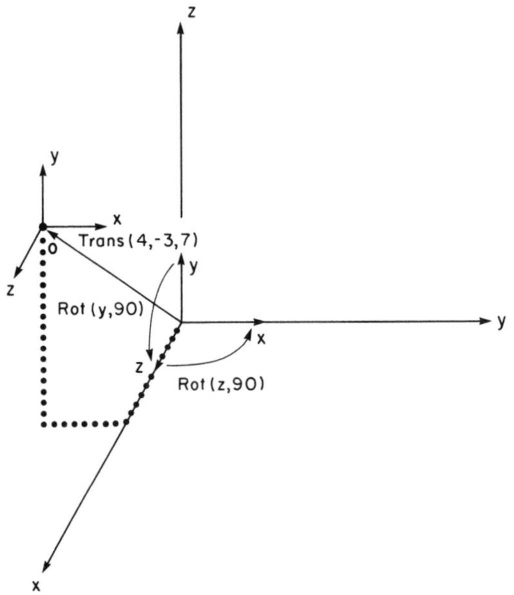

Figure 1.5. The Interpretation of a Transform as a Frame

obtain $[4, -2, 7, 1]^T$, $[4, -3, 8, 1]^T$, and $[5, -3, 7, 1]^T$, respectively. These four vectors are plotted in Figure 1.5 and form a coordinate frame.

The direction of these unit vectors is formed by subtracting the vector representing the origin of this coordinate frame and extending the vectors to infinity by reducing their scale factors to zero. The direction of the x, y, and z axes of this frame are $[0, 1, 0, 0]^T$, $[0, 0, 1, 0]^T$, and $[1, 0, 0, 0]^T$, respectively. These direction vectors correspond to the first three columns of the transformation matrix. The transformation matrix thus describes the three axis directions and the position of the origin of a coordinate frame rotated and translated away from the reference coordinate frame (see Figure 1.4). When a vector is transformed, as in Equation 1.47, the original vector can be considered as a vector described in the coordinate frame. The transformed vector is the same vector described with respect to the reference coordinate frame (see Figure 1.6).

1.9 Relative Transformations

The rotations and translations we have been describing have all been made with respect to the fixed reference coordinate frame. Thus, in the example given,

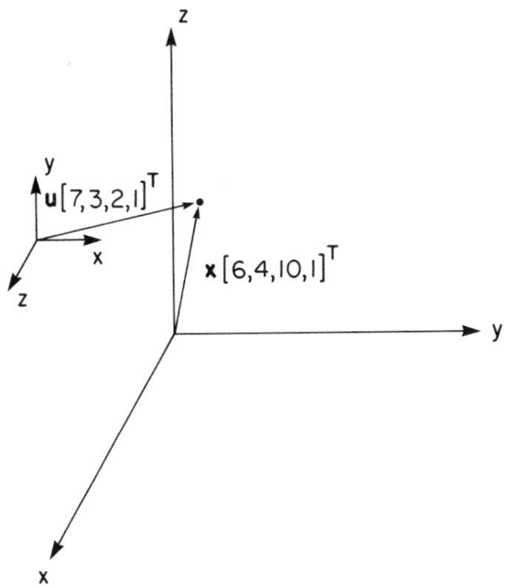

Figure 1.6. The Transformation of a Vector

$$\text{Trans}(4, -3, 7)\ \text{Rot}(y, 90)\ \text{Rot}(z, 90) = \begin{bmatrix} 0 & 0 & 1 & 4 \\ 1 & 0 & 0 & -3 \\ 0 & 1 & 0 & 7 \\ 0 & 0 & 0 & 1 \end{bmatrix} \tag{1.49}$$

the frame is first rotated around the reference z axis by 90°, then rotated 90° around the reference y axis, and finally translated by $4\mathbf{i} - 3\mathbf{j} + 7\mathbf{k}$, as shown in Figure 1.5. We may also interpret the operation in the reverse order, from left to right, as follows: the object is first translated by $4\mathbf{i} - 3\mathbf{j} + 7\mathbf{k}$; it is then rotated 90° around the current frame axes, which in this case are the same as the reference axes; it is then rotated 90° about the newly rotated (current) frame axes (see Figure 1.7).

In general, if we postmultiply a transform representing a frame by a second transformation describing a rotation and/or translation, we make that translation and/or rotation with respect to the frame axes described by the first transformation. If we premultiply the frame transformation by a transformation representing a translation and/or rotation, then that translation and/or rotation is made with respect to the base reference coordinate frame. Thus, given a frame **C** and a transformation **T**, corresponding to a rotation of 90° about the z axis, and a translation of 10 units in the x direction, we obtain a new position **X** when the change is made in base coordinates $\mathbf{X} = \mathbf{T}\,\mathbf{C}$

$$\begin{bmatrix} 0 & 0 & 1 & 0 \\ 1 & 0 & 0 & 20 \\ 0 & 1 & 0 & 0 \\ 0 & 0 & 0 & 1 \end{bmatrix} = \begin{bmatrix} 0 & -1 & 0 & 10 \\ 1 & 0 & 0 & 0 \\ 0 & 0 & 1 & 0 \\ 0 & 0 & 0 & 1 \end{bmatrix} \begin{bmatrix} 1 & 0 & 0 & 20 \\ 0 & 0 & -1 & 10 \\ 0 & 1 & 0 & 0 \\ 0 & 0 & 0 & 1 \end{bmatrix} \tag{1.50}$$

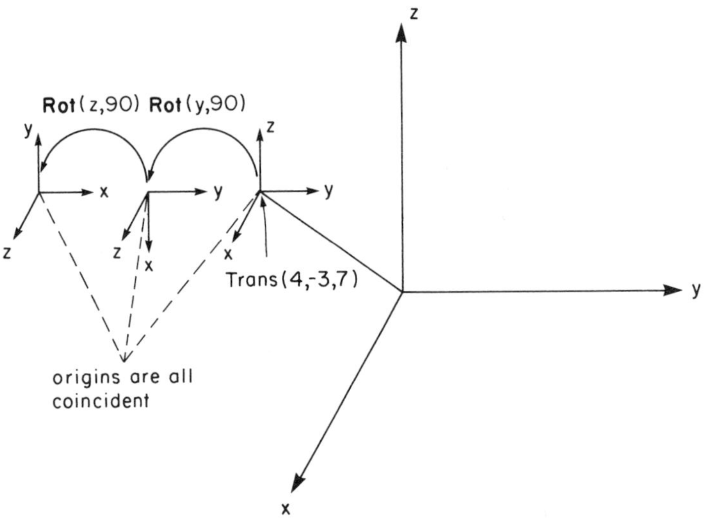

Figure 1.7. Relative Transformations

and a new position **Y** when the change is made relative to the frame axes as $\mathbf{Y} = \mathbf{C}\mathbf{T}$

$$\begin{bmatrix} 0 & -1 & 0 & 30 \\ 0 & 0 & -1 & 10 \\ 1 & 0 & 0 & 0 \\ 0 & 0 & 0 & 1 \end{bmatrix} = \begin{bmatrix} 1 & 0 & 0 & 20 \\ 0 & 0 & -1 & 10 \\ 0 & 1 & 0 & 0 \\ 0 & 0 & 0 & 1 \end{bmatrix} \begin{bmatrix} 0 & -1 & 0 & 10 \\ 1 & 0 & 0 & 0 \\ 0 & 0 & 1 & 0 \\ 0 & 0 & 0 & 1 \end{bmatrix} \tag{1.51}$$

The results are shown in Figure 1.8.

1.10 Objects

Transformations are used to describe the position and orientation of objects. An object shown in Figure 1.9 is described by six points with respect to a coordinate frame fixed in the object.

If we rotate the object 90° about the z axis and then 90° about the y axis, followed by a translation of four units in the x direction, we can describe the transformation as

$$\mathrm{Trans}(4,0,0)\,\mathrm{Rot}(y,90)\,\mathrm{Rot}(z,90) = \begin{bmatrix} 0 & 0 & 1 & 4 \\ 1 & 0 & 0 & 0 \\ 0 & 1 & 0 & 0 \\ 0 & 0 & 0 & 1 \end{bmatrix} \tag{1.52}$$

The transformation matrix represents the operation of rotation and translation on a coordinate frame originally aligned with the reference coordinate frame. We

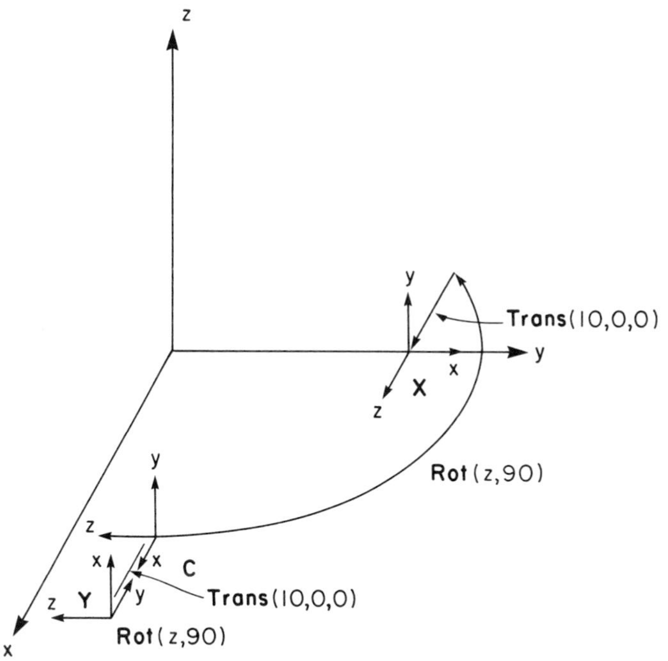

Figure 1.8. Transformations with Respect to Base and Frame Coordinates

may transform the six points of the object as

$$\begin{bmatrix} 4 & 4 & 6 & 6 & 4 & 4 \\ 1 & -1 & -1 & 1 & 1 & -1 \\ 0 & 0 & 0 & 0 & 4 & 4 \\ 1 & 1 & 1 & 1 & 1 & 1 \end{bmatrix} = \begin{bmatrix} 0 & 0 & 1 & 4 \\ 1 & 0 & 0 & 0 \\ 0 & 1 & 0 & 0 \\ 0 & 0 & 0 & 1 \end{bmatrix} \begin{bmatrix} 1 & -1 & -1 & 1 & 1 & -1 \\ 0 & 0 & 0 & 0 & 4 & 4 \\ 0 & 0 & 2 & 2 & 0 & 0 \\ 1 & 1 & 1 & 1 & 1 & 1 \end{bmatrix} \tag{1.53}$$

The results are plotted in Figure 1.10.

It can be seen that the object described in the figure bears the same fixed relationship to its coordinate frame, whose position and orientation are described by the transformation. Given an object described by a reference coordinate frame as in Figure 1.9, and a transformation representing the position and orientation of the object's axes, the object can be simply reconstructed, without the necessity of transforming all the points, by noting the direction and orientation of key features with respect to the describing frame's coordinate axes. By drawing the transformed coordinate frame, the object can be related to the new axis directions. In the example given, the long axis of the wedge lies along the y axis of the describing frame and, as the transformed y axis is in the z direction, the long axis will be upright in the transformed state, etc.

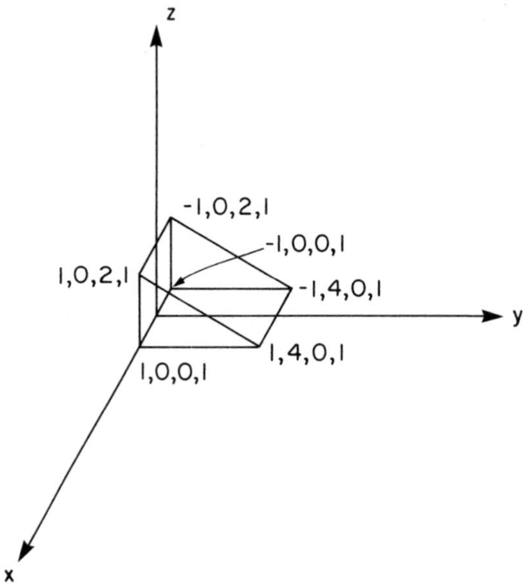

Figure 1.9. An Object

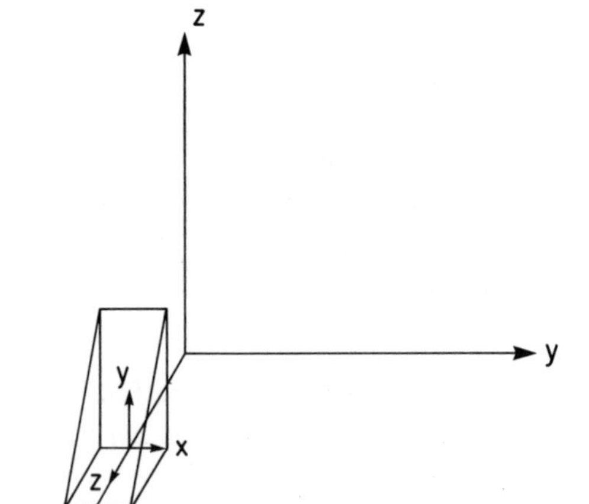

Figure 1.10. Transformed Wedge

1.11 Inverse Transformations

We are now in a position to develop the inverse transformation as the transform which carries the transformed coordinate frame back to the original frame. This is simply the description of the reference coordinate frame with respect to the transformed frame. Consider the example given in Figure 1.10. The direction of the reference frame x axis is $[0, 0, 1, 0]^T$ with respect to the transformed frame. The y and z axes are $[1, 0, 0, 0]^T$ and $[0, 1, 0, 0]^T$, respectively. The location of the origin is $[0, 0, -4, 1]^T$ with respect to the transformed frame and thus the inverse transform is

$$T^{-1} = \begin{bmatrix} 0 & 1 & 0 & 0 \\ 0 & 0 & 1 & 0 \\ 1 & 0 & 0 & -4 \\ 0 & 0 & 0 & 1 \end{bmatrix} \tag{1.54}$$

That this is indeed the transform inverse is easily verified by multiplying it by the transform T to obtain an identity transform

$$\begin{bmatrix} 1 & 0 & 0 & 0 \\ 0 & 1 & 0 & 0 \\ 0 & 0 & 1 & 0 \\ 0 & 0 & 0 & 1 \end{bmatrix} = \begin{bmatrix} 0 & 1 & 0 & 0 \\ 0 & 0 & 1 & 0 \\ 1 & 0 & 0 & -4 \\ 0 & 0 & 0 & 1 \end{bmatrix} \begin{bmatrix} 0 & 0 & 1 & 4 \\ 1 & 0 & 0 & 0 \\ 0 & 1 & 0 & 0 \\ 0 & 0 & 0 & 1 \end{bmatrix} \tag{1.55}$$

In general, given a transform with elements

$$T = \begin{bmatrix} n_x & o_x & a_x & p_x \\ n_y & o_y & a_y & p_y \\ n_z & o_z & a_z & p_z \\ 0 & 0 & 0 & 1 \end{bmatrix} \tag{1.56}$$

then the inverse is

$$T^{-1} = \begin{bmatrix} n_x & n_y & n_z & -\mathbf{p} \cdot \mathbf{n} \\ o_x & o_y & o_z & -\mathbf{p} \cdot \mathbf{o} \\ a_x & a_y & a_z & -\mathbf{p} \cdot \mathbf{a} \\ 0 & 0 & 0 & 1 \end{bmatrix} \tag{1.57}$$

where **p**, **n**, **o**, and **a** are the four column vectors and "·" represents the vector dot product. This result is easily verified by postmultiplying Equation 1.56 by Equation 1.57.

1.12 General Rotation Transformation

We stated the rotation transformations for rotations about the x, y, and z axes (Equations 1.32, 1.33, and 1.34). These transformations have a simple geometric

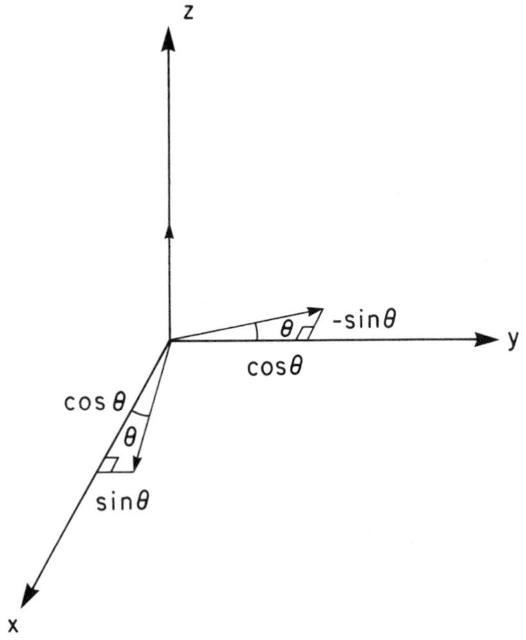

Figure 1.11. A Rotation about the z axis

interpretation. For example, in the case of a rotation about the z axis, the column representing the z axis will remain constant, while the column elements representing the x and y axes will vary as shown in Figure 1.11.

We will now develop the transformation matrix representing a rotation around an arbitrary vector **k** located at the origin. (See [Hamilton] for a full discussion of this subject.) In order to do this we will imagine that **k** is the z axis unit vector of a coordinate frame **C**

$$\mathbf{C} = \begin{bmatrix} n_x & o_x & a_x & 0 \\ n_y & o_y & a_y & 0 \\ n_z & o_z & a_z & 0 \\ 0 & 0 & 0 & 1 \end{bmatrix} \tag{1.58}$$

$$\mathbf{k} = a_x\mathbf{i} + a_y\mathbf{j} + a_z\mathbf{k} \tag{1.59}$$

Rotating around the vector **k** is then equivalent to rotating around the z axis of the frame **C**.

$$\mathrm{Rot}(\mathbf{k}, \theta) = \mathrm{Rot}({}^{C}z, \theta) \tag{1.60}$$

If we are given a frame T described with respect to the reference coordinate frame, we can find a frame **X** which describes the same frame with respect to frame C as

$$\mathrm{T} = \mathrm{C\,X} \tag{1.61}$$

where X describes the position of T with respect to frame C. Solving for X we obtain

$$\mathrm{X} = \mathrm{C}^{-1}\,\mathrm{T} \tag{1.62}$$

Rotating T around k is equivalent to rotating X around the z axis of frame C

$$\mathrm{Rot}(\mathrm{k}, \theta)\,\mathrm{T} = \mathrm{C\,Rot}(z, \theta)\,\mathrm{X} \tag{1.63}$$

$$\mathrm{Rot}(\mathrm{k}, \theta)\,\mathrm{T} = \mathrm{C\,Rot}(z, \theta)\,\mathrm{C}^{-1}\,\mathrm{T}. \tag{1.64}$$

Thus

$$\mathrm{Rot}(\mathrm{k}, \theta) = \mathrm{C\,Rot}(z, \theta)\,\mathrm{C}^{-1} \tag{1.65}$$

However, we have only k, the z axis of the frame C. By expanding Equation 1.65 we will discover that $\mathrm{C\,Rot}(z, \theta)\,\mathrm{C}^{-1}$ is a function of k only.

Multiplying $\mathrm{Rot}(z, \theta)$ on the right by C^{-1} we obtain

$$\mathrm{Rot}(z, \theta)\,\mathrm{C}^{-1} = \begin{bmatrix} \cos\theta & -\sin\theta & 0 & 0 \\ \sin\theta & \cos\theta & 0 & 0 \\ 0 & 0 & 1 & 0 \\ 0 & 0 & 0 & 1 \end{bmatrix} \begin{bmatrix} n_x & n_y & n_z & 0 \\ o_x & o_y & o_z & 0 \\ a_x & a_y & a_z & 0 \\ 0 & 0 & 0 & 1 \end{bmatrix}$$

$$= \begin{bmatrix} n_x\cos\theta - o_x\sin\theta & n_y\cos\theta - o_y\sin\theta & n_z\cos\theta - o_z\sin\theta & 0 \\ n_x\sin\theta + o_x\cos\theta & n_y\sin\theta + o_y\cos\theta & n_z\sin\theta + o_z\cos\theta & 0 \\ a_x & a_y & a_z & 0 \\ 0 & 0 & 0 & 1 \end{bmatrix} \tag{1.66}$$

premultiplying by

$$\mathrm{C} = \begin{bmatrix} n_x & o_x & a_x & 0 \\ n_y & o_y & a_y & 0 \\ n_z & o_z & a_y & 0 \\ 0 & 0 & 0 & 1 \end{bmatrix} \tag{1.67}$$

we obtain $\mathbf{C}\,\mathbf{Rot}(z,\theta)\,\mathbf{C}^{-1} =$

$$
\begin{bmatrix}
n_x n_x \cos\theta - n_x o_x \sin\theta + n_x o_x \sin\theta + o_x o_x \cos\theta + a_x a_x \\
n_y n_x \cos\theta - n_y o_x \sin\theta + n_x o_y \sin\theta + o_y o_x \cos\theta + a_y a_x \\
n_z n_x \cos\theta - n_z o_x \sin\theta + n_x o_z \sin\theta + o_z o_x \cos\theta + a_z a_x \\
0 \\
n_x n_y \cos\theta - n_x o_y \sin\theta + n_y o_x \sin\theta + o_y o_x \cos\theta + a_x a_y \\
n_y n_y \cos\theta - n_y o_y \sin\theta + n_y o_y \sin\theta + o_y o_y \cos\theta + a_y a_y \\
n_z n_y \cos\theta - n_z o_y \sin\theta + n_y o_z \sin\theta + o_y o_z \cos\theta + a_z a_y \\
0 \\
n_x n_z \cos\theta - n_x o_z \sin\theta + n_z o_x \sin\theta + o_z o_x \cos\theta + a_x a_z \quad 0 \\
n_y n_z \cos\theta - n_y o_z \sin\theta + n_z o_y \sin\theta + o_z o_y \cos\theta + a_y a_z \quad 0 \\
n_z n_z \cos\theta - n_z o_z \sin\theta + n_z o_z \sin\theta + o_z o_z \cos\theta + a_z a_z \quad 0 \\
0 \qquad\qquad\qquad 1
\end{bmatrix}
\tag{1.68}
$$

Simplifying, using the following relationships:
the dot product of any row or column of **C** with any other row or column is zero, as the vectors are orthogonal;
the dot product of any row or column of **C** with itself is 1 as the vectors are of unit magnitude;
the z unit vector is the vector cross product of the x and y vectors or

$$\mathbf{a} = \mathbf{n} \times \mathbf{o} \tag{1.69}$$

which has components

$$
\begin{aligned}
a_x &= n_y o_z - n_z o_y \\
a_y &= n_z o_x - n_x o_z. \\
a_z &= n_x o_y - n_y o_x
\end{aligned}
$$

the versine, abbreviated as $\operatorname{vers}\theta$, is defined as $\operatorname{vers}\theta = (1 - \cos\theta)$,
$k_x = a_x$, $k_y = a_y$, and $k_z = a_z$.
We obtain $Rot(k,\theta) =$

$$
\begin{bmatrix}
k_x k_x \operatorname{vers}\theta + \cos\theta & k_y k_x \operatorname{vers}\theta - k_z \sin\theta & k_z k_x \operatorname{vers}\theta + k_y \sin\theta & 0 \\
k_x k_y \operatorname{vers}\theta + k_z \sin\theta & k_y k_y \operatorname{vers}\theta + \cos\theta & k_z k_y \operatorname{vers}\theta - k_x \sin\theta & 0 \\
k_x k_z \operatorname{vers}\theta - k_y \sin\theta & k_y k_z \operatorname{vers}\theta + k_x \sin\theta & k_z k_z \operatorname{vers}\theta + \cos\theta & 0 \\
0 & 0 & 0 & 1
\end{bmatrix}
\tag{1.70}
$$

This is an important result and should be thoroughly understood before proceeding further.

From this general rotation transformation we can obtain each of the elementary rotation transforms. For example $\mathbf{Rot}(x,\theta)$ is $\mathbf{Rot}(\mathbf{k},\theta)$ where $k_x = 1$, $k_y = 0$,

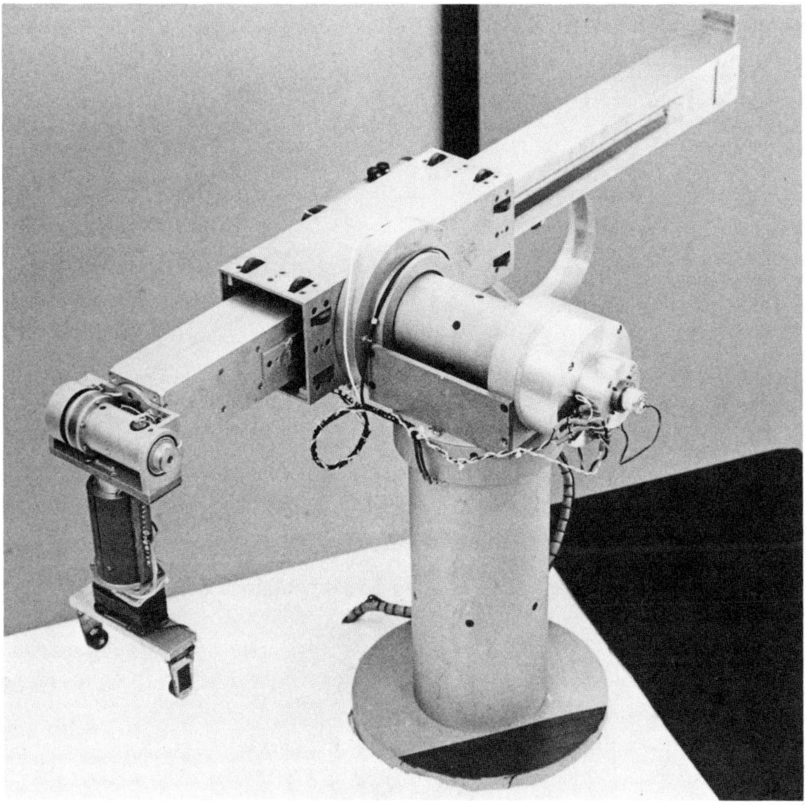

Figure 1.12. The Stanford Manipulator

and $k_z = 0$. Substituting these values of k into Equation 1.70 we obtain

$$\mathrm{Rot}(x,\theta) = \begin{bmatrix} 1 & 0 & 0 & 0 \\ 0 & \cos\theta & -\sin\theta & 0 \\ 0 & \sin\theta & \cos\theta & 0 \\ 0 & 0 & 0 & 1 \end{bmatrix} \tag{1.71}$$

as before.

1.13 Equivalent Angle and Axis of Rotation

Given any arbitrary rotational transformation, we can use Equation 1.70 to obtain an axis about which an equivalent rotation θ is made as follows. Given a rotational transformation **R**

$$\mathbf{R} = \begin{bmatrix} n_x & o_x & a_x & 0 \\ n_y & o_y & a_y & 0 \\ n_z & o_z & a_z & 0 \\ 0 & 0 & 0 & 1 \end{bmatrix} \tag{1.72}$$

we may equate **R** to $\mathbf{Rot}(\mathbf{k}, \theta)$

$$\begin{bmatrix} n_x & o_x & a_x & 0 \\ n_y & o_y & a_y & 0 \\ n_z & o_z & a_z & 0 \\ 0 & 0 & 0 & 1 \end{bmatrix} =$$

$$\begin{bmatrix} k_x k_x \operatorname{vers}\theta + \cos\theta & k_y k_x \operatorname{vers}\theta - k_z \sin\theta & k_z k_x \operatorname{vers}\theta + k_y \sin\theta & 0 \\ k_x k_y \operatorname{vers}\theta + k_z \sin\theta & k_y k_y \operatorname{vers}\theta + \cos\theta & k_z k_y \operatorname{vers}\theta - k_x \sin\theta & 0 \\ k_x k_z \operatorname{vers}\theta - k_y \sin\theta & k_y k_z \operatorname{vers}\theta + k_x \sin\theta & k_z k_z \operatorname{vers}\theta + \cos\theta & 0 \\ 0 & 0 & 0 & 1 \end{bmatrix} \tag{1.73}$$

Summing the diagonal terms of Equation 1.73 we obtain

$$n_x + o_y + a_z + 1 = k_x^2 \operatorname{vers}\theta + \cos\theta + k_y^2 \operatorname{vers}\theta + \cos\theta + k_z^2 \operatorname{vers}\theta + \cos\theta + 1 \tag{1.74}$$

$$\begin{aligned} n_x + o_y + a_z &= (k_x^2 + k_y^2 + k_z^2) \operatorname{vers}\theta + 3\cos\theta \\ &= 1 + 2\cos\theta \end{aligned} \tag{1.75}$$

and the cosine of the angle of rotation is

$$\cos\theta = \frac{1}{2}(n_x + o_y + a_z - 1) \tag{1.76}$$

Differencing pairs of off-diagonal terms in Equation 1.73 we obtain

$$o_z - a_y = 2k_x \sin\theta \tag{1.77}$$

$$a_x - n_z = 2k_y \sin\theta \tag{1.78}$$

$$n_y - o_x = 2k_z \sin\theta \tag{1.79}$$

Squaring and adding Equations 1.77 – 1.79 we obtain an expression for $\sin\theta$

$$(o_z - a_y)^2 + (a_x - n_z)^2 + (n_y - o_x)^2 = 4\sin^2\theta \tag{1.80}$$

and the sine of the angle of rotation is

$$\sin\theta = \pm\frac{1}{2}\sqrt{(o_z - a_y)^2 + (a_x - n_z)^2 + (n_y - o_x)^2} \tag{1.81}$$

We may define the rotation to be positive about the vector **k** such that $0 \leq \theta \leq 180°$. In this case the + sign is appropriate in Equation 1.81 and thus the angle of rotation θ is uniquely defined as

$$\tan\theta = \frac{\sqrt{(o_z - a_y)^2 + (a_x - n_z)^2 + (n_y - o_x)^2}}{(n_x + o_y + a_z - 1)} \tag{1.82}$$

The components of **k** may be obtained from Equations 1.77 – 1.79 as

$$k_x = \frac{o_z - a_y}{2\sin\theta} \tag{1.83}$$

$$k_y = \frac{a_x - n_z}{2\sin\theta} \tag{1.84}$$

$$k_z = \frac{n_y - o_x}{2\sin\theta} \tag{1.85}$$

When the angle of rotation is very small, the axis of rotation is physically not well defined due to the small magnitude of both numerator and denominator in Equations 1.83–1.85. If the resulting angle is small, the vector **k** should be renormalized to ensure that $|\mathbf{k}| = 1$. When the angle of rotation approaches 180° the vector **k** is once again poorly defined by Equation 1.83–1.85 as the magnitude of the sine is again decreasing [Klump]. The axis of rotation is, however, physically well defined in this case. When $\theta > 150°$, the denominator of Equations 1.83-1.85 is less than 1. As the angle increases to 180° the rapidly decreasing magnitude of both numerator and denominator leads to considerable inaccuracies in the determination of **k**. At $\theta = 180°$, Equations 1.83–1.85 are of the form $0/0$, yielding no information at all about a physically well defined vector **k**. If the angle of rotation is greater than 90°, then we must follow a different approach in determining **k**. Equating the diagonal elements of Equation 1.73 we obtain

$$k_x^2 \operatorname{vers}\theta + \cos\theta = n_x \tag{1.86}$$
$$k_y^2 \operatorname{vers}\theta + \cos\theta = o_y \tag{1.87}$$
$$k_z^2 \operatorname{vers}\theta + \cos\theta = a_z \tag{1.88}$$

Substituting for $\cos\theta$ and $\operatorname{vers}\theta$ from Equation 1.76 and solving for the elements of **k** we obtain further

$$k_x = \pm\sqrt{\frac{n_x - \cos\theta}{1 - \cos\theta}} \tag{1.89}$$

$$k_y = \pm\sqrt{\frac{o_y - \cos\theta}{1 - \cos\theta}} \tag{1.90}$$

$$k_z = \pm\sqrt{\frac{a_z - \cos\theta}{1 - \cos\theta}} \tag{1.91}$$

The largest component of k defined by Equations 1.89 – 1.91 corresponds to the most positive component of n_x, o_y, and a_z. For this largest element, the sign of the radical can be obtained from Equations 1.77 – 1.79. As the sine of the angle of rotation θ must be positive, then the sign of the component of **k** defined by Equations 1.77 – 1.79 must be the same as the sign of the left hand side of these equations. Thus we may combine Equations 1.89–1.91 with the information contained in Equations 1.77–1.79 as follows

$$k_x = \operatorname{sgn}(o_z - a_y)\sqrt{\frac{n_x - \cos\theta}{1 - \cos\theta}} \tag{1.92}$$

$$k_y = \operatorname{sgn}(a_x - n_z)\sqrt{\frac{o_y - \cos\theta}{1 - \cos\theta}} \tag{1.93}$$

$$k_z = \operatorname{sgn}(n_y - o_x)\sqrt{\frac{a_z - \cos\theta}{1 - \cos\theta}} \tag{1.94}$$

where $\operatorname{sgn}(e) = +1$ if $e \geq 0$ and $\operatorname{sgn}(e) = -1$ if $e \leq 0$.

Only the largest element of k is determined from Equations 1.92–1.94, corresponding to the most positive element of n_x, o_y, and a_z. The remaining elements are more accurately determined by the following equations formed by summing pairs of off-diagonal elements of Equation 1.73

$$n_y + o_x = 2k_x k_y \operatorname{vers}\theta \tag{1.95}$$

$$o_z + a_y = 2k_y k_z \operatorname{vers}\theta \tag{1.96}$$

$$n_z + a_x = 2k_z k_x \operatorname{vers}\theta \tag{1.97}$$

If k_x is largest then

$$k_y = \frac{n_y + o_x}{2k_x \operatorname{vers}\theta} \quad \text{from Equation 1.95} \tag{1.98}$$

$$k_z = \frac{a_x + n_z}{2k_x \operatorname{vers}\theta} \quad \text{from Equation 1.97} \tag{1.99}$$

If k_y is largest then

$$k_x = \frac{n_y + o_x}{2k_y \operatorname{vers}\theta} \quad \text{from Equation 1.95} \tag{1.100}$$

$$k_z = \frac{o_z + a_y}{2k_y \operatorname{vers}\theta} \quad \text{from Equation 1.96} \tag{1.101}$$

If k_z is largest then

$$k_x = \frac{a_x + n_z}{2k_z \operatorname{vers}\theta} \quad \text{from Equation 1.97} \tag{1.102}$$

$$k_y = \frac{o_z + a_y}{2k_z \operatorname{vers}\theta} \quad \text{from Equation 1.96} \tag{1.103}$$

(See [Whitney] for an alternate approach to this problem.)

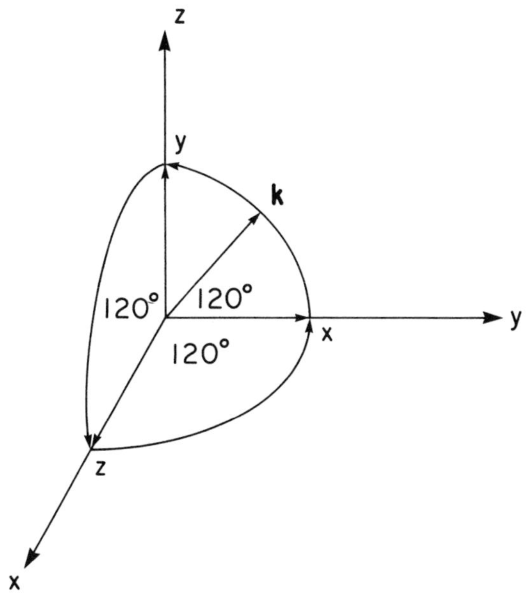

Figure 1.13. Rotation about **k** of 120°

Example 1.1

Determine the equivalent axis and angle of rotation for the matrix given in Equation 1.41

$$\mathrm{Rot}(y,90)\mathrm{Rot}(z,90) = \begin{bmatrix} 0 & 0 & 1 & 0 \\ 1 & 0 & 0 & 0 \\ 0 & 1 & 0 & 0 \\ 0 & 0 & 0 & 1 \end{bmatrix} \tag{1.104}$$

We first determine $\cos\theta$ from Equation 1.76

$$\cos\theta = \frac{1}{2}(0+0+0-1) = -\frac{1}{2} \tag{1.105}$$

and $\sin\theta$ from Equation 1.81

$$\sin\theta = \frac{1}{2}\sqrt{(1-0)^2+(1-0)^2+(1-0)^2} = \frac{\sqrt{3}}{2} \tag{1.106}$$

Thus

$$\theta = \tan^{-1}\left(\frac{\sqrt{3}}{2}\bigg/\frac{-1}{2}\right) = 120^\circ \tag{1.107}$$

As $\theta > 90$, we determine the largest component of k corresponding to the largest element on the diagonal. As all diagonal elements are equal in this example we may pick any one. We will pick k_x given by Equation 1.92

$$k_x = +\sqrt{0 + \frac{1}{2} \Big/ 1 + \frac{1}{2}} = \frac{1}{\sqrt{3}} \tag{1.108}$$

As we have determined k_x we may now determine k_y and k_z from Equations 1.98 and 1.99, respectively

$$k_y = \frac{1+0}{\sqrt{3}} = \frac{1}{\sqrt{3}} \tag{1.109}$$

$$k_z = \frac{1+0}{\sqrt{3}} = \frac{1}{\sqrt{3}} \tag{1.110}$$

In summary, then

$$\text{Rot}(y, 90)\text{Rot}(z, 90) = \text{Rot}(\mathbf{k}, 120) \tag{1.111}$$

where

$$\mathbf{k} = \frac{1}{\sqrt{3}}\mathbf{i} + \frac{1}{\sqrt{3}}\mathbf{j} + \frac{1}{\sqrt{3}}\mathbf{k} \quad \text{(see Figure 1.13)} \tag{1.112}$$

Any combination of rotations is always equivalent to a single rotation about some axis k by an angle θ, an important result that we will make use of later.

1.14 Stretching and Scaling

Although we will not use these deforming transformations in manipulation, we include them here to complete the subject of transformations.

A transform T

$$\mathbf{T} = \begin{bmatrix} a & 0 & 0 & 0 \\ 0 & b & 0 & 0 \\ 0 & 0 & c & 0 \\ 0 & 0 & 0 & 1 \end{bmatrix} \tag{1.113}$$

will stretch objects uniformly along the x axis by a factor a, along the y axis by a factor b, and along the z axis by a factor c. Consider any point on an object $x\mathbf{i} + y\mathbf{j} + z\mathbf{k}$; its transform is

$$\begin{bmatrix} ax \\ by \\ cz \\ 1 \end{bmatrix} = \begin{bmatrix} a & 0 & 0 & 0 \\ 0 & b & 0 & 0 \\ 0 & 0 & c & 0 \\ 0 & 0 & 0 & 1 \end{bmatrix} \begin{bmatrix} x \\ y \\ z \\ 1 \end{bmatrix} \tag{1.114}$$

indicating stretching as stated. Thus a cube could be transformed into a rectangular parallelepiped by such a transform.

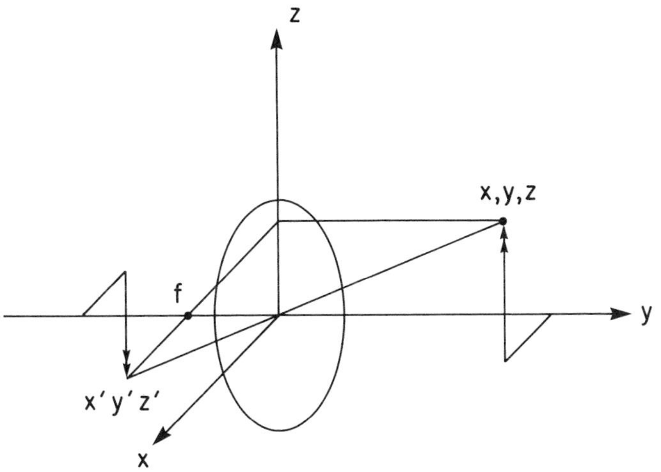

Figure 1.14. Perspective Transformation

The transform S where

$$S = \begin{bmatrix} s & 0 & 0 & 0 \\ 0 & s & 0 & 0 \\ 0 & 0 & s & 0 \\ 0 & 0 & 0 & 1 \end{bmatrix} \tag{1.115}$$

will scale any object by the factor s.

1.15 Perspective Transformations

Consider the image formed of an object by a simple lens as shown in Figure 1.14.

The axis of the lens is shown along the y axis for convenience. An object point x, y, z is imaged at x' y' z' if the lens has a focal length f (f is considered positive). y' represents the image distance and varies with object distance y. If we plot points on a plane perpendicular to the y axis located at y' (the film plane in a camera), then a perspective image is formed.

We will first obtain values of x', y', and z', then introduce a perspective transformation and show that the same values are obtained.

Based on the fact that a ray passing through the center of the lens is undeviated, we may write

$$\frac{z}{y} = \frac{z'}{y'} \tag{1.116}$$

and

$$\frac{x}{y} = \frac{x'}{y'} \tag{1.117}$$

Based on the additional fact that a ray parallel to the lens axis passes through the focal point f, we may write

$$\frac{z}{f} = \frac{z'}{y' + f} \tag{1.118}$$

and

$$\frac{x}{f} = \frac{x'}{y' + f} \tag{1.119}$$

Notice that x', y', and z' are negative and that f is positive. Eliminating y' between Equations 1.116 and 1.118 we obtain

$$\frac{z}{f} = \frac{z'}{(\frac{z'y}{z} + f)} \tag{1.120}$$

and solving for z' we obtain the result

$$z' = \frac{z}{(1 - \frac{y}{f})} \tag{1.121}$$

Working with Equations 1.117 and 1.119 we can similarly obtain

$$x' = \frac{x}{(1 - \frac{y}{f})} \tag{1.122}$$

In order to obtain the image distance y' we rewrite Equations 1.116 and 1.118 as

$$\frac{z}{z'} = \frac{y}{y'} \tag{1.123}$$

and

$$\frac{z}{z'} = \frac{f}{y' + f} \tag{1.124}$$

thus

$$\frac{y}{y'} = \frac{f}{y' + f} \tag{1.125}$$

and solving for y' we obtain the result

$$y' = \frac{y}{(1 - \frac{y}{f})} \tag{1.126}$$

The homogeneous transformation **P** which produces the same result is

$$\mathbf{P} = \begin{bmatrix} 1 & 0 & 0 & 0 \\ 0 & 1 & 0 & 0 \\ 0 & 0 & 1 & 0 \\ 0 & -\frac{1}{f} & 0 & 1 \end{bmatrix} \tag{1.127}$$

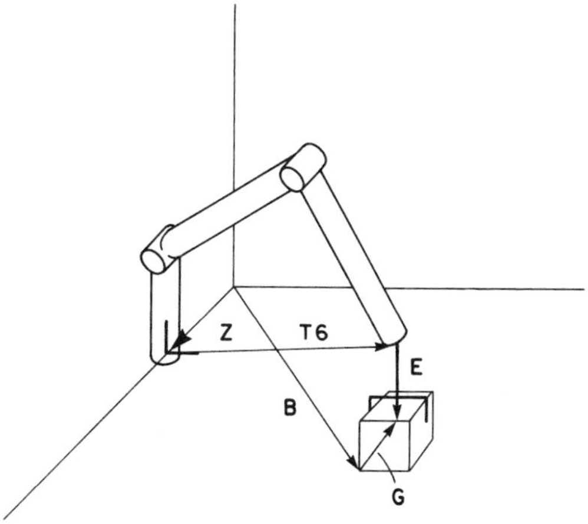

Figure 1.15. An Object and Manipulator

as any point $x\mathbf{i} + y\mathbf{j} + z\mathbf{k}$ transforms as

$$\begin{bmatrix} x \\ y \\ z \\ 1-\frac{y}{f} \end{bmatrix} = \begin{bmatrix} 1 & 0 & 0 & 0 \\ 0 & 1 & 0 & 0 \\ 0 & 0 & 1 & 0 \\ 0 & -\frac{1}{f} & 0 & 1 \end{bmatrix} \begin{bmatrix} x \\ y \\ z \\ 1 \end{bmatrix} \tag{1.128}$$

The image point x', y', z', obtained by dividing through by the weight factor $(1 - y/f)$, is

$$\frac{x}{(1-y/f)}\mathbf{i} + \frac{y}{(1-y/f)}\mathbf{j} + \frac{z}{(1-y/f)}\mathbf{k} \tag{1.129}$$

This is the same result that we obtained above.

A transform similar to $\mathbf{P}$ but with $-1/f$ at the bottom of the first column produces a perspective transformation along the x axis. If the $-1/f$ term is in the third column then the projection is along the z axis.

1.16 Transform Equations

We will frequently be required to deal with transform equations in which a coordinate frame is described in two or more ways. Consider the situation described in Figure 1.15. A manipulator is positioned with respect to base coordinates by a transform $\mathbf{Z}$. The end of the manipulator is described by a transform ${}^{Z}\mathbf{T}_6$, and the end effector is described by ${}^{T_6}\mathbf{E}$. An object is positioned with respect to base coordinates by a transform $\mathbf{B}$, and finally the manipulator end effector is positioned with respect to the object by ${}^{B}\mathbf{G}$. We have two descriptions of the position of the end effector, one with respect to the object and one with respect to the

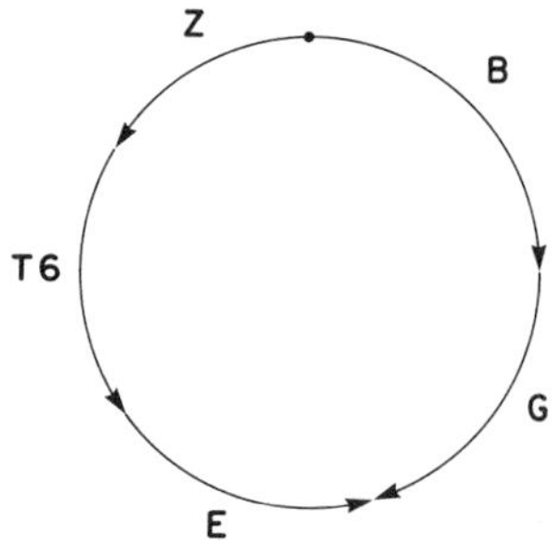

Figure 1.16. Directed Transform Graph

manipulator. As both positions are the same, we may equate the two descriptions

$$\mathbf{Z}\, {}^{Z}\mathbf{T}_6\, {}^{T_6}\mathbf{E} = \mathbf{B}\, {}^{B}\mathbf{G} \tag{1.130}$$

This equation may be represented by the directed transform graph (see Figure 1.16). Each link of the graph represents a transform and is directed from its defining coordinate frame.

If we wish to solve Equation 1.130 for the manipulator transform T_6 we must premultiply Equation 1.130 by $\mathbf{Z}^{-1}$ and postmultiply by E^{-1} to obtain

$$\mathrm{T}_6 = \mathbf{Z}^{-1}\, \mathbf{B}\, \mathbf{G}\, \mathbf{E}^{-1} \tag{1.131}$$

We may obtain this result from the transform graph by starting at the base of the T_6 link and listing the transforms as we traverse the graph in order until we reach the head of link T_6. If, as we list transforms, we move from a head to a tail (in the reverse direction of the directed link), we list the inverse of the transform. From the graph we thus obtain

$$\mathrm{T}_6 = \mathbf{Z}^{-1}\, \mathbf{B}\, \mathbf{G}\, \mathbf{E}^{-1} \tag{1.132}$$

as before.

As a further example, consider that the position of the object **B** is unknown, but that the manipulator is moved such that the end effector is positioned over the object correctly. We may then solve for **B** from Equation 1.130 by postmultiplying by $\mathbf{G}^{-1}$ or obtain the same result directly from the graph by tracing the path from the tail of **B** back around the graph to the head of link **B**

$$\mathbf{B} = \mathbf{Z}\, \mathrm{T}_6\, \mathbf{E}\, \mathbf{G}^{-1} \tag{1.133}$$

We may also use the graph to solve for connected groups of transforms, for example

$$\mathbf{Z}\, \mathrm{T}_6 = \mathbf{B}\, \mathbf{G}\, \mathbf{E}^{-1} \tag{1.134}$$

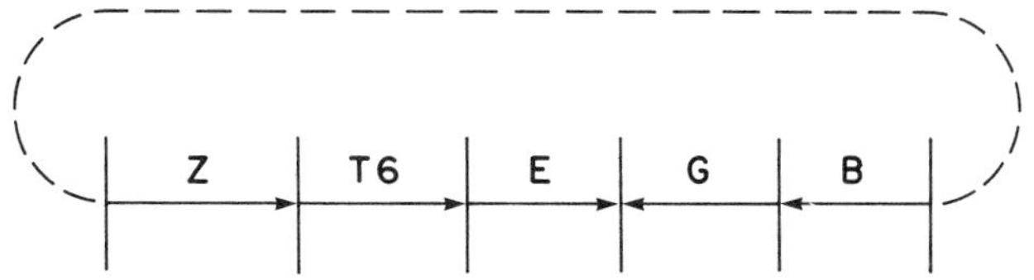

Figure 1.17. An Alternative Form of Figure 1.16

The use of a transform graph simplifies the solution of transform equations, allowing the results to be written directly. In order to avoid drawing circles, we will represent the transform graph as shown in Figure 1.17, where the dashed line indicates that two nodes are connected together.

Intermediate vertical lines represent individual coordinate frames.

1.17 Summary

Homogeneous transformations may be readily used to describe the positions and orientations of coordinate frames in space. If a coordinate frame is embedded in an object then the position and orientation of the object are also readily described.

The description of object A in terms of object B by means of a homogeneous transformation may be inverted to obtain the description of object B in terms of object A. This is not a property of a simple vector description of the relative displacement of one object with respect to another.

Transformations may be interpreted as a product of rotation and translation transformations. If they are interpreted from left to right, then the rotations and translations are in terms of the currently defined coordinate frame. If they are interpreted from right to left, then the rotations and translations are described with respect to the reference coordinate frame.

Homogeneous transformations describe coordinate frames in terms of rectangular components, which are the sines and cosines of angles. This description may be related to rotations in which case the description is in terms of a vector and angle of rotation.

1.18 References

Denavit, J. & Hartenberg, R. S. "A Kinematic Notation for Lower-Pair Mechanisms Based on Matrices," *ASME Journal of Applied Mechanics* (June 1955), 215–221.

Duda, R. O. & Hart, P. E. *Pattern Classification and Scene Analysis*, Wiley, New York, 1972.

Hamilton, W. R. *Elements of Quaternions*, Chelsea Publishing Co., New York, 1969.

Klumpp, A. R. "Singularity-Free Extraction of a Quaternion from a Direction Cosine Matrix," *Journal of Spacecraft* 13, 12 (Dec. 1976), 754–755.

Paul, R. P. Modeling, Trajectory Calculation and Servoing of a Computer Controlled Arm, Stanford Artificial Intelligence Laboratory, Stanford University, AIM 177, 1972.

Paul, R. P. "The Mathematics of Computer Controlled Manipulation," *The 1977 Joint Automatic Control Conference*, July 1977, 124–131.

Pieper, D. L. The Kinematics of Manipulators Under Computer Control, Stanford Artificial Intelligence Laboratory, Stanford University, AIM 72, 1968.

Roberts, L. G. Machine Perception of Three-Dimensional Solids, Lincoln Laboratory, Massachusetts Institute of Technology, Report No. 315, 1963.

Roberts, L. G. Homogeneous Matrix Representation and Manipulation of N-Dimensional Constructs, Lincoln Laboratory, Massachusetts Institute of Technology, Document No. MS1045, 1965.

Whitney, D. E. "The Mathematics of Coordinated Control of Prosthetic Arms and Manipulators," *Trans. ASME, Journal of Dynamic Systems, Measurement, and Control* (Dec. 1972), 303–309.

CHAPTER 2

KINEMATIC EQUATIONS

2.1 Introduction

In this chapter we will develop homogeneous transformations to represent various coordinate frames and formulate methods of assigning coordinate frames to mechanical linkages representing manipulators. We will first define various methods of describing the position and orientation of a manipulator and then develop this description in terms of the joint coordinates.

Any manipulator can be considered to consist of a series of links connected together by joints. We will embed a coordinate frame in each link of the manipulator. Using homogeneous transformations, we can describe the relative position and orientation between these coordinate frames [Pieper]. Historically, the homogeneous transformation describing the relation between one link and the next has been called an A matrix [Denavit]. An A matrix is simply a homogeneous transformation describing the relative translation and rotation between link coordinate systems. A_1 describes the position and orientation of the first link. A_2 describes the position and orientation of the second link with respect to the first. Thus the position and orientation of the second link in base coordinates are given by the matrix product

$$T_2 = A_1 A_2 \tag{2.1}$$

Similarly, A_3 describes the third link in terms of the second and

$$T_3 = A_1 A_2 A_3 \tag{2.2}$$

These products of A matrices have historically been called T matrices, with the leading superscript omitted if it is 0. Given a six link manipulator we have

$$T_6 = A_1 A_2 A_3 A_4 A_5 A_6 \tag{2.3}$$

A six link manipulator can have six degrees of freedom, one for each link, and can be positioned and oriented arbitrarily within its range of motion. Three degrees of freedom are required to specify position and three more to specify orientation. T_6 represents the position and orientation of the manipulator. This can be thought of

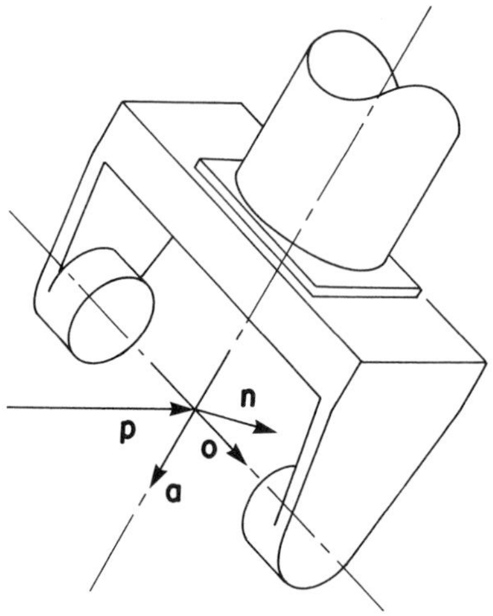

Figure 2.1. **o**, **a**, and **p** Vectors

in terms of a hand, as shown in Figure 2.1. We locate the origin of a describing coordinate frame centrally between the finger tips. This origin is described by a vector **p**.

The three unit vectors describing the hand orientation are directed as follows. The z vector lies in the direction from which the hand would approach an object and is known as the approach vector, **a**. The y vector, known as the orientation vector **o**, is in the direction specifying the orientation of the hand, from fingertip to fingertip. The final vector, known as the normal vector, **n**, forms a right-handed set of vectors and is thus specified by the vector cross-product

$$\mathbf{n} = \mathbf{o} \times \mathbf{a}$$

The transform T_6 thus has elements

$$T_6 = \begin{bmatrix} n_x & o_x & a_x & p_x \\ n_y & o_y & a_y & p_y \\ n_z & o_z & a_z & p_z \\ 0 & 0 & 0 & 1 \end{bmatrix} \tag{2.4}$$

as shown in Figure 2.1.

2.2 Specification of Orientation

T_6 is fully specified by assigning values to each of its 16 elements. Of these 16 elements only 12 have any real meaning. The bottom row consists of three zeros and a one. The left hand column vector is the vector cross product of the **o** and **a** column vectors. The remaining nine numbers represent three vectors **o**, **a**, and **p**. While there is no restriction on the value of **p**, provided the manipulator can reach the desired position, the vectors **o** and **a** must both be of unit magnitude and perpendicular, i.e.

$$\mathbf{o} \cdot \mathbf{o} = 1 \tag{2.5}$$

$$\mathbf{a} \cdot \mathbf{a} = 1 \tag{2.6}$$

$$\mathbf{o} \cdot \mathbf{a} = 0 \tag{2.7}$$

These restrictions on **o** and **a** make it difficult to assign components to the vectors except in simple cases when the end effector is aligned with the coordinate axes. If there is any doubt that **o** and **a** meet these conditions, the vectors may be modified to satisfy the conditions as follows. Make **a** of unit magnitude

$$\mathbf{a} \leftarrow \frac{\mathbf{a}}{|\mathbf{a}|} \tag{2.8}$$

construct **n** perpendicular to **o** and **a**

$$\mathbf{n} \leftarrow \mathbf{o} \times \mathbf{a} \tag{2.9}$$

rotate **o** in the plane formed by **o** and **a**, so that it is perpendicular to both **n** and **a**

$$\mathbf{o} \leftarrow \mathbf{a} \times \mathbf{n} \tag{2.10}$$

and make **o** of unit magnitude

$$\mathbf{o} \leftarrow \frac{\mathbf{o}}{|\mathbf{o}|} \tag{2.11}$$

We may also specify the orientation of the end of the manipulator as a rotation θ about an axis **k** using the generalized rotation matrix, $\mathbf{Rot}(\mathbf{k}, \theta)$, developed in Chapter 1. Unfortunately, the axis of rotation to achieve some desired orientations is not intuitively obvious.

2.3 Euler Angles

Orientation is more frequently specified by a sequence of rotations about the x, y, or z axes. Euler angles describe any possible orientation in terms of a rotation ϕ about the z axis, then a rotation θ about the new y axis, y', and finally, a rotation about the new z axis, z'', of ψ. (See Figure 2.2).

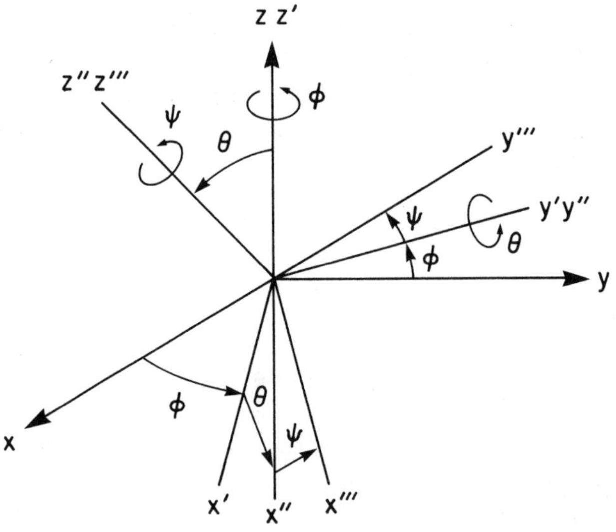

Figure 2.2. Euler Angles

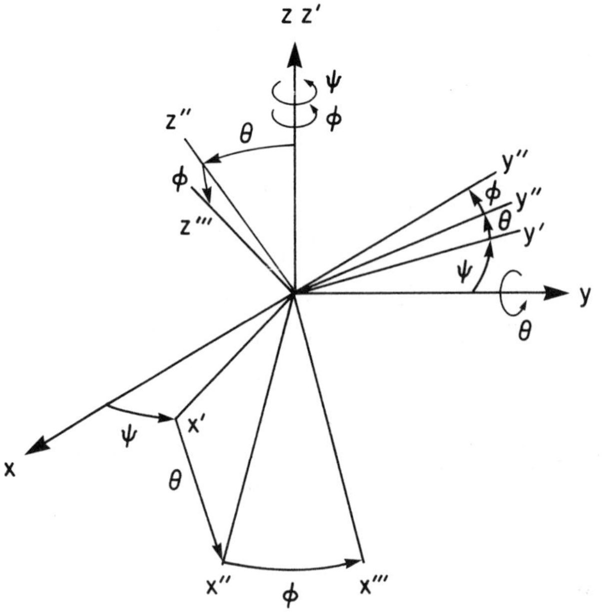

Figure 2.3. Euler Angles Interpreted in Base Coordinates

$$\mathrm{Euler}(\phi, \theta, \psi) = \mathrm{Rot}(z, \phi)\ \mathrm{Rot}(y, \theta)\ \mathrm{Rot}(z, \psi) \tag{2.12}$$

As in every case of a sequence of rotations, the order in which the rotations are made is important. Notice that this sequence of rotations can be interpreted in the reverse order as rotations in base coordinates: a rotation ψ about the z axis, followed by a rotation θ about the base y axis, and finally a rotation ϕ, once again about the base z axis (see Figure 2.3).

The Euler transformation, **Euler**(ϕ, θ, ψ), can be evaluated by multiplying the three rotation matrices together

$$\mathbf{Euler}(\phi,\theta,\psi) = \mathbf{Rot}(z,\phi)\,\mathbf{Rot}(y,\theta)\,\mathbf{Rot}(z,\psi) \tag{2.13}$$

$$\mathbf{Euler}(\phi,\theta,\psi) = \mathbf{Rot}(z,\phi)\begin{bmatrix} \cos\theta & 0 & \sin\theta & 0 \\ 0 & 1 & 0 & 0 \\ -\sin\theta & 0 & \cos\theta & 0 \\ 0 & 0 & 0 & 1 \end{bmatrix}\begin{bmatrix} \cos\psi & -\sin\psi & 0 & 0 \\ \sin\psi & \cos\psi & 0 & 0 \\ 0 & 0 & 1 & 0 \\ 0 & 0 & 0 & 1 \end{bmatrix}. \tag{2.14}$$

$$\mathbf{Euler}(\phi,\theta,\psi) = \begin{bmatrix} \cos\phi & -\sin\phi & 0 & 0 \\ \sin\phi & \cos\phi & 0 & 0 \\ 0 & 0 & 1 & 0 \\ 0 & 0 & 0 & 1 \end{bmatrix}\begin{bmatrix} \cos\theta\cos\psi & -\cos\theta\sin\psi & \sin\theta & 0 \\ \sin\psi & \cos\psi & 0 & 0 \\ -\sin\theta\cos\psi & \sin\theta\sin\psi & \cos\theta & 0 \\ 0 & 0 & 0 & 1 \end{bmatrix} \tag{2.15}$$

$$\mathbf{Euler}(\phi,\theta,\psi) = \begin{bmatrix} \cos\phi\cos\theta\cos\psi - \sin\phi\sin\psi & -\cos\phi\cos\theta\sin\psi - \sin\phi\cos\psi & \cos\phi\sin\theta & 0 \\ \sin\phi\cos\theta\cos\psi + \cos\phi\sin\psi & -\sin\phi\cos\theta\sin\psi + \cos\phi\cos\psi & \sin\phi\sin\theta & 0 \\ -\sin\theta\cos\psi & \sin\theta\sin\psi & \cos\theta & 0 \\ 0 & 0 & 0 & 1 \end{bmatrix} \tag{2.16}$$

2.4 Roll, Pitch, and Yaw

Another frequently used set of rotations is roll, pitch, and yaw.

If we imagine a ship steaming along the z axis, then roll corresponds to a rotation ϕ about the z axis, pitch corresponds to a rotation θ about the y axis, and yaw corresponds to a rotation ψ about the x axis (see Figure 2.4). The rotations applied to a manipulator end effector are shown in Figure 2.5.

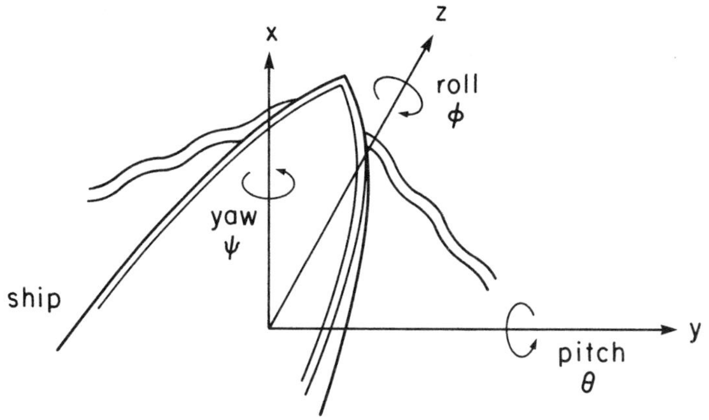

Figure 2.4. Roll, Pitch, and Yaw Angles

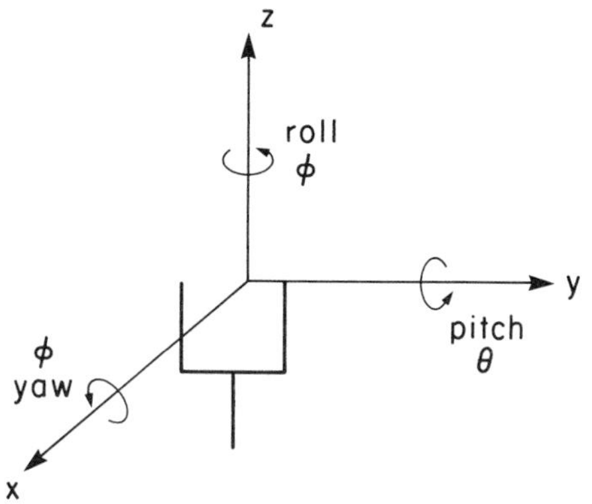

Figure 2.5. Roll, Pitch, and Yaw Coordinates for a Manipulator

We will specify the order of rotation as

$$\text{RPY}(\phi, \theta, \psi) = \text{Rot}(z, \phi)\ \text{Rot}(y, \theta)\ \text{Rot}(x, \psi) \tag{2.17}$$

that is, a rotation of ψ about station x, followed by a rotation θ about station y, and finally, a rotation ϕ about station z. The transformation is as follows

$$\text{RPY}(\phi, \theta, \psi) = \text{Rot}(z, \phi) \begin{bmatrix} \cos\theta & 0 & \sin\theta & 0 \\ 0 & 1 & 0 & 0 \\ -\sin\theta & 0 & \cos\theta & 0 \\ 0 & 0 & 0 & 1 \end{bmatrix} \begin{bmatrix} 1 & 0 & 0 & 0 \\ 0 & \cos\psi & -\sin\psi & 0 \\ 0 & \sin\psi & \cos\psi & 0 \\ 0 & 0 & 0 & 1 \end{bmatrix} \tag{2.18}$$

$$\mathrm{RPY}(\phi,\theta,\psi) = \begin{bmatrix} \cos\phi & -\sin\phi & 0 & 0 \\ \sin\phi & \cos\phi & 0 & 0 \\ 0 & 0 & 1 & 0 \\ 0 & 0 & 0 & 1 \end{bmatrix} \begin{bmatrix} \cos\theta & \sin\theta\sin\psi & \sin\theta\cos\psi & 0 \\ 0 & \cos\psi & -\sin\psi & 0 \\ -\sin\theta & \cos\theta\sin\psi & \cos\theta\cos\psi & 0 \\ 0 & 0 & 0 & 1 \end{bmatrix} \tag{2.19}$$

$$\mathrm{RPY}(\phi,\theta,\psi) = \begin{bmatrix} \cos\phi\cos\theta & \cos\phi\sin\theta\sin\psi - \sin\phi\cos\psi & \cos\phi\sin\theta\cos\psi + \sin\phi\sin\psi & 0 \\ \sin\phi\cos\theta & \sin\phi\sin\theta\sin\psi + \cos\phi\cos\psi & \sin\phi\sin\theta\cos\psi - \cos\phi\sin\psi & 0 \\ -\sin\theta & \cos\theta\sin\psi & \cos\theta\cos\psi & 0 \\ 0 & 0 & 0 & 1 \end{bmatrix} \tag{2.20}$$

2.5 Specification of Position

Once its orientation is specified, the hand may be positioned in station coordinates by multiplying by a translation transform corresponding to the vector **p**

$$T_6 = \begin{bmatrix} 1 & 0 & 0 & p_x \\ 0 & 1 & 0 & p_y \\ 0 & 0 & 1 & p_z \\ 0 & 0 & 0 & 1 \end{bmatrix} \begin{bmatrix} \text{Some} \\ \text{orientation} \\ \text{transformation} \end{bmatrix} \tag{2.21}$$

2.6 Cylindrical Coordinates

We might, however, wish to specify the position of the hand in cylindrical coordinates. This corresponds to a translation r along the x axis, followed by a rotation a about the z axis, and finally a translation z along the z axis (see Figure 2.6).

$$\mathrm{Cyl}(z,a,r) = \mathrm{Trans}(0,0,z)\ \mathrm{Rot}(z,a)\ \mathrm{Trans}(r,0,0)$$

$$\mathrm{Cyl}(z,a,r) = \mathrm{Trans}(0,0,z) \begin{bmatrix} \cos a & -\sin a & 0 & 0 \\ \sin a & \cos a & 0 & 0 \\ 0 & 0 & 1 & 0 \\ 0 & 0 & 0 & 1 \end{bmatrix} \begin{bmatrix} 1 & 0 & 0 & r \\ 0 & 1 & 0 & 0 \\ 0 & 0 & 1 & 0 \\ 0 & 0 & 0 & 1 \end{bmatrix} \tag{2.22}$$

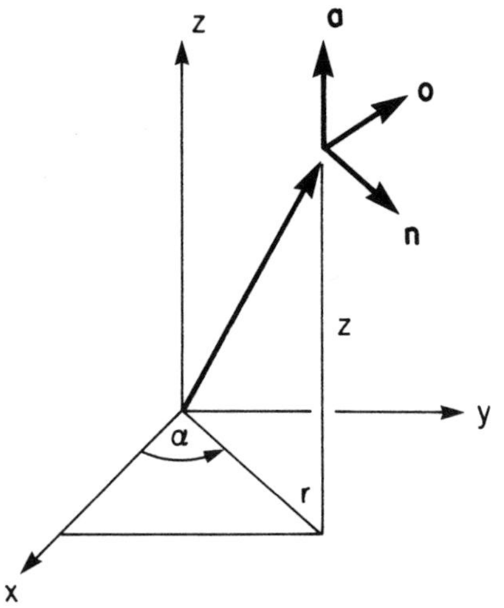

Figure 2.6. Cylindrical Polar Coordinates

$$\mathrm{Cyl}(z, \alpha, r) = \begin{bmatrix} 1 & 0 & 0 & 0 \\ 0 & 1 & 0 & 0 \\ 0 & 0 & 1 & z \\ 0 & 0 & 0 & 1 \end{bmatrix} \begin{bmatrix} \cos\alpha & -\sin\alpha & 0 & r\cos\alpha \\ \sin\alpha & \cos\alpha & 0 & r\sin\alpha \\ 0 & 0 & 1 & 0 \\ 0 & 0 & 0 & 1 \end{bmatrix} \tag{2.23}$$

$$\mathrm{Cyl}(z, \alpha, r) = \begin{bmatrix} \cos\alpha & -\sin\alpha & 0 & r\cos\alpha \\ \sin\alpha & \cos\alpha & 0 & r\sin\alpha \\ 0 & 0 & 1 & z \\ 0 & 0 & 0 & 1 \end{bmatrix} \tag{2.24}$$

If we were to postmultiply this transformation by an orientation transform, as in Equation 2.21, then the orientation of the hand would be with respect to the station coordinates rotated α about the z axis. If it were desired to specify orientation with respect to unrotated station coordinates, then we would rotate 2.24 by $-\alpha$ about its z axis or

$$\mathrm{Cyl}(z, \alpha, r) = \begin{bmatrix} \cos\alpha & -\sin\alpha & 0 & r\cos\alpha \\ \sin\alpha & \cos\alpha & 0 & r\sin\alpha \\ 0 & 0 & 1 & z \\ 0 & 0 & 1 & 1 \end{bmatrix} \begin{bmatrix} \cos(-\alpha) & -\sin(-\alpha) & 0 & 0 \\ \sin(-\alpha) & \cos(-\alpha) & 0 & 0 \\ 0 & 0 & 1 & 0 \\ 0 & 0 & 0 & 1 \end{bmatrix} \tag{2.25}$$

$$\mathrm{Cyl}(z, \alpha, r) = \begin{bmatrix} \cos\alpha & -\sin\alpha & 0 & r\cos\alpha \\ \sin\alpha & \cos\alpha & 0 & r\sin\alpha \\ 0 & 0 & 1 & z \\ 0 & 0 & 0 & 1 \end{bmatrix} \begin{bmatrix} \cos\alpha & \sin\alpha & 0 & 0 \\ -\sin\alpha & \cos\alpha & 0 & 0 \\ 0 & 0 & 1 & 0 \\ 0 & 0 & 0 & 1 \end{bmatrix} \tag{2.26}$$

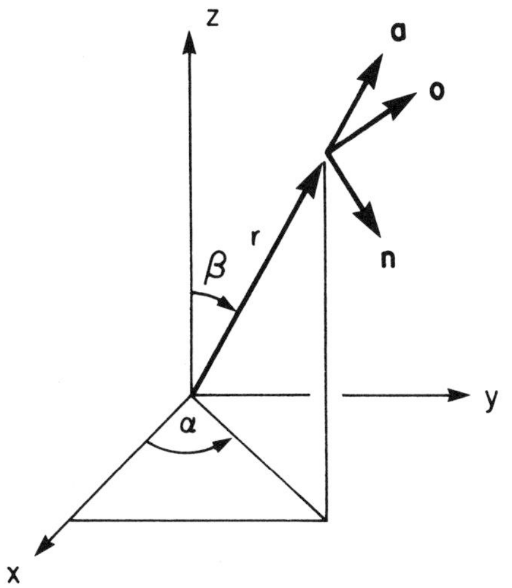

Figure 2.7. Spherical Polar Coordinates

$$\mathrm{Cyl}(z, a, r) = \begin{bmatrix} 1 & 0 & 0 & r\cos a \\ 0 & 1 & 0 & r\sin a \\ 0 & 0 & 1 & z \\ 0 & 0 & 0 & 1 \end{bmatrix} \tag{2.27}$$

This is the form in which we will interpret $\mathbf{Cyl}(z, a, r)$.

2.7 Spherical Coordinates

Finally, we will consider the method of specifying the position vector by means of spherical coordinates. This method corresponds to a translation r along the z axis, followed by a rotation β about station y, and then a rotation a about station z (see Figure 2.7).

$$\mathrm{Sph}(a, \beta, r) = \mathrm{Rot}(z, a)\, \mathrm{Rot}(y, \beta)\, \mathrm{Trans}(0, 0, r) \tag{2.28}$$

$$\mathrm{Sph}(a, \beta, r) = \mathrm{Rot}(z, a) \begin{bmatrix} \cos\beta & 0 & \sin\beta & 0 \\ 0 & 1 & 0 & 0 \\ -\sin\beta & 0 & \cos\beta & 0 \\ 0 & 0 & 0 & 1 \end{bmatrix} \begin{bmatrix} 1 & 0 & 0 & 0 \\ 0 & 1 & 0 & 0 \\ 0 & 0 & 1 & r \\ 0 & 0 & 0 & 1 \end{bmatrix} \tag{2.29}$$

$$\mathrm{Sph}(a, \beta, r) = \begin{bmatrix} \cos a & -\sin a & 0 & 0 \\ \sin a & \cos a & 0 & 0 \\ 0 & 0 & 1 & 0 \\ 0 & 0 & 0 & 1 \end{bmatrix} \begin{bmatrix} \cos\beta & 0 & \sin\beta & r\sin\beta \\ 0 & 1 & 0 & 0 \\ -\sin\beta & 0 & \cos\beta & r\cos\beta \\ 0 & 0 & 0 & 1 \end{bmatrix} \tag{2.30}$$

Table 2.1

[Translation]	Eqn.	[Rotation]	Eqn.
p_x, p_y, p_z		$o_x o_y o_z a_x a_y a_z$	
		$\mathbf{Rot}(\mathbf{k}, \theta)$	1.70
$\mathbf{Cyl}(r, a, r)$	2.27	$\mathbf{Euler}(\phi, \theta, \psi)$	2.16
$\mathbf{Sph}(a, \beta, r)$	2.33	$\mathbf{RPY}(\phi, \theta, \psi)$	2.20

$$\mathbf{Sph}(a, \beta, r) = \begin{bmatrix} \cos a \cos \beta & -\sin a & \cos a \sin \beta & r \cos a \sin \beta \\ \sin a \cos \beta & \cos a & \sin a \sin \beta & r \sin a \sin \beta \\ -\sin \beta & 0 & \cos \beta & r \cos \beta \\ 0 & 0 & 0 & 1 \end{bmatrix} \tag{2.31}$$

Once again, if we do not wish the orientation to be expressed with respect to this rotated coordinate frame, we must postmultiply by $\mathbf{Rot}(y, -\beta)$ and $\mathbf{Rot}(z, -a)$

$$\mathbf{Sph}(a, \beta, r) = \mathbf{Rot}(z, a)\mathbf{Rot}(y, \beta)\mathbf{Trans}(0, 0, r)\mathbf{Rot}(y, -\beta)\mathbf{Rot}(z, -a) \tag{2.32}$$

$$\mathbf{Sph}(a, \beta, r) = \begin{bmatrix} 1 & 0 & 0 & r \cos a \sin \beta \\ 0 & 1 & 0 & r \sin a \sin \beta \\ 0 & 0 & 1 & r \cos \beta \\ 0 & 0 & 0 & 1 \end{bmatrix} \tag{2.33}$$

2.8 Specification of T_6

T_6 can be specified in many ways in the form of a rotation and a translation

$$T_6 = [Translation][Rotation] \tag{2.34}$$

The various forms of translation and rotation that we have investigated are summarized in Table 2.1. If we use the unrotated version of **Cyl** or **Sph**, then the matrix product 2.32 is simply the rotation transform with its right hand column replaced by the right hand column of the translation transformation.

2.9 Specification of A matrices

We will now consider the specification of the A matrices on the right hand side of Equation 2.3. A serial link manipulator consists of a sequence of links connected together by actuated joints. For an n degree of freedom manipulator, there will be n links and n joints. The base of the manipulator is link 0 and is not considered one of the six links. Link 1 is connected to the base link by joint 1. There is no joint at the end of the final link. The only significance of links is that they maintain a fixed relationship between the manipulator joints at each end of the link.

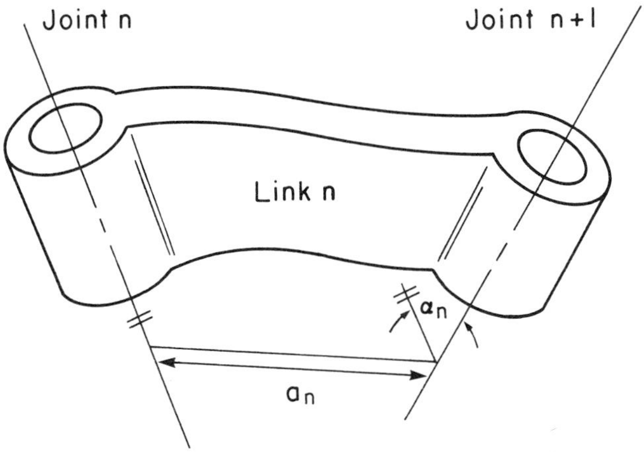

Figure 2.8. The Length a and Twist α of a Link

Any link can be characterized by two dimensions: the common normal distance a_n, and the angle α_n between the axes in a plane perpendicular to a_n. It is customary to call a_n the length and α_n the twist of the link (see Figure 2.8). Generally, two links are connected at each joint axis (see Figure 2.9).

The axis will have two normals to it, one for each link. The relative position of two such connected links is given by d_n, the distance between the normals along the joint n axis, and θ_n the angle between the normals measured in a plane normal to the axis. d_n and θ_n are called the distance and the angle between the links, respectively.

In order to describe the relationship between links, we will assign coordinate frames to each link. We will first consider revolute joints in which θ_n is the joint variable. The origin of the coordinate frame of link n is set to be at the intersection of the common normal between the axes of joints n and $n+1$ and the axis of joint $n+1$. In the case of intersecting joint axes, the origin is at the point of intersection of the joint axes. If the axes are parallel, the origin is chosen to make the joint distance zero for the next link whose coordinate origin is defined. The z axis for link n will be aligned with the axis of joint $n+1$. The x axis will be aligned with any common normal which exists and is directed along the normal from joint n to joint $n+1$. In the case of intersecting joints, the direction of the x axis is parallel or antiparallel to the vector cross product $\mathbf{z}_{n-1} \times \mathbf{z}_n$. Notice that this condition is also satisfied for the x axis directed along the normal between joints n and $n+1$. θ_n is zero for the nth revolute joint when $\mathbf{x}_{n-1}$ and $\mathbf{x}_n$ are parallel and have the same direction.

In the case of a prismatic joint, the distance d_n is the joint variable. The direction of the joint axis is the direction in which the joint moves. The direction of the axis is defined but, unlike a revolute joint, the position in space is not defined (see

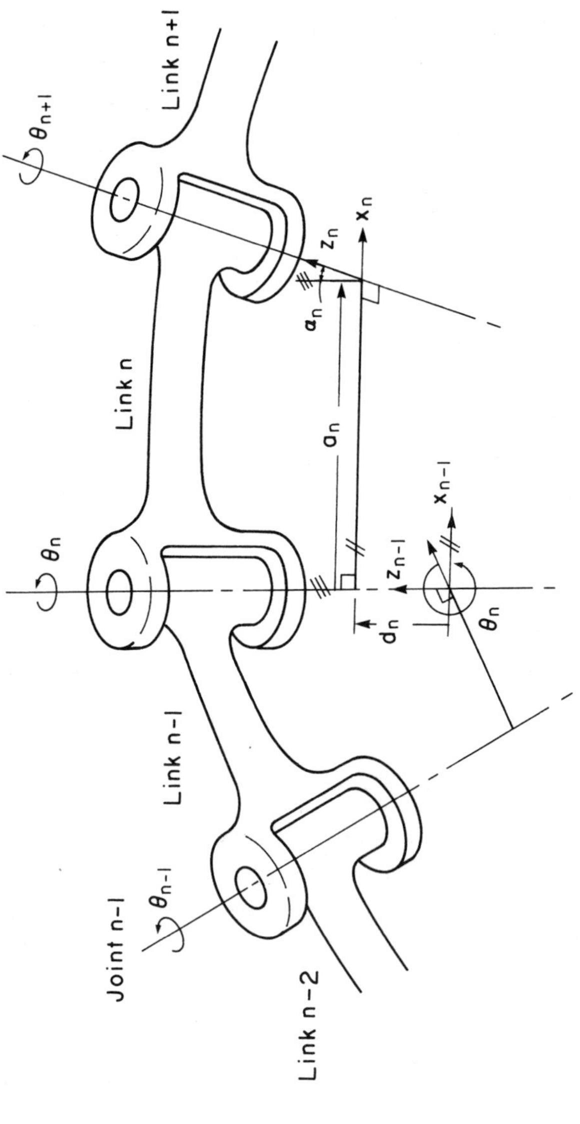

Figure 2.9. Link Parameters θ, d, a, and α

Figure 2.10). In the case of a prismatic joint, the length a_n has no meaning and is set to zero. The origin of the coordinate frame for a prismatic joint is coincident with the next defined link origin. The z axis of the prismatic link is aligned with the axis of joint $n+1$. The x_n axis is parallel or antiparallel to the vector cross product of the direction of the prismatic joint and $\mathbf{z}_n$. For a prismatic joint, we will define the zero position when $d_n = 0$.

With the manipulator in its zero position, the positive sense of rotation for revolute joints or displacement for prismatic joints can be decided and the sense of the direction of the z axes determined. The origin of the base link (zero) will be coincident with the origin of link 1. If it is desired to define a different reference coordinate system, then the relationship between the reference and base coordinate systems can be described by a fixed homogeneous transformation. At the end of the manipulator, the final displacement d_6 or rotation θ_6 occurs with respect to $\mathbf{z}_5$. The origin of the coordinate system for link 6 is chosen to be coincident with that of the link 5 coordinate system. If a tool (or end effector) is used whose origin and axes do not coincide with the coordinate system of link 6, the tool can be related by a fixed homogeneous transformation to link 6 [Paul81a].

Having assigned coordinate frames to all links according to the preceding scheme, we can establish the relationship between successive frames $n-1, n$ by the following rotations and translations:

rotate about $\mathbf{z}_{n-1}$, an angle, θ_n;
translate along $\mathbf{z}_{n-1}$, a distance d_n;
translate along rotated $\mathbf{x}_{n-1} = \mathbf{x}_n$ a length a_n;
rotate about $\mathbf{x}_n$, the twist angle α_n.

This may be expressed as the product of four homogeneous transformations relating the coordinate frame of link n to the coordinate frame of link $n-1$. This relationship is called an A matrix

$$\mathrm{A}_n = \mathrm{Rot}(z, \theta)\ \mathrm{Trans}(0, 0, d)\ \mathrm{Trans}(a, 0, 0)\ \mathrm{Rot}(x, \alpha) \tag{2.35}$$

$$\mathrm{A}_n = \begin{bmatrix} \cos\theta & -\sin\theta & 0 & 0 \\ \sin\theta & \cos\theta & 0 & 0 \\ 0 & 0 & 1 & 0 \\ 0 & 0 & 0 & 1 \end{bmatrix} \begin{bmatrix} 1 & 0 & 0 & a \\ 0 & 1 & 0 & 0 \\ 0 & 0 & 1 & d \\ 0 & 0 & 0 & 1 \end{bmatrix} \begin{bmatrix} 1 & 0 & 0 & 0 \\ 0 & \cos\alpha & -\sin\alpha & 0 \\ 0 & \sin\alpha & \cos\alpha & 0 \\ 0 & 0 & 0 & 1 \end{bmatrix} \tag{2.36}$$

$$\mathrm{A}_n = \begin{bmatrix} \cos\theta & -\sin\theta\cos\alpha & \sin\theta\sin\alpha & a\cos\theta \\ \sin\theta & \cos\theta\cos\alpha & -\cos\theta\sin\alpha & a\sin\theta \\ 0 & \sin\alpha & \cos\alpha & d \\ 0 & 0 & 0 & 1 \end{bmatrix} \tag{2.37}$$

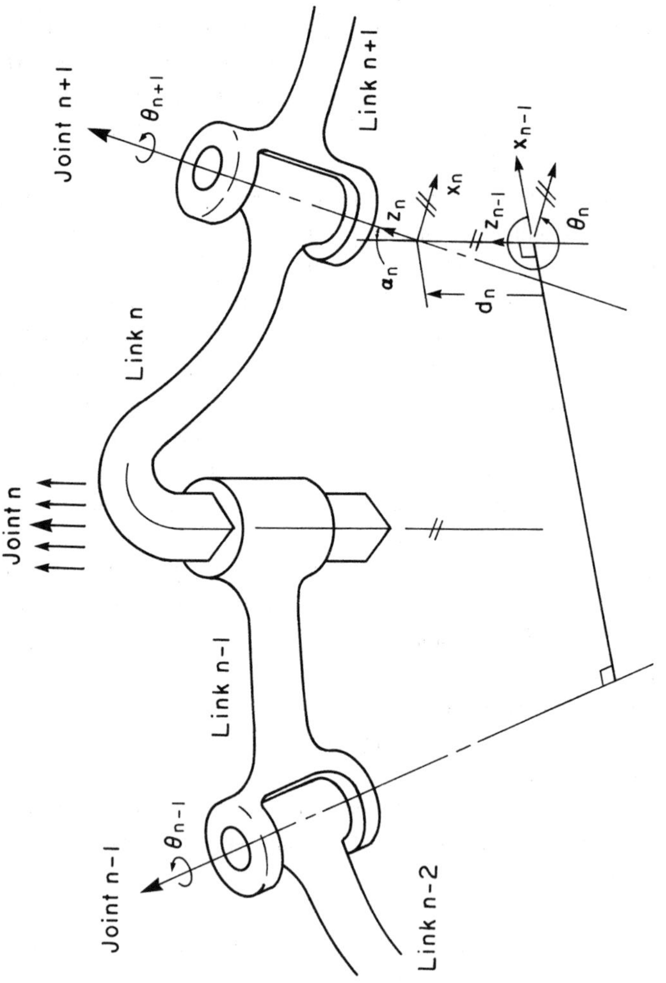

Figure 2.10. Link Parameters θ, d, and α for a Prismatic Joint

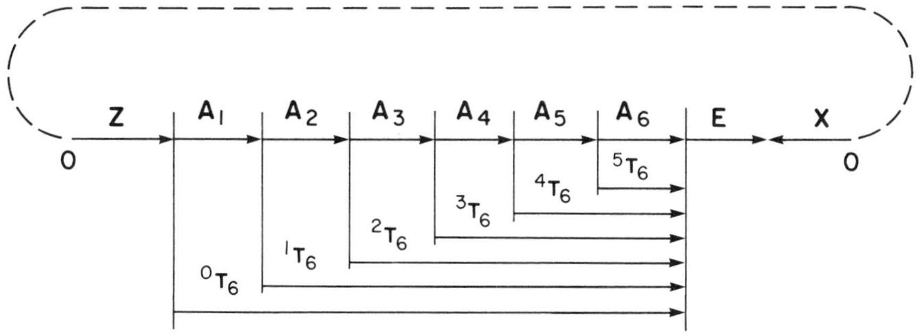

Figure 2.11. The Manipulator Transform Graph

For a prismatic joint the A matrix reduces to

$$A_n = \begin{bmatrix} \cos\theta & -\sin\theta\cos\alpha & \sin\theta\sin\alpha & 0 \\ \sin\theta & \cos\theta\cos\alpha & -\cos\theta\sin\alpha & 0 \\ 0 & \sin\alpha & \cos\alpha & d \\ 0 & 0 & 0 & 1 \end{bmatrix} \tag{2.38}$$

Once the link coordinate frames have been assigned to the manipulator, the various constant link parameters can be tabulated: d, a, and α for a link following a revolute joint, and θ and α for a link following a prismatic joint. Based on these parameters the constant sine and cosine values of the α's may be evaluated. The A matrices then become a function of the joint variable θ or, in the case of a prismatic joint, d. Once these values are known, the values for the six $\mathbf{A}_i$ transformation matrices can be determined.

2.10 Specification of T6 in Terms of the A matrices

The description of the end of the manipulator, link coordinate frame 6, with respect to link coordinate frame $n-1$ is given by ${}^{n-1}T_6$ where

$${}^{n-1}T_6 = A_n\, A_{n+1} \ldots A_6. \tag{2.39}$$

The end of the manipulator with respect to the base, known as T_6, is given by

$$T_6 = A_1\, A_2\, A_3\, A_4\, A_5\, A_6. \tag{2.40}$$

If the manipulator is related to a reference coordinate frame by a transformation Z, and has a tool attached to its end whose attachment is described by E, the position and orientation of the end of the tool with respect to the reference coordinate system are then described by **X** as

$$X = Z\, T_6\, E \tag{2.41}$$

The transform graph is shown in Figure 2.11, from which we may obtain

$$T_6 = Z^{-1}\, X\, E^{-1} \tag{2.42}$$

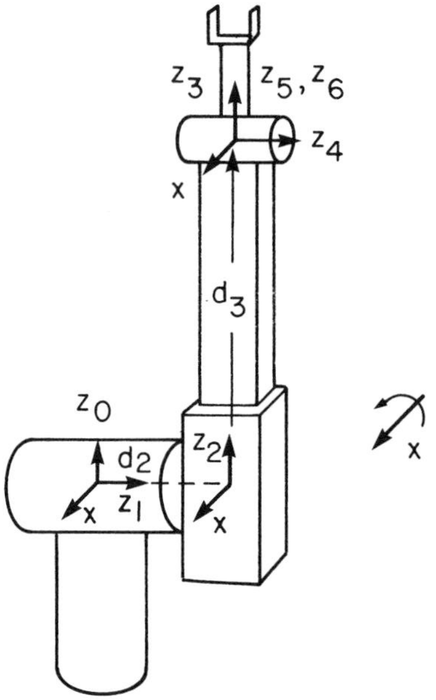

Figure 2.12. Coordinate Frames for the Stanford Manipulator

2.11 Kinematic Equations for the Stanford Manipulator

In Figure 2.12 the Stanford manipulator [Scheinman] is shown with coordinate frames assigned to the links. A picture of this manipulator is shown in Figure 1.12.

We will use the following abbreviations for the sine and cosine of the angle θ

$$\sin \theta_i = \mathrm{S}_i,$$

$$\cos \theta_i = \mathrm{C}_i,$$

$$\sin(\theta_i + \theta_j) = \mathrm{S}_{ij},$$

$$\cos(\theta_i + \theta_j) = \mathrm{C}_{ij},$$

The parameters are shown in Table 2.2.

Table 2.2 Link parameters for the Stanford Manipulator

Link	Variable	α	a	d	$\cos\alpha$	$\sin\alpha$
1	θ_1	$-90°$	0	0	0	-1
2	θ_2	$90°$	0	d_2	0	1
3	d_3	$0°$	0	d_3	1	0
4	θ_4	$-90°$	0	0	0	-1
5	θ_5	$90°$	0	0	0	1
6	θ_6	$0°$	0	0	1	0

The A transformations for the Stanford manipulator are as follows:

$$A_1 = \begin{bmatrix} C_1 & 0 & -S_1 & 0 \\ S_1 & 0 & C_1 & 0 \\ 0 & -1 & 0 & 0 \\ 0 & 0 & 0 & 1 \end{bmatrix} \tag{2.43}$$

$$A_2 = \begin{bmatrix} C_2 & 0 & S_2 & 0 \\ S_2 & 0 & -C_2 & 0 \\ 0 & 1 & 0 & d_2 \\ 0 & 0 & 0 & 1 \end{bmatrix} \tag{2.44}$$

$$A_3 = \begin{bmatrix} 1 & 0 & 0 & 0 \\ 0 & 1 & 0 & 0 \\ 0 & 0 & 1 & d_3 \\ 0 & 0 & 0 & 1 \end{bmatrix} \tag{2.45}$$

$$A_4 = \begin{bmatrix} C_4 & 0 & -S_4 & 0 \\ S_4 & 0 & C_4 & 0 \\ 0 & -1 & 0 & 0 \\ 0 & 0 & 0 & 1 \end{bmatrix} \tag{2.46}$$

$$A_5 = \begin{bmatrix} C_5 & 0 & S_5 & 0 \\ S_5 & 0 & -C_5 & 0 \\ 0 & 1 & 0 & 0 \\ 0 & 0 & 0 & 1 \end{bmatrix} \tag{2.47}$$

$$A_6 = \begin{bmatrix} C_6 & -S_6 & 0 & 0 \\ S_6 & C_6 & 0 & 0 \\ 0 & 0 & 1 & 0 \\ 0 & 0 & 0 & 1 \end{bmatrix} \tag{2.48}$$

The products of the A transformations for the Stanford manipulator, starting at link six and working back to the base, are

$$
{}^5T_6 = \begin{bmatrix} C_6 & -S_6 & 0 & 0 \\ S_6 & C_6 & 0 & 0 \\ 0 & 0 & 1 & 0 \\ 0 & 0 & 0 & 1 \end{bmatrix} \tag{2.49}
$$

$$
{}^4T_6 = \begin{bmatrix} C_5 C_6 & -C_5 S_6 & S_5 & 0 \\ S_5 C_6 & -S_5 S_6 & -C_5 & 0 \\ S_6 & C_6 & 0 & 0 \\ 0 & 0 & 0 & 1 \end{bmatrix} \tag{2.50}
$$

$$
{}^3T_6 = \begin{bmatrix} C_4 C_5 C_6 - S_4 S_6 & -C_4 C_5 S_6 - S_4 C_6 & C_4 S_5 & 0 \\ S_4 C_5 C_6 + C_4 S_6 & -S_4 C_5 S_6 + C_4 C_6 & S_4 S_5 & 0 \\ -S_5 C_6 & S_5 S_6 & C_5 & 0 \\ 0 & 0 & 0 & 1 \end{bmatrix} \tag{2.51}
$$

$$
{}^2T_6 = \begin{bmatrix} C_4 C_5 C_6 - S_4 S_6 & -C_4 C_5 S_6 - S_4 C_6 & C_4 S_5 & 0 \\ S_4 C_5 C_6 + C_4 S_6 & -S_4 C_5 S_6 + C_4 C_6 & S_4 S_5 & 0 \\ -S_5 C_6 & S_5 S_6 & C_5 & d_3 \\ 0 & 0 & 0 & 1 \end{bmatrix} \tag{2.52}
$$

$$
{}^1T_6 = \begin{bmatrix} C_2(C_4 C_5 C_6 - S_4 S_6) - S_2 S_5 C_6 & -C_2(C_4 C_5 S_6 + S_4 C_6) + S_2 S_5 S_6 & C_2 C_4 S_5 + S_2 C_5 & S_2 d_3 \\ S_2(C_4 C_5 C_6 - S_4 S_6) + C_2 S_5 C_6 & -S_2(C_4 C_5 S_6 + S_4 C_6) - C_2 S_5 S_6 & S_2 C_4 S_5 - C_2 C_5 & -C_2 d_3 \\ S_4 C_5 C_6 + C_4 S_6 & -S_4 C_5 S_6 + C_4 C_6 & S_4 S_5 & d_2 \\ 0 & 0 & 0 & 1 \end{bmatrix} \tag{2.53}
$$

$$
T_6 = \begin{bmatrix} n_x & o_x & a_x & p_x \\ n_y & o_y & a_y & p_y \\ n_z & o_z & a_z & p_z \\ 0 & 0 & 0 & 1 \end{bmatrix} \tag{2.54}
$$

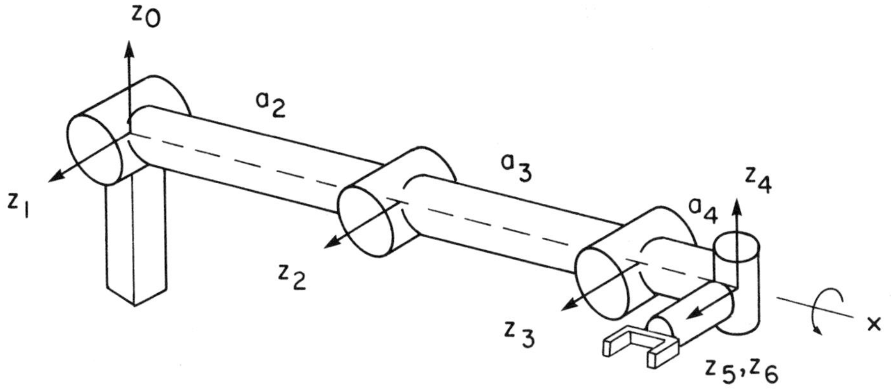

Figure 2.13. Coordinate Frames for The Elbow Manipulator

where

$$
\begin{aligned}
n_x &= C_1[C_2(C_4C_5C_6 - S_4S_6) - S_2S_5C_6] - S_1(S_4C_5C_6 + C_4S_6)\\
n_y &= S_1[C_2(C_4C_5C_6 - S_4S_6) - S_2S_5C_6] + C_1(S_4C_5C_6 + C_4S_6)\\
n_z &= -S_2(C_4C_5C_6 - S_4S_6) - C_2S_5C_6\\
o_x &= C_1[-C_2(C_4C_5S_6 + S_4C_6) + S_2S_5S_6] - S_1(-S_4C_5S_6 + C_4C_6)\\
o_y &= S_1[-C_2(C_4C_5S_6 + S_4C_6) + S_2S_5S_6] + C_1(-S_4C_5S_6 + C_4C_6)\\
o_z &= S_2(C_4C_5S_6 + S_4C_6) + C_2S_5S_6\\
a_x &= C_1(C_2C_4S_5 + S_2C_5) - S_1S_4S_5\\
a_y &= S_1(C_2C_4S_5 + S_2C_5) + C_1S_4S_5\\
a_z &= -S_2C_4S_5 + C_2C_5\\
p_x &= C_1S_2d_3 - S_1d_2\\
p_y &= S_1S_2d_3 + C_1d_2\\
p_z &= C_2d_3
\end{aligned}
\tag{2.55}
$$

In order to compute the right hand three columns of T_6, we require 10 transcendental function calls, 30 multiplies, and 12 additions. The first column of T_6 can be obtained as the vector cross product of the second and third columns. If the joint coordinates are given, the position and orientation of the hand are obtained by evaluating these equations to obtain T_6.

2.12 Kinematic Equations for an Elbow Manipulator

As a further example of this method of obtaining a solution, we will investigate another frequently occurring configuration, shown in Figure 2.13, described by the link parameters in Table 2.3 and the A matrices (Equations 2.56 – 2.61).

Table 2.3 Link parameters for the Elbow Manipulator

Link	Variable	α	a	d	$\cos\alpha$	$\sin\alpha$
1	θ_1	90°	0	0	0	1
2	θ_2	0°	a_2	0	1	0
3	θ_3	0°	a_3	0	1	0
4	θ_4	−90°	a_4	0	0	−1
5	θ_5	90°	0	0	0	1
6	θ_6	0°	0	0	1	0

The T matrices (Equations 2.62 – 2.68) are simplified by the introduction of variables $\theta_{23} = \theta_2 + \theta_3$ and $\theta_{234} = \theta_{23} + \theta_4$. This should be done whenever manipulator joint axes are parallel.

$$A_1 = \begin{bmatrix} C_1 & 0 & S_1 & 0 \\ S_1 & 0 & -C_1 & 0 \\ 0 & 1 & 0 & 0 \\ 0 & 0 & 0 & 1 \end{bmatrix} \tag{2.56}$$

$$A_2 = \begin{bmatrix} C_2 & -S_2 & 0 & C_2a_2 \\ S_2 & C_2 & 0 & S_2a_2 \\ 0 & 0 & 1 & 0 \\ 0 & 0 & 0 & 1 \end{bmatrix} \tag{2.57}$$

$$A_3 = \begin{bmatrix} C_3 & -S_3 & 0 & C_3a_3 \\ S_3 & C_3 & 0 & S_3a_3 \\ 0 & 0 & 1 & 0 \\ 0 & 0 & 0 & 1 \end{bmatrix} \tag{2.58}$$

$$A_4 = \begin{bmatrix} C_4 & 0 & -S_4 & C_4a_4 \\ S_4 & 0 & C_4 & S_4a_4 \\ 0 & -1 & 0 & 0 \\ 0 & 0 & 0 & 1 \end{bmatrix} \tag{2.59}$$

$$A_5 = \begin{bmatrix} C_5 & 0 & S_5 & 0 \\ S_5 & 0 & -C_5 & 0 \\ 0 & 1 & 0 & 0 \\ 0 & 0 & 0 & 1 \end{bmatrix} \tag{2.60}$$

$$A_6 = \begin{bmatrix} C_6 & -S_6 & 0 & 0 \\ S_6 & C_6 & 0 & 0 \\ 0 & 0 & 1 & 0 \\ 0 & 0 & 0 & 1 \end{bmatrix} \tag{2.61}$$

We now evaluate the products of the A matrices, starting at link six and working back towards the base in order to obtain T_6.

$$^{5}T_6 = \begin{bmatrix} C_6 & -S_6 & 0 & 0 \\ S_6 & C_6 & 0 & 0 \\ 0 & 0 & 1 & 0 \\ 0 & 0 & 0 & 1 \end{bmatrix} \tag{2.62}$$

$$^{4}T_6 = \begin{bmatrix} C_5C_6 & -C_5S_6 & S_5 & 0 \\ S_5C_6 & -S_5S_6 & -C_5 & 0 \\ S_6 & C_6 & 0 & 0 \\ 0 & 0 & 0 & 1 \end{bmatrix} \tag{2.63}$$

$$^{3}T_6 = \begin{bmatrix} C_4C_5C_6 - S_4S_6 & -C_4C_5S_6 - S_4C_6 & C_4S_5 & C_4a_4 \\ S_4C_5C_6 + C_4S_6 & -S_4C_5S_6 + C_4C_6 & S_4S_5 & S_4a_4 \\ -S_5C_6 & S_5S_6 & C_5 & 0 \\ 0 & 0 & 0 & 1 \end{bmatrix} \tag{2.64}$$

$$^{2}T_6 = \begin{bmatrix} C_{34}C_5C_6 - S_{34}S_6 & -C_{34}C_5S_6 - S_{34}C_6 & C_{34}S_5 & C_{34}a_4 + C_3a_3 \\ S_{34}C_5C_6 + C_{34}S_6 & -S_{34}C_5S_6 + C_{34}C_6 & S_{34}S_5 & S_{34}a_4 + S_3a_3 \\ -S_5C_6 & S_5S_6 & C_5 & 0 \\ 0 & 0 & 0 & 1 \end{bmatrix} \tag{2.65}$$

$$^{1}T_6 = \begin{bmatrix} C_{234}C_5C_6 - S_{234}S_6 & -C_{234}C_5G_6 - S_{234}C_6 & C_{234}S_5 & C_{234}a_4 + C_{23}a_3 + C_2a_2 \\ S_{234}C_5C_6 + C_{234}S_6 & -S_{234}C_5S_6 + C_{234}C_6 & S_{234}S_5 & S_{234}a_4 + S_{23}a_3 + S_2a_2 \\ -S_5C_6 & S_5S_6 & C_5 & 0 \\ 0 & 0 & 0 & 1 \end{bmatrix} \tag{2.66}$$

$$T_6 = \begin{bmatrix} n_x & o_x & a_x & p_x \\ n_y & o_y & a_y & p_y \\ n_z & o_z & a_z & p_z \\ 0 & 0 & 0 & 1 \end{bmatrix} \tag{2.67}$$

where

$$
\begin{aligned}
o_x &= -C_1[C_{234}C_5S_6 + S_{234}C_6] + S_1S_5S_6\\
o_y &= -S_1[C_{234}C_5S_6 + S_{234}C_6] - C_1S_5S_6\\
o_z &= -S_{234}C_5S_6 + C_{234}C_6\\
a_x &= C_1C_{234}S_5 + S_1C_5\\
a_y &= S_1C_{234}S_5 - C_1C_5\\
a_z &= S_{234}S_5\\
p_x &= C_1[C_{234}a_4 + C_{23}a_3 + C_2a_2]\\
p_y &= S_1[C_{234}a_4 + C_{23}a_3 + C_2a_2]\\
p_z &= S_{234}a_4 + S_{23}a_3 + S_2a_2
\end{aligned}
\tag{2.68}
$$

The evaluation of the right hand three columns of T_6 from the joint angles represents 12 transcendental function calls, 34 multiplies, and 14 additions.

2.13 Summary

We have employed homogeneous transformations in this chapter in order to describe the position and orientation of a manipulator in terms of various coordinate systems. We first developed transformations between various orthogonal coordinate systems and homogeneous transformations. We then developed the important relationship between the non-orthogonal joint coordinates and the homogeneous transformation describing the end of the manipulator. Notice that this may be done for any manipulator of any number of joints.

2.14 References

Denavit, J. & Hartenberg, R. S. "A Kinematic Notation for Lower-Pair Mechanisms Based on Matrices," *ASME Journal of Applied Mechanics* (June 1955), 215–221.

Paul, R. P. "Kinematic Control Equations for Manipulators," *IEEE Trans. on Systems, Man, and Cybernetics* (1981), to appear.

Pieper, D. L. The Kinematics of Manipulators Under Computer Control, Stanford Artificial Intelligence Laboratory, Stanford University, AIM 72, 1968.

Scheinman, V. D. Design of a Computer Manipulator, Stanford Artificial Intelligence Laboratory, Stanford University, AIM 92, 1969.

CHAPTER 3

SOLVING KINEMATIC EQUATIONS

3.1 Introduction

In the last chapter we developed a method for writing the kinematic equations for any manipulator specifying T_6, given the joint coordinates as arguments. We also studied different methods for specifying the position and orientation of the end effector T_6 by means of Euler angles, roll, pitch, and yaw, etc. We are concerned here with obtaining a solution to the kinematic equations obtained in Chapter 2 and we will start by obtaining solutions to some of the specifications of T_6. That is,for example, given numeric values for T_6, we will obtain the Euler angles. We will then proceed to the more difficult problem of solving for the joint coordinates, once again given T_6 as input. Obtaining a solution for the joint coordinates is of the utmost importance in robot manipulator control. We normally know where we want to move the manipulator in terms of T_6 and we need to obtain the joint coordinates in order to make the move. Obtaining a solution for the joint coordinates requires intuition and is the most difficult problem we will encounter.

We obtain these joint coordinate solutions by equating transform expressions. For each transform equation we obtain 12 non-trivial equations and it is these equations which will yield the required solution. The solution is obtained in a sequential manner, isolating each variable by premultiplication by a number of the transforms in each equation.

3.2 Euler Transform Solution

We will first obtain a solution for a transform specified by Euler angles

$$\mathbf{Euler}(\phi, \theta, \psi) = \mathbf{T} \tag{3.1}$$

where

$$\mathbf{Euler}(\phi, \theta, \psi) = \mathbf{Rot}(z, \phi)\, \mathbf{Rot}(y, \theta)\, \mathbf{Rot}(z, \psi) \tag{3.2}$$

We wish to obtain ϕ, θ, and ψ given any transformation $\mathbf{T}$. That is, if we have numeric values for each of the elements of $\mathbf{T}$, then what are the corresponding values of ϕ, θ, and ψ? We already have an expression for $\mathbf{Euler}(\phi, \theta, \psi)$ from

Equation 2.16 and we can equate this to T to obtain 16 equations, as matrix equality implies element-by-element equality

$$\begin{bmatrix} n_x & o_x & a_x & p_x \\ n_y & o_y & a_y & p_y \\ n_z & o_z & a_z & p_z \\ 0 & 0 & 0 & 1 \end{bmatrix} =$$

$$\begin{bmatrix} \cos\phi\cos\theta\cos\psi - \sin\phi\sin\psi & -\cos\phi\cos\theta\sin\psi - \sin\phi\cos\psi & \cos\phi\sin\theta & 0 \\ \sin\phi\cos\theta\cos\psi + \cos\phi\sin\psi & -\sin\phi\cos\theta\sin\psi + \cos\phi\cos\psi & \sin\phi\sin\theta & 0 \\ -\sin\theta\cos\psi & \sin\theta\sin\psi & \cos\theta & 0 \\ 0 & 0 & 0 & 1 \end{bmatrix} \tag{3.3}$$

The non-trivial equations are

$$n_x = \cos\phi\cos\theta\cos\psi - \sin\phi\sin\psi \tag{3.4}$$
$$n_y = \sin\phi\cos\theta\cos\psi + \cos\phi\sin\psi \tag{3.5}$$
$$n_z = -\sin\theta\cos\psi \tag{3.6}$$
$$o_x = -\cos\phi\cos\theta\sin\psi - \sin\phi\cos\psi \tag{3.7}$$
$$o_y = -\sin\phi\cos\theta\sin\psi + \cos\phi\cos\psi \tag{3.8}$$
$$o_z = \sin\theta\sin\psi \tag{3.9}$$
$$a_x = \cos\phi\sin\theta \tag{3.10}$$
$$a_y = \sin\phi\sin\theta \tag{3.11}$$
$$a_z = \cos\theta \tag{3.12}$$

We might be tempted to solve these equations for ϕ, θ, and ψ as follows

$$\theta = \cos^{-1}(a_z) \qquad \text{from 3.12} \tag{3.13}$$
$$\phi = \cos^{-1}(a_x/\sin\theta) \qquad \text{from 3.10 and 3.13} \tag{3.14}$$
$$\psi = \cos^{-1}(-n_z/\sin\theta) \qquad \text{from 3.6 and 3.13} \tag{3.15}$$

but this is useless for the following reasons:

a) In attempting to obtain an angle using the arc cosine function not only is the sign of the angle undefined but accuracy in determining the angle is itself dependent on the angle, i.e., $\cos(\theta) = \cos(-\theta)$ and $\frac{d\cos(\theta)}{d\theta}|_{0,180} = 0$.

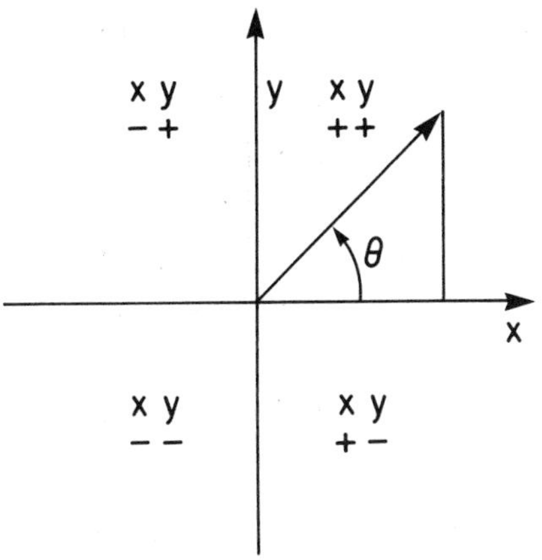

Figure 3.1. The atan2 Function

b) In the solution for ϕ and ψ (Equations 3.14, 3.15), we again use the arc cosine function but we divide by $\sin\theta$. This leads to inaccuracy whenever $\sin\theta$ is close to **0**.

c) Equations 3.14 and 3.15 are undefined when $\theta = 0$ or $\pm 180°$.

We must therefore be more careful in obtaining a solution. In determining angles we will always use the arc tangent function atan2 which is supplied two arguments, the ordinate y, and the abscissa x (see Figure 3.1). This function returns angles in the range of $-\pi \leq \theta < \pi$ by examining the sign of both y and x. The function also detects when either x or y is zero and returns the correct result. The accuracy of this function is uniform over its full range of definition. We should, of course, never divide by the sine of an angle as in the case of Equations 3.14 and 3.15.

In order to obtain the equations, we will employ a different approach which usually results in explicit solutions. We premultiply the given equation successively by the unknown inverse transforms. In the case of $\mathbf{Euler}(\phi, \theta, \psi)$

$$\mathbf{Rot}(z, \phi)^{-1}\,\mathbf{T} = \mathbf{Rot}(y, \theta)\,\mathbf{Rot}(z, \psi) \tag{3.16}$$

$$\mathbf{Rot}(y, \theta)^{-1}\,\mathbf{Rot}(z, \phi)^{-1}\,\mathbf{T} = \mathbf{Rot}(z, \psi) \tag{3.17}$$

The left hand side of Equation 3.16 is a function of the given transform **T** and ϕ. We examine the elements of the right hand side of the equation, find those which are either zero or constant, and equate these elements to the elements of the left hand side. In the case of Equation 3.16 we have

$$\begin{bmatrix} \cos\phi & \sin\phi & 0 & 0 \\ -\sin\phi & \cos\phi & 0 & 0 \\ 0 & 0 & 1 & 0 \\ 0 & 0 & 0 & 1 \end{bmatrix} \begin{bmatrix} n_x & o_x & a_x & p_x \\ n_y & o_y & a_y & p_y \\ n_z & o_z & a_z & p_z \\ 0 & 0 & 0 & 1 \end{bmatrix} = \begin{bmatrix} \cos\theta\cos\psi & -\cos\theta\sin\psi & \sin\theta & 0 \\ \sin\psi & \cos\psi & 0 & 0 \\ -\sin\theta\cos\psi & \sin\theta\sin\psi & \cos\theta & 0 \\ 0 & 0 & 0 & 1 \end{bmatrix} \tag{3.18}$$

Before we evaluate the left hand side of the equation, notice that we may write the product in the form

$$\begin{bmatrix} f_{11}(\mathrm{n}) & f_{11}(\mathrm{o}) & f_{11}(\mathrm{a}) & f_{11}(\mathrm{p}) \\ f_{12}(\mathrm{n}) & f_{12}(\mathrm{o}) & f_{12}(\mathrm{a}) & f_{12}(\mathrm{p}) \\ f_{13}(\mathrm{n}) & f_{13}(\mathrm{o}) & f_{13}(\mathrm{a}) & f_{13}(\mathrm{p}) \\ 0 & 0 & 0 & 1 \end{bmatrix} \tag{3.19}$$

where

$$f_{11} = \cos\phi\, x + \sin\phi\, y \tag{3.20}$$

$$f_{12} = -\sin\phi\, x + \cos\phi\, y \tag{3.21}$$

$$f_{13} = z \tag{3.22}$$

and x, y, z refer to components of the vectors given as arguments to f_{11}, f_{12}, and f_{13}. For example

$$f_{12}(\mathrm{a}) = -\sin\phi a_x + \cos\phi a_y \tag{3.23}$$

Thus we may rewrite Equation 3.18 as

$$\begin{bmatrix} f_{11}(\mathrm{n}) & f_{11}(\mathrm{o}) & f_{11}(\mathrm{a}) & f_{11}(\mathrm{p}) \\ f_{12}(\mathrm{n}) & f_{12}(\mathrm{o}) & f_{12}(\mathrm{a}) & f_{12}(\mathrm{p}) \\ f_{13}(\mathrm{n}) & f_{13}(\mathrm{o}) & f_{13}(\mathrm{a}) & f_{13}(\mathrm{p}) \\ 0 & 0 & 0 & 1 \end{bmatrix} = \begin{bmatrix} \cos\theta\cos\psi & -\cos\theta\sin\psi & \sin\theta & 0 \\ \sin\psi & \cos\psi & 0 & 0 \\ -\sin\theta\cos\psi & \sin\theta\sin\psi & \cos\theta & 0 \\ 0 & 0 & 0 & 1 \end{bmatrix} \tag{3.24}$$

where f_{11}, f_{12}, and f_{13} are defined above.

On examining the right hand side, we notice immediately that p_x, p_y, and p_z must be zero. This is to be expected, as the Euler transformation does not provide for any translation. The second row, third column element is also zero. Equating this to $f_{12}(\mathrm{a})$ we obtain

$$-\sin\phi a_x + \cos\phi a_y = 0 \tag{3.25}$$

Adding $\sin\phi a_x$ to both sides and dividing through by $\cos\phi a_x$ we obtain an expression for the tangent

$$\tan\phi = \frac{\sin\phi}{\cos\phi} = \frac{a_y}{a_x} \tag{3.26}$$

The angle ϕ is obtained from the computer atan2 function of two arguments y,x

$$\phi = \text{atan2}(a_y, a_x) \tag{3.27}$$

We can, however, obtain another solution to Equation 3.25 by adding $-\cos\phi a_y$ to both sides, dividing through by $-\cos\phi a_x$, and canceling $-a_x$ on the left hand side and $\cos\phi$ on the right hand side

$$\tan\phi = \frac{\sin\phi}{\cos\phi} = \frac{-a_y}{-a_x} \tag{3.28}$$

The angle ϕ is in this case

$$\phi = \text{atan2}(-a_y, -a_x) \tag{3.29}$$

which is a difference of 180° from the first solution.

Whenever we have an equation of the form of Equation 3.25 there will be two solutions, each 180° apart. If both a_y and a_x are zero, then the angle is undefined. This occurs when the hand is pointing straight up or down and both ϕ and ψ correspond to the same rotation. This is known as a degeneracy and in this case we will arbitrarily set ϕ to zero.

With the value of ϕ obtained, all the elements of the left hand side of Equation 3.24 are now defined. Examining the right hand side of the equation reveals that

$$\sin\theta = f_{11}(\mathrm{a}) \tag{3.30}$$
$$\cos\theta = f_{13}(\mathrm{a}) \tag{3.31}$$

or

$$\sin\theta = \cos\phi a_x + \sin\phi a_y \tag{3.32}$$
$$\cos\theta = a_z \tag{3.33}$$

thus

$$\theta = \text{atan2}(\cos\phi a_x + \sin\phi a_y, a_z) \tag{3.34}$$

When both the sine and cosine are defined, as in the above case, the angle is always uniquely defined and there is no problem of degeneracy as in the case ot the previous angle ϕ.

We also have the equation for ψ from Equation 3.24

$$\sin\psi = f_{12}(\mathbf{n}) \tag{3.35}$$
$$\cos\psi = f_{12}(\mathbf{o}) \tag{3.35}$$

or

$$\sin\psi = -\sin\phi n_x + \cos\phi n_y \tag{3.37}$$
$$\cos\psi = -\sin\phi o_x + \cos\phi o_y \tag{3.38}$$

and

$$\psi = \text{atan2}(-\sin\phi n_x + \cos\phi n_y, -\sin\phi o_x + \cos\phi o_y) \tag{3.39}$$

In summary, then: given a homogeneous transformation representing any rotation, we can determine the equivalent Euler angles as

$$\phi = \text{atan2}(a_y, a_x) \tag{3.40}$$

and

$$\phi = \phi + 180^\circ \tag{3.41}$$

$$\theta = \text{atan2}(\cos\phi a_x + \sin\phi a_y, a_z) \tag{3.42}$$

$$\psi = \text{atan2}(-\sin\phi n_x + \cos\phi n_y, -\sin\phi o_x + \cos\phi o_y) \tag{3.43}$$

representing 6 multiplies, 3 additions, and 3 transcendental function calls.

3.3 RPY Transform Solution

In the case of RPY(ϕ, θ, ψ), defined by Equations 2.17 – 2.20, we will solve the equation

$$\text{Rot}(z, \phi)^{-1}\,\text{T} = \text{Rot}(y, \theta)\,\text{Rot}(x, \psi) \tag{3.44}$$

$$\begin{bmatrix} f_{11}(\mathbf{n}) & f_{11}(\mathbf{o}) & f_{11}(\mathbf{a}) & 0 \\ f_{12}(\mathbf{n}) & f_{12}(\mathbf{o}) & f_{12}(\mathbf{a}) & 0 \\ f_{13}(\mathbf{n}) & f_{13}(\mathbf{o}) & f_{13}(\mathbf{a}) & 0 \\ 0 & 0 & 0 & 1 \end{bmatrix} = \begin{bmatrix} \cos\theta & \sin\theta\sin\psi & \sin\theta\cos\psi & 0 \\ 0 & \cos\psi & -\sin\psi & 0 \\ -\sin\theta & \cos\theta\sin\psi & \cos\theta\cos\psi & 0 \\ 0 & 0 & 0 & 1 \end{bmatrix} \tag{3.45}$$

where

$$f_{11} = \cos\phi x + \sin\phi y \tag{3.46}$$
$$f_{12} = -\sin\phi x + \cos\phi y \tag{3.47}$$
$$f_{13} = z \tag{3.48}$$

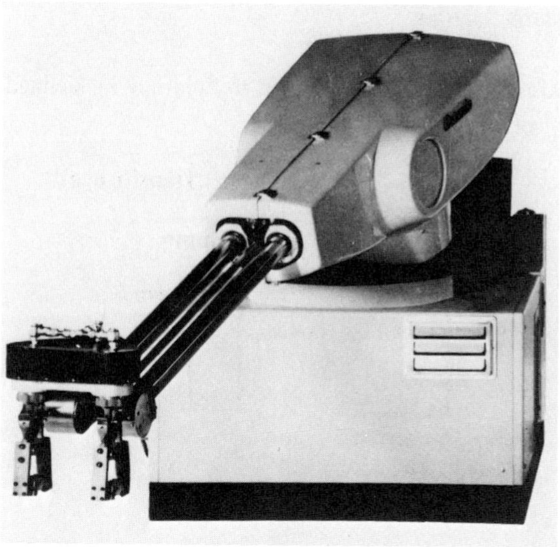

Figure 3.2. The Unimate 2100G (Courtesy of Unimation Inc.)

equating $f_{12}(\mathbf{n})$ yields

$$-\sin\phi n_x + \cos\phi n_y = 0 \tag{3.49}$$

and thus

$$\phi = \mathrm{atan2}(n_y, n_x) \tag{3.50}$$

and

$$\phi = \phi + 180^\circ \tag{3.51}$$

By equating the 3,1 and 1,1 elements from the right hand side of Equation 3.45 we now obtain

$$-\sin\theta = n_z \tag{3.52}$$

$$\cos\theta = \cos\phi n_x + \sin\phi n_y \tag{3.53}$$

and

$$\theta = \mathrm{atan2}(-n_z, \cos\phi n_x + \sin\phi n_y) \tag{3.54}$$

and further by equating the 2,3 and 2,2 elements we obtain

$$-\sin\psi = -\sin\phi a_x + \cos\phi a_y \tag{3.55}$$

$$\cos\psi = -\sin\phi o_x + \cos\phi o_y \tag{3.56}$$

and

$$\psi = \mathrm{atan2}(\sin\phi a_x - \cos\phi a_y, -\sin\phi o_x + \cos\phi o_y) \tag{3.57}$$

representing 6 multiplies, 3 additions, and 3 transcendental function calls.

3.4 Sph Transform Solution

The above technique may also be applied to $\mathrm{Sph}(a, \beta, r)$, defined by Equations 2.28 – 2.31, by solving

$$\mathrm{Rot}(z, a)^{-1}\,\mathrm{T} = \mathrm{Rot}(y, \beta)\,\mathrm{Trans}(0, 0, z) \tag{3.58}$$

In this case we will need only the right hand column

$$\begin{bmatrix} \cos a p_x + \sin a p_y \\ - \sin a p_x \cos a p_y \\ p_z \\ 1 \end{bmatrix} = \begin{bmatrix} r \sin \beta \\ 0 \\ r \cos \beta \\ 1 \end{bmatrix} \tag{3.59}$$

thus

$$- \sin a p_x + \cos a p_y = 0 \tag{3.60}$$

and

$$a = \mathrm{atan2}(p_y, p_x) \tag{3.61}$$

$$a = a + 180^{\circ} \tag{3.62}$$

and as $r > 0$ by definition

$$r \sin \beta = \cos a p_x + \sin a p_y \tag{3.63}$$

$$r \cos \beta = p_z \tag{3.64}$$

and

$$\beta = \mathrm{atan2}(\cos a p_x + \sin a p_y, p_z) \tag{3.65}$$

In order to obtain z we must premultiply both sides of Equation 3.58 by $\mathrm{Rot}(y, -\beta)$ to obtain

$$\mathrm{Rot}(y, \beta)^{-1}\,\mathrm{Rot}(x, a)^{-1}\,\mathrm{T} = \mathrm{Trans}(0, 0, z) \tag{3.66}$$

The right hand column is

$$\begin{bmatrix} \cos \beta(\cos a p_x + \sin a p_y) - \sin \beta p_z \\ - \sin a p_x + \cos a p_y \\ \sin \beta(\cos a p_x + \sin a p_y) + \cos \beta p_z \\ 1 \end{bmatrix} = \begin{bmatrix} 0 \\ 0 \\ z \\ 1 \end{bmatrix} \tag{3.67}$$

and thus

$$z = \sin \beta(\cos a p_x + \sin a p_y) + \cos \beta p_z \tag{3.68}$$

representing 6 multiplies, 3 additions, and 2 transcendental function calls.

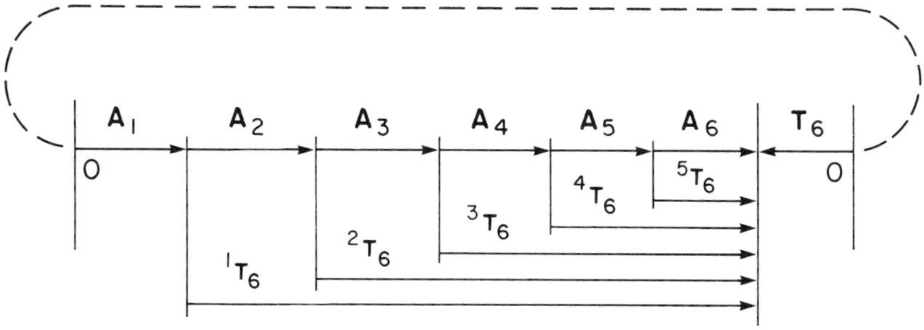

Figure 3.3. The Manipulator Transform Graph

3.5 Stanford Manipulator Solution

For manipulators, T_6 is known and is equal to the product of the six A matrices (see Figure 3.3).

$$T_6 = A_1\, A_2\, A_3\, A_4\, A_5\, A_6 \tag{3.69}$$

Six matrix equations are then obtained by successively premultiplying Equation 3.69 by the A matrix inverses

$$A_1^{-1}\, T_6 = {}^1T_6 \tag{3.70}$$
$$A_2^{-1}\, A_1^{-1}\, T_6 = {}^2T_6 \tag{3.71}$$
$$A_3^{-1}\, A_2^{-1}\, A_1^{-1} T_6 = {}^3T_6 \tag{3.72}$$
$$A_4^{-1}\, A_3^{-1}\, A_2^{-1}\, A_1^{-1}\, T_6 = {}^4T_6 \tag{3.73}$$
$$A_5^{-1}\, A_4^{-1}\, A_3^{-1}\, A_2^{-1}\, A_1^{-1}\, T_6 = {}^5T_6 \tag{3.74}$$

The matrix elements of the left hand sides of these equations are functions of the elements of T_6 and of the first $n - 1$ joint variables. The matrix elements of the right hand sides are either zero, constants, or functions of the nth to 6th joint variables. As matrix equality implies element-by-element, equality we obtain 12 equations from each matrix equation, that is, one equation for each of the components of the four vectors **n**, **o**, **a** and **p**. We will illustrate the various forms of these equations by developing the equations for the Stanford Manipulator (see Chapter 2, Equations 2.43 – 2.55, Figure 2.12).

If we premultiply Equation 3.69 by A_1^{-1} we obtain

$$A_1^{-1}\, T_6 = A_2\, A_3\, A_4\, A_5\, A_6 \tag{3.75}$$

$$A_1^{-1}\, T_6 = {}^1\, T_6 \tag{3.76}$$

The left hand side of Equation 3.76 is given by

$$A_1^{-1}\,T_6 = \begin{bmatrix} C_1 & S_1 & 0 & 0 \\ 0 & 0 & -1 & 0 \\ -S_1 & C_1 & 0 & 0 \\ 0 & 0 & 0 & 1 \end{bmatrix} \begin{bmatrix} n_x & o_x & a_x & p_x \\ n_y & o_y & a_y & p_y \\ n_z & o_z & a_z & p_z \\ 0 & 0 & 0 & 1 \end{bmatrix} \tag{3.77}$$

$$A_1^{-1}\,T_6 = \begin{bmatrix} f_{11}(\mathbf{n}) & f_{11}(\mathbf{o}) & f_{11}(\mathbf{a}) & f_{11}(\mathbf{p}) \\ f_{12}(\mathbf{n}) & f_{12}(\mathbf{o}) & f_{12}(\mathbf{a}) & f_{12}(\mathbf{p}) \\ f_{13}(\mathbf{n}) & f_{13}(\mathbf{o}) & f_{13}(\mathbf{a}) & f_{13}(\mathbf{p}) \\ 0 & 0 & 0 & 1 \end{bmatrix} \tag{3.78}$$

where

$$f_{11} = C_1\,x + S_1\,y \tag{3.79}$$

$$f_{12} = -z \tag{3.80}$$

$$f_{13} = -S_1\,x + C_1\,y \tag{3.81}$$

The right hand side of Equation 3.76 is obtained from Equation 2.53 and is given by

$$^1T_6 = \begin{bmatrix} C_2(C_4C_5C_6 - S_4S_6) - S_2S_5C_6 & -C_2(C_4C_5S_6 + S_4C_6) + S_2S_5S_6 & C_2C_4S_5 + S_2C_5 & S_2d_3 \\ S_2(C_4C_5C_6 - S_4S_6) + C_2S_5C_6 & -S_2(C_4C_5S_6 + S_4C_6) - C_2S_5S_6 & S_2C_4S_5 - C_2C_5 & -C_2d_3 \\ S_4C_5C_6 + C_4S_6 & -S_4C_5S_6 + C_4C_6 & S_4S_5 & d_2 \\ 0 & 0 & 0 & 1 \end{bmatrix} \tag{3.82}$$

All the elements of the right hand side of Equation 3.82 are functions of θ_2, d_3, θ_4, θ_5, and θ_6, except for the row 3 column 4 element. We may equate the 3,4 elements to obtain

$$f_{13}(\mathbf{p}) = d_2 \tag{3.83}$$

$$\text{or} \qquad -S_1\,p_x + C_1\,p_y = d_2 \tag{3.84}$$

In order to solve equations of this form, we make the following trigonometric substitutions

$$p_x = r\cos\phi \tag{3.85}$$

$$p_y = r\sin\phi \tag{3.86}$$

where

$$r = +\sqrt{p_x^2 + p_y^2} \tag{3.87}$$

$$\phi = \tan^{-1}\left(\frac{p_y}{p_x}\right) \tag{3.88}$$

Substituting for p_x and p_y in Equation 3.84 we obtain

$$\sin\phi\cos\theta_1 - \cos\phi\sin\theta_1 = d_2/r \tag{3.89}$$

with

$$0 < d_2/r \leq 1$$

Equation 3.89 reduces to

$$\sin(\phi - \theta_1) = d_2/r \tag{3.90}$$

with

$$0 < \phi - \theta_1 < \pi$$

We may obtain the cosine as

$$\cos(\phi - \theta_1) = \pm\sqrt{1 - (d_2/r)^2} \tag{3.91}$$

where the - sign corresponds to a left hand shoulder configuration of the manipulator and the + sign corresponds to a right hand shoulder configuration. Finally

$$\theta_1 = \tan^{-1}\left(\frac{p_y}{p_x}\right) - \tan^{-1}\frac{d_2}{\pm\sqrt{r^2 - d_2^2}} \tag{3.92}$$

Having determined θ_1, the left hand side of Equation 3.76 is now defined. Whenever we have the left hand side of one of Equations 3.70-3.74 defined, we look for elements on the right hand side which are a function of the individual joint coordinates. In this case, the 1,4 and 2,4 elements are functions of $S_2 d_3$ and $C_2 d_3$ and we have

$$S_2 d_3 = C_1 p_x + S_1 p_y \tag{3.93}$$

$$-C_2 d_3 = -p_z \tag{3.94}$$

As we require d_3, the extension of the prismatic joint, to be greater than zero, we have values proportional to the sine and cosine of θ_2 and may obtain a unique value for θ_2 as

$$\theta_2 = \tan^{-1}\frac{C_1 p_x + S_1 p_y}{p_z} \tag{3.95}$$

Evaluating the elements of Equation 3.71 we obtain

$$\begin{bmatrix} f_{21}(\mathbf{n}) & f_{21}(\mathbf{o}) & f_{21}(\mathbf{a}) & 0 \\ f_{22}(\mathbf{n}) & f_{22}(\mathbf{o}) & f_{22}(\mathbf{a}) & 0 \\ f_{23}(\mathbf{n}) & f_{23}(\mathbf{o}) & f_{23}(\mathbf{a}) & f_{23}(\mathbf{p}) \\ 0 & 0 & 0 & 1 \end{bmatrix} = \begin{bmatrix} C_4C_5C_6 - S_4S_6 & -C_4C_5S_6 - S_4C_6 & C_4S_5 & 0 \\ S_4C_5C_6 + C_4S_6 & -S_4C_5S_6 + C_4C_6 & S_4S_5 & 0 \\ S_5S_6 & S_5S_6 & C_5 & d_3 \\ 0 & 0 & 0 & 1 \end{bmatrix} \tag{3.96}$$

where

$$f_{21} = C_2(C_1 x + S_1 y) - S_2 z \tag{3.97}$$
$$f_{22} = -S_1 x + C_1 y \tag{3.98}$$
$$f_{23} = S_2(C_1 x + S_1 y) + C_2 z \tag{3.99}$$

and we can obtain an equation for d_3 by equating the 3,4 elements as

$$d_3 = S_2(C_1 p_x + S_1 p_y) + C_2 p_z \tag{3.100}$$

With the left hand side of Equation 3.96 now defined, we check the right hand side for functions of single variables. Finding none, we evaluate Equation 3.72, which provides no new information.

Evaluating the elements of Equation 3.73 we obtain

$$\begin{bmatrix} f_{41}(\mathbf{n}) & f_{41}(\mathbf{o}) & f_{41}(\mathbf{a}) & 0 \\ f_{42}(\mathbf{n}) & f_{42}(\mathbf{o}) & f_{42}(\mathbf{a}) & 0 \\ f_{43}(\mathbf{n}) & f_{43}(\mathbf{o}) & f_{43}(\mathbf{a}) & 0 \\ 0 & 0 & 0 & 1 \end{bmatrix} = \begin{bmatrix} C_5C_6 & -C_5S_6 & S_5 & 0 \\ S_5C_6 & -S_5S_6 & -C_5 & 0 \\ S_6 & C_6 & 0 & 0 \\ 0 & 0 & 0 & 1 \end{bmatrix} \tag{3.101}$$

where

$$f_{41} = C_4[C_2(C_1 x + S_1 y) - S_2 z] + S_4[-S_1 x + C_1 y] \tag{3.102}$$
$$f_{42} = -S_2(C_1 x + S_1 y) - C_2 z \tag{3.103}$$
$$f_{43} = -S_4[C_2(C_1 x + S_1 y) - S_2 z] + C_4[-S_1 x + C_1 y] \tag{3.104}$$

The 3,3 elements give us an equation for θ_4

$$-S_4[C_2(C_1 x + S_1 y) - S_2 z] + C_4[-S_1 x + C_1 y] = 0 \tag{3.105}$$

This equation is of the same form as Equation 3.25, leading to two solutions

$$\theta_4 = \tan^{-1} \frac{-S_1 a_x + C_1 a_y}{C_2(C_1 a_x + S_1 a_y) - S_2 a_z} \tag{3.106}$$

and

$$\theta_4 = \theta_4 + 180^\circ \tag{3.107}$$

If both numerator and denominator of Equation 3.106 go to zero, the manipulator becomes degenerate. Examining the 1,3 and 2,3 elements of Equation 3.96 reveals that our solution for θ_4 is in terms of $S_4 S_5$ and $C_4 S_5$ as

$$C_4 S_5 = C_2(C_1 a_x + S_1 a_y) - S_2 a_z \tag{3.108}$$

$$S_4 S_5 = -S_1 a_x + C_1 a_y \tag{3.109}$$

and thus

$$\theta_4 = \tan^{-1} \frac{-S_1 a_x + C_1 a_y}{C_2(C_1 a_x + S_1 a_y) - S_2 a_z} \tag{3.110}$$

if $\theta_5 > 0$ and

$$\theta_4 = \theta_4 + 180^\circ \tag{3.111}$$

if $\theta_5 < 0$.

This corresponds to two configurations of the manipulator. When $S_5 = 0, \theta_5 = 0$ the manipulator becomes degenerate with both the axes of joint 4 and joint 6 aligned. In this state only the sum of θ_4 and θ_6 is significant. If θ_5 is zero, we are free to choose any value for θ_4. The current value is frequently assigned.

From the right hand side of Equation 3.101 we can then obtain equations for S_5, C_5, S_6 and C_6 by inspection. When both sine and cosine are defined, we obtain a unique value for the joint angle. We obtain a value for θ_5 by equating the 1,3 and 2,3 elements of Equation 3.101

$$S_5 = C_4[C_2(C_1 a_x + S_1 a_y) - S_2 a_z] + S_4[-S_1 a_x + C_1 a_y] \tag{3.112}$$

$$C_5 = S_2(C_1 a_x + S_1 a_y) + C_2 a_z \tag{3.113}$$

and obtain θ_5 as

$$\theta_5 = \tan^{-1} \frac{C_4[C_2(C_1 a_x + S_1 a_y) - S_2 a_z] + S_4[-S_1 a_x + C_1 a_y]}{S_2(C_1 a_x + S_1 a_y) + C_2 a_z} \tag{3.114}$$

While we have equations for both S_6 and C_6, the equation for S_6 is in terms of elements of the first column, which involves the use of the **n** vector of T_6. The **n** vector of T_6 is not usually made available as it represents redundant information. It can always be computed by the vector cross-product of the **o** and **a** vectors. By evaluating the elements of Equation 3.74 we can obtain equations for S_6 and C_6 as functions of the **o** vector

$$\begin{bmatrix} f_{51}(\mathbf{n}) & f_{51}(\mathbf{o}) & 0 & 0 \\ f_{52}(\mathbf{n}) & f_{52}(\mathbf{o}) & 0 & 0 \\ f_{53}(\mathbf{n}) & f_{53}(\mathbf{o}) & 1 & 0 \\ 0 & 0 & 0 & 1 \end{bmatrix} = \begin{bmatrix} C_6 & -S_6 & 0 & 0 \\ S_6 & C_6 & 0 & 0 \\ 0 & 0 & 1 & 0 \\ 0 & 0 & 0 & 1 \end{bmatrix} \tag{3.115}$$

where

$$f_{51} = C_5\{C_4[C_2(C_1 x + S_1 y) - S_2 z] + S_4[-S_1 x + C_1 y]\} + S_5\{-S_2(C_1 x + S_1 y) - C_2 z\} \tag{3.116}$$

$$f_{52} = -S_4[C_2(C_1 x + S_1 y) - S_2 z] + C_4[-S_1 x + C_1 y] \tag{3.117}$$

$$f_{53} = S_5\{C_4[C_2(C_1 x + S_1 y) - S_2 z] + S_4[-S_1 x + C_1 y]\} + C_5\{S_2(C_1 x + S_1 y) + C_2 z\} \tag{3.118}$$

By equating the 1,2 and 2,2 elements we obtain expressions for S_6 and C_6

$$S_6 = - C_5\{C_4[C_2(C_1 o_x + S_1 o_y) - S_2 o_z] + S_4[-S_1 o_x + C_1 o_y]\} + S_5\{S_2(C_1 o_x + S_1 o_y) + C_2 o_z\} \tag{3.119}$$

$$C_6 = -S_4[C_2(C_1 o_x + S_1 o_y) - S_2 o_z] + C_4[-S_1 o_x + C_1 o_y] \tag{3.120}$$

We obtain an equation for θ_6 as

$$\theta_6 = \tan^{-1} \frac{S_6}{C_6} \tag{3.121}$$

Even in the case where θ_4 is undefined because the manipulator configuration is degenerate, once a value is assigned to θ_4 then the correct values for θ_5 and θ_6 are determined by these equations. This solution corresponds to 14 transcendental function calls, 31 multiplies, and 15 additions.

3.6 Elbow Manipulator Solution

As a further example of this method of obtaining a solution, we will investigate the solution of the Elbow Manipulator (see Chapter 2, Equations 2.56 – 2.68, Figure 2.13). In order to obtain a solution, we proceed as before, premultiplying both sides of the equation defining T_6 by A_1 inverse

$$A_1^{-1}\, T_6 = {}^1T_6 \tag{3.122}$$

$$
\begin{bmatrix} f_{11}(n) & f_{11}(o) & f_{11}(a) & f_{11}(p) \\ f_{12}(n) & f_{12}(o) & f_{12}(a) & f_{12}(p) \\ f_{13}(n) & f_{13}(o) & f_{13}(a) & f_{13}(p) \\ 0 & 0 & 0 & 1 \end{bmatrix} =
$$

$$
\begin{bmatrix} C_{234}C_5C_6 - S_{234}S_6 & -C_{234}C_5C_6 - S_{234}C_6 & C_{234}S_5 & C_{234}a_4 + C_{23}a_3 + C_2a_2 \\ S_{234}C_5C_6 + C_{234}S_6 & -S_{234}C_5S_6 + C_{234}C_6 & S_{234}S_5 & S_{234}a_4 + S_{23}a_3 + S_2a_2 \\ -S_5C_6 & S_5S_6 & C_5 & 0 \\ 0 & 0 & 0 & 1 \end{bmatrix} \tag{3.123}
$$

where

$$
f_{11} = C_1\,x + S_1\,y \tag{3.124}
$$

$$
f_{12} = z \tag{3.125}
$$

$$
f_{13} = S_1\,x - C_1\,y \tag{3.126}
$$

C_{234} represents $\cos(\theta_2 + \theta_3 + \theta_4)$ and S_{234} represents $\sin(\theta_2 + \theta_3 + \theta_4)$. Equating the 34 elements gives us an equation for θ_1

$$
S_1\,p_x - C_1\,p_y = 0 \tag{3.127}
$$

$$
\theta_1 = \tan^{-1}\left(\frac{p_y}{p_x}\right) \tag{3.128}
$$

and

$$
\theta_1 = \theta_1 + 180^\circ \tag{3.129}
$$

Note that we also have an equation for C_5 from the 33 element

$$
C_5 = S_1\,a_x - C_1\,a_y \tag{3.130}
$$

In the case of this manipulator, the next three joints are parallel and no results are obtained by premultiplying by the A matrix inverses until link 4 is constrained. This is given by

$$
A_4^{-1}\,A_3^{-1}\,A_2^{-1}\,A_1^{-1}\,T_6 = {}^4T_6 \tag{3.131}
$$

$$\begin{bmatrix} f_{41}(\mathbf{n}) & f_{41}(\mathbf{o}) & f_{41}(\mathbf{a}) & f_{41}(\mathbf{p}) - C_{34}a_2 - C_4a_3 - a_4 \\ f_{42}(\mathbf{n}) & f_{42}(\mathbf{o}) & f_{42}(\mathbf{a}) & 0 \\ f_{43}(\mathbf{n}) & f_{43}(\mathbf{o}) & f_{43}(\mathbf{a}) & f_{43}(\mathbf{p}) + S_{34}a_2 + S_4a_3 \\ 0 & 0 & 0 & 1 \end{bmatrix} = \begin{bmatrix} C_5C_6 & -C_5S_6 & S_5 & 0 \\ S_5C_6 & -S_5S_6 & -C_5 & 0 \\ S_6 & C_6 & 0 & 0 \\ 0 & 0 & 0 & 1 \end{bmatrix} \tag{3.132}$$

where

$$f_{41} = C_{234}(C_1x + S_1y) + S_{234}z \tag{3.133}$$
$$f_{42} = -(S_1x - C_1y) \tag{3.134}$$
$$f_{43} = -S_{234}(C_1x + S_1y) + C_{234}z \tag{3.135}$$

Equating the 33 elements gives us an equation for θ_{234}

$$-S_{234}(C_1a_x + S_1a_y) + C_{234}a_z = 0 \tag{3.136}$$

$$\theta_{234} = \tan^{-1}\frac{a_z}{C_1a_x + S_1a_y} \tag{3.137}$$

and

$$\theta_{234} = \theta_{234} + 180^\circ \tag{3.138}$$

In this manipulator, θ_3 controls the reach and we can expect a cosine relationship with the reach squared. This can be obtained by solving equations obtained from the 1,4 and 2,4 elements of Equation 3.123 simultaneously

$$C_1p_x + S_1p_y = C_{234}a_4 + C_{23}a_3 + C_2a_2 \tag{3.139}$$

$$p_z = S_{234}a_4 + S_{23}a_3 + S_2a_2 \tag{3.140}$$

Let

$$p'_x = C_1p_x + S_1p_y - C_{234}a_4 \tag{3.141}$$
$$p'_y = p_z - S_{234}a_4 \tag{3.142}$$

Substituting Equations 3.141 and 3.142 into 3.139 and 3.140, respectively, we obtain

$$p'_x = C_{23}\, a_3 + C_2\, a_2 \tag{3.143}$$
$$p'_y = S_{23}\, a_3 + S_2\, a_2 \tag{3.144}$$

Squaring both equations and adding will yield

$$C_3 = \frac{p'^{\,2}_x + p'^{\,2}_y - a_3^2 - a_2^2}{2a_2a_3} \tag{3.145}$$

While we could obtain θ_3 from the arc cosine, we will obtain a value S_3 and use the tangent routine as usual

$$S_3 = \pm(1 - C_3^2)^{1/2} \tag{3.146}$$

where the two solutions correspond to an elbow up and an elbow down configuration.

$$\theta_3 = \tan^{-1}\frac{S_3}{C_3} \tag{3.147}$$

Expressions for S_2 and C_2 are then obtained by solving Equations 3.143 and 3.144 simultaneously

$$S_2 = \frac{(C_3\, a_3 + a_2)p'_y - S_3\, a_3 p'_x}{(C_3\, a_3 + a_2)^2 + S_3^2\, a_3^2} \tag{3.148}$$
$$C_2 = \frac{(C_3\, a_3 + a_2)p'_x + S_3\, a_3 p'_y}{(C_3\, a_3 + a_2)^2 + S_3^2\, a_3^2} \tag{3.149}$$

As the denominators are both equal and positive, we obtain

$$\theta_2 = \tan^{-1}\frac{(C_3\, a_3 + a_2)p'_y - S_3\, a_3 p'_x}{(C_3\, a_3 + a_2)p'_x + S_3\, a_3 p'_y} \tag{3.150}$$

θ_4 is now given by

$$\theta_4 = \theta_{234} - \theta_3 - \theta_2 \tag{3.151}$$

Equations for θ_5 are obtained by equating the 1,3 and 2,3 elements of Equation 3.132

$$S_5 = C_{234}(C_1\, a_x + S_1\, a_y) + S_{234}\, a_z \tag{3.152}$$
$$C_5 = S_1\, a_x - C_1\, a_y \tag{3.153}$$

Thus

$$\theta_5 = \tan^{-1}\frac{C_{234}(C_1\, a_x + S_1\, a_y) + S_{234}\, a_z}{S_1\, a_x - C_1\, a_y} \tag{3.154}$$

Premultiplying by A_5^{-1} we obtain

$$A_5^{-1}\,A_4^{-1}\,A_3^{-1}\,A_2^{-1}\,A_1^{-1}\,T_6 = {}^5T_6 \tag{3.155}$$

$$\begin{bmatrix} f_{51}(n) & f_{51}(o) & 0 & 0 \\ f_{52}(n) & f_{52}(o) & 0 & 0 \\ 0 & 0 & 1 & 0 \\ 0 & 0 & 0 & 1 \end{bmatrix} = \begin{bmatrix} C_6 & -S_6 & 0 & 0 \\ S_6 & C_6 & 0 & 0 \\ 0 & 0 & 1 & 0 \\ 0 & 0 & 0 & 1 \end{bmatrix} \tag{3.156}$$

where

$$f_{51} = C_5[C_{234}(C_1\,x + S_1\,y) + S_{234}z] - S_5(S_1\,x - C_1\,y) \tag{3.157}$$
$$f_{52} = -S_{234}(C_1\,x + S_1\,y) + C_{234}z \tag{3.158}$$

and by inspection

$$S_6 = -C_5[C_{234}(C_1\,o_x + S_1\,o_y) + S_{234}\,o_z] + S_5(S_1\,o_x - C_1\,o_y) \tag{3.159}$$
$$C_6 = -S_{234}(C_1\,o_x + S_1\,o_y) + C_{234}\,o_z \tag{3.160}$$

with

$$\theta_6 = \tan^{-1}\left(\frac{-C_5[C_{234}(C_1\,o_x + S_1\,o_y) + S_{234}\,o_z] + S_5(S_1\,o_x - C_1\,o_y)}{-S_{234}(C_1\,o_x + S_1\,o_y) + C_{234}\,o_z}\right) \tag{3.161}$$

This solution represents 13 transcendental function calls, 27 multiplies, and 20 additions.

3.7 Summary

The solution method outlined in this chapter is trigonometric in nature. In this method we make use of homogeneous transforms which provide equations for all the rectangular components, both the sine and cosine of all angles. These component equations are then combined with the exclusive use of the arc tangent function of two arguments in order to avoid problems of angle quadrant ambiguity inherent in trigonometry. The method [Pieper] works well for most simple manipulators, yielding solutions in the simplest form almost directly [Paul81a]. In some cases geometric intuition is required, but that intuition can still be expressed in the approach outlined in this chapter. For example, a manipulator with a final prismatic joint requires that the extension of the final link be solved for first by postmultiplying to obtain

$$T_6\,A_6^{-1} = A_1\,A_2\,A_3\,A_4\,A_5$$

In another case of a very simple manipulator, it was necessary to invert the problem and to solve to position the base of the manipulator at T_6^{-1}.

In obtaining solutions, we encountered four types of equation, each with kinematic significance. The first type is of the form of Equation 3.25

$$-\sin\phi a_x + \cos\phi a_y = 0 \tag{3.25}$$

This equation has two solutions 180° apart, representing two configurations of a manipulator. The possibility that both numerator and denominator may become zero must be investigated, as this represents a degeneracy, with the manipulator losing a degree of freedom. The second type of equation is of the form of Equation 3.84

$$-S_1 p_x + C_1 p_y = d_2 \tag{3.84}$$

This equation also has two solutions, each of which is less than 180°. Once again the possibility of degeneracy exists if both numerator and denominator become zero. Equations expressing the sine and cosine of an angle, both multiplied by a joint extension or offset which could be considered greater than zero, represent the third form of equation. Equations 3.93 and 3.94 are of this form

$$S_2 d_3 = C_1 p_x + S_1 p_y \tag{3.93}$$

$$-C_2 d_3 = -p_z \tag{3.94}$$

These equations can be used to obtain the angle uniquely, as in the final case when equations for both sine and cosine were obtained, leading to a unique value for an angle. Finally, in the case of manipulators which have two or more parallel joints, the joint angles must be solved for simultaneously in terms of sums of joint angles. The interior angle between the two links is obtained as an arc cosine (see Equations 3.143–3.150).

Obtaining a solution to a given manipulator configuration is the most difficult problem we have encountered thus far. There is no algorithm by which we can obtain solutions. Geometric intuition is required to direct the solution. However, once a solution is conceived, the methods outlined in this chapter will produce the equations in a direct, unambiguous manner.

3.8 References

Pieper, D. L. The Kinematics of Manipulators Under Computer Control, Stanford Artificial Intelligence Laboratory, Stanford University, AIM 72, 1968.

Paul, R. P. "Kinematic Control Equations for Manipulators," *IEEE Trans. on Systems, Man, and Cybernetics* (1981), to appear.

CHAPTER 4

DIFFERENTIAL RELATIONSHIPS

4.1 Introduction

Differential relationships are of importance to manipulation in a number of ways. The most obvious is in the case of motions of accommodation [Whitney72] for instance, when a camera observes the manipulator end effector position and calculates differential changes in position and orientation in order to accomplish some goal. In this case we will want to be able to transform differential changes in one coordinate frame into changes in another — from the camera frame into T_6, for example. Another use of differential relationships follows directly. Given a differential change in T_6, we employ differential relationships to find the corresponding changes in the joint coordinates. These differential relationships will be equally important in understanding subsequent chapters where we examine the dynamics of manipulators, making extensive use of velocities, which are the time derivatives, and where we consider forces and show that differential relationships are the basis for force transformations.

4.2 Derivative

Given a transformation whose elements are functions of some variable, the differential transformation with respect to that variable is the transformation whose elements are the derivatives of the original transformation elements. For example, given a transform T

$$\mathrm{T} = \begin{bmatrix} t_{1,1} & t_{1,2} & t_{1,3} & t_{1,4} \\ t_{2,1} & t_{2,2} & t_{2,3} & t_{2,4} \\ t_{3,1} & t_{3,2} & t_{3,3} & t_{3,4} \\ t_{4,1} & t_{4,2} & t_{4,3} & t_{4,4} \end{bmatrix} \tag{4.1}$$

whose elements are a function of some variable x, then its derivative is

$$d\mathrm{T} = \begin{bmatrix} \frac{\partial t_{1,1}}{\partial x} & \frac{\partial t_{1,2}}{\partial x} & \frac{\partial t_{1,3}}{\partial x} & \frac{\partial t_{1,4}}{\partial x} \\ \frac{\partial t_{2,1}}{\partial x} & \frac{\partial t_{2,2}}{\partial x} & \frac{\partial t_{2,3}}{\partial x} & \frac{\partial t_{2,4}}{\partial x} \\ \frac{\partial t_{3,1}}{\partial x} & \frac{\partial t_{3,2}}{\partial x} & \frac{\partial t_{3,3}}{\partial x} & \frac{\partial t_{3,4}}{\partial x} \\ \frac{\partial t_{4,1}}{\partial x} & \frac{\partial t_{4,2}}{\partial x} & \frac{\partial t_{4,3}}{\partial x} & \frac{\partial t_{4,4}}{\partial x} \end{bmatrix} dx \tag{4.2}$$

The obvious example that comes to mind is that of the manipulator link **A** transformations given by

$$A = \begin{bmatrix} \cos\theta & -\sin\theta\cos\alpha & \sin\theta\sin\alpha & a\cos\theta \\ \sin\theta & \cos\theta\cos\alpha & -\cos\theta\sin\alpha & a\sin\theta \\ 0 & \sin\alpha & \cos\alpha & d \\ 0 & 0 & 0 & 1 \end{bmatrix} \tag{4.3}$$

If this represents a revolute joint, then the transformation is a function of θ. The derivative is obtained by differentiating each element of the transformation with respect to θ

$$dA = \begin{bmatrix} -\sin\theta & -\cos\theta\cos\alpha & \cos\theta\sin\alpha & -a\sin\theta \\ \cos\theta & -\sin\theta\cos\alpha & \sin\theta\sin\alpha & a\cos\theta \\ 0 & 0 & 0 & 0 \\ 0 & 0 & 0 & 0 \end{bmatrix} d\theta \tag{4.4}$$

4.3 Differential Translation and Rotation

If we restrict ourselves to transformations which represent only translation and rotation, excluding perspective and scaling transformations, etc., then we can express the derivative as a differential translation and rotation. Further, we may express the differential translation and rotation in terms of either the given coordinate frame or the base coordinate frame. That is, given a coordinate frame **T**, we can express $T + dT$ as

$$T + dT = \mathrm{Trans}(dx, dy, dz)\,\mathrm{Rot}(k, d\theta)\,T \tag{4.5}$$

where

$\mathrm{Trans}(dx, dy, dz)$	is a transformation representing a translation of dx, dy, dz in base coordinates.
$\mathrm{Rot}(k, d\theta)$	is a transformation representing a differential rotation $d\theta$ about a vector **k** also in base coordinates.

dT is given by

$$dT = (\mathrm{Trans}(dx, dy, dz)\,\mathrm{Rot}(k, d\theta) - I)\,T \tag{4.6}$$

Alternatively, we can express the differential change in terms of a differential translation and rotation in the given coordinate frame **T**

$$T + dT = T\,\mathrm{Trans}(dx, dy, dz)\,\mathrm{Rot}(k, d\theta) \tag{4.7}$$

where

Trans(dx, dy, dz) is now a transformation representing the differential translation with respect to coordinate frame T

Rot($\mathbf{k}, d\theta$) represents the differential rotation $d\theta$ about a vector $\mathbf{k}$ described in coordinate frame T.

dT is now given by

$$\mathrm{dT} = \mathrm{T}(\mathrm{Trans}(dx, dy, dz)\ \mathrm{Rot}(\mathbf{k}, d\theta) - \mathbf{I}) \tag{4.8}$$

4.3.1 The Differential Translation and Rotation Transformation Δ

The common subexpression which appears in Equations 4.6 and 4.8

$$\mathrm{Trans}(dx, dy, dz)\ \mathrm{Rot}(\mathbf{k}, d\theta) - \mathbf{I}$$

represents a differential translation and rotation transformation. We will denote this by the symbol Δ.

$$\Delta = \mathrm{Trans}(dx, dy, dz)\mathrm{Rot}(\mathbf{k}, d\theta) - \mathbf{I} \tag{4.9}$$

As with other transformations, a leading superscript will describe the coordinate frame with respect to which the differential transformation is made. A following subscript will denote the differential variable causing the change. For example, we could rewrite Equation 4.6 as

$$\mathrm{dT} = \Delta \mathrm{T} \tag{4.10}$$

The change here is with respect to the base coordinate frame. Equation 4.8 becomes

$$\mathrm{dT} = \mathrm{T}\,{}^{T}\Delta \tag{4.11}$$

In this case the change is made with respect to coordinate frame T, which is indicated by the leading superscript. In both cases the cause of the differential change was not made explicit and thus no following subscript was used.

In Chapter 1 we developed transformations representing translation and rotation θ about a vector $\mathbf{k}$

$$\mathrm{Trans}(\mathrm{d}) = \begin{bmatrix} 1 & 0 & 0 & d_x \\ 0 & 1 & 0 & d_y \\ 0 & 0 & 1 & d_z \\ 0 & 0 & 0 & 1 \end{bmatrix} \tag{4.12}$$

The argument to **Trans** is in this case a differential vector **d** representing the differential change $d_x\mathbf{i} + d_y\mathbf{j} + d_z\mathbf{k}$.

$$\mathbf{Rot}(\mathbf{k}, \theta) =$$
$$\begin{bmatrix} k_x k_x \operatorname{vers}\theta + \cos\theta & k_y k_x \operatorname{vers}\theta - k_z \sin\theta & k_z k_x \operatorname{vers}\theta + k_y \sin\theta & 0 \\ k_x k_y \operatorname{vers}\theta + k_z \sin\theta & k_y k_y \operatorname{vers}\theta + \cos\theta & k_z k_y \operatorname{vers}\theta - k_x \sin\theta & 0 \\ k_x k_z \operatorname{vers}\theta - k_y \sin\theta & k_y k_z \operatorname{vers}\theta + k_x \sin\theta & k_z k_z \operatorname{vers}\theta + \cos\theta & 0 \\ 0 & 0. & 0 & 1 \end{bmatrix} \tag{4.13}$$

θ is in this case finite. For a differential change $d\theta$ the corresponding trigonometric functions become

$$\lim_{\theta \to 0} \sin\theta \to d\theta$$

$$\lim_{\theta \to 0} \cos\theta \to 1$$

$$\lim_{\theta \to 0} \operatorname{vers}\theta \to 0$$

and Equation 4.13 becomes

$$\mathbf{Rot}(\mathbf{k}, d\theta) = \begin{bmatrix} 1 & -k_z d\theta & k_y d\theta & 0 \\ k_z d\theta & 1 & -k_x d\theta & 0 \\ -k_y d\theta & k_x d\theta & 1 & 0 \\ 0 & 0 & 0 & 1 \end{bmatrix} \tag{4.14}$$

Equation 4.9 then becomes

$$\Delta = \begin{bmatrix} 1 & 0 & 0 & d_x \\ 0 & 1 & 0 & d_y \\ 0 & 0 & 1 & d_z \\ 0 & 0 & 0 & 1 \end{bmatrix} \begin{bmatrix} 1 & -k_z d\theta & k_y d\theta & 0 \\ k_z d\theta & 1 & -k_x d\theta & 0 \\ -k_y d\theta & k_x d\theta & 1 & 0 \\ 0 & 0 & 0 & 1 \end{bmatrix} - \begin{bmatrix} 1 & 0 & 0 & 0 \\ 0 & 1 & 0 & 0 \\ 0 & 0 & 1 & 0 \\ 0 & 0 & 0 & 1 \end{bmatrix}$$

$$\Delta = \begin{bmatrix} 0 & -k_z d\theta & k_y d\theta & d_x \\ k_z d\theta & 0 & -k_x d\theta & d_y \\ -k_y d\theta & k_x d\theta & 0 & d_z \\ 0 & 0 & 0 & 0 \end{bmatrix} \tag{4.15}$$

4.3.2 Equivalence of Differential Rotations

Δ was defined in the previous section in terms of a differential rotation $d\theta$ about an axis defined by a vector **k**. We could also have defined Δ in terms of differential rotations δ_x,δ_y, and δ_z about the x,y, and z axes, respectively. In this subsection we will establish a relationship between the two forms and will show that in the case of differential rotations the result is independent of the order in which the rotations are made.

In Chapter 1, Section 1.7 we developed rotation transformations about the x,y, and z axes

$$\mathrm{Rot}(x,\theta)=\begin{bmatrix}1 & 0 & 0 & 0\\ 0 & \cos\theta & -\sin\theta & 0\\ 0 & \sin\theta & \cos\theta & 0\\ 0 & 0 & 0 & 1\end{bmatrix} \tag{4.16}$$

$$\mathrm{Rot}(y,\theta)=\begin{bmatrix}\cos\theta & 0 & \sin\theta & 0\\ 0 & 1 & 0 & 0\\ -\sin\theta & 0 & \cos\theta & 0\\ 0 & 0 & 0 & 1\end{bmatrix} \tag{4.17}$$

$$\mathrm{Rot}(z,\theta)=\begin{bmatrix}\cos\theta & -\sin\theta & 0 & 0\\ \sin\theta & \cos\theta & 0 & 0\\ 0 & 0 & 1 & 0\\ 0 & 0 & 0 & 1\end{bmatrix} \tag{4.18}$$

In the case of differential changes, $\sin\theta \rightarrow d\theta$ and $\cos\theta \rightarrow 1$ and Equations 4.16 - 4.18 become

$$\mathrm{Rot}(x,\delta_x)=\begin{bmatrix}1 & 0 & 0 & 0\\ 0 & 1 & -\delta_x & 0\\ 0 & \delta_x & 1 & 0\\ 0 & 0 & 0 & 1\end{bmatrix} \tag{4.19}$$

$$\mathrm{Rot}(y,\delta_y)=\begin{bmatrix}1 & 0 & \delta_y & 0\\ 0 & 1 & 0 & 0\\ -\delta_y & 0 & 1 & 0\\ 0 & 0 & 0 & 1\end{bmatrix} \tag{4.20}$$

$$\mathrm{Rot}(z,\delta_z)=\begin{bmatrix}1 & -\delta_z & 0 & 0\\ \delta_z & 1 & 0 & 0\\ 0 & 0 & 1 & 0\\ 0 & 0 & 0 & 1\end{bmatrix} \tag{4.21}$$

If we now consider a differential rotation δ_x and δ_y about the x and y axes, respectively

$$\mathrm{Rot}(x,\delta_x)\,\mathrm{Rot}(y,\delta_y)=\begin{bmatrix}1 & 0 & 0 & 0\\ 0 & 1 & -\delta_x & 0\\ 0 & \delta_x & 1 & 0\\ 0 & 0 & 0 & 1\end{bmatrix}\begin{bmatrix}1 & 0 & \delta_y & 0\\ 0 & 1 & 0 & 0\\ -\delta_y & 0 & 1 & 0\\ 0 & 0 & 0 & 1\end{bmatrix} \tag{4.22}$$

Neglecting second order terms such as $\delta_x \delta_y$ we obtain

$$\mathrm{Rot}(x, \delta_x)\,\mathrm{Rot}(y, \delta_y) = \begin{bmatrix} 1 & 0 & \delta_y & 0 \\ 0 & 1 & -\delta_x & 0 \\ -\delta_y & \delta_x & 1 & 0 \\ 0 & 0 & 0 & 1 \end{bmatrix} \tag{4.23}$$

The above result is independent of the order in which the differential rotations are made

$$\mathrm{Rot}(x, \delta_x)\,\mathrm{Rot}(y, \delta_y) = \mathrm{Rot}(y, \delta_y)\,\mathrm{Rot}(x, \delta_x) \tag{4.24}$$

Finally, premultiplying or postmultiplying by $\mathrm{Rot}(z, \delta_z)$

$$\mathrm{Rot}(x, \delta_x)\,\mathrm{Rot}(y, \delta_y)\,\mathrm{Rot}(z, \delta_z) = \begin{bmatrix} 1 & 0 & \delta_y & 0 \\ 0 & 1 & -\delta_x & 0 \\ -\delta_y & \delta_x & 1 & 0 \\ 0 & 0 & 0 & 1 \end{bmatrix} \begin{bmatrix} 1 & -\delta_z & 0 & 0 \\ \delta_z & 1 & 0 & 0 \\ 0 & 0 & 1 & 0 \\ 0 & 0 & 0 & 1 \end{bmatrix} \tag{4.25}$$

and again ignoring second order terms, we obtain

$$\mathrm{Rot}(x, \delta_x)\,\mathrm{Rot}(y, \delta_y)\,\mathrm{Rot}(z, \delta_z) = \begin{bmatrix} 1 & -\delta_z & \delta_y & 0 \\ \delta_z & 1 & -\delta_x & 0 \\ -\delta_y & \delta_x & 1 & 0 \\ 0 & 0 & 0 & 1 \end{bmatrix} \tag{4.26}$$

Comparison of the elements of Equation 4.26 with the elements of Equation 4.14 shows that a differential rotation $d\theta$ about an axis **k** is equivalent to three differential rotations δ_x,δ_y, and δ_z made in any order about the x,y, and z axes, respectively, where

$$\begin{aligned} k_x d\theta &= \delta_x \\ k_y d\theta &= \delta_y \\ k_z d\theta &= \delta_z \end{aligned} \tag{4.27}$$

We may then rewrite Equation 4.15 as

$$\Delta = \begin{bmatrix} 0 & -\delta_z & \delta_y & d_x \\ \delta_z & 0 & -\delta_x & d_y \\ -\delta_y & \delta_x & 0 & d_z \\ 0 & 0 & 0 & 0 \end{bmatrix} \tag{4.28}$$

The differential translation and rotation transformation Δ can be considered to be made up from two vectors **d** and δ known as the differential translation and differential rotation vectors, respectively

$$\begin{aligned} \mathbf{d} &= d_x\mathbf{i} + d_y\mathbf{j} + d_z\mathbf{k} \\ \delta &= \delta_x\mathbf{i} + \delta_y\mathbf{j} + \delta_z\mathbf{k} \end{aligned} \tag{4.29}$$

We will also have occasion to refer to these two vectors collectively in the form of a column matrix known as the differential motion vector. In this case we will use an upper case bold face character to name the vector. Thus

$$\mathbf{D} = \begin{bmatrix} d_x \\ d_y \\ d_z \\ \delta_x \\ \delta_y \\ \delta_z \end{bmatrix} \tag{4.30}$$

When referring to these vectors we will also apply the superscripts and subscripts that we would apply to Δ. Thus ${}^T\Delta$ of Equation 4.11 is made up from two vectors, ${}^T\mathbf{d}$ and ${}^T\delta$, as is ${}^T\mathbf{D}$.

Example 4.1

Given a coordinate frame **A**

$$\mathbf{A} = \begin{bmatrix} 0 & 0 & 1 & 10 \\ 1 & 0 & 0 & 5 \\ 0 & 1 & 0 & 0 \\ 0 & 0 & 0 & 1 \end{bmatrix}$$

what is the differential transformation **dA** corresponding to a differential translation $\mathbf{d} = 1\mathbf{i} + 0\mathbf{j} + 0.5\mathbf{k}$ and rotation $\delta = 0\mathbf{i} + 0.1\mathbf{j} + 0\mathbf{k}$ made with respect to base coordinates?

Solution:

We first construct the differential translation and rotation transformation Δ, as in Equation 4.28.

$$\Delta = \begin{bmatrix} 0 & 0 & 0.1 & 1 \\ 0 & 0 & 0 & 0 \\ -0.1 & 0 & 0 & 0.5 \\ 0 & 0 & 0 & 0 \end{bmatrix}$$

and then use Equation 4.10 of subsection 4.3.1 to solve for **dA**

$$\mathbf{dA} = \Delta\mathbf{A}$$

$$\mathbf{dA} = \begin{bmatrix} 0 & 0 & 0.1 & 1 \\ 0 & 0 & 0 & 0 \\ -0.1 & 0 & 0 & 0.5 \\ 0 & 0 & 0 & 0 \end{bmatrix} \begin{bmatrix} 0 & 0 & 1 & 10 \\ 1 & 0 & 0 & 5 \\ 0 & 1 & 0 & 0 \\ 0 & 0 & 0 & 1 \end{bmatrix}$$

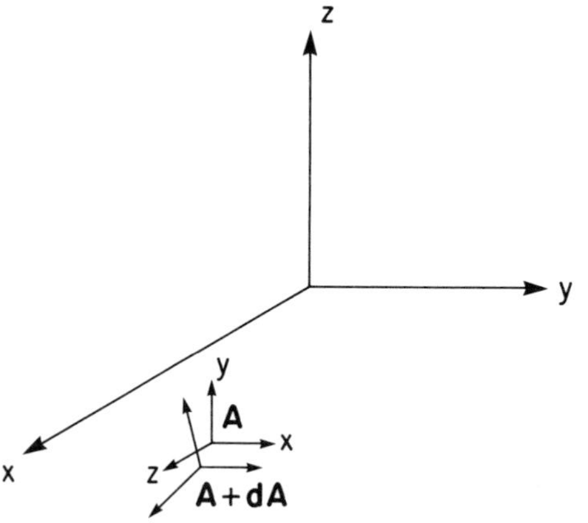

Figure 4.1. The Differential Change in Coordinate Frame **A**

$$dA = \begin{bmatrix} 0 & 0.1 & 0 & 1 \\ 0 & 0 & 0 & 0 \\ 0 & 0 & -0.1 & -0.5 \\ 0 & 0 & 0 & 0 \end{bmatrix}$$

see Figure 4.1.

4.4 Transforming Differential Changes between Coordinate Frames

We have been discussing differential changes made with respect to a given coordinate frame or with respect to base coordinates (Equations 4.10 and 4.11). In this section we will evaluate the transformation of differential changes between coordinate frames. That is, given Δ what is ${}^{T}\Delta$?

Equations 4.10 and 4.11 both give us an expression for **dT** which we may equate to obtain a relation between Δ and ${}^{T}\Delta$

$$\Delta\, T = T\, {}^{T}\Delta \tag{4.31}$$

This transform equation, like any other transform equation, may be represented by a transform graph. This is shown in Figure 4.2 from which we may obtain ${}^{T}\Delta$ directly as

$${}^{T}\Delta = T^{-1}\, \Delta\, T \tag{4.32}$$

The above equation is important as it relates differential changes between coordinate frames. Before we use this result we will first expand the matrix product on the right hand side of the above equation. In doing this, a great deal of simplification occurs, giving us a direct relationship between elements of the

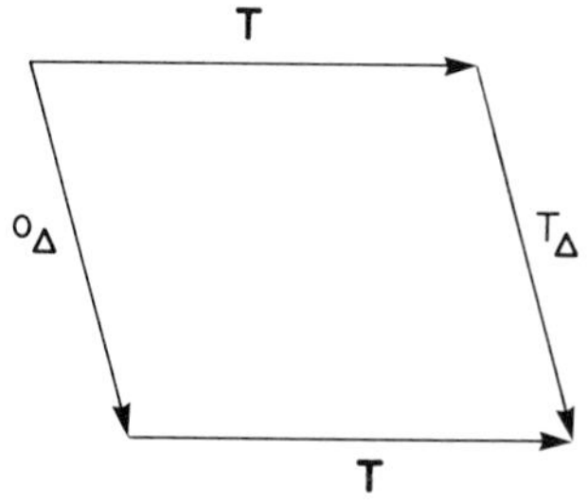

Figure 4.2. Transform Graph for Differential Changes

differential change vectors **d** and δ. The transformation T in Equation 4.32 is known as the differential coordinate transformation.

If we represent the elements of the differential coordinate transformation T in terms of the vectors **n**,**o**,**a**, and **p**, as follows

$$\mathrm{T} = \begin{bmatrix} n_x & o_x & a_x & p_x \\ n_y & o_y & a_y & p_y \\ n_z & o_z & a_z & p_z \\ 0 & 0 & 0 & 1 \end{bmatrix} \tag{4.33}$$

we can express the product of the right hand two transformations of Equation 4.32 as

$$\Delta\mathrm{T} = \begin{bmatrix} (\delta\times\mathbf{n})_x & (\delta\times\mathbf{o})_x & (\delta\times\mathbf{a})_x & ((\delta\times\mathbf{p})+\mathbf{d})_x \\ (\delta\times\mathbf{n})_y & (\delta\times\mathbf{o})_y & (\delta\times\mathbf{a})_y & ((\delta\times\mathbf{p})+\mathbf{d})_y \\ (\delta\times\mathbf{n})_z & (\delta\times\mathbf{o})_z & (\delta\times\mathbf{a})_z & ((\delta\times\mathbf{p})+\mathbf{d})_z \\ 0 & 0 & 0 & 0 \end{bmatrix} \tag{4.34}$$

δ and **d** are the differential rotation and translation vectors as before. Premultiplying by T^{-1} we obtain

$$\mathrm{T}^{-1}\Delta\mathrm{T} = \begin{bmatrix} \mathbf{n}\cdot(\delta\times\mathbf{n}) & \mathbf{n}\cdot(\delta\times\mathbf{o}) & \mathbf{n}\cdot(\delta\times\mathbf{a}) & \mathbf{n}\cdot((\delta\times\mathbf{p})+\mathbf{d}) \\ \mathbf{o}\cdot(\delta\times\mathbf{n}) & \mathbf{o}\cdot(\delta\times\mathbf{o}) & \mathbf{o}\cdot(\delta\times\mathbf{a}) & \mathbf{o}\cdot((\delta\times\mathbf{p})+\mathbf{d}) \\ \mathbf{a}\cdot(\delta\times\mathbf{n}) & \mathbf{a}\cdot(\delta\times\mathbf{o}) & \mathbf{a}\cdot(\delta\times\mathbf{a}) & \mathbf{a}\cdot((\delta\times\mathbf{p})+\mathbf{d}) \\ 0 & 0 & 0 & 0 \end{bmatrix} \tag{4.35}$$

The transform elements of Equation 4.35 are of the form of vector triple products

$$\mathbf{a}\cdot(\mathbf{b}\times\mathbf{c}).$$

In such a triple product, pairs of vectors may be interchanged if the sign of the triple product is changed for each interchange. For example,

$$\mathbf{a}\cdot(\mathbf{b}\times\mathbf{c}) = -\mathbf{b}\cdot(\mathbf{a}\times\mathbf{c}) = \mathbf{b}\cdot(\mathbf{c}\times\mathbf{a}). \tag{4.36}$$

Also, if any two vectors are the same, the value of the triple product is zero. For example,

$$\mathbf{a} \cdot (\mathbf{a} \times \mathbf{c}) = 0 \tag{4.37}$$

Thus the diagonal terms of Equation 4.35 are all zero.

Rearranging the terms of the triple products in Equation 4.35 we obtain

$$^{T}\Delta = \begin{bmatrix} 0 & -\boldsymbol{\delta} \cdot (\mathbf{n} \times \mathbf{o}) & \boldsymbol{\delta} \cdot (\mathbf{a} \times \mathbf{n}) & \boldsymbol{\delta} \cdot (\mathbf{p} \times \mathbf{n}) + \mathbf{d} \cdot \mathbf{n} \\ \boldsymbol{\delta} \cdot (\mathbf{n} \times \mathbf{o}) & 0 & -\boldsymbol{\delta} \cdot (\mathbf{o} \times \mathbf{a}) & \boldsymbol{\delta} \cdot (\mathbf{p} \times \mathbf{o}) + \mathbf{d} \cdot \mathbf{o} \\ -\boldsymbol{\delta} \cdot (\mathbf{a} \times \mathbf{n}) & \boldsymbol{\delta} \cdot (\mathbf{o} \times \mathbf{a}) & 0 & \boldsymbol{\delta} \cdot (\mathbf{p} \times \mathbf{a}) + \mathbf{d} \cdot \mathbf{a} \\ 0 & 0 & 0 & 0 \end{bmatrix} \tag{4.38}$$

Further, as

$$\begin{aligned} \mathbf{n} \times \mathbf{o} &= \mathbf{a}; \\ \mathbf{a} \times \mathbf{n} &= \mathbf{o}; \\ \mathbf{o} \times \mathbf{a} &= \mathbf{n}. \end{aligned} \tag{4.39}$$

we may finally write Equation 4.35 as

$$^{T}\Delta = \begin{bmatrix} 0 & -\boldsymbol{\delta} \cdot \mathbf{a} & \boldsymbol{\delta} \cdot \mathbf{o} & \boldsymbol{\delta} \cdot (\mathbf{p} \times \mathbf{n}) + \mathbf{d} \cdot \mathbf{n} \\ \boldsymbol{\delta} \cdot \mathbf{a} & 0 & -\boldsymbol{\delta} \cdot \mathbf{n} & \boldsymbol{\delta} \cdot (\mathbf{p} \times \mathbf{o}) + \mathbf{d} \cdot \mathbf{o} \\ -\boldsymbol{\delta} \cdot \mathbf{o} & \boldsymbol{\delta} \cdot \mathbf{n} & 0 & \boldsymbol{\delta} \cdot (\mathbf{p} \times \mathbf{a}) + \mathbf{d} \cdot \mathbf{a} \\ 0 & 0 & 0 & 0 \end{bmatrix} \tag{4.40}$$

However, $^{T}\Delta$ is defined to be

$$^{T}\Delta = \begin{bmatrix} 0 & -{}^{T}\delta_z & {}^{T}\delta_y & {}^{T}\mathbf{d}_x \\ {}^{T}\delta_z & 0 & -{}^{T}\delta_x & {}^{T}\mathbf{d}_y \\ -{}^{T}\delta_y & {}^{T}\delta_x & 0 & {}^{T}\mathbf{d}_z \\ 0 & 0 & 0 & 0 \end{bmatrix} \tag{4.41}$$

By equating transform elements between Equations 4.40 and 4.41 we obtain the differential translation and rotation vectors described with respect to coordinate frame T($^{T}\boldsymbol{\delta}$, and $^{T}\mathbf{d}$) in terms of the differential translation and rotation vectors described with respect to base coordinates ($\boldsymbol{\delta}$, and **d**).

$$\begin{aligned} {}^{T}\mathbf{d}_x &= \boldsymbol{\delta} \cdot (\mathbf{p} \times \mathbf{n}) + \mathbf{d} \cdot \mathbf{n} \\ {}^{T}\mathbf{d}_y &= \boldsymbol{\delta} \cdot (\mathbf{p} \times \mathbf{o}) + \mathbf{d} \cdot \mathbf{o} \\ {}^{T}\mathbf{d}_z &= \boldsymbol{\delta} \cdot (\mathbf{p} \times \mathbf{a}) + \mathbf{d} \cdot \mathbf{a} \end{aligned} \tag{4.42}$$

$$\begin{aligned} {}^{T}\delta_x &= \boldsymbol{\delta} \cdot \mathbf{n} \\ {}^{T}\delta_y &= \boldsymbol{\delta} \cdot \mathbf{o} \\ {}^{T}\delta_z &= \boldsymbol{\delta} \cdot \mathbf{a} \end{aligned} \tag{4.43}$$

where **n**, **o**, **a**, and **p** are the column vectors of the differential coordinate transformation **T**.

Equations 4.42 and 4.43 can also be expressed in six-by-six matrix form

$$\begin{bmatrix} {}^T\mathbf{d}_x \\ {}^T\mathbf{d}_y \\ {}^T\mathbf{d}_z \\ {}^T\delta_x \\ {}^T\delta_y \\ {}^T\delta_z \end{bmatrix} = \begin{bmatrix} n_x & n_y & n_z & (\mathbf{p}\times\mathbf{n})_x & (\mathbf{p}\times\mathbf{n})_y & (\mathbf{p}\times\mathbf{n})_z \\ o_x & o_y & o_z & (\mathbf{p}\times\mathbf{o})_x & (\mathbf{p}\times\mathbf{o})_y & (\mathbf{p}\times\mathbf{o})_z \\ a_x & a_y & a_z & (\mathbf{p}\times\mathbf{a})_x & (\mathbf{p}\times\mathbf{a})_y & (\mathbf{p}\times\mathbf{a})_z \\ 0 & 0 & 0 & n_x & n_y & n_z \\ 0 & 0 & 0 & o_x & o_y & o_z \\ 0 & 0 & 0 & a_x & a_y & a_z \end{bmatrix} \begin{bmatrix} \mathbf{d}_x \\ \mathbf{d}_y \\ \mathbf{d}_z \\ \delta_x \\ \delta_y \\ \delta_z \end{bmatrix} \tag{4.44}$$

Computationally, we would write Equations 4.42 and 4.43 as

$$\begin{aligned} {}^T\mathbf{d}_x &= \mathbf{n}\cdot((\delta\times\mathbf{p})+\mathbf{d}) \\ {}^T\mathbf{d}_y &= \mathbf{o}\cdot((\delta\times\mathbf{p})+\mathbf{d}) \\ {}^T\mathbf{d}_z &= \mathbf{a}\cdot((\delta\times\mathbf{p})+\mathbf{d}) \end{aligned} \tag{4.45}$$

$$\begin{aligned} {}^T\delta_x &= \mathbf{n}\cdot\delta \\ {}^T\delta_y &= \mathbf{o}\cdot\delta \\ {}^T\delta_z &= \mathbf{a}\cdot\delta \end{aligned} \tag{4.46}$$

Equations 4.45 and 4.46 represent an important result of which we will make much use as we go on.

Example 4.2

Given the same coordinate frame and differential translation and rotation as in Example 4.1

$$\mathrm{A} = \begin{bmatrix} 0 & 0 & 1 & 10 \\ 1 & 0 & 0 & 5 \\ 0 & 1 & 0 & 0 \\ 0 & 0 & 0 & 1 \end{bmatrix}$$

$$\mathbf{d} = 1\mathbf{i} + 0\mathbf{j} + 0.5\mathbf{k}$$

$$\delta = 0\mathbf{i} + 0.1\mathbf{j} + 0\mathbf{k}$$

what is the equivalent differential translation and rotation in coordinate frame A?

Solution:

With

$$\begin{aligned} \mathbf{n} &= 0\mathbf{i} + 1\mathbf{j} + 0\mathbf{k}; \\ \mathbf{o} &= 0\mathbf{i} + 0\mathbf{j} + 1\mathbf{k}; \\ \mathbf{a} &= 1\mathbf{i} + 0\mathbf{j} + 0\mathbf{k}; \\ \mathbf{p} &= 10\mathbf{i} + 5\mathbf{j} + 0\mathbf{k}. \end{aligned}$$

we first form $\delta \times \mathbf{p}$

$$\delta \times \mathbf{p} = \begin{vmatrix} \mathbf{i} & \mathbf{j} & \mathbf{k} \\ 0 & 0.1 & 0 \\ 10 & 5 & 0 \end{vmatrix}$$

$$\delta \times \mathbf{p} = 0\mathbf{i} + 0\mathbf{j} - 1\mathbf{k}$$

then add $\mathbf{d}$ to it

$$\delta \times \mathbf{p} + \mathbf{d} = 1\mathbf{i} + 0\mathbf{j} - 0.5\mathbf{k}$$

We now use Equations 4.45 and 4.46 to evaluate ${}^{A}\mathbf{d}$ and ${}^{A}\delta$

$$ {}^{A}\mathbf{d} = 0\mathbf{i} - 0.5\mathbf{j} + 1\mathbf{k}; $$
$$ {}^{A}\delta = 0.1\mathbf{i} + 0\mathbf{j} + 0\mathbf{k}. $$

We can check this result by using Equation 4.11 to evaluate $\mathbf{dA}$

$$\mathrm{dA} = \mathrm{A}\,{}^{A}\Delta$$

Forming ${}^{A}\Delta$ from ${}^{A}\delta$ and ${}^{A}\mathbf{d}$ we have

$$ {}^{A}\Delta = \begin{bmatrix} 0 & 0 & 0 & 0 \\ 0 & 0 & -0.1 & -0.5 \\ 0 & 0.1 & 0 & 1 \\ 0 & 0 & 0 & 0 \end{bmatrix} $$

and

$$\mathrm{dA} = \begin{bmatrix} 0 & 0 & 1 & 10 \\ 1 & 0 & 0 & .5 \\ 0 & 1 & 0 & 0 \\ 0 & 0 & 0 & 1 \end{bmatrix} \begin{bmatrix} 0 & 0 & 0 & 0 \\ 0 & 0 & -0.1 & -0.5 \\ 0 & 0.1 & 0 & 1 \\ 0 & 0 & 0 & 0 \end{bmatrix}$$

and as in Example 1

$$\mathrm{dA} = \begin{bmatrix} 0 & 0.1 & 0 & 1 \\ 0 & 0 & 0 & 0 \\ 0 & 0 & -0.1 & -0.5 \\ 0 & 0 & 0 & 0 \end{bmatrix}$$

(see Figure 4.1).

Figure 4.3. The Cincinnati Milacron T3 Robot (Courtesy of Cincinnati Milacron)

4.5 Differential Relationships in Transform Expressions

Equations 4.45 and 4.46 specify the elements of ${}^{T}\Delta$ in terms of elements of the differential coordinate transformation T and the differential translation and rotation transformation Δ. If we require the differential vectors of Δ given the differential vectors of ${}^{T}\Delta$, we can obtain a transform expression directly from Figure 4.2 as

$$\Delta = \mathrm{T}\,{}^{T}\Delta\,\mathrm{T}^{-1} \tag{4.47}$$

If we rewrite this equation as

$$\Delta = (\mathrm{T}^{-1})^{-1}\,{}^{T}\Delta(\mathrm{T}^{-1}) \tag{4.48}$$

it now has the same form as Equation 4.32 of Section 4.4. We may now use Equations 4.45 and 4.46 to obtain the differential vectors of Δ if we use the elements of T^{-1} as the differential coordinate transformation.

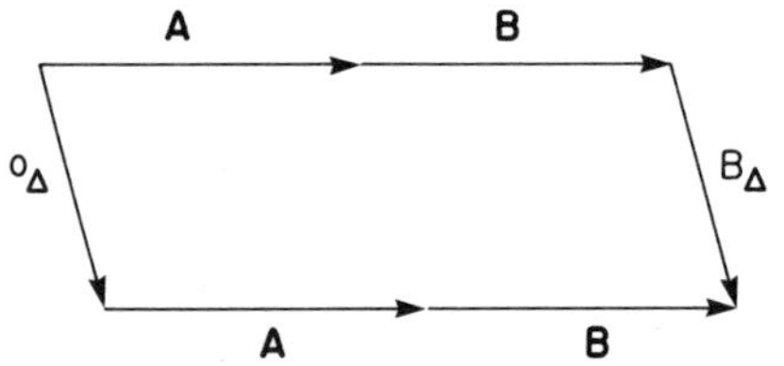

Figure 4.4. Differential Changes between Two Coordinate Frames

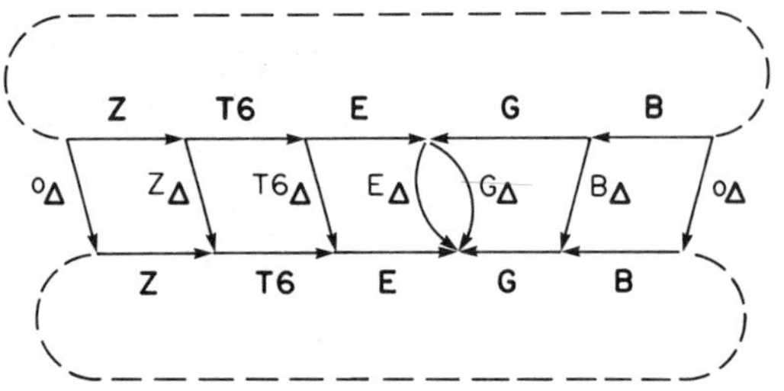

Figure 4.5. General Differential Change Graph

In order to relate differential changes between two coordinate frames A and $^{A}\mathbf{B}$ to obtain Δ given $^{B}\Delta$ we have

$$\Delta \, \mathrm{A} \, \mathrm{B} = \mathrm{A} \, \mathrm{B} \, ^{B}\Delta \tag{4.49}$$

for which the transform graph is shown in Figure 4.4.

We can, once again, obtain the required expression directly from the graph as

$$\Delta = \mathrm{A} \, \mathrm{B} \, ^{B}\Delta \, \mathrm{B}^{-1} \, \mathrm{A}^{-1} \tag{4.50}$$

or rearranged in the form of Equation 4.32

$$\Delta = (\mathrm{B}^{-1}\mathrm{A}^{-1})^{-1} \, ^{B}\Delta(\mathrm{B}^{-1}\mathrm{A}^{-1}) \tag{4.51}$$

We then use $\mathbf{B}^{-1}\mathbf{A}^{-1}$ as the differential coordinate transformation in place of the elements of T, as shown in Equations 4.45 and 4.46, to obtain the elements of Δ. We may obtain this expression for the differential coordinate transformation directly from Figure 4.4 by tracing the path back from the head of the given differential change transformation, $^{B}\Delta$ in this case, to the head of the required equivalent differential change transformation, Δ. From the figure, this is seen to be $\mathbf{B}^{-1}\mathbf{A}^{-1}$.

A general differential change graph is shown in Figure 4.5 which illustrates the following transform equation

$$\mathrm{Z} \, \mathrm{T}_6 \, \mathrm{E} = \mathrm{B} \, \mathrm{G} \tag{4.52}$$

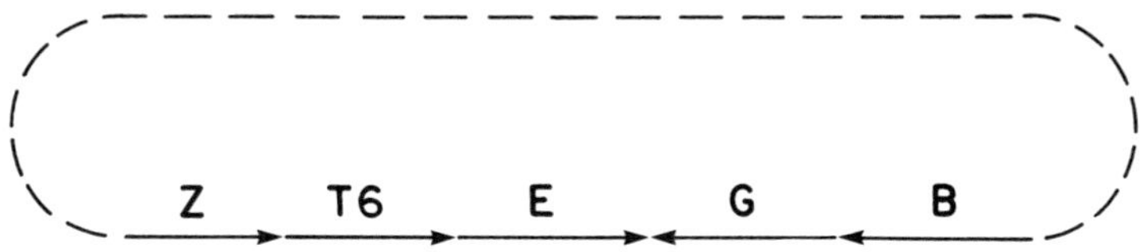

Figure 4.6. Transform Graph

The relationship between all possible differential changes may be obtained from the figure. A differential change in only one coordinate frame is considered to cause a resulting change in only one other coordinate frame. For example, the change ${}^{T_6}\Delta$ as a result of a change ${}^{B}\Delta$ is obtained directly, involving the transform expression $\mathbf{G}\,\mathbf{E}^{-1}$ as the differential coordinate transformation, to be used in place of T as shown in Equations 4.45 and 4.46 of the previous section. We could also have gone the other way around the transform graph and obtained an equivalent expression for the differential coordinate transformation as $\mathbf{B}^{-1}\,\mathbf{Z}\,\mathbf{T}_6$. In a transform equation there are always two paths, resulting in two equivalent expressions. As a further example, the differential coordinate transformation to use for a change ${}^{Z}\Delta$ as a result of a change ${}^{B}\Delta$ is either $\mathbf{G}\,\mathbf{E}^{-1}\,\mathbf{T}_6^{-1}$ or $\mathbf{B}^{-1}\,\mathbf{Z}$.

There is no need to draw the full differential change graph as the differential change transform links always point away from the head of their respective transform links and both transform graphs separated by the differential change links are the same. The transform graph of Figure 4.5 is redrawn in Figure 4.6. From this redrawn figure the differential coordinate transform is obtained directly as the path from the head of the link representing the transform in which the change occurred to the head of the transform in which the equivalent change is desired. The differential coordinate transformation to use in place of T in Equations 4.45 and 4.46 in order to evaluate Δ as a result of a change ${}^{T_6}\Delta$ is obtained from Figure 4.6 directly as

$$\mathrm{T} = \mathrm{T}_6^{-1}\mathrm{Z}^{-1} \tag{4.53}$$

or

$$\mathrm{T} = \mathrm{E}\,\mathrm{G}^{-1}\mathrm{B}^{-1} \tag{4.54}$$

Example 4.3

A camera is attached to link 5 of a manipulator. The connection is defined by

$$^{T_5}\mathrm{CAM} = \begin{bmatrix} 0 & 0 & -1 & 5 \\ 0 & -1 & 0 & 0 \\ -1 & 0 & 0 & 10 \\ 0 & 0 & 0 & 1 \end{bmatrix}$$

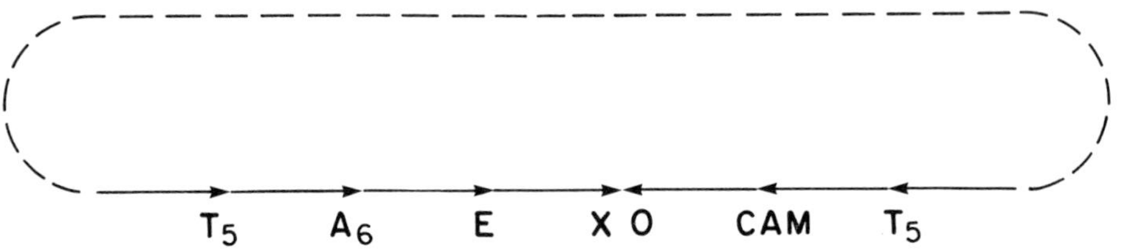

Figure 4.7. Transform Graph for Example 3

The last link of the manipulator is described, in its current position, by

$$A_6 = \begin{bmatrix} 0 & -1 & 0 & 0 \\ 1 & 0 & 0 & 0 \\ 0 & 0 & 1 & 8 \\ 0 & 0 & 0 & 1 \end{bmatrix}$$

An object ${}^{CAM}\mathbf{O}$ is observed and differential changes in CAM coordinates are given in order to bring the end effector into contact with the object.

$${}^{CAM}\mathbf{d} = -1\mathbf{i} + 1\mathbf{j} + 0\mathbf{k} \qquad {}^{CAM}\boldsymbol{\delta} = 0\mathbf{i} + 0\mathbf{j} + 0.1\mathbf{k}$$

What are the required changes in T_6 coordinates?

The situation is described by the following transform equation

$$T_5 A_6 E\, X = T_5 CAM\, \mathbf{O}$$

- T_5 describes link 5 with respect to base coordinates
- A_6 describes link 6 in terms of link 5 coordinates
- E describes the end effector
- X is an unknown transformation describing the object with respect to the end effector
- **O** describes the object in camera coordinates

Solution:

The transform graph is shown in Figure 4.7 from which we obtain the differential coordinate transformation T relating ${}^{T_6}\Delta$ to ${}^{CAM}\Delta$ as

$$T = CAM^{-1} T_5^{-1} T_5 A_6$$

$$T = CAM^{-1} A_6$$

$$\mathrm{CAM}^{-1} = \begin{bmatrix} 0 & 0 & -1 & 10 \\ 0 & -1 & 0 & 0 \\ -1 & 0 & 0 & 5 \\ 0 & 0 & 0 & 1 \end{bmatrix}$$

The differential coordinate transformation is then

$$\mathrm{T} = \begin{bmatrix} 0 & 0 & -1 & 10 \\ 0 & -1 & 0 & 0 \\ -1 & 0 & 0 & 5 \\ 0 & 0 & 0 & 1 \end{bmatrix} \begin{bmatrix} 0 & -1 & 0 & 0 \\ 1 & 0 & 0 & 0 \\ 0 & 0 & 1 & 8 \\ 0 & 0 & 0 & 1 \end{bmatrix}$$

$$\mathrm{T} = \begin{bmatrix} 0 & 0 & -1 & 2 \\ -1 & 0 & 0 & 0 \\ 0 & 1 & 0 & 5 \\ 0 & 0 & 0 & 1 \end{bmatrix}$$

Using Equations 4.45 and 4.46 we form

$$\delta \times \mathbf{p} = \begin{vmatrix} \mathbf{i} & \mathbf{j} & \mathbf{k} \\ 0 & 0 & 0.1 \\ 2 & 0 & 5 \end{vmatrix} = 0\mathbf{i} + 0.2\mathbf{j} + 0\mathbf{k}$$

$$\delta \times \mathbf{p} + \mathbf{d} = -1\mathbf{i} + 0.2\mathbf{j} + 0\mathbf{k}$$

obtaining finally

$$^{T_6}\mathbf{d} = -0.2\mathbf{i} + 0\mathbf{j} + 1\mathbf{k} \qquad ^{T_6}\delta = 0\mathbf{i} + 0.1\mathbf{j} + 0\mathbf{k}$$

4.6 The Manipulator Jacobian

In the case of the manipulator, differential changes in position and orientation of T_6 are caused by differential changes in joint coordinates dq_i. In the case of a revolute joint, dq_i corresponds to a differential rotation $d\theta_i$; and in the case of a prismatic joint, dq_i corresponds to a differential change in the joint distance dd_i. In Chapter 2 we developed the transformation expression for the position and orientation of the end of the manipulator T_6 in terms of a product of the A transformations

$$T_6 = A_1\, A_2\, A_3\, A_4\, A_5\, A_6 \tag{4.55}$$

The transformation graph for this equation is shown in Figure 4.8.

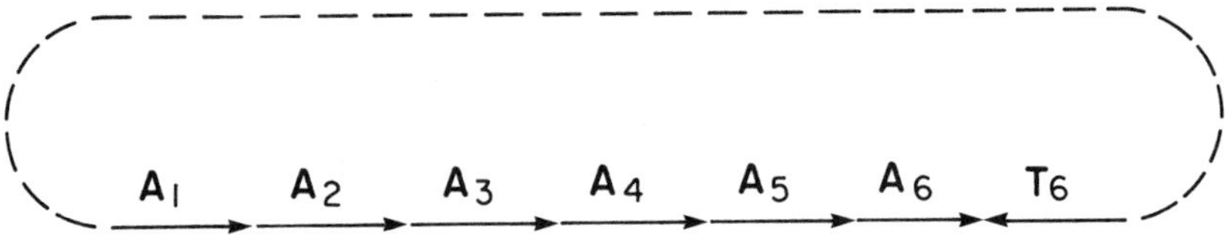

Figure 4.8. The Manipulator Transform Graph

The A transformations were set up in such a manner that, in the case of a revolute joint, the joint variable θ corresponded to a rotation about the z axis of the previous link coordinate frame. In the case of a prismatic joint, the joint variable d corresponded to a translation along the z axis of the previous link coordinate frame. For example, joint 3 of the Stanford manipulator translates along the z axis of coordinate frame A_2 and joint 2 rotates about the z axis of coordinate frame A_1. We will define a differential change transformation Δ_i to correspond to a unit differential rotation about the z axis if joint i is revolute, and to a unit differential translation along the z axis if the joint is prismatic. In both cases the differential change transformation is applied to link $i-1$ coordinates and is written as ${}^{i-1}\Delta_i$. See [Groome] for a vectorial approach to this problem.

We may write an equation for a differential change dT_6 in terms of a differential change in T_6 coordinates ${}^{T_6}\Delta$ and in terms of the differential change of any joint coordinate i as

$$dT_6 = T_6\, {}^{T_6}\Delta_i dq_i = A_1A_2\ldots A_{i-1}\, {}^{i-1}\Delta_i\, A_i\ldots A_6 dq_i \tag{4.56}$$

and thus

$$\frac{\partial T_6}{\partial q_i} = T_6\, {}^{T_6}\Delta_i \tag{4.57}$$

where

$${}^{T_6}\Delta = (A_iA_{i+1}\ldots A_6)^{-1}\, {}^{i-1}\Delta_i\, (A_iA_{i+1}\ldots A_6) \tag{4.58}$$

the differential coordinate transform is thus

$$T = (A_iA_{i+1}\ldots A_6) = {}^{i-1}T_6 \tag{4.59}$$

We could have obtained this directly from Figure 4.8 by tracing the path from the head of the link representing A_i to the head of the link representing T_6.

If joint i is revolute, then as $\mathbf{d}_i = 0$ Equations 4.45 and 4.46 become

$$\begin{aligned} {}^{T_6}\mathbf{d}_{i_x} &= \mathbf{n}\cdot(\delta\times\mathbf{p}) \\ {}^{T_6}\mathbf{d}_{i_y} &= \mathbf{o}\cdot(\delta\times\mathbf{p}) \\ {}^{T_6}\mathbf{d}_{i_z} &= \mathbf{a}\cdot(\delta\times\mathbf{p}) \end{aligned} \tag{4.60}$$

$$
\begin{aligned}
{}^{T_6}\delta_{i_x} &= \mathbf{n} \cdot \delta \\
{}^{T_6}\delta_{i_y} &= \mathbf{o} \cdot \delta \\
{}^{T_6}\delta_{i_z} &= \mathbf{a} \cdot \delta
\end{aligned} \tag{4.61}
$$

However, $\delta_i = 0\mathbf{i} + 0\mathbf{j} + 1\mathbf{k}$ and thus Equations 4.60 and 4.61 are further simplified to

$$ {}^{T_6}\mathbf{d}_i = (-n_x p_y + n_y p_x)\mathbf{i}\ (-o_x p_y + o_y p_x)\mathbf{j}\ (-a_x p_y + a_y p_x)\mathbf{k} \tag{4.62} $$

$$ {}^{T_6}\delta_i = n_z\mathbf{i} + o_z\mathbf{j} + a_z\mathbf{k} \tag{4.63} $$

If the joint is prismatic, $\delta = 0$, $\mathbf{d} = 0\mathbf{i} + 0\mathbf{j} + 1\mathbf{k}$ and Equations 4.45 and 4.46 become

$$ {}^{T_6}\mathbf{d}_i = n_z\mathbf{i} + o_z\mathbf{j} + z_z\mathbf{k} \tag{4.64} $$

$$ {}^{T_6}\delta_i = 0\mathbf{i} + 0\mathbf{j} + 0\mathbf{k} \tag{4.65} $$

The differential change in position and orientation of T_6 as a function of all six joint coordinates is written as a six-by-six matrix consisting of differential rotation and translation vector elements and is known as the Jacobian. Each column of the Jacobian consists of the differential translation and rotation vector corresponding to differential changes of each of the joint coordinates [Paul81b].

$$
\begin{bmatrix} {}^{T_6}\mathbf{d}_x \\ {}^{T_6}\mathbf{d}_y \\ {}^{T_6}\mathbf{d}_z \\ {}^{T_6}\delta_x \\ {}^{T_6}\delta_y \\ {}^{T_6}\delta_z \end{bmatrix}
=
\begin{bmatrix}
{}^{T_6}\mathbf{d}_{1_x} & {}^{T_6}\mathbf{d}_{2_x} & {}^{T_6}\mathbf{d}_{3_x} & {}^{T_6}\mathbf{d}_{4_x} & {}^{T_6}\mathbf{d}_{5_x} & {}^{T_6}\mathbf{d}_{6_x} \\
{}^{T_6}\mathbf{d}_{1_y} & {}^{T_6}\mathbf{d}_{2_y} & {}^{T_6}\mathbf{d}_{3_y} & {}^{T_6}\mathbf{d}_{4_y} & {}^{T_6}\mathbf{d}_{5_y} & {}^{T_6}\mathbf{d}_{6_y} \\
{}^{T_6}\mathbf{d}_{1_z} & {}^{T_6}\mathbf{d}_{2_z} & {}^{T_6}\mathbf{d}_{3_z} & {}^{T_6}\mathbf{d}_{4_z} & {}^{T_6}\mathbf{d}_{5_z} & {}^{T_6}\mathbf{d}_{6_z} \\
{}^{T_6}\delta_{1_x} & {}^{T_6}\delta_{2_x} & {}^{T_6}\delta_{3_x} & {}^{T_6}\delta_{4_x} & {}^{T_6}\delta_{5_x} & {}^{T_6}\delta_{6_x} \\
{}^{T_6}\delta_{1_y} & {}^{T_6}\delta_{2_y} & {}^{T_6}\delta_{3_y} & {}^{T_6}\delta_{4_y} & {}^{T_6}\delta_{5_y} & {}^{T_6}\delta_{6_y} \\
{}^{T_6}\delta_{1_z} & {}^{T_6}\delta_{2_z} & {}^{T_6}\delta_{3_z} & {}^{T_6}\delta_{4_z} & {}^{T_6}\delta_{5_z} & {}^{T_6}\delta_{6_z}
\end{bmatrix}
\begin{bmatrix} dq_1 \\ dq_2 \\ dq_3 \\ dq_4 \\ dq_5 \\ dq_6 \end{bmatrix} \tag{4.66}
$$

4.6.1 The Jacobian for the Stanford Manipulator

We will illustrate the above methods by computing the Jacobian for the Stanford manipulator. This manipulator was defined in Chapter 2 by the A transformations (Equations 2.43 – 2.48). In order to compute the columns of the Jacobian we will need the differential coordinate transformations corresponding to all six differential changes $d\theta_1$, $d\theta_2$, dd_3, $d\theta_4$, $d\theta_5$, $d\theta_6$; these are T_6, ${}^1T_6$, ${}^2T_6$, ${}^3T_6$, ${}^4T_6$, ${}^5T_6$, respectively. These are the same six transformations which we used in order to compute the solution to the kinematic equations and are also given in Chapter 2, Section 2.11, Equations 2.49 – 2.55.

The first column of the Jacobian corresponds to $\partial T_6/\partial\theta_1$; the differential coordinate transformation is T_6, given by Equations 2.54 – 2.55. We will use

Equations 4.62 and 4.63 to compute the differential translation and rotation vectors whose elements make up the first column

$$
\begin{aligned}
{}^{T_6}\mathbf{d}_{1_x} = & -\{C_1[C_2(C_4 C_5 C_6 - S_4 S_6) - S_2 S_5 C_6] - S_1(S_4 C_5 C_6 + C_4 S_6)\} \\
& \quad \times \{S_1 S_2 d_3 + C_1 d_2\} \\
& + \{S_1[C_2(C_4 C_5 C_6 - S_4 S_6) - S_2 S_5 C_6] + C_1(S_4 C_5 C_6 + C_4 S_6)\} \\
& \quad \times \{C_1 S_2 d_3 - S_1 d_2\}
\end{aligned} \tag{4.67}
$$

$$
\begin{aligned}
{}^{T_6}\mathbf{d}_{1_y} = & -\{C_1[-C_2(C_4 C_5 S_6 + S_4 C_6) + S_2 S_5 S_6] \\
& \qquad - S_1(-S_4 C_5 S_6 + C_4 C_6)\} \\
& \quad \times \{S_1 S_2 d_3 + C_1 d_2\} \\
& + \{S_1[-C_2(C_4 C_5 S_6 + S_4 C_6) + S_2 S_5 S_6] \\
& \qquad + C_1(-S_4 C_5 S_6 + C_4 C_6)\} \\
& \quad \times \{C_1 S_2 d_3 - S_1 d_2\}
\end{aligned} \tag{4.68}
$$

$$
\begin{aligned}
{}^{T_6}\mathbf{d}_{1_z} = & -\{C_1(C_2 C_4 S_5 + S_2 C_5) - S_1 S_4 S_5\}\{S_1 S_2 d_3 + C_1 d_2\} \\
& + \{S_1(C_2 C_4 S_5 + S_2 C_5) + C_1 S_4 S_5\}\{C_1 S_2 d_3 - S_1 d_2\}
\end{aligned} \tag{4.69}
$$

$$
{}^{T_6}\delta_{1_x} = -S_2(C_4 C_5 C_6 - S_4 S_6) - C_2 S_5 C_6 \tag{4.70}
$$

$$
{}^{T_6}\delta_{1_y} = S_2(C_4 C_5 S_6 + S_4 C_6) + C_2 S_5 S_6 \tag{4.71}
$$

$$
{}^{T_6}\delta_{1_z} = -S_2 C_4 S_5 + C_2 C_5 \tag{4.72}
$$

On simplification, we obtain the first column as

$$
\partial T_6/\partial\theta_1 =
\begin{bmatrix}
-d_2[C_2(C_4 C_5 C_6 - S_4 S_6) - S_2 S_5 C_6] + S_2 d_3(S_4 C_5 C_6 + C_4 S_6) \\
-d_2[-C_2(C_4 C_5 S_6 + S_4 C_6) + S_2 S_5 S_6] + S_2 d_3(-S_4 C_5 S_6 + C_4 C_6) \\
-d_2(C_2 C_4 S_5 + S_2 C_5) + S_2 d_3 S_4 S_5 \\
-S_2(C_4 C_5 C_6 - S_4 S_6) - C_2 S_5 C_6 \\
S_2(C_4 C_5 S_6 + S_4 C_6) + C_2 S_5 S_6 \\
-S_2 C_4 S_5 + C_2 C_5
\end{bmatrix} \tag{4.73}
$$

The second column of the Jacobian corresponds to $\partial T_6/\partial\theta_2$; the differential coordinate transform is ${}^1T_6$, as shown in Equation 2.53. Again the joint is revolute and the differential translation and rotation vectors are given by Equations 4.62 and 4.63

$$
\begin{aligned}
{}^{T_6}\mathbf{d}_{2_x} = & -\{C_2(C_4 C_5 C_6 - S_4 S_6) - S_2 S_5 C_6\}\{-C_2 d_3\} \\
& + \{S_2(C_4 C_5 C_6 - S_4 S_6) + C_2 S_5 C_6\}\{S_2 d_3\}
\end{aligned}
\tag{4.74}
$$

$$
\begin{aligned}
{}^{T_6}\mathbf{d}_{2_y} = & -\{-C_2(C_4 C_5 C_6 + S_4 C_6) + S_2 S_5 S_6\}\{-C_2 d_3\} \\
& + \{-S_2(C_4 C_5 C_6 + S_4 C_6) - C_2 S_5 S_6\}\{S_2 d_3\}
\end{aligned}
\tag{4.75}
$$

$$
\begin{aligned}
{}^{T_6}\mathbf{d}_{2_z} = & -\{C_2 C_4 S_5 + S_2 C_5\}\{-C_2 d_3\} \\
& + \{S_2 C_4 S_5 - C_2 C_5\}\{S_2 d_3\}
\end{aligned}
\tag{4.76}
$$

$$
{}^{T_6}\delta_{2_x} = S_4 C_5 C_6 + C_4 S_6 \tag{4.77}
$$

$$
{}^{T_6}\delta_{2_y} = -S_4 C_5 S_6 + C_4 C_6 \tag{4.78}
$$

$$
{}^{T_6}\delta_{2_z} = S_4 S_5 \tag{4.79}
$$

Upon simplification, the second column of the Jacobian becomes

$$
\partial T_6/\partial \theta_2 = \begin{bmatrix} d_3(C_4 C_5 C_6 - S_4 S_6) \\ -d_3(C_4 C_5 C_6 + S_4 C_6) \\ d_3 C_4 S_5 \\ S_4 C_5 C_6 + C_4 S_6 \\ -S_4 C_5 S_6 + C_4 C_6 \\ S_4 S_5 \end{bmatrix} \tag{4.80}
$$

The differential coordinate transformation for the third column is ${}^2T_6$, given by Equation 2.52. As this joint is prismatic, we will use Equations 4.64 and 4.65 to obtain the elements of the third column, which we may write directly as

$$
\partial T_6/\partial d_3 = \begin{bmatrix} -S_5 C_6 \\ S_5 S_6 \\ C_5 \\ 0 \\ 0 \\ 0 \end{bmatrix} \tag{4.81}
$$

The equations become much simpler as we move closer to link 6. The next column, which corresponds to the revolute joint 4, is defined once again by Equations 4.62 and 4.63 with ${}^3T_6$ as the differential coordinate transformation. In this case the **p** vector is zero and we have directly

$$\partial T_6/\partial\theta_4 = \begin{bmatrix} 0 \\ 0 \\ 0 \\ -S_5\,C_6 \\ S_5\,S_6 \\ C_5 \end{bmatrix} \tag{4.82}$$

The differential coordinate transformation for joint 5 is given by Equation 2.50 and the result is

$$\partial T_6/\partial\theta_5 = \begin{bmatrix} 0 \\ 0 \\ 0 \\ S_6 \\ C_6 \\ 0 \end{bmatrix} \tag{4.83}$$

Finally, $\partial T_6/\partial\theta_6$ is defined by the differential coordinate transformation ${}^5T_6$, as shown in Equation 2.49, and the result is simply

$$\partial T_6/\partial\theta_6 = \begin{bmatrix} 0 \\ 0 \\ 0 \\ 0 \\ 0 \\ 1 \end{bmatrix} \tag{4.84}$$

Example 4.4

The Stanford manipulator is in the following state

$$T_6 = \begin{bmatrix} 0 & 1 & 0 & 20 \\ 1 & 0 & 0 & 6.0 \\ 0 & 0 & -1 & 0 \\ 0 & 0 & 0 & 1 \end{bmatrix}$$

which corresponds to the joint coordinates shown in Table 4.1.

Table 4.1 Manipulator State

Coordinate	Value	Sine	Cosine
θ_1	$0°$	0	1
θ_2	$90°$	1	0
d_3	20in.		
θ_4	$0°$	0	1
θ_5	$90°$	1	0
θ_6	$90°$	1	0

The value of $d_2 = 6.0$.

Compute the Jacobian and evaluate the differential change $\mathbf{dT_6}$ for the following differential change in joint coordinates

$$dq_i = \begin{bmatrix} 0.1 \\ -0.1 \\ 2.0 \\ 0.1 \\ 0.1 \\ 0.1 \end{bmatrix}$$

Solution:

We compute the columns of the Jacobian using Equations 4.73, and 4.80 – 4.84 to obtain

$$\frac{\partial \mathrm{T}_6}{\partial q_i} = \begin{bmatrix} 20.0 & 0.0 & 0.0 & 0.0 & 0.0 & 0.0 \\ -6.0 & 0.0 & 1.0 & 0.0 & 0.0 & 0.0 \\ 0.0 & 20.0 & 0.0 & 0.0 & 0.0 & 0.0 \\ 0.0 & 1.0 & 0.0 & 0.0 & 1.0 & 0.0 \\ 0.0 & 0.0 & 0.0 & 1.0 & 0.0 & 0.0 \\ -1.0 & 0.0 & 0.0 & 0.0 & 0.0 & 1.0 \end{bmatrix}$$

The differential change in position and orientation is then given by

$$\begin{bmatrix} 2.0 \\ 1.4 \\ -2.0 \\ 0.0 \\ 0.1 \\ 0.0 \end{bmatrix} = \begin{bmatrix} 20.0 & 0.0 & 0.0 & 0.0 & 0.0 & 0.0 \\ -6.0 & 0.0 & 1.0 & 0.0 & 0.0 & 0.0 \\ 0.0 & 20.0 & 0.0 & 0.0 & 0.0 & 0.0 \\ 0.0 & 1.0 & 0.0 & 0.0 & 1.0 & 0.0 \\ 0.0 & 0.0 & 0.0 & 1.0 & 0.0 & 0.0 \\ -1.0 & 0.0 & 0.0 & 0.0 & 0.0 & 1.0 \end{bmatrix} \begin{bmatrix} 0.1 \\ -0.1 \\ 2.0 \\ 0.1 \\ 0.1 \\ 0.1 \end{bmatrix}$$

Thus

$$^{T_6}\mathbf{d} = 2.0\mathbf{i} + 1.4\mathbf{j} - 2.0\mathbf{k}$$
$$^{T_6}\delta = 0.0\mathbf{i} + 0.1\mathbf{j} + 0.0\mathbf{k}$$

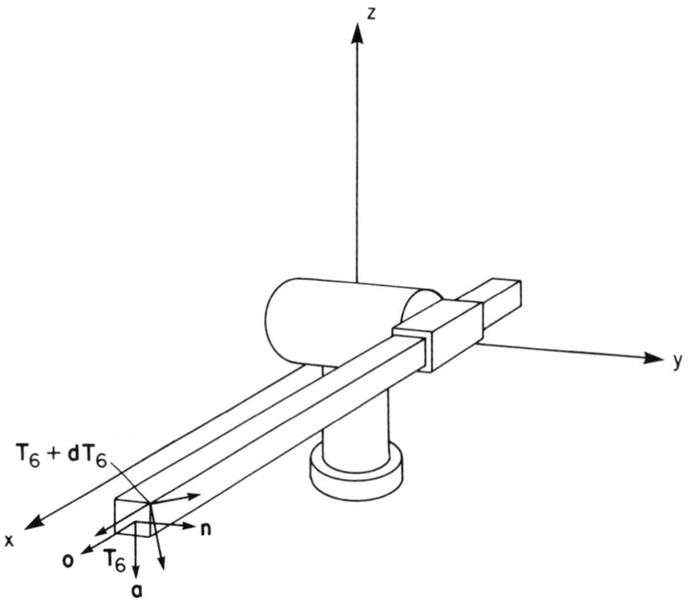

Figure 4.9. The Change in Position and Orientation of $\mathbf{T_6}$

Forming ${}^{T_6}\Delta$ we obtain

$$
{}^{T_6}\Delta = \begin{bmatrix} 0 & 0 & 0.1 & 2.0 \\ 0 & 0 & 0 & 1.4 \\ -0.1 & 0 & 0 & -2.0 \\ 0 & 0 & 0 & 0 \end{bmatrix}
$$

Postmultiplying T_6 by ${}^{T_6}\Delta$ we obtain $\mathbf{dT_6}$

$$
dT_6 = \begin{bmatrix} 0 & 1 & 0 & 20 \\ 1 & 0 & 0 & 6.0 \\ 0 & 0 & -1 & 0 \\ 0 & 0 & 0 & 1 \end{bmatrix} \begin{bmatrix} 0 & 0 & 0.1 & 2.0 \\ 0 & 0 & 0 & 1.4 \\ -0.1 & 0 & 0 & -2.0 \\ 0 & 0 & 0 & 0 \end{bmatrix}
$$

$$
dT_6 = \begin{bmatrix} 0 & 0 & 0 & 1.4 \\ 0 & 0 & 0.1 & 2.0 \\ 0.1 & 0 & 0 & 2.0 \\ 0 & 0 & 0 & 0 \end{bmatrix}
$$

See Figure 4.9.

4.7 The Inverse Jacobian

In manipulation we occasionally need a solution to Equation 4.66. That is, given a desired differential change in position and orientation d_x, d_y, d_z, δ_x, δ_y, and δ_z, what are the required changes in joint coordinates dq_i? We may write the solution to this problem as

$$\begin{bmatrix} dq_1 \\ dq_2 \\ dq_3 \\ dq_4 \\ dq_5 \\ dq_6 \end{bmatrix} = \begin{bmatrix} {}^{T_6}\mathbf{d}_{1_x} & {}^{T_6}\mathbf{d}_{2_x} & {}^{T_6}\mathbf{d}_{3_x} & {}^{T_6}\mathbf{d}_{4_x} & {}^{T_6}\mathbf{d}_{5_x} & {}^{T_6}\mathbf{d}_{6_x} \\ {}^{T_6}\mathbf{d}_{1_y} & {}^{T_6}\mathbf{d}_{2_y} & {}^{T_6}\mathbf{d}_{3_y} & {}^{T_6}\mathbf{d}_{4_y} & {}^{T_6}\mathbf{d}_{5_y} & {}^{T_6}\mathbf{d}_{6_y} \\ {}^{T_6}\mathbf{d}_{1_z} & {}^{T_6}\mathbf{d}_{2_z} & {}^{T_6}\mathbf{d}_{3_z} & {}^{T_6}\mathbf{d}_{4_z} & {}^{T_6}\mathbf{d}_{5_z} & {}^{T_6}\mathbf{d}_{6_z} \\ {}^{T_6}\delta_{1_x} & {}^{T_6}\delta_{2_x} & {}^{T_6}\delta_{3_x} & {}^{T_6}\delta_{4_x} & {}^{T_6}\delta_{5_x} & {}^{T_6}\delta_{6_x} \\ {}^{T_6}\delta_{1_y} & {}^{T_6}\delta_{2_y} & {}^{T_6}\delta_{3_y} & {}^{T_6}\delta_{4_y} & {}^{T_6}\delta_{5_y} & {}^{T_6}\delta_{6_y} \\ {}^{T_6}\delta_{1_z} & {}^{T_6}\delta_{2_z} & {}^{T_6}\delta_{3_z} & {}^{T_6}\delta_{4_z} & {}^{T_6}\delta_{5_z} & {}^{T_6}\delta_{6_z} \end{bmatrix}^{-1} \begin{bmatrix} {}^{T_6}\mathbf{d}_x \\ {}^{T_6}\mathbf{d}_y \\ {}^{T_6}\mathbf{d}_z \\ {}^{T_6}\delta_x \\ {}^{T_6}\delta_y \\ {}^{T_6}\delta_z x \end{bmatrix} \tag{4.85}$$

While it is sometimes possible to invert the Jacobian symbolically, this is usually very difficult due to the complexity of the Jacobian itself, whose columns were defined in the previous example. For a systematic approach to this problem see [Renaud] who performs this symbolic inversion in terms of an intermediate coordinate frame. Given a required differential change, we can obtain a numeric solution, but this usually requires far too many arithmetic operations and the procedure is complicated by singularities which occur whenever the manipulator becomes degenerate. An even worse approach is to invert the Jacobian numerically, as this requires six solutions to Equation 4.66 of the previous section.

The approach we will follow is to differentiate the solution we obtained for the joint coordinates given a value of T_6 (see Chapter 3). This method gives us expressions for differential changes in the same order as we obtained the joint coordinates. The expressions for each differential change in joint coordinates are functions of the differential changes in the elements of $\mathbf{d}T_6$ and also of the differential joint coordinate changes already obtained. This approach frequently results in simpler expressions for the differential changes and if, due to joint limit constraints, a change is not possible, then the change may be set to zero, resulting in a correct solution for the following joints. We will assume in the discussion that follows that a symbolic solution exists for the manipulator and that a solution has been obtained such that the sines and cosines of the joint coordinates are available.

In order to compute $\mathbf{d}T_6$ given differential translation and rotation vectors ${}^{T}\mathbf{d}$, and ${}^{T}\delta$, we first transform them into a differential translation and rotation with respect to T_6, ${}^{T_6}\mathbf{d}$ and ${}^{T_6}\delta$, by means of Equations 4.45 and 4.46 of Section 4.5. We then form ${}^{T_6}\Delta$ (see Equation 4.28) and finally compute $\mathbf{d}T_6$ using Equation 4.11.

We will demonstrate the method by differentiating the solution obtained for the Stanford manipulator in Chapter 3. We will start with θ_1, which is specified implicitly by Equation 3.84 of Chapter 3

$$-\mathrm{S}_1 p_x + \mathrm{C}_1 p_y = d_2 \tag{4.86}$$

We may differentiate this directly to obtain

$$d\theta_1 = \frac{\mathrm{C}_1\, dp_y - \mathrm{S}_1\, dp_x}{C_1 p_x + S_1 p_y} \tag{4.87}$$

the differential change of θ_1. We check as we obtain each differential change in case $q_i + dq_i$ violates a joint motion limit. If this happens, we set dq_i to

$$dq_i = \text{joint motion limit} - q_i \tag{4.88}.$$

As we obtain each differential joint angle change $d\theta_i$, we also evaluate $d(\sin\theta_1)$ and $d(\cos\theta_i)$

$$d\sin\theta_i = \cos\theta_i d\theta_i \tag{4.89}$$
$$d\cos\theta_i = -\sin\theta_i d\theta_i \tag{4.90}$$

The solution for θ_2 is given by Equation 3.95 of Chapter 3

$$\theta_2 = \tan^{-1}\frac{\mathrm{C}_1 p_x + S_1 p_y}{p_z} \tag{4.91}$$

In order to differentiate the arctangent we note that if

$$\tan\theta_i = \frac{N\sin\theta_i}{N\cos\theta_i} \tag{4.92}$$

then

$$d\theta = \frac{N\cos\theta d(N\sin\theta) - N\sin\theta d(N\cos\theta)}{(N\sin\theta)^2 + (N\cos\theta)^2} \tag{4.93}$$

We have $N\,\mathrm{S}_2$ and $N\,\mathrm{C}_2$ from Equations 3.93 and 3.94, respectively

$$N\,\mathrm{S}_2 = \mathrm{S}_2 d_3 = \mathrm{C}_1 p_x + \mathrm{S}_1 p_y \tag{4.94}$$
$$N\,\mathrm{C}_2 = \mathrm{C}_2 d_3 = p_z \tag{4.95}$$

We then obtain the derivatives $d(N\,\mathrm{S}_2)$ and $d(N\,\mathrm{C}_2)$ as

$$d(N\,\mathrm{S}_2) = d\,\mathrm{C}_1 p_x + \mathrm{C}_1\, dp_x + d\,\mathrm{S}_1 p_y + \mathrm{S}_1\, dp_y \tag{4.96}$$
$$d(N\,\mathrm{C}_2) = dp_z \tag{4.97}$$

Thus

$$d\theta_2 = \frac{C_2\, d(N\, S_2) - S_2\, dp_z}{d_3} \tag{4.98}$$

Substituting from Equation 3.93 into Equation 3.100, we obtain an expression for d_3 as

$$d_3 = S_2\, N\, S_2 + C_2\, p_z \tag{4.99}$$

and

$$dd_3 = d\, S_2\, N\, S_2 + S_2\, d(N\, S_2) + d\, C_2\, p_z + C_2\, dp_z \tag{4.100}$$

The equations for $N\, S_4$ and $N\, C_4$ are given by Equations 3.108 and 3.109

$$N\, S_4 = -S_1\, a_x + C_1\, a_y \tag{4.101}$$

$$N\, C_4 = C_2 D_{41} - S_2\, a_z \tag{4.102}$$

where

$$D_{41} = C_1\, a_x + S_1\, a_y \tag{4.103}$$

The derivatives are then

$$dD_{41} = d\, C_1\, a_x + C_1\, da_x + d\, S_1\, a_y + S_1\, da_y \tag{4.104}$$

and

$$d(N\, S_4) = -d\, S_1\, a_x - S_1\, da_x + d\, C_1\, a_y + C_1\, da_y \tag{4.105}$$

$$d(N\, C_4) = d\, C_2 D_{41} + C_2\, dD_{41} - d\, S_2\, a_z - S_2\, da_z \tag{4.106}$$

We then obtain $d\theta_4$ from Equation 4.93. Notice that we create variables for each independent subexpression and for its derivative. As a result we need only differentiate expressions in the form of a sum of product terms.

In the case of θ_5 we have expressions for both the sine and cosine and we may simplify Equation 4.93 to become

$$d\theta = \cos\theta d(\sin\theta) - \sin\theta d(\cos\theta) \tag{4.107}$$

We have from Equations 3.112 and 3.113

$$S_5 = C_4 N\, C_4 + N\, S_4 \tag{4.108}$$

$$C_5 = S_2 D_{41} + C_2\, a_z \tag{4.109}$$

where $N\, S_4$, $N\, C_4$, and D_{41} are defined in Equations 4.101 – 4.103. The derivatives are

$$d\, S_5 = d\, C_4 N\, C_4 + C_4\, d(N\, C_4) + d\, S_4\, N\, S_4 + S_4\, d(N\, S_4) \tag{4.110}$$

$$d\, C_5 = d\, S_2 D_{41} + S_2\, dD_{41} + d\, C_2\, a_z + C_2\, da_z \tag{4.111}$$

$d\theta_5$ is then obtained from Equation 4.107. In this case we do not need to evaluate $d\, S_5$ and $d\, C_5$, as they are given above.

Finally, for θ_6 we obtain from Equations 3.119 and 3.120

$$\mathrm{S}_6 = -\,\mathrm{C}_5\, N_{61} - \mathrm{S}_5\, N_{612} \tag{4.112}$$
$$\mathrm{C}_6 = -\,\mathrm{S}_4\, N_{611} + \mathrm{C}_4\, N_{6112} \tag{4.113}$$

where

$$N_{6111} = \mathrm{C}_1\, o_x + \mathrm{S}_1\, o_y \tag{4.114}$$
$$dN_{6111} = d\,\mathrm{C}_1\, o_x + \mathrm{C}_1\, do_x + d\,\mathrm{S}_1\, o_y + \mathrm{S}_1\, do_y \tag{4.115}$$
$$N_{6112} = -\,\mathrm{S}_1\, o_x + \mathrm{C}_1\, o_y \tag{4.116}$$
$$dN_{6112} = -d\,\mathrm{S}_1\, o_x - \mathrm{S}_1\, do_x + d\,\mathrm{C}_1\, o_y + \mathrm{C}_1\, do_y \tag{4.117}$$
$$N_{611} = \mathrm{C}_2\, N_{6111} - \mathrm{S}_2\, o_z \tag{4.118}$$
$$dN_{611} = d\,\mathrm{C}_2\, N_{6111} + \mathrm{C}_2\, dN_{6111} - d\,\mathrm{S}_2\, o_z - \mathrm{S}_2\, do_z \tag{4.119}$$
$$N_{612} = -\,\mathrm{S}_2\, N_{6111} - \mathrm{C}_2\, o_z \tag{4.120}$$
$$dN_{612} = -d\,\mathrm{S}_2\, N_{6111} - \mathrm{S}_2\, dN_{6111} - d\,\mathrm{C}_2\, o_z - \mathrm{C}_2\, do_z \tag{4.121}$$
$$N_{61} = \mathrm{C}_4\, N_{611} + \mathrm{S}_4\, N_{6112} \tag{4.122}$$
$$dN_{61} = d\,\mathrm{C}_4\, N_{611} + \mathrm{C}_4\, dN_{611} + d\,\mathrm{S}_4\, N_{6112} + \mathrm{S}_4\, dN_{6112} \tag{4.123}$$

then

$$d\,\mathrm{S}_6 = -d\,\mathrm{C}_5\, N_{61} - \mathrm{C}_5\, dN_{61} - d\,\mathrm{S}_5\, N_{612} - \mathrm{S}_5\, dN_{612} \tag{4.124}$$
$$d\,\mathrm{C}_6 = -d\,\mathrm{S}_4\, N_{611} - \mathrm{S}_4\, dN_{611} + d\,\mathrm{C}_4\, N_{6112} + \mathrm{C}_4\, dN_{6112} \tag{4.125}$$

and $d\theta_6$ is obtained from Equation 4.107.

The differential solution to obtain $d\theta_i$ given $\mathbf{dT}_6$ requires 78 multiplies, 47 additions, and no transcendental function calls, assuming that the solution yielding θ_i given T_6 has been evaluated.

Example 4.5

The Stanford manipulator is in the state given in the previous example

$$\mathrm{T}_6 = \begin{bmatrix} 0 & 1 & 0 & 20 \\ 1 & 0 & 0 & 6.0 \\ 0 & 0 & -1 & 0 \\ 0 & 0 & 0 & 1 \end{bmatrix}$$

which corresponds to the following joint coordinates whose sines and cosines are as follows

Table 4.2 Manipulator State

Coordinate	Value	Sine	Cosine
θ_1	0°	0	1
θ_2	90°	1	0
d_3	20in.		
θ_4	0°	0	1
θ_5	90°	1	0
θ_6	90°	1	0

Compute the differential change in joint coordinates corresponding to a differential translation ${}^{T_6}\mathbf{d} = 2.0\mathbf{i} + 1.4\mathbf{j} + -2.0\mathbf{k}$ and differential rotation ${}^{T_6}\delta = 0.0\mathbf{i} + 0.1\mathbf{j} + 0.0\mathbf{k}$.

Solution:

We first form ${}^{T_6}\Delta$ and premultiply by T_6 in order to obtain $\mathbf{dT_6}$

$$
{}^{T_6}\Delta = \begin{bmatrix} 0 & 0 & 0.1 & 2.0 \\ 0 & 0 & 0 & 1.4 \\ -0.1 & 0 & 0 & -2.0 \\ 0 & 0 & 0 & 0 \end{bmatrix}
$$

Premultiplying by T_6 we obtain $\mathbf{dT_6}$

$$
dT_6 = \begin{bmatrix} 0 & 1 & 0 & 20 \\ 1 & 0 & 0 & 6.0 \\ 0 & 0 & -1 & 0 \\ 0 & 0 & 0 & 1 \end{bmatrix} \begin{bmatrix} 0 & 0 & 0.1 & 2.0 \\ 0 & 0 & 0 & 1.4 \\ -0.1 & 0 & 0 & -2.0 \\ 0 & 0 & 0 & 0 \end{bmatrix}
$$

$$
dT_6 = \begin{bmatrix} 0 & 0 & 0 & 1.4 \\ 0 & 0 & 0.1 & 2.0 \\ 0.1 & 0 & 0 & 2.0 \\ 0 & 0 & 0 & 0 \end{bmatrix}
$$

Thus

$$
\begin{aligned}
dn_x &= 0.0\\
dn_y &= 0.0\\
dn_z &= 0.1\\
do_x &= 0.0\\
do_y &= 0.0\\
do_z &= 0.0\\
da_x &= 0.0\\
da_y &= 0.1\\
da_z &= 0.0\\
dp_x &= 1.4\\
dp_y &= 2.0\\
dp_z &= 2.0
\end{aligned}
$$

We now evaluate the equations given in the previous section in order to obtain the differential changes in joint coordinates.
$d\theta_1$ is given directly by equation 4.87

$$
\begin{aligned}
d\theta_1 &= \frac{\mathrm{C}_1\, dp_y - \mathrm{S}_1\, dp_x}{C_1 p_x + S_1 p_y}\\
d\theta_1 &= \frac{2.0 - 0.0}{20.0 + 0.0}\\
d\theta_1 &= 0.1
\end{aligned}
$$

As we obtain each differential change in a joint angle, we use Equations 4.89 and 4.90 to evaluate the differential change $d\sin\theta$ and $d\cos\theta$.

$$
\begin{aligned}
d\,\mathrm{S}_1 &= 0.1\\
d\,\mathrm{C}_1 &= 0
\end{aligned}
$$

Evaluating Equations 4.94 – 4.98 we obtain $d\theta_2$

$$
\begin{aligned}
N\,\mathrm{S}_2 &= 20.0\\
N\,\mathrm{C}_2 &= 0\\
dN\,\mathrm{S}_2 &= 2.0\\
dN\,\mathrm{C}_2 &= 2.0
\end{aligned}
$$

$$
d\theta_2 = \frac{-2.0}{20.0} = -0.1
$$

We then evaluate

$$
\begin{aligned}
d\,\mathrm{S}_2 &= 0\\
d\,\mathrm{C}_2 &= 0.1
\end{aligned}
$$

dd_3 is given directly by Equation 4.100

$$dd_3 = 2.0$$

Evaluating Equations 4.101 – 4.106 we obtain $d\theta_4$

$$\begin{aligned} N\,S_4 &= 0 \\ D_{41} &= 0.0 \\ N\,C_4 &= 1.0 \\ dD_{41} &= 0 \\ dN\,S_4 &= 0.1 \\ dN\,C_4 &= 0 \end{aligned}$$

and then from Equation 4.93 we obtain

$$d\theta_4 = \frac{0.1 - 0.0}{1.0 + 0.0} = 0.1$$

Equations 4.110 and 4.111 give us $d \sin \theta_5$ and $d \cos \theta_5$ directly

$$\begin{aligned} d\,S_5 &= 0 \\ d\,C_5 &= -\,0.1 \end{aligned}$$

and from Equation 4.107 we obtain

$$d\theta_5 = 0.1$$

In this case there is no need to use Equations 4.89 and 4.90 as we already have values for $d\,S_5$ and $d\,C_5$. Finally, we evaluate equations 4.112 – 4.125 in order to obtain $d\theta_6$

$$\begin{aligned} N_{6111} &= 1.0 \\ dN_{6111} &= 0 \\ N_{6112} &= 0 \\ dN_{6112} &= -\,0.1 \\ N_{611} &= 0 \\ dN_{611} &= 0 \\ N_{612} &= -\,1.0 \\ dN_{612} &= 0 \\ N_{61} &= 0 \\ dN_{61} &= -\,0.1 \\ d\,S_6 &= 0 \\ d\,C_6 &= -\,0.1 \end{aligned}$$

and from Equation 4.107 we obtain

$$d\theta_6 = 0.1$$

In summary, then

$$dq = \begin{bmatrix} 0.1 \\ -0.1 \\ 2.0 \\ 0.1 \\ 0.1 \\ 0.1 \end{bmatrix}$$

4.8 Summary

We have seen that the derivative of a transformation **dT**, representing rotation and translation, can be expressed in terms of a matrix product

$$\mathrm{dT} = \Delta \mathrm{T} \tag{4.10}$$

where the differential change is expressed with respect to base coordinates, and

$$\mathrm{dT} = \mathrm{T}\,{}^{T}\!\Delta \tag{4.11}$$

where the differential change is expressed with respect to coordinate frame T coordinates.

The differential rotation and translation transformation Δ is composed from the elements of two vectors: **d**, the differential translation vector, and δ, the differential rotation vector

$$\Delta = \begin{bmatrix} 0 & -\delta_z & \delta_y & d_x \\ \delta_z & 0 & -\delta_x & d_y \\ -\delta_y & \delta_x & 0 & d_z \\ 0 & 0 & 0 & 0 \end{bmatrix} \tag{4.28}$$

The elements of δ represent differential rotations about the x, y, and z axes. In the case of differential rotations it was shown that the result is independent of the order of rotation and that differential rotations δ_x, δ_y, and δ_z made about the x, y, and z axes, respectively, are equivalent to a differential rotation $d\theta$ made about a unit magnitude vector **k** if

$$\begin{aligned} \delta_x &= \mathrm{k}_x d\theta \\ \delta_y &= \mathrm{k}_y d\theta \\ \delta_z &= \mathrm{k}_z d\theta \end{aligned} \tag{4.27}$$

The relationship between ${}^{T}\Delta$ and Δ was shown to be

$$ {}^{T}\Delta = \mathrm{T}^{-1}\Delta\mathrm{T} \tag{4.32} $$

where the transformation T, composed of columns **n**, **o**, **a**, and **p**, is known as the differential coordinate transformation. The elements of ${}^{T}\Delta$, in terms of the elements of Δ, were shown to be

$$ \begin{aligned} {}^{T}\mathbf{d}_x &= \mathbf{n} \cdot ((\boldsymbol{\delta} \times \mathbf{p}) + \mathbf{d}) \\ {}^{T}\mathbf{d}_y &= \mathbf{o} \cdot ((\boldsymbol{\delta} \times \mathbf{p}) + \mathbf{d}) \\ {}^{T}\mathbf{d}_z &= \mathbf{a} \cdot ((\boldsymbol{\delta} \times \mathbf{p}) + \mathbf{d}) \end{aligned} \tag{4.45} $$

$$ \begin{aligned} {}^{T}\delta_x &= \mathbf{n} \cdot \boldsymbol{\delta} \\ {}^{T}\delta_y &= \mathbf{o} \cdot \boldsymbol{\delta} \\ {}^{T}\delta_z &= \mathbf{a} \cdot \boldsymbol{\delta} \end{aligned} \tag{4.46} $$

Given any transformation expression represented by a transformation graph, the differential coordinate transformation T, which relates differential changes between coordinate frames, is the path traced from the head of the link representing the transform in which the change occurred to the head of the transform in which the equivalent change is desired.

These methods were applied to develop the manipulator Jacobian, in which case the differential coordinate transformation for a differential change in coordinate frame T_6 caused by a differential change in joint coordinate i was ${}^{i-1}\mathrm{T}_6$. The differential translation and rotation vectors representing the column of the Jacobian for a revolute joint were further simplified to

$$ {}^{T_6}\mathbf{d} = (-n_x p_y + n_y p_x)\mathbf{i}\ (-o_x p_y + o_y p_x)\mathbf{j}\ (-a_x p_y + a_y p_x)\mathbf{k} \tag{4.62} $$

$$ {}^{T_6}\delta = n_z\mathbf{i} + o_z\mathbf{j} + a_z\mathbf{k} \tag{4.63} $$

and where the joint was prismatic the differential translation and rotation vectors became

$$ {}^{T_6}\mathbf{d} = n_z\mathbf{i} + o_z\mathbf{j} + z_z\mathbf{k} \tag{4.64} $$

$$ {}^{T_6}\delta = 0\mathbf{i} + 0\mathbf{j} + 0\mathbf{k} \tag{4.65} $$

As an example, the Jacobian was then developed for the Stanford manipulator. In order to obtain the inverse Jacobian, the six-by-six matrix representing the Jacobian must be symbolically inverted. This represents considerable effort and results in very complicated mathematical expressions which make it impractical for all but the simplest manipulators. We have presented a method of differentiating the solution to the kinematics equations to obtain a solution to the inverse Jacobian which is easy to evaluate and results in simple mathematical expressions.

4.9 References

Groome, R. C. Jr. Force Feedback Steering of a Teleoperator System, M.Sc. Thesis, Massachusetts Institute of Technology, Aug 1972.

Paul, R. P. "Differential Kinematic Control Equations for Manipulators," *IEEE Trans. on Systems, Man, and Cybernetics* (1981), to appear.

Renaud, M. Contribution a la Modelisation et a la Commande Dynamique des Robots Manipulators, Ph.D. Thesis, l'Universite Paul Sabatier de Toulouse, 1980.

Whitney, D. E. "The Mathematics of Coordinated Control of Prosthetic Arms and Manipulators," *Trans. ASME, Journal of Dynamic Systems, Measurement, and Control* (Dec. 1972), 303–309.

CHAPTER 5

MOTION TRAJECTORIES

5.1 Introduction

This chapter describes the basis for a robot motion control system. It is divided into four main parts. The first part deals with a structural task description in terms of homogeneous coordinate transforms, some of which are defined symbolically and some defined by teaching-by-doing [Grossman] [Takase]. The second part of the chapter describes a motion control scheme based on time coordinated trajectories. These trajectories are simple, provide for continuity of position, velocity, and acceleration, and require no precomputation. The third part of the chapter describes motion executed in joint coordinates. The fourth part describes a Cartesian motion control scheme, conceptually simpler than the joint motion scheme, but computationally more expensive.

5.2 Object Description

As we have seen in Chapter 1, any rigid object can be described in terms of a coordinate system bearing a fixed relationship to the object. As described in Section 1.10, points of the object can be described in terms of vectors from the origin of the fixed coordinate system, and directions described in terms of direction cosines from the coordinate system axes. Given a graphic representation of such an object and its coordinate system, a specification of the position and orientation of the coordinate system will be sufficient to reconstruct the object in any other position and orientation.

Consider the pin described graphically in Figure 5.1. The axis of the pin lies along the z axis; the pin is of radius 0.5 and length 6. If we have knowledge of an object relative to a defining coordinate system as shown in the figure, then the only information necessary to define the object in space is the location and orientation of the object's coordinate system.

5.3 Task Description

Let us use these transformations to describe a task. The task consists in picking up pins, such as described in Figure 5.1, and inserting them into holes in a subas-

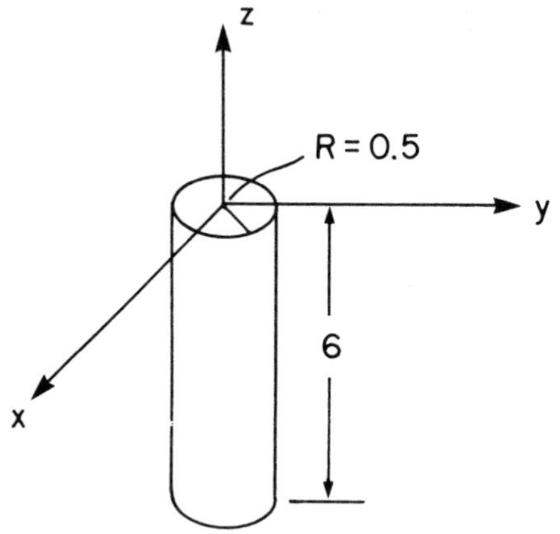

Figure 5.1. Pin Definition

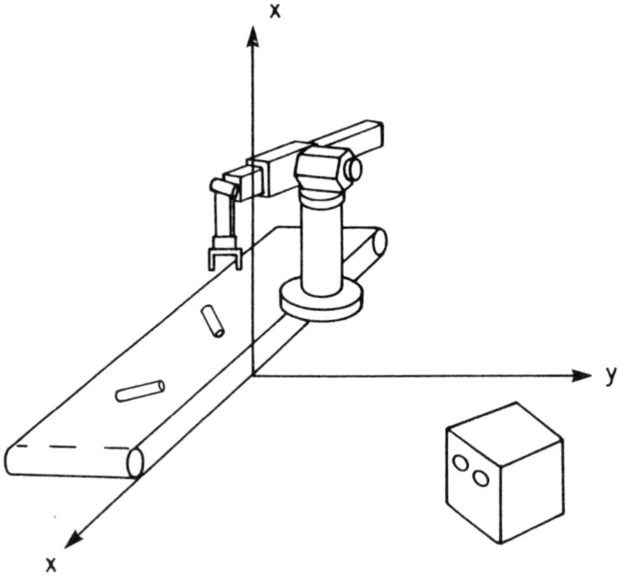

Figure 5.2. Task

sembly (see Figure 5.2). By defining a series of manipulator end effector positions pn (see Figure 5.3), we can describe the task as a sequence of manipulator moves and actions referring to these numbered positions

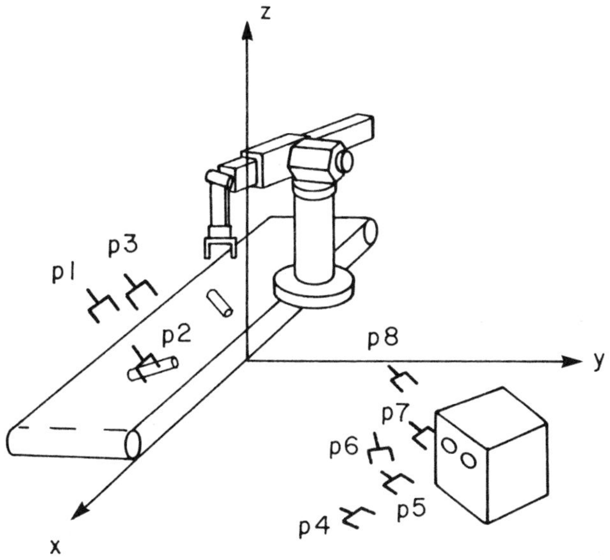

Figure 5.3. Task Positions

MOVE	p1	Approach pin
MOVE	p2	Move over pin
GRASP		Grasp the pin
MOVE	p3	Lift it vertically
MOVE	p4	Approach hole at an angle
MOVE	p5	Stop on contact with hole
MOVE	p6	Stand the pin up
MOVE	p7	Insert the pin
RELEASE		Let go of the pin
MOVE	p8	Move away

Such a program could be executed by any one of a number of commercially available industrial robots, and it also exhibits all the limitations of such robots. There is no provision for compliance, such as is required during the pin insertion or the contact between the pin and the hole. No provision is made for storing information related to the actual position of any objects. After the pin is inserted in the first hole, information relating to the position of the hole needs to be retained in order to simplify the insertion of the second pin. If the manipulator is moved, the entire program must be retaught. To insert the second pin, the entire program must be repeated, but with slightly different positions relating to the second hole. What is missing is the structure of the task.

Let us begin to define the structure of the task by defining the structure of the manipulator. We will describe the manipulator by the product of three transformations such that the positions in the task description are replaced by

$$\texttt{MOVE pn} = \texttt{MOVE}\ Z\,T_6\,E \tag{5.1}$$

where

Z represents the position of the manipulator with respect to the base coordinate system;

T_6 represents the end of the manipulator with respect to its base. T_6 is a computable function of joint coordinates;

E represents a tool or end effector at the end of the manipulator.

With such a description, the calibration of a manipulator to the work station is represented by Z. If the task is to be performed with a change of tool, only E must be changed.

We will now represent the structure of the task in terms of the following transforms:

P the position of the pin in base coordinates;

H the position of the block with the two holes;

$^{H}HR_i$ the position of the ith hole in the block with respect to the H coordinate system;

^{P}PG the position of the gripper holding the pin with respect to the pin;

^{P}PA the gripper approaching the pin;

^{P}PD the gripper departing with the pin;

^{HR}PHA the pin approaching the ith hole;

^{HR}PCH the pin at contact with the hole;

^{HR}PAL the pin at the beginning of insertion;

^{HR}PN the pin inserted.

The task can now be represented as a series of transform equations solvable for T6, the manipulator control input, as follows:

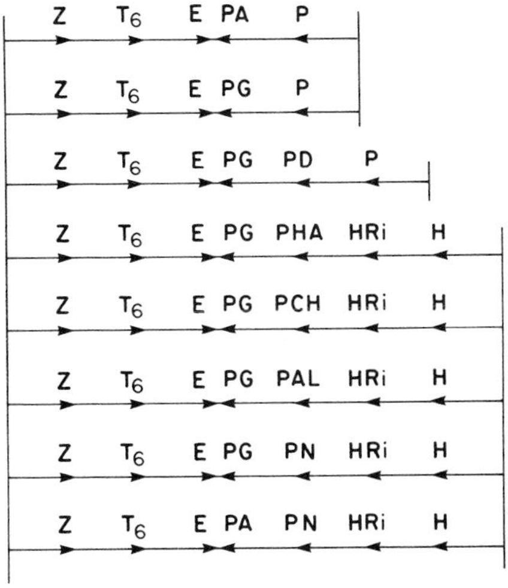

Figure 5.4. Task Position Transform Graphs

p1: $Z\,T_6\,E = P\,PA$
p2: $Z\,T_6\,E = P\,PG$
GRASP
p3: $Z\,T_6\,E = P\,PD\,PG$
p4: $Z\,T_6\,E = H\,HR_i\,PHA\,PG$
p5: $Z\,T_6\,E = H\,HR_i\,PCH\,PG$
p6: $Z\,T_6\,E = H\,HR_i\,PAL\,PG$
p7: $Z\,T_6\,E = H\,HR_i\,PN\,PG$
RELEASE
p8: $Z\,T_6\,E = H\,HR_i\,PN\,PA$

as shown in Figure 5.4.

While this may appear complicated, it represents the essential structure of the task, and each transformation represents a separate piece of information. In order to define the transforms we will use a combination of definition and teaching-by-doing. Some of the transforms are logically defined symbolically, such as $\mathbf{HR}_i$, which may be obtained from engineering drawings. It is important that transformations representing pure translation or rotation are defined as such, for this information can be used to speed up and simplify matrix multiplication during task execution. Other transforms are logically defined by moving the manipulator from position to position, obtaining T_6, and solving for the required transforms.

The coordinate frames corresponding to **P**, **H**, and **Z** are shown in Figure 5.5. While the interrelationship of these three coordinate frames is fixed by the physical objects, the location of the base coordinate system is arbitrary, and can be

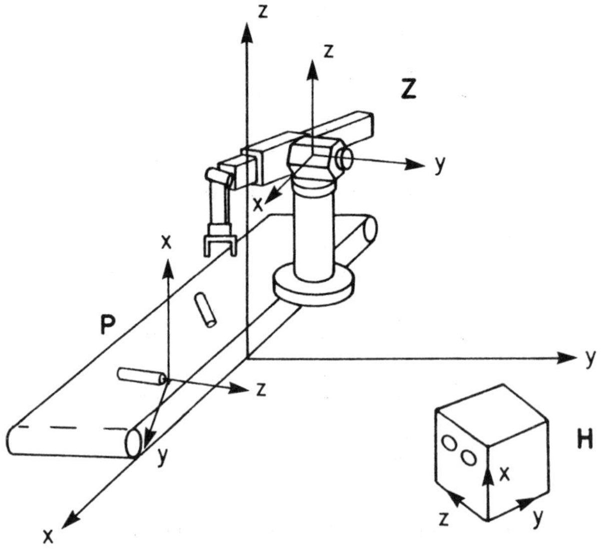

Figure 5.5. Task Frames P, H and Z

specified in terms of any of the three frames. We will specify the base frame in terms of Z. While the manipulator coordinate frame is located in the shoulder, we would like the base coordinate frame to be at the base of the manipulator, or at ${}^{T_6}\mathbf{p}_z = -50$. The manipulator cannot reach back to its own base, so we will set it behind the origin of base coordinates such that ${}^{T_6}\mathbf{p}_x = 30$. Leaving ${}^{T_6}\mathbf{p}_y = 0$ and keeping both frames aligned, we have

$$\mathbf{Z}\begin{bmatrix} 1 & 0 & 0 & 30 \\ 0 & 1 & 0 & 0 \\ 0 & 0 & 1 & -50 \\ 0 & 0 & 0 & 1 \end{bmatrix} = \mathbf{I} \tag{5.2}$$

where $\mathbf{I}$ is the identity transform, and thus

$$\mathbf{Z} = \begin{bmatrix} 1 & 0 & 0 & -30 \\ 0 & 1 & 0 & 0 \\ 0 & 0 & 1 & 50 \\ 0 & 0 & 0 & 1 \end{bmatrix} \tag{5.3}$$

This allows the manipulator working range to be positive x and $\pm y$ with $z = 0$ at the base of the manipulator.

We will define the end effector by a transform with respect to the end of the manipulator. Using the convention that the z axis of the end effector is in its

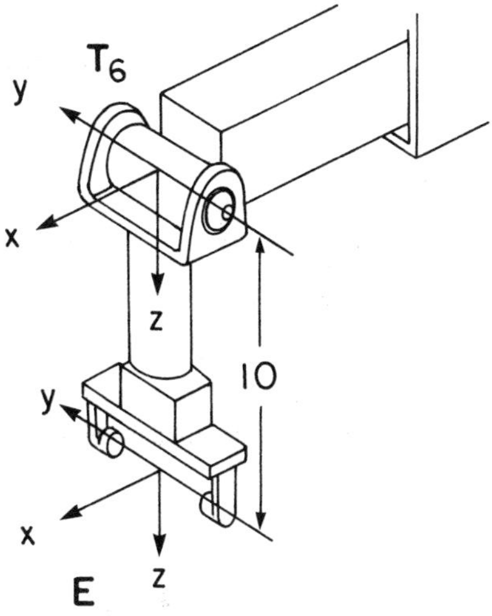

Figure 5.6. Tool Transformation

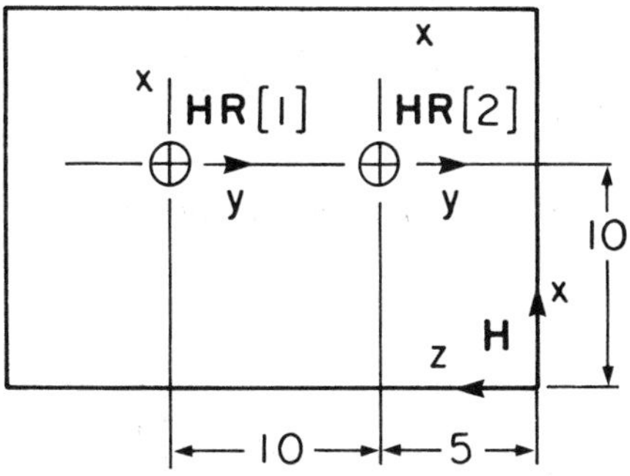

Figure 5.7. Block With Two Holes

principal direction of approach to a task and the y axis describes its orientation, we can describe the tool shown in Figure 5.6 as

$$^{T_6}\text{E} = \begin{bmatrix} 1 & 0 & 0 & 0 \\ 0 & 1 & 0 & 0 \\ 0 & 0 & 1 & 10 \\ 0 & 0 & 0 & 1 \end{bmatrix} \qquad (5.4)$$

While we have described the pin in Figure 5.1, we need to look at the part with the two holes, H. A front elevation will enable us to define its features by means of a transform array HR (see Figure 5.7)

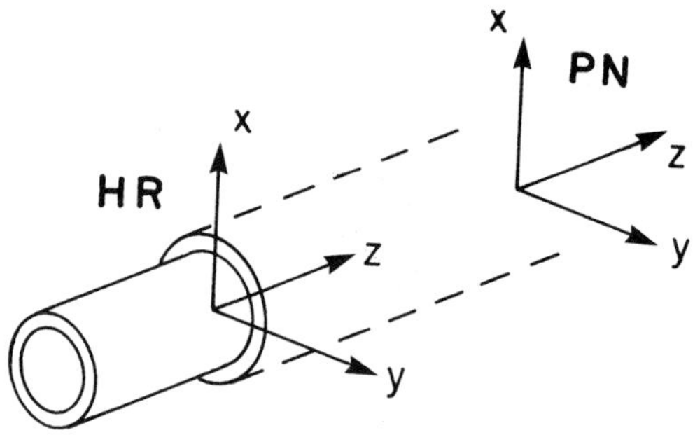

Figure 5.8. Pin Inserted in Hole

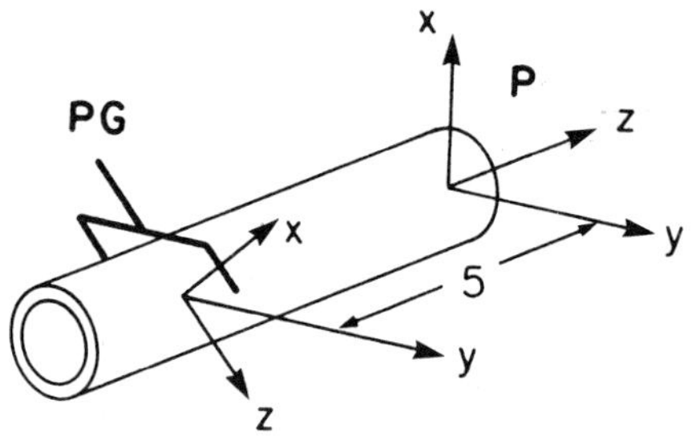

Figure 5.9. Placement of Gripper on Pin

$$\mathrm{HR}_1 = \begin{bmatrix} 1 & 0 & 0 & 10 \\ 0 & 0 & 1 & 0 \\ 0 & -1 & 0 & 15 \\ 0 & 0 & 0 & 1 \end{bmatrix} \quad (5.5) \qquad \mathrm{HR}_2 = \begin{bmatrix} 1 & 0 & 0 & 10 \\ 0 & 0 & 1 & 0 \\ 0 & -1 & 0 & 5 \\ 0 & 0 & 0 & 1 \end{bmatrix} \quad (5.6)$$

The most important transform is the pin inserted in a hole (see Figure 5.8). The z axis of the pin must agree with the axis of the hole. As the pin has cylindrical symmetry, the direction of the x and y axes is arbitrary. We will define the x axis to be up when the pin is lying on its side about to be picked up, and we will keep x up as the pin is inserted

$$^{HR}\mathrm{PN} = \begin{bmatrix} 1 & 0 & 0 & 0 \\ 0 & 1 & 0 & 0 \\ 0 & 0 & 1 & 4 \\ 0 & 0 & 0 & 1 \end{bmatrix} \quad (5.7)$$

One last transform must be defined in this manner: the placement of the gripper on the pin (see Figure 5.9)

$$
{}^{P}\mathrm{PG} = \begin{bmatrix} .7 & 0 & -.7 & 0 \\ 0 & 1 & 0 & 0 \\ .7 & 0 & .7 & -5 \\ 0 & 0 & 0 & 1 \end{bmatrix} \tag{5.8}
$$

We can now define the remaining transforms by using the manipulator. The end effector is placed on the pin at its pick up position and the following transform equation is true

$$\mathrm{Z\,T_6\,E = P\,PG} \tag{5.9}$$

which defines **P**

$$\mathrm{P = Z\,T_6\,E\,PG^{-1}} \tag{5.10}$$

The gripper is moved back to the approach position `p1` and we have

$$\mathrm{Z\,T_6\,E = P\,PA} \tag{5.11}$$

defining **PA**

$$\mathrm{PA = P^{-1}\,Z\,T_6\,E} \tag{5.12}$$

A departure point relative to **P** is now defined by lifting the pin in the gripper to the departure position **PD**

$$\mathrm{Z\,T_6\,E = P\,PD\,PG} \tag{5.13}$$

which defines **PD**

$$\mathrm{PD = P^{-1}Z\,T_6\,E\,PG^{-1}} \tag{5.14}$$

The position of the block H is defined by

$$\mathrm{Z\,T_6\,E = H\,HR_1\,PN\,PG} \tag{5.15}$$

and solving for H

$$\mathrm{H = Z\,T_6\,E(HR_1\,PN\,PG)^{-1}} \tag{5.16}$$

The pin at the beginning of insertion **PAL** (see Figure 5.10.) is defined by

$$\mathrm{Z\,T_6\,E = H\,HR_1\,PAL\,PG} \tag{5.17}$$

and

$$\mathrm{PAL = (H\,HR_1)^{-1}\,Z\,T_6\,E\,PG^{-1}} \tag{5.18}$$

The pin on first contact with the hole **PCH** and an approach point **PHA** to the contact point are defined by

$$\mathrm{PCH = (H\,HR_1)^{-1}\,Z\,T_6\,E\,PG^{-1}} \tag{5.19}$$

$$\mathrm{PHA = (H\,HR_1)^{-1}\,Z\,T_6\,E\,PG^{-1}} \tag{5.20}$$

which completes the definition of all transforms.

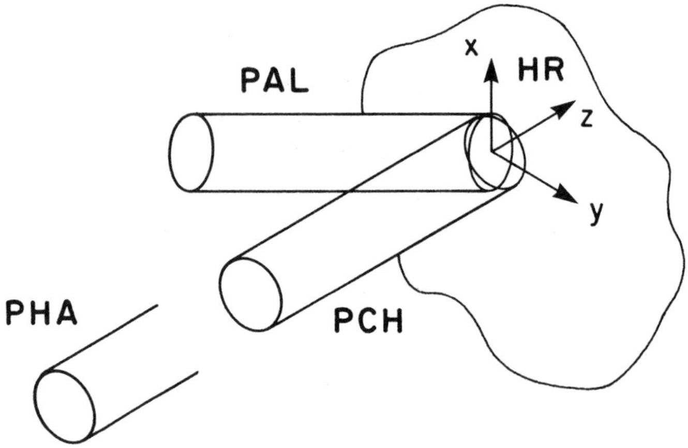

Figure 5.10. Approach Contact and Beginning of Insert

5.4 Vision

In obtaining the position of the pin for the task, we placed the manipulator over the pin in the correct grasping position and then solved the transformation equation for **P**. In actual practice, we will expect the position of objects, such as the pin, to be obtained visually. Given a camera in a fixed position such that it can specify the position and orientation of the pin as a homogeneous transform relative to its own coordinate system, say, **PC**, then the position of the pin relative to base coordinates can be expressed as

$$\mathbf{P} = \mathbf{CAM\ PC} \tag{5.21}$$

where **CAM** is a transformation representing the camera coordinate system in base coordinates.

The value of **CAM** can be obtained after **P** is defined by the manipulator by taking a picture, obtaining **PC**, and solving for **CAM**

$$\mathbf{CAM} = \mathbf{P\ PC}^{-1} \tag{5.22}$$

Input from the camera will be obtained by a READ procedure, with arguments the device and the transform. Thus in the task program we could write

```
READ(CAMERA, PC);
P := CAM + PC;
```

and **P** will be defined. We refer to transforms in programs by the use of identifiers using the + symbol to indicate matrix multiplication and — to indicate multiplication by the matrix inverse

5.5 Program

We can now define each position `p1:` – `p8:` in the task program in terms of a transform equation solvable for T_6 (see Figure 5.4).

To move the manipulator to `p1` requires that

$$Z\,T_6\,E = P\,PA \tag{5.23}$$

which implies that

$$T_6 = Z^{-1}\,P\,PA\,E^{-1} \tag{5.24}$$

to reach `p2` requires that

$$Z\,T_6\,E = P\,PG \tag{5.25}$$

and so forth.

Before we replace the positions `p1` – `p8` in the program with transform expressions for T_6, we will first define two transform expression variables, **COORD** and **TOOL**, representing a general expression for a working coordinate system and a general expression for the tool, respectively. We can then write all the position equations in the form

$$T_6\,\text{TOOL} = \text{COORD POS} \tag{5.26}$$

For the first move we will define **COORD** and **TOOL** as

```
COORD:=-Z+P;
TOOL:=E;
```

and the first move as

```
MOVE PA;
```

The tool is as before, but examination of the **COORD** expression reveals that the position is now defined with respect to the pin. After the pin is grasped we redefine **TOOL** as

```
TOOL := E - PG
```

This has the effect of redefining the end of the manipulator to be the end of the pin. The program to insert the two pins becomes

```
TOOL := E;                              Attach tool
FOR I := 1,2 DO
BEGIN
    READ(CAMERA, PC);                   Read in position of pin
    P := CAM + PC;                      Set P
    COORD := -Z + P;                    Coord wrt pin
    MOVE PA;                            Approach
    MOVE PG;                            Over pin
    GRASP;
    TOOL := E - PG;                     Tool now end of pin
    MOVE PD;                            Departure position
    HT := HR[I];                        Temp position of hole
    COORD := -Z + H + HT;               Coord wrt hole
    MOVE PHA;                           Hole approach
    MOVE PCH;                           Contact hole
    MOVE PAL;                           Stand up
    MOVE PN;                            Insert pin
    RELEASE;
    COORD := -Z + H + HT + PN;          Coord wrt pin
    TOOL := E;
    MOVE PA                             Depart from pin
END;
```

While we will not discuss compliance in this chapter, we will note that any compliance will be specified in the coordinate frame of the right hand most transform of the TOOL, while the effects of compliance are accounted for by modifying one of the transforms of the **COORD** expression.

5.6 Conveyor Tracking

In the task we are describing, the pins lie on a moving conveyor, so we must now consider the problem of working in a moving coordinate frame. With the pin moving, we must be able to track the motion of the conveyor during the approach to the pin, the grasp, and the departure. In our original definition of the task, the pin **P** was defined with respect to base coordinates. In order to perform the task with the pin on the conveyor, all we need do, in principle, is create a transform $\mathbf{CONV}(s)$, a function of conveyor position s, and then describe the pin ${}^{CONV}\mathbf{P}$ with respect to the conveyor $\mathbf{CONV}(s)$. That is, the position of the pin in base coordinates is

$$\mathbf{P} = \mathbf{CONV}(s)\,{}^{CONV}\mathbf{P} \tag{5.27}$$

Positions are then described as homogeneous transformations with respect to the conveyor, and the conveyor is in turn described as a homogeneous transformation with respect to base coordinates. The transformation which describes the conveyor is a function of conveyor position (s). If the object **OBJ** is placed on a conveyor, a transform equation may be written in terms of an additional transform describing the conveyor.
Thus

$$\mathbf{Z}\,\mathbf{T}_6\,\mathbf{E} = \mathbf{CONV}(s)\,\mathbf{OBJ}\,\mathbf{F}\,\mathbf{G} \tag{5.28}$$

where

CONV is a function of some scalar variable s describing the conveyor position;

${}^{CONV}\mathbf{OBJ}$ describes the object with respect to the conveyor;

${}^{OBJ}\mathbf{F}$ describes the feature in terms of the assembly;

${}^{F}\mathbf{G}$ describes the end effector in terms of the feature.

If the object on the conveyor is stopped in some position and the end effector placed in the grasping position, **OBJ** may be defined as

$$\mathbf{OBJ} = \mathbf{CONV}^{-1}(s)\,\mathbf{Z}\,\mathbf{T}_6\,\mathbf{E}\,(\mathbf{F}\,\mathbf{G})^{-1} \tag{5.29}$$

In execution, T6 becomes a function of the conveyor variable

$$\mathbf{T}_6 = \mathbf{Z}^{-1}\,\mathbf{CONV}(s)\,\mathbf{OBJ}\,\mathbf{F}\,\mathbf{G}\,\mathbf{E}^{-1} \tag{5.30}$$

If T_6 were evaluated continuously and converted into joint angles, and the manipulator servoed to those joint angles, then the manipulator would track the moving object. If the conveyor were to stop, then the manipulator would also stop. Such a tracking motion is not limited to conveyors, but can be applied to any system in which the relative displacement between the object and the manipulator can be expressed in the form of a homogeneous transformation, such as docking tasks in space and at sea.

The program to perform the task can then be rewritten as

```
TOOL := E;                                   Attach tool
FOR I := 1,2 DO
BEGIN
    READ(CAMERA, PC);                        Read in position of pin
    P := -CONV[S] + CAM + PC;                Set P
    COORD := -Z + CONV[S] + P;               Coord wrt pin
    MOVE PA;                                 Approach
    MOVE PG;                                 Over pin
    GRASP;
    TOOL := E - PG;                          Tool now end of pin
    MOVE PD;                                 Departure position
    HT := HR[I];                             Temp position of hole
    COORD := -Z + H + HT;                    Coord wrt hole
    MOVE PHA;                                Hole approach
    MOVE PCH;                                Contact hole
    MOVE PAL;                                Stand up
    MOVE PN;                                 Insert pin
    RELEASE;
    COORD := -Z + H + HT + PN;               Coord wrt pin
    TOOL := E;
    MOVE PA                                  Depart from pin
END;
```

5.7 Motion Between Positions

Manipulator task positions can be expressed in the general form

$$T_6\ TOOL = COORD\ POS \tag{5.31}$$

where

T_6 represents the six links of the manipulator;

TOOL represents the transform expression describing the tool end point or object whose motion is to be controlled;

COORD is the transform expression which represents the working coordinate system;

POS is the remaining transform expression describing the desired position of the tool tip or object.

If there is no working coordinate system, then COORD will be missing. If T_6 is defined to describe the tool tip, then TOOL will also be missing. Execution of any position defined manipulator task will then consist of moving the manipulator through a series of position defined equations such as

$$\begin{aligned} \mathrm{T_6\,TOOL_1} &= \mathrm{COORD_1\,POS_1} \\ \mathrm{T_6\,TOOL_2} &= \mathrm{COORD_2\,POS_2} \\ \mathrm{T_6\,TOOL_3} &= \mathrm{COORD_3\,POS_3} \\ \text{etc.} & \end{aligned} \tag{5.32}$$

While the sequence of task positions defines the task, it does not specify how the manipulator is to be moved from position to position. We have already seen the need to evaluate the expression for T_6 repeatedly in order to provide tracking. Between any two positions defined by $\mathbf{COORD}_i\ \mathbf{POS}_i\ \mathbf{TOOL}_i^{-1}$ and $\mathbf{COORD}_{i+1}\ \mathbf{POS}_{i+1}\ \mathbf{TOOL}_{i+1}^{-1}$ we can obtain the distance between points and also, as we will show later, the angular distance between points. We could also solve Equation 5.32 for T_6 for both positions and obtain the change in joint coordinates between positions. Given a desired linear and angular velocity and/or joint coordinate velocity, we can then obtain the time T_i to move from point i to point i+1 as the maximum of any of these times. We must also be careful to allow time for the manipulator to decelerate and accelerate between trajectory segments. Given a time t_{acc} necessary to accelerate the manipulator from rest to maximum velocity, we must ensure that $T_i > 2t_{acc}$ in order to execute the worst case trajectory. We will define time t to run from 0 to T_i between each pair of points. As tools and coordinate systems are specified at positions, we may choose to move between two positions with any combination of tools and/or coordinate systems. We will choose to move from one position to the next in the coordinate system, and with the tool specified at the destination position. In order to do this we must redefine the present position in terms of the subsequent coordinate systems and tools. We will do this by defining a second **POS** transformation for each position, in terms of the next coordinate system and tool. At position 1 we have

$$^{1}\mathrm{T_6\,TOOL_1} = \mathrm{COORD_1}(s\mid_{t=0})\ ^{1}\mathrm{POS_1} \tag{5.33}$$

We have added a leading superscript to T_6 and to **POS** to indicate that they are defined with respect to $\mathbf{TOOL}_1$ and $\mathbf{COORD}_1$. We have also added an argument $(s\mid_{t=0})$ to **COORD** to indicate that the transformation expression is to be evaluated for time $t = 0$, that is, at the beginning of the motion from point 1 to 2. We may write a second transform expression involving the same manipulator transform $^{1}T_6$ but in terms of the destination position $\mathbf{TOOL}_2$ and $\mathbf{COORD}_2$

$$^{1}\mathrm{T_6\,TOOL_2} = \mathrm{COORD_2}(s\mid_{t=0})\ ^{2}\mathrm{POS_1} \tag{5.34}$$

where $^{1}T_6$ is the same transformation in both Equations 5.33 and 5.34. We can solve these equations for $^{2}\mathbf{POS}_1$, the transformation for position 1 defined in

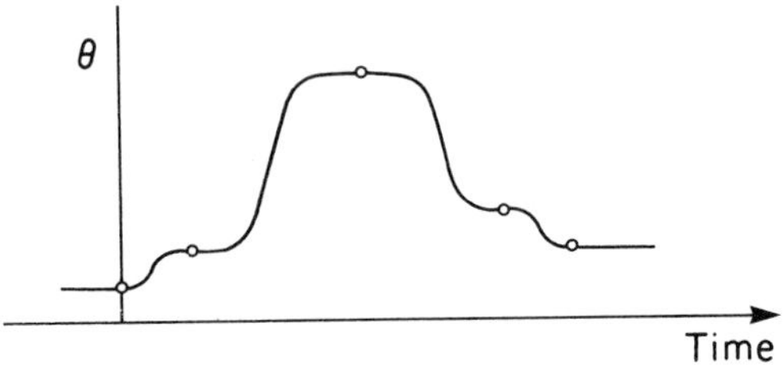

Figure 5.11. Starting and Stopping Motion

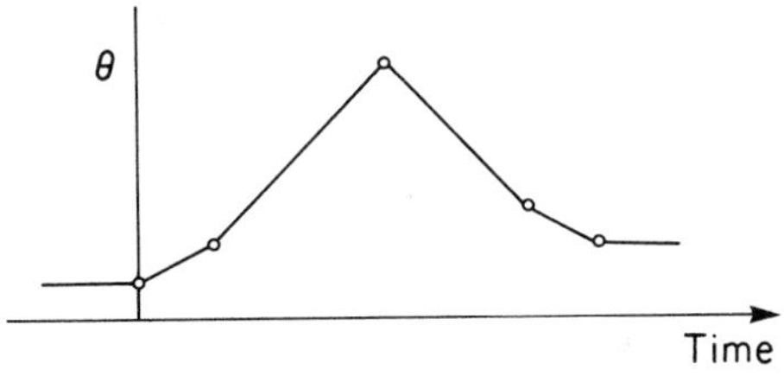

Figure 5.12. Piecewise Linear Approximation

terms of $\mathbf{COORD_2}$ and $\mathbf{TOOL_2}$

$$^2\mathbf{POS}_1 = \mathbf{COORD}_2^{-1}(s\,|_{t=0})\,\mathbf{COORD}_1(s\,|_{t=0})\,{}^1\mathbf{POS}_1\,\mathbf{TOOL}_1^{-1}\,\mathbf{TOOL}_2 \tag{5.35}$$

The motion between any two points i and i+1 is then a motion from

$$\mathbf{T}_6 = \mathbf{COORD}_2(s)\,{}^2\mathbf{POS}_1\,\mathbf{TOOL}_2^{-1} \tag{5.36}$$

to

$$\mathbf{T}_6 = \mathbf{COORD}_2(s)\,{}^2\mathbf{POS}_2\,\mathbf{TOOL}_2^{-1} \tag{5.37}$$

Notice that in these equations $COORD_{i+1}$ is a function of (s), the moving coordinate system variable. If we can arrange to change from $^2\mathbf{POS}_1$ to $^2\mathbf{POS}_2$ in some controlled manner, then the motion of the tool with respect to the moving coordinate system is independent of s, just as it is in the case of a tracking motion, when the tool appears at rest from the moving coordinate system.

There are, of course, many ways in which to move a manipulator from one position to the next. Every system must, however, provide for continuity of position and velocity. In order to prevent vibration and jerk we also require continuity of acceleration in making any motion. Midrange motion should be predictable and motion should stop only when necessary [Paul72].

Based on times T_i to move from position to position, we can plot linear coordinates, angular coordinates, or joint coordinates as a function of time. A plot for a typical coordinate is shown in Figure 5.11. As there is no need to stop at each intermediate point, we may first replace this trajectory with a linear approximation as shown in Figure 5.12. We cannot, however, execute such a trajectory, as both velocity and acceleration are discontinuous at all the trajectory definition points. In order to provide for continuity of position, velocity, and acceleration during the transition from one trajectory segment to another, we may define position as some appropriate function of time $f(t)$ over the interval $-t_{acc} < t < t_{acc}$. We will start the transition from one segment to the next t_{acc} before the end of the segment and will complete the transition t_{acc} after the start of the new segment. Consider the following part of a trajectory shown in Figure 5.13. The manipulator has just passed point A on its way to B. The time is $-t_{acc}$ at the beginning of the transition to the new path segment to point C. In estimating the time for trajectory path segments we allowed t_{acc} to accelerate the manipulator from rest to maximum velocity. In a transition between path segments we have $2t_{acc}$, which allows us to accelerate from maximum negative velocity to maximum positive velocity if necessary. If we were to pick $f(t)$ to be a polynomial then, as we have six boundary conditions (position, velocity, and acceleration at both ends of the transition), we would require a fifth degree polynomial. However, due to the symmetry of the transition, a quartic polynomial will suffice

$$q = a_4t^4 + a_3t^3 + a_2t^2 + a_1t + a_0 \tag{5.38}$$

where q is the generalized position, joint, linear, or angular. By obtaining the derivatives and applying the boundary conditions, we obtain the following functions specifying position q, velocity $\dot{q}$, and acceleration $\ddot{q}$ for the transition

$$q = \left[(\Delta\mathrm{C}\frac{t_{acc}}{T_1} + \Delta\mathrm{B})(2-h)h^2 - 2\Delta\mathrm{B}\right]h + \mathrm{B} + \Delta\mathrm{B} \tag{5.39}$$

$$\dot{q} = \left[(\Delta\mathrm{C}\frac{t_{acc}}{T_1} + \Delta\mathrm{B})(1.5-h)2h^2 - \Delta\mathrm{B}\right]\frac{1}{t_{acc}} \tag{5.40}$$

$$\ddot{q} = (\Delta\mathrm{C}\frac{t_{acc}}{T_1} + \Delta\mathrm{B})(1-h)\frac{3h}{t_{acc}^2} \tag{5.41}$$

where

$$\Delta C = C - B \tag{5.42}$$

$$\Delta B = A - B \tag{5.43}$$

$$h = \frac{t + t_{acc}}{2t_{acc}} \tag{5.44}$$

After the transition at time $t = t_{acc}$ the set points are given by

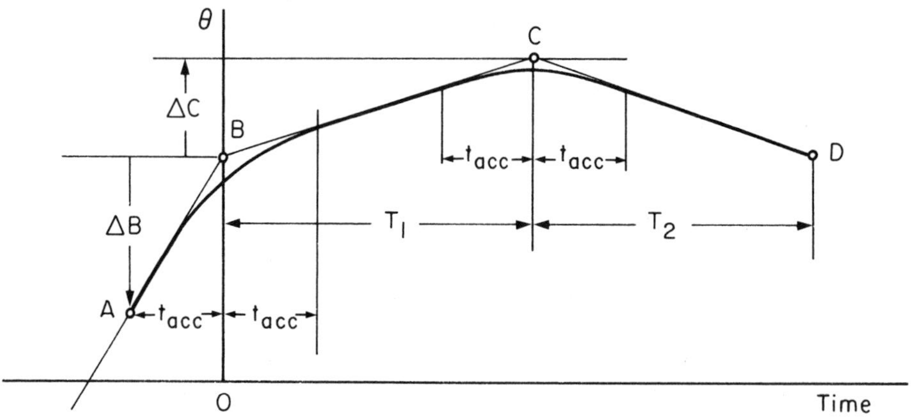

Figure 5.13. Path Transitions

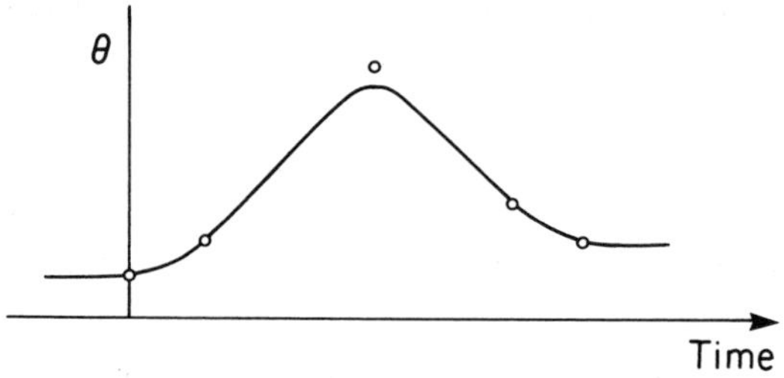

Figure 5.14. Motion With Smooth Transitions

$$q = \Delta C h + \mathbf{B} \tag{5.45}$$

$$\dot{q} = \frac{\Delta \mathbf{C}}{T_1} \tag{5.46}$$

$$\ddot{q} = 0 \tag{5.47}$$

$$h = \frac{t}{T_1} \tag{5.48}$$

Based on a fixed acceleration time t_{acc} we can obtain a coordinated trajectory that we can execute for the entire manipulator (see Figure 5.14). It is not necessary to plan an entire motion, but only to look ahead one position. As soon as the transition is started (point A) we may begin to evaluate the motion from point C to point D. This will involve evaluating the transform expression for point D, obtaining T_6, and then obtaining the time, T_2, to move from C to D. When the time $t = T_1 - t_{acc}$ then the following assignments take place to initiate the transition to the next path segment

```
T1  := T2;
A  := X;            The present position
B  := C;
C  := D;
ΔC  := C-B;
ΔB  := A-B;
t  := -TACC;        Reset time
```

5.8 Joint Motion

In this section we will consider manipulator motion when the motion variables q, $\dot{q}$, and $\ddot{q}$, given by Equations 5.39 — 5.48, represent joint coordinates, joint angles θ_i in the case of revolute joints, and joint distances d_i in the case of prismatic joints. This type of motion is very efficient, being limited only by joint accelerations and maximum joint velocities. While the motion is coordinated, it is not along straight lines or along any other simple, well defined path. Degeneracies of the manipulator do not cause any problem in this type of motion, and it is used in moving from one solution state to another. It is used in the large motion parts of manipulator trajectories when the manipulator is moving clear of any objects and when minimum time is of importance.

We will describe this type of motion at the beginning of a transition, point A in Figure 5.13, and assume that we have the following information: **J**, the current joint coordinates at time $t = T_1 - t_{acc}$, and $\mathbf{J}_C$, the joint coordinates corresponding to point C at the end of the current path segment evaluated for time $t = T_1$. We first evaluate the joint coordinates at point D. If point D is in terms of a moving coordinate system **COORD**(s) then we evaluate **COORD**(s) with $s = s1$ the value of s at the present time $t = T_1 - t_{acc}$. Thus

$$\mathbf{J}_D = \mathrm{solve}(\mathbf{COORD}(s1)\ \mathbf{POS}\ \mathbf{TOOL}^{-1}) \tag{5.49}$$

where solve is a function returning the joint coordinates with a transform expression as argument.

The time to move to point D is then calculated for each joint as

$$t_i = |\mathbf{J}_{Di} - \mathbf{J}_{Ci}|/v_i \tag{5.50}$$

where v_i is the maximum velocity for joint i. The segment time is picked as

$$T_2 = \max t_i, 2t_{acc} \tag{5.51}$$

We then make the end of segment assignments

```
T1  := T2;
JA  := J;              The present position
JB  := JC;
JC  := JD;
ΔJC  := JC-JB;
ΔJB  := JA-JB;
t  := -TACC;           Reset time
```

and use Equations 5.39 — 5.48 to evaluate the manipulator joint set points using `JA, JB, ... ΔJB` in place of A, B, ... ΔB.

We have, however, failed to take into account the motion due to the moving coordinate system COORD(s). We do this by reevaluating the joint coordinates corresponding to the final point D, which has now become point C, which we will call J_{C2}, for time $t = T_1$ when we expect to reach the end of the new segment. At this time we will estimate the moving coordinate variable s to be $s2 = s\ |_{t=T_1}$

$$J_{C2} = \text{solve}(\text{COORD}(s2)\ \text{POS}\ \text{TOOL}^{-1}) \tag{5.52}$$

If, as we calculate set points J, we simply add to J a correction term to account for the motion of point C, we will obtain a motion which will track point C when the manipulator arrives there

```
J:=J+(JC2-JC)*((S-S1)/(S2-S1));
```

This modification to account for the motion of point C introduces one further minor problem: at the beginning of the transition, point A, we change the velocity discontinously by

$$(J_{C2} - J_C)\frac{s0 - s1}{s2 - s1}\frac{1}{t_{acc}}$$

where $s0$ is $s\ |_{t=0}$. This problem is simply corrected by modifying point B to

```
JB:=JB-(JC2-JC)*((SO-S1)/(S2-S1));
```

such that if the initial conditions continue to hold the manipulator will still move towards point B as before. If the initial conditions do not hold, we will still have provided for continuity of velocity, which is all that was necessary, as the manipulator is meant to be tracking point C. We must, of course, also recompute ΔJ_B and ΔJ_C after we have modified the value of point B. Finally, as we approach point C at time $t = T_1 - t_{acc}$ we are at J, and we evaluate the point we are apparently approaching as

```
JC:=JC+(JC2-JC)*((S3-S1)/(S2-S1));
```

where $s3 = s \mid_{t=T_1}$. Thus the end-of-segment assignments become

```
JA  := J;                                          The present position
JB  := JC+(JC2-JC)*((S3-S1)/(S2-S1));
JC  := solve(COORD(S1)+POS-TOOL);
T1  := T2;
JC2:= solve(COORD(S2)+POS-TOOL);
JB  := JB-(JC2-JC)*((SO-S1)/(S2-S1));
ΔJC  := JC-JB;
ΔJB  := JA-JB;
t := -TACC;                                        Reset time
```

5.9 Cartesian Motion

In this section we will describe Cartesian coordinate motion [Paul79]. This is a form of motion which is natural to Cartesian coordinates with the manipulator moving along straight lines and rotating about fixed axes in space. The extension of Cartesian motion to include motion in cylindrical, spherical, and other orthogonal coordinate systems is very simple. As in joint coordinate motion, trajectory segments are defined between positions described by homogeneous transform expressions. The difference between Cartesian and joint coordinate motion is that in the former the motion is natural to Cartesian coordinates (straight lines), while in the latter the motion is linear in joint coordinates. The advantage of Cartesian motion as compared to joint motion is that the motion between trajectory segment end points is well defined and thus is particularly suited to the initial and final trajectory segments.

Cartesian motion has, however, a number of disadvantages. It involves the continuous evaluation of the manipulator set point and its subsequent transformation into joint coordinates. For motion in joint coordinates it is only necessary to interpolate, in joint coordinates, between segment end points. This involves roughly 1% of the computation necessary for Cartesian motion. The continuous evaluation of a Cartesian set point and subsequent transformation into joint coordinates is useful, however, in providing for functionally defined motion (see Chapter 10). A second disadvantage is that Cartesian motion breaks down whenever the manipulator becomes degenerate. Joint rates are unbounded in Cartesian motion, becoming infinite as a manipulator moves into a degeneracy. Furthermore, in Cartesian motion it is not possible to predict whether a trajectory segment will involve excessive joint rates before it is executed. It is difficult to estimate motion times and accelerations as Cartesian velocities and accelerations are related to the limiting joint velocities and accelerations in a complicated manner, dependent on manipulator configuration.

The first problem in developing Cartesian motion is to generate intermediate points between the beginning and end of a path segment defined by two transformation expressions.

5.9.1 Motion Between Positions

One of the simplest ways to change from one transform to the other is by a straight line translation and a rotation about some fixed axis in space. If we can find such a line and axis, then we can produce a motion of controlled linear and angular velocity. We will, however, develop a system in which the motion is made in terms of a translation and two rotations. The first rotation will serve to align the tool in the required final direction, and the second rotation will control the orientation of the tool about its axis. As all manipulators end in a rotary joint, this second rotation in space corresponds to a rotation of the final joint of the manipulator. In many manipulator tasks, such as picking up objects randomly placed on a conveyor, the tool direction is fixed but the tool orientation varies from cycle to cycle. By using the proposed two-rotation scheme, the change from cycle to cycle of the manipulator configuration is confined to the final joint rotation. This causes no change in the space volume swept out by the manipulator as it moves. The range of joint motions is thus simple and predictable.

The motion from a point 1 to a point 2 can be expressed in terms of a drive transform $\mathbf{D}(r)$, a function of relative motion r, as

$$\mathbf{T}_6 = \mathbf{COORD}_2(s)\, {}^2\mathbf{POS}_1\, \mathbf{D}(r)\, \mathbf{TOOL}_2^{-1} \tag{5.53}$$

where $r = t/T$, t is the time since the beginning of the motion, and T is the total time for the move. When $r = 0$ at the start of the motion we require that $\mathbf{D}(0) = \mathbf{I}$, the identity transform. At the end of the motion $r = 1$, we require that

$${}^2\mathbf{POS}_2 = {}^2\mathbf{POS}_1\, \mathbf{D}(1) \tag{5.54}$$

and thus

$$\mathbf{D}(1) = {}^2\mathbf{POS}_1^{-1}\, {}^2\mathbf{POS}_2 \tag{5.55}$$

If we let ${}^2\mathbf{POS}_1 = \mathbf{P1}$ and ${}^2\mathbf{POS}_2 = \mathbf{P2}$ and express the columns of $\mathbf{P1}$ and $\mathbf{P2}$ as vectors ${}^{P1}\mathbf{n}$, ${}^{P1}\mathbf{o}$, ${}^{P1}\mathbf{a}$, ${}^{P1}\mathbf{p}$, and ${}^{P2}\mathbf{n}$, ${}^{P2}\mathbf{o}$, ${}^{P2}\mathbf{a}$, ${}^{P2}\mathbf{p}$, such that

$$\mathbf{P1} = \begin{bmatrix} {}^{P1}\mathbf{n}_x & {}^{P1}\mathbf{o}_x & {}^{P1}\mathbf{a}_x & {}^{P1}\mathbf{p}_x \\ {}^{P1}\mathbf{n}_y & {}^{P1}\mathbf{o}_y & {}^{P1}\mathbf{a}_y & {}^{P1}\mathbf{p}_y \\ {}^{P1}\mathbf{n}_z & {}^{P1}\mathbf{o}_z & {}^{P1}\mathbf{a}_z & {}^{P1}\mathbf{p}_z \\ 0 & 0 & 0 & 1 \end{bmatrix} \tag{5.56}$$

$$\mathbf{P2} = \begin{bmatrix} {}^{P2}\mathbf{n}_x & {}^{P2}\mathbf{o}_x & {}^{P2}\mathbf{a}_x & {}^{P2}\mathbf{p}_x \\ {}^{P2}\mathbf{n}_y & {}^{P2}\mathbf{o}_y & {}^{P2}\mathbf{a}_y & {}^{P2}\mathbf{p}_y \\ {}^{P2}\mathbf{n}_z & {}^{P2}\mathbf{o}_z & {}^{P2}\mathbf{a}_z & {}^{P2}\mathbf{p}_z \\ 0 & 0 & 0 & 1 \end{bmatrix} \tag{5.57}$$

then, by symbolically inverting **P1** and postmultiplying by **P2**, we obtain

$$\mathbf{D}(1) = \begin{bmatrix} {}^{P1}\mathbf{n} \cdot {}^{P2}\mathbf{n} & {}^{P1}\mathbf{n} \cdot {}^{P2}\mathbf{o} & {}^{P1}\mathbf{n} \cdot {}^{P2}\mathbf{a} & {}^{P1}\mathbf{n} \cdot ({}^{P2}\mathbf{p} - {}^{P1}\mathbf{p}) \\ {}^{P1}\mathbf{o} \cdot {}^{P2}\mathbf{n} & {}^{P1}\mathbf{o} \cdot {}^{P2}\mathbf{o} & {}^{P1}\mathbf{o} \cdot {}^{P2}\mathbf{a} & {}^{P1}\mathbf{o} \cdot ({}^{P2}\mathbf{p} - {}^{P1}\mathbf{p}) \\ {}^{P1}\mathbf{a} \cdot {}^{P2}\mathbf{n} & {}^{P1}\mathbf{a} \cdot {}^{P2}\mathbf{o} & {}^{P1}\mathbf{a} \cdot {}^{P2}\mathbf{a} & {}^{P1}\mathbf{a} \cdot ({}^{P2}\mathbf{p} - {}^{P1}\mathbf{p}) \\ 0 & 0 & 0 & 1 \end{bmatrix} \tag{5.58}$$

We will choose intermediate values of **D** to represent a translation and two rotations. Both the translation and the rotations will be directly proportional to r, so that if r varies linearly with respect to time, then the motion represented by **D** will correspond to a constant linear and two constant angular velocities. The translation will be along the line joining **P1** and **P2** and will be represented by the transformation $\mathbf{T}(r)$. The first rotation will serve to rotate the approach vector ${}^{P1}\mathbf{a}$, the direction in which the tool is pointing, from **P1** into the approach vector ${}^{P2}\mathbf{a}$ at **P2**. This rotation will be about a vector **k**, obtained by rotating the y axis of **P1** an angle ψ about the z axis. The vector ${}^{P1}\mathbf{k}$ is thus given by

$${}^{P1}\mathbf{k} = \begin{bmatrix} -\mathrm{S}\,\psi \\ \mathrm{C}\,\psi \\ 0 \\ 1 \end{bmatrix} = \begin{bmatrix} \mathrm{C}\,\psi & -\mathrm{S}\,\psi & 0 & 0 \\ \mathrm{S}\,\psi & \mathrm{C}\,\psi & 0 & 0 \\ 0 & 0 & 1 & 0 \\ 0 & 0 & 0 & 1 \end{bmatrix} \begin{bmatrix} 0 \\ 1 \\ 0 \\ 1 \end{bmatrix} \tag{5.59}$$

This rotation will be represented by $\mathbf{Ra}(r)$ and is given by Equation 1.70 with **k** given above. The second rotation will rotate the orientation vector ${}^{P1}\mathbf{o}$, representing the orientation of the tool, from **P1** into the orientation vector ${}^{P2}\mathbf{o}$ at **P2** $\mathbf{Ro}(r)$. We will then represent $\mathbf{D}(r)$ as

$$\mathbf{D}(r) = \mathbf{T}(r)\,\mathbf{Ra}(r)\,\mathbf{Ro}(r) \tag{5.60}$$

where **T**, **Ra**, and **Ro** have the following form

$$\mathbf{T}(r) = \begin{bmatrix} 1 & 0 & 0 & rx \\ 0 & 1 & 0 & ry \\ 0 & 0 & 1 & rz \\ 0 & 0 & 0 & 1 \end{bmatrix} \tag{5.61}$$

where x, y, and z represents the components of the translation from **P1** to **P2**.

$$\mathbf{Ra}(r) = \begin{bmatrix} \mathrm{S}\,\psi^2\,\mathrm{V}(r\theta) + \mathrm{C}(r\theta) & -\mathrm{S}\,\psi\,\mathrm{C}\,\psi\,\mathrm{V}(r\theta) & \mathrm{C}\,\psi\,\mathrm{S}(r\theta) & 0 \\ -\mathrm{S}\,\psi\,\mathrm{C}\,\psi\,\mathrm{V}(r\theta) & \mathrm{C}\,\psi^2\,\mathrm{V}(r\theta) + \mathrm{C}(r\theta) & \mathrm{S}\,\psi\,\mathrm{S}(r\theta) & 0 \\ -\mathrm{C}\,\psi\,\mathrm{S}(r\theta) & -\mathrm{S}\,\psi\,\mathrm{S}(r\theta) & \mathrm{C}(r\theta) & 0 \\ 0 & 0 & 0 & 1 \end{bmatrix} \tag{5.62}$$

and where

$$V(r\theta) = \text{vers}(r\theta) = (1 - \cos(r\theta)) \tag{5.63}$$
$$C(r\theta) = \cos(r\theta) \tag{5.64}$$
$$S(r\theta) = \sin(r\theta) \tag{5.65}$$

$Ra(r)$ represents a rotation of θ about ${}^{P1}\mathbf{k}$ (see Equation 5.59). The rotation about the approach vector $\mathbf{Ro}(r)$ is simply a rotation about the z axis given by Equation 1.34

$$\mathbf{Ro}(r) = \begin{bmatrix} C(r\phi) & -S(r\phi) & 0 & 0 \\ S(r\phi) & C(r\phi) & 0 & 0 \\ 0 & 0 & 1 & 0 \\ 0 & 0 & 0 & 1 \end{bmatrix} \tag{5.66}$$

where

$$S(r\phi) = \sin(r\phi) \tag{5.67}$$
$$C(r\phi) = \cos(r\phi) \tag{5.68}$$

$\mathbf{Ro}(r)$ represents a rotation of ϕ about the approach vector of the tool. The right hand three columns of $\mathbf{D}(r)$ are

$$D(r) = \begin{bmatrix} ? & -S(r\phi)[S\,\psi^2\,V(r\theta) + C(r\theta)] + C(r\phi)[-S\,\psi\,C\,\psi\,V(r\theta)] & C\,\psi\,S(r\theta) & rx \\ ? & -S(r\phi)[-S\,\psi\,C\,\psi\,V(r\theta)] + C(r\phi)[C^2\,\psi\,V(r\theta) + C(r\theta)] & S\,\psi\,S(r\theta) & ry \\ ? & -S(r\phi)[-C\,\psi\,S(r\theta)] + C(r\phi)[-S\,\psi\,S(r\theta)] & C(r\theta) & rz \\ 0 & 0 & 0 & 1 \end{bmatrix} \tag{5.69}$$

The left hand column can be retrieved from the vector cross product of the second two columns treated as vectors. The function $\mathbf{D}(r)$ corresponds to 4 transcendental function calls, 15 multiplies, and 6 additions.

If we set $r = 1$, we may solve for x, y, z, θ, ψ and ϕ as follows. Postmultiplying both sides of Equation 5.60 by $\mathbf{Ro}(1)^{-1}\,\mathbf{Ra}(1)^{-1}$ and equating elements of the right hand column with elements of Equation 5.58, we obtain values for x, y, and z of the translation transformation $\mathbf{T}$

$$\mathbf{D}(1)\,\mathbf{Ro}(1)^{-1}\,\mathbf{Ra}(1)^{-1} = \mathbf{T}(1) \tag{5.70}$$

and

$$x = {}^{P1}\mathbf{n} \cdot ({}^{P2}\mathbf{p} - {}^{P1}\mathbf{p}) \tag{5.71}$$
$$y = {}^{P1}\mathbf{o} \cdot ({}^{P2}\mathbf{p} - {}^{P1}\mathbf{p}) \tag{5.72}$$
$$x = {}^{P1}\mathbf{a} \cdot ({}^{P2}\mathbf{p} - {}^{P1}\mathbf{p}) \tag{5.73}$$

By postmultiplying both sides of Equation 5.60 by $\mathrm{Ro}(1)^{-1}$ and then premultiplying by T(1), we may solve for θ and ψ by equating elements of the third column with the elements from Equation 5.58

$$\mathrm{T}(1)^{-1}\,\mathrm{D}(1)\,\mathrm{Ro}(1)^{-1} = \mathrm{Ra}(1) \tag{5.74}$$

$$\mathrm{C}\,\psi\,\mathrm{S}(\theta) = {}^{P1}\mathbf{n}\cdot{}^{P2}\mathbf{a} \tag{5.75}$$
$$\mathrm{S}\,\psi\,\mathrm{S}(\theta) = {}^{P1}\mathbf{o}\cdot{}^{P2}\mathbf{a} \tag{5.76}$$
$$\mathrm{C}(\theta) = {}^{P1}\mathbf{a}\cdot{}^{P2}\mathbf{a} \tag{5.77}$$

Thus

$$\tan\psi = \frac{{}^{P1}\mathbf{o}\cdot{}^{P2}\mathbf{a}}{{}^{P1}\mathbf{n}\cdot{}^{P2}\mathbf{a}} \qquad -\pi \le \psi < \pi \tag{5.78}$$

and

$$\tan\theta = \frac{\left(({}^{P1}\mathbf{n}\cdot{}^{P2}\mathbf{a})^2 + ({}^{P1}\mathbf{o}\cdot{}^{P2}\mathbf{a})^2\right)^{1/2}}{{}^{P1}\mathbf{a}\cdot{}^{P2}\mathbf{a}} \qquad 0 \le \theta \le \pi \tag{5.79}$$

Finally, by premultiplying both sides of Equation 5.60 by $\mathrm{T}(1)^{-1}$ and then $\mathrm{Ra}(1)^{-1}$, we obtain

$$\mathrm{Ra}(1)^{-1}\,\mathrm{T}(1)^{-1}\,\mathrm{D}(1) = \mathrm{Ro}(1) \tag{5.80}$$

or

$$\begin{bmatrix} \mathrm{S}\,\psi^2\,\mathrm{V}\,\theta + \mathrm{C}\,\theta & -\mathrm{S}\,\psi\,\mathrm{C}\,\psi\,\mathrm{V}\,\theta & -\mathrm{C}\,\psi\,\mathrm{S}\,\theta & 0 \\ -\mathrm{S}\,\psi\,\mathrm{C}\,\psi\,\mathrm{V}\,\theta & \mathrm{C}\,\psi^2\,\mathrm{V}\,\theta + \mathrm{C}\,\theta & -\mathrm{S}\,\psi\,\mathrm{S}\,\theta & 0 \\ \mathrm{C}\,\psi\,\mathrm{S}\,\theta & \mathrm{S}\,\psi\,\mathrm{S}\,\theta & \mathrm{C}\,\theta & 0 \\ 0 & 0 & 0 & 1 \end{bmatrix} \mathrm{D}(1)$$

$$= \begin{bmatrix} \mathrm{C}\,\phi & -\mathrm{S}\,\phi & 0 & 0 \\ \mathrm{S}\,\phi & \mathrm{C}\,\phi & 0 & 0 \\ 0 & 0 & 1 & 0 \\ 0 & 0 & 0 & 1 \end{bmatrix} \tag{5.81}$$

and by equating the 2, 1 and 2, 2 elements we obtain

$$\begin{aligned} \mathrm{S}\,\phi = &- \mathrm{S}\,\psi\,\mathrm{C}\,\psi\,\mathrm{V}\,\theta({}^{P1}\mathbf{n}\cdot{}^{P2}\mathbf{n}) \\ &+ (\mathrm{C}\,\psi^2\,\mathrm{V}\,\theta + \mathrm{C}\,\theta)({}^{P1}\mathbf{o}\cdot{}^{P2}\mathbf{n}) \\ &- \mathrm{S}\,\psi\,\mathrm{S}\,\theta({}^{P1}\mathbf{a}\cdot{}^{P2}\mathbf{n}) \\ \mathrm{C}\,\phi = &- \mathrm{S}\,\psi\,\mathrm{C}\,\psi\,\mathrm{V}\,\theta({}^{P1}\mathbf{n}\cdot{}^{P2}\mathbf{o}) \\ &+ (\mathrm{C}\,\psi^2\,\mathrm{V}\,\theta + \mathrm{C}\,\theta)({}^{P1}\mathbf{o}\cdot{}^{P2}\mathbf{o}) \\ &- \mathrm{S}\,\psi\,\mathrm{S}\,\theta({}^{P1}\mathbf{a}\cdot{}^{P2}\mathbf{o}) \end{aligned} \tag{5.82}$$

and

$$\tan\phi = \frac{\mathrm{S}\,\phi}{\mathrm{C}\,\phi} \qquad -\pi \le \phi < \pi \tag{5.83}$$

5.9.2 Transitions Between Path Segments

In the last subsection we described path motion in terms of a translation and two rotations controlled by a drive transformation $\mathbf{D}(r)$

$$T_6 = \mathbf{COORD}_2(s)\, {}^2\mathbf{POS}_1\, \mathbf{D}(r)\, \mathbf{TOOL}_2^{-1} \tag{5.84}$$

In this subsection we will describe the transition between path segments. We will describe it in a manner similar to that in which we described path transitions in joint coordinates (Section 5.8). That is, we will consider the manipulator to be at a position described by $\mathbf{J}_A$ at time $T_1 - t_{acc}$, moving towards $\mathbf{J}_B$, to arrive at time T_1. At time T_1 the manipulator will move to a position $\mathbf{POS}_C$ described by

$$T_{6C}\, \mathbf{TOOL} = \mathbf{COORD}(s)\, \mathbf{POS}_C \tag{5.85}$$

where T_{6C} is the value of T_6 when the manipulator will be at $\mathbf{POS}_C$.

We must first evaluate positions A and B in terms of the new moving coordinate system **COORD** and tool **TOOL**. We do this by evaluating T_6 for the two positions T_{6A} and T_{6B}, represented by $\mathbf{J}_A$ and $\mathbf{J}_B$, respectively. We then solve for the corresponding position transformations $\mathbf{POS}_A$ and $\mathbf{POS}_B$

$$\mathbf{POS}_A = \mathbf{COORD}(s\, |_{t=-t_{acc}})^{-1}\, T_{6A}\, \mathbf{TOOL} \tag{5.86}$$

$$\mathbf{POS}_B = \mathbf{COORD}(s\, |_{t=0})^{-1}\, T_{6B}\, \mathbf{TOOL} \tag{5.87}$$

As shown in the previous section, the motion from point B to point C would be described by a drive transformation $\mathbf{D}_{BC}$ defined by

$$\mathbf{D}_{BC}(1) = \mathbf{POS}_B^{-1}\, \mathbf{POS}_C \tag{5.88}$$

and would then specify intermediate set points by

$$T_6 = \mathbf{COORD}(s)\, \mathbf{POS}_B\, \mathbf{D}_{BC}(r)\, \mathbf{TOOL}_C^{-1} \tag{5.89}$$

We could also describe a motion from point B back to point A in terms of position $\mathbf{POS}_B$ by another drive transformation $\mathbf{D}_{BA}$ defined by

$$\mathbf{D}_{BA}(1) = \mathbf{POS}_B^{-1}\, \mathbf{POS}_A \tag{5.90}$$

From each of the two drive transformations we obtain variables x, y, z, θ, ϕ, and ψ. We will distinguish between them by a subscript A or C. As both sets of drive variables are described with respect to the same coordinate system $\mathbf{POS}_B$, we can describe the motion from point A through point B to point C by varying rx, ry, rz, $r\theta$, and $r\phi$ in $\mathrm{D}(r)$ from x_A, y_A, z_A, θ_A, and ϕ_A through zero to x_C, y_C, z_C, θ_C, and ϕ_C. Assume for the moment that the first rotation described by θ is around the same axis for both drive transformations, or, in other words, that ψ is the same for both drive transformations. We may then plot the coordinates as a function of time, as shown in Figure 5.15.

We can now define a ΔB and ΔC as we did for joint motion and use Equations 5.39 — 5.48 to describe the transition and linear motion to point C. In this case, the generalized coordinates q become rx, ry, rz, $r\theta$, and $r\phi$; ψ is assumed the same for both motions and is thus not a motion variable. ΔC is given directly by x_C, y_C, z_C, θ_C, and ϕ_C. ΔB is given by x_A, y_A, z_A, θ_A, and ϕ_A. Notice further that the motion passes through the origin, so that B in Equations 5.39 — 5.48 is zero. For example, the rx coordinate of the drive transformation is given by

$$rx = \left[(\Delta C\frac{t_{acc}}{T_1} + \Delta B)(2-h)h^2 - 2\Delta B\right]h + \Delta B \tag{5.91}$$

$$r\dot{x} = \left[(\Delta C\frac{t_{acc}}{T_1} + \Delta B)(1.5-h)2h^2 - \Delta B\right]\frac{1}{t_{acc}} \tag{5.92}$$

$$r\ddot{x} = (\Delta C\frac{t_{acc}}{T_1} + \Delta B)(1-h)\frac{3h}{t_{acc}^2} \tag{5.93}$$

$$h = \frac{t + t_{acc}}{2t_{acc}} \tag{5.94}$$

After the transition at time $t = t_{acc}$ the set points are given by

$$rx = \Delta C h \tag{5.95}$$

$$r\dot{x} = \frac{\Delta C}{T_1} \tag{5.96}$$

$$r\ddot{x} = 0 \tag{5.97}$$

$$h = \frac{t}{T_1} \tag{5.98}$$

If ψ is not the same for both drive transformations then we must vary ψ from ψ_A to ψ_C during the transition. We may do this linearly as

$$\psi = (\psi_C - \psi_A)h + \psi_A \tag{5.99}$$

where h is given by Equation 5.94 during the transition. This corresponds to an additional angular acceleration. Note that the value for ψ from Equation 5.78 was based on a positive value of θ. In determining ψ_A we will add or subtract 180° in order to make the change $|\psi_C - \psi_A| < 90°$ and change the sign of θ if ψ is so adjusted. ϕ obtained from Equation 5.83 is unaffected by these changes. This change to ψ_A will minimize the effects of the additional acceleration corresponding to the rotation of ψ.

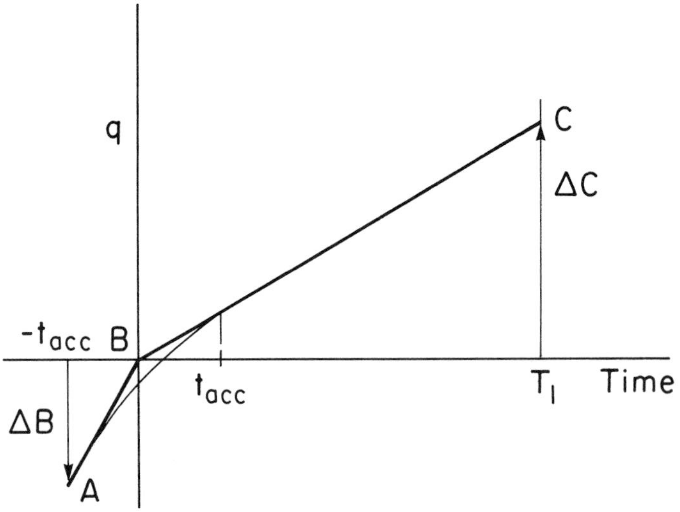

Figure 5.15. Cartesian Path Transition

Example 5.1

This is an example of a manipulator motion from a point POS1 through POS2 to POS3. Where

$$\mathrm{POS1} = \begin{bmatrix} -1 & 0 & 0 & 0 \\ 0 & 1 & 0 & 10 \\ 0 & 0 & -1 & 10 \\ 0 & 0 & 0 & 1 \end{bmatrix}$$

$$\mathrm{POS2} = \begin{bmatrix} 0 & 0 & 1 & 0 \\ 1 & 0 & 0 & 0 \\ 0 & 1 & 0 & 10 \\ 0 & 0 & 0 & 1 \end{bmatrix}$$

$$\mathrm{POS3} = \begin{bmatrix} -1 & 0 & 0 & 10 \\ 0 & -1 & 0 & 0 \\ 0 & 0 & 1 & 10 \\ 0 & 0 & 0 & 1 \end{bmatrix}$$

as is shown in Figure 5.16.

In the motion from point POS1 to POS2 we use Equations 5.71 —5.83 to define x, y, z, ψ, θ, and ϕ

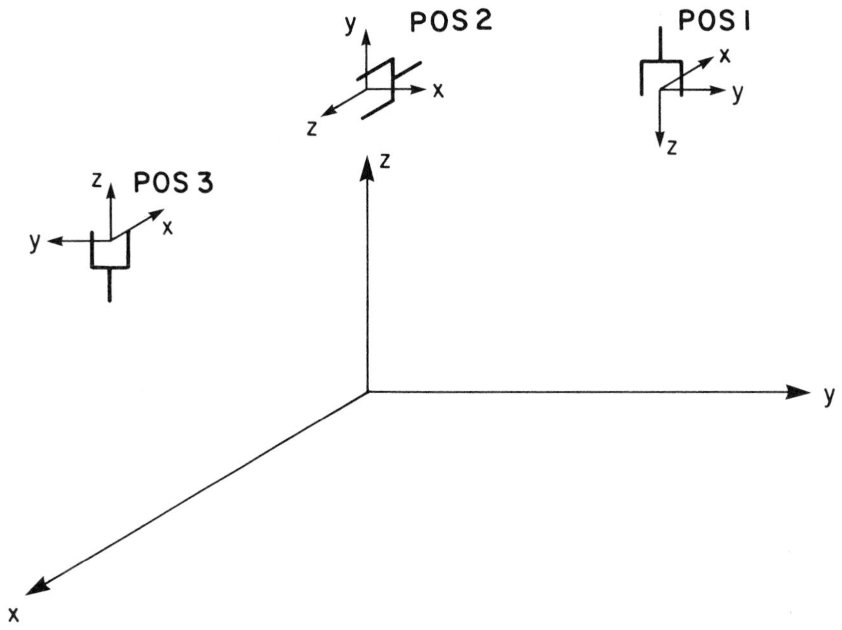

Figure 5.16. Cartesian Motion Example

$$x = 0 \qquad y = -10 \qquad z = 0$$
$$\tan\psi = 0/-1 \qquad \Rightarrow \psi = -180^\circ$$
$$\tan\theta = (1+0)/0 \qquad \Rightarrow \theta = 90^\circ$$
$$\tan\phi = 1/0 \qquad \Rightarrow \phi = 90^\circ$$

Let us assume that the manipulator is approaching point POS2 from POS1 and that $r = 0.9$. The drive transform will then be given by Equation 5.69 as

$$D = \begin{bmatrix} .024 & -.155 & -.988 & 0 \\ .988 & .156 & 0 & -9.00 \\ .155 & -.976 & .156 & 0 \\ 0 & 0 & 0 & 1 \end{bmatrix}$$

and the manipulator position as

$$\text{POS1 } D(0.9) = \begin{bmatrix} -.024 & .155 & .988 & 0 \\ .988 & .156 & 0 & 1.00 \\ -.155 & .976 & -.156 & 10.00 \\ 0 & 0 & 0 & 1 \end{bmatrix}$$

The motion is then from the present position through point POS2 to point POS3 corresponding to positions A, B, and C in Subsection 5.9.2. The drive transformation D_{BA} is defined by a motion from

$$B = POS1 = \begin{bmatrix} 0 & 0 & 1 & 0 \\ 1 & 0 & 0 & 0 \\ 0 & 1 & 0 & 10 \\ 0 & 0 & 0 & 1 \end{bmatrix}$$

to

$$A = POS2 = \begin{bmatrix} -.024 & .155 & .988 & 0 \\ .988 & .156 & 0 & 1.00 \\ -.155 & .976 & -.156 & 10.00 \\ 0 & 0 & 0 & 1 \end{bmatrix}$$

The drive parameters x_A, y_A, z_A, ψ_A, θ_A, and ϕ_A can be obtained from Equations 5.71 — 5.83 with B = POS1 and A = POS2

$$x_A = 1.00 \qquad y_A = 0 \qquad z_A = 0$$
$$\tan\psi_A = -.156/0 \qquad \Rightarrow \psi_A = -90^\circ$$
$$\tan\theta_A = .156/.988 \qquad \Rightarrow \theta_A = 9^\circ$$
$$\tan\phi_A = -.179/.988 \qquad \Rightarrow \phi_A = -9^\circ$$

The motion from point B to point C is described by drive transformation D_{BC} and is defined by the motion from

$$B = POS1 = \begin{bmatrix} 0 & 0 & 1 & 0 \\ 1 & 0 & 0 & 0 \\ 0 & 1 & 0 & 10 \\ 0 & 0 & 0 & 1 \end{bmatrix}$$

to

$$C = POS2 = \begin{bmatrix} -1 & 0 & 0 & 10 \\ 0 & -1 & 0 & 0 \\ 0 & 0 & 1 & 10 \\ 0 & 0 & 0 & 1 \end{bmatrix}$$

Again employing Equations 5.71 — 5.83, we obtain

$$x_C = 0 \qquad y_C = 0 \qquad z_C = 10.00$$
$$\tan\psi_C = 1/0 \qquad \Rightarrow \psi_C = 90^\circ$$
$$\tan\theta_C = 1/0 \qquad \Rightarrow \theta_C = 90^\circ$$
$$\tan\phi_C = 1/0 \qquad \Rightarrow \phi_C = 90^\circ$$

As $|\psi_C - \psi_A| > 90^\circ$ we add 180° to ψ_A and change the sign of θ_A to obtain

$$x_A = 1.00 \qquad y_A = 0 \qquad z_A = 0$$
$$\psi_A = 90^\circ \qquad \theta_A = -9^\circ \qquad \phi_A = -9^\circ$$

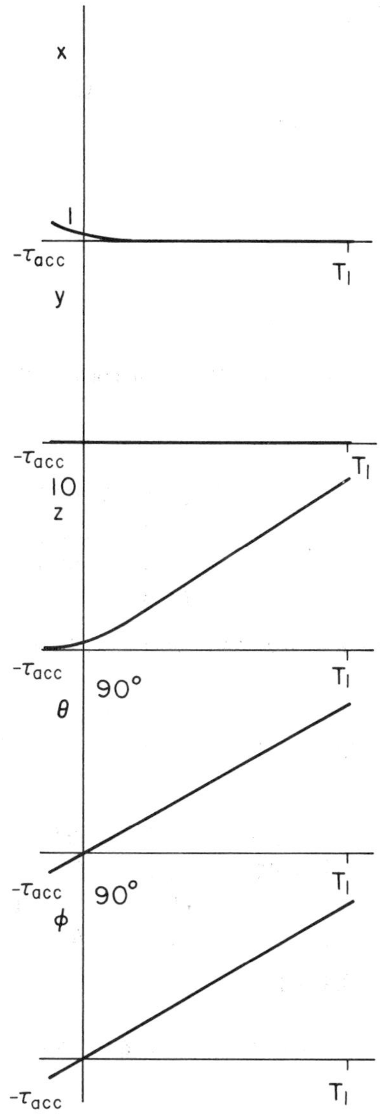

Figure 5.17. Cartesian Motion Variables

We can now evaluate the motion for any points of the transition from A to C (see Figure 5.17). For example, when time $t = 0$, $T_1 = 10t_{acc}$, and r given by Equation 5.94 is 0.5, then component values given by Equation 5.91 are

$$rx = 0.188 \quad ry = 0.000 \quad rz = 0.188 \quad r\theta = 0 \quad r\phi = 0$$

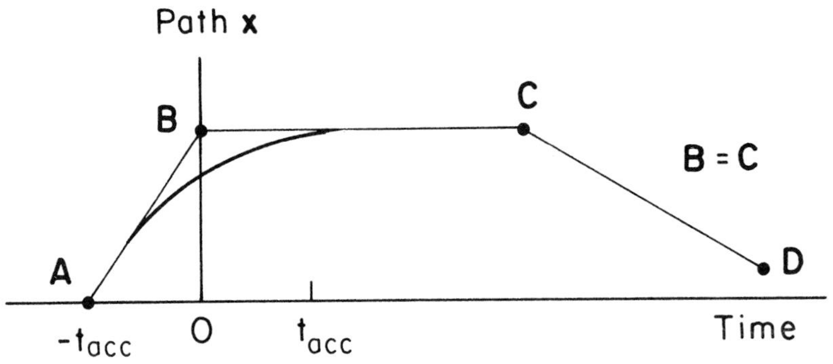

Figure 5.18. Motion Stopping at **B**

and

$$\mathrm{B\,D}(r) = \begin{bmatrix} 0 & 0 & 1 & 0.188 \\ 1 & 0 & 0 & 0.188 \\ 0 & 1 & 0 & 10.000 \\ 0 & 0 & 0 & 1 \end{bmatrix}$$

When $t = t_{acc}$ we have $r = 0.1$ from Equation 5.98 and motion variables given by Equation 5.95 as

$$rx = 0.000 \quad ry = 0.000 \quad rz = 1.000 \quad r\theta = 9^\circ \quad r\phi = 9^\circ$$

and

$$\mathrm{B\,D}(r) = \begin{bmatrix} -0.024 & -0.155 & 0.988 & 1.000 \\ 0.988 & -0.156 & 0 & 0 \\ 0.154 & 0.976 & 0.156 & 10.000 \\ 0 & 0 & 0 & 1 \end{bmatrix}$$

At $t = T_1 - t_{acc}$, $r = 0.9$ and

$$rx = 0.000 \quad ry = 0.000 \quad rz = 9.000 \quad r\theta = 81^\circ \quad r\phi = 81^\circ$$

and

$$\mathrm{B\,D}(r) = \begin{bmatrix} -0.976 & -0.155 & 0.156 & 9.000 \\ 0.157 & -0.988 & 0 & 0 \\ 0.154 & 0.024 & 0.988 & 10.000 \\ 0 & 0 & 0 & 1 \end{bmatrix}$$

With this motion scheme, the manipulator does not in fact pass through any of the points, but passes close by. The only time that the manipulator passes through a trajectory point is when it stops at that point. In order to bring the manipulator to rest, a trajectory point is repeated in the path specification (see Figure 5.18).

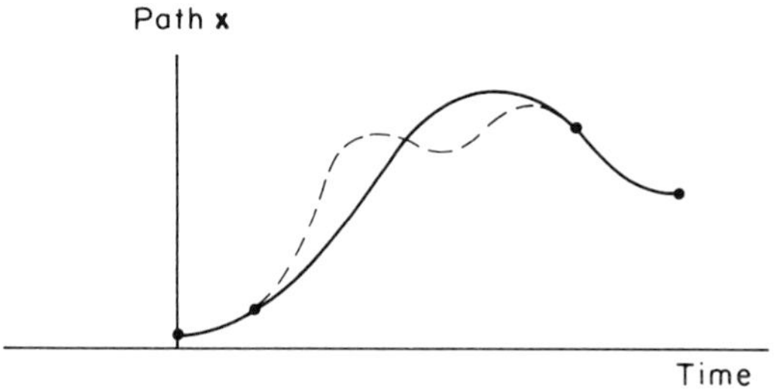

Figure 5.19. Overshooting Motion

If we attempted to pass the manipulator through intermediate trajectory points with non-zero velocity, then at all trajectory extremum points the manipulator would overshoot the trajectory point, as the velocity must change sign either before or after the point (see Figure 5.19). The solution to this problem is to require zero velocity at each trajectory extremum; this is, of course, equivalent to the method described above.

5.9.3 Solution Evaluation Period

If the manipulator has a solution relating joint angles to T_6, we can obtain a set of joint coordinates corresponding to values of T_6. Obtaining values of the joint coordinates is a discrete operation; the transforms representing **COORD**, **POS**, **TOOL** and $D(r)$ are evaluated and multiplied together to form T_6, the joint coordinates J are then obtained from T_6. In order to drive the manipulator, we will perform these operations at some fixed sample rate f_{solve}. We are concerned in this section with estimating f_{solve} for any manipulator.

A serial link manipulator is an extremely complicated mechanical structure and its description is dependent on configuration, which is infinitely variable. A gross simplification of the description of a manipulator is to characterize it as a structure with some resonant frequency $f_{structural}$ and damping coefficient. Indeed, most manipulators are designed to have some minimum resonant frequency. We will use this gross simplification here to obtain a minimum bound on f_{solve}. We will assume that it takes $1/f_{solve}$ to compute a solution J. Between solutions we will interpolate linearly to obtain intermediate manipulator position set points. This interpolation corresponds to constant velocity between solutions and to impulsive accelerations occurring at f_{solve}. In order that the impulses not excite any structural resonances in the manipulator we should ensure that

$$f_{solve} > 10 f_{structural} \tag{5.100}$$

The Stanford manipulator might be optimistically characterized by a structural frequency of 5hz. and thus we should obtain solutions at a 50hz. rate.

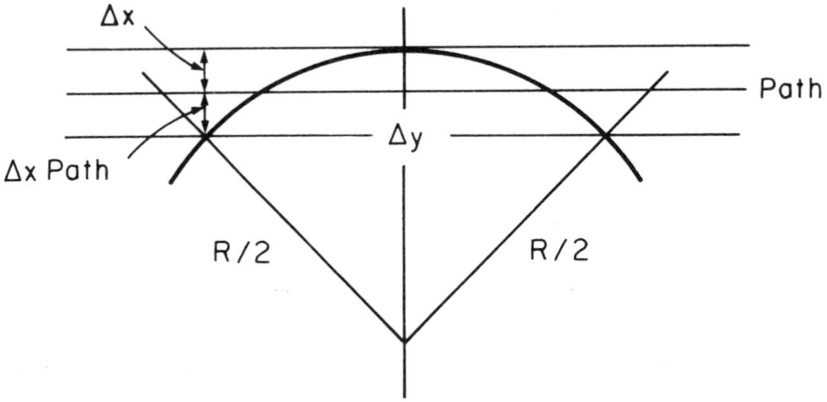

Figure 5.20. Tracking Accuracy

Having determined f_{solve}, we can estimate the tracking accuracy in the important situation where the manipulator is working on a moving conveyor. That is, if we consider joint rates to be constant between solutions and the manipulator to be at rest relative to a coordinate system moving at constant velocity, then we can ascertain the maximum path deviation. If we consider the manipulator to consist of a link of radius R, as shown in Figure 5.20, situated a distance $R/2$ from an object moving past in the y direction at constant velocity, it can be shown that the maximum tracking error Δx is a function of the distance between solutions Δy

$$\Delta x = \frac{\Delta y^2}{8R} \tag{5.101}$$

If the object tracked moves at constant velocity v_c, then the error is related to the solution frequency as

$$\Delta x = \frac{v_c^2}{8Rf_{solve}^2} \tag{5.102}$$

Thus, for the Stanford manipulator, if $R = 1$m. and $v_c = 10$cm.sec.$^{-1}$ then $\Delta x = 5 \times 10^{-4}$mm., a very small number.

5.9.4 Interpolation

While it is sufficient to obtain manipulation solutions at a sample rate f_{solve} to describe the set point, a joint servo system should have a sample rate of approximately $15 f_{structural}$ for any link of the manipulator. In the case of the Stanford manipulator, this rate is as high as 300hz. We obtain these intermediate servo set points by interpolating between solution set points obtained every $1/f_{solve}$. Assuming that it takes $1/f_{solve}$ to obtain a solution, we must start the solution for a point at a time $2/f_{solve}$ before we will reach that position. This can cause problems if the moving coordinate system suddenly stops, as the manipulator will overshoot the correct position by

$$dy = \frac{2v_c}{f_{solve}} \tag{5.103}$$

In the case of the Stanford manipulator tracking a conveyor which is moving at 10cm.sec^{-1}, the overshoot would be 4mm.

5.10 Summary

We have introduced three main subjects in this chapter: a structured task description, a coordinated joint motion control scheme suitable for mid-path motion, and Cartesian motion control suitable for terminal motion control. By employing a structural task description expressed in terms of homogeneous transform equations, it is possible to isolate individual positional components and to incorporate changes in such components appropriately throughout the task. By structuring the task, it is also possible to identify those transforms which should be defined symbolically and those which should be defined by teaching.

The above system provides for motion through intermediate points without stopping and can be adapted to large distance Cartesian motion as described in Equations 5.39 – 5.48

$$q = \left[(\Delta C \frac{t_{acc}}{T_1} + \Delta B)(2 - h)h^2 - 2\Delta B \right] h + B + \Delta B \tag{5.39}$$

$$\dot{q} = \left[(\Delta C \frac{t_{acc}}{T_1} + \Delta B)(1.5 - h)2h^2 - \Delta B \right] \frac{1}{t_{acc}} \tag{5.40}$$

$$\ddot{q} = (\Delta C \frac{t_{acc}}{T_1} + \Delta B)(1 - h)\frac{3h}{t_{acc}^2} \tag{5.41}$$

where

$$\Delta C = C - B \tag{5.42}$$

$$\Delta B = A - B \tag{5.43}$$

$$h = \frac{t + t_{acc}}{2t_{acc}} \tag{5.44}$$

After the transition at time $t = t_{acc}$ the set points are given by

$$q = \Delta Ch + B \tag{5.45}$$

$$\dot{q} = \frac{\Delta C}{T_1} \tag{5.46}$$

$$\ddot{q} = 0 \tag{5.47}$$

$$h = \frac{t}{T_1} \tag{5.48}$$

Motion in Cartesian coordinates is controlled by a drive transformation $\mathbf{D}(r)$ where

$$D(r) = \begin{bmatrix} ? & -\mathrm{S}(r\phi)[\mathrm{S}\,\psi^2\,\mathrm{V}(r\theta) + \mathrm{C}(r\theta)] + \mathrm{C}(r\phi)[-\mathrm{S}\,\psi\,\mathrm{C}\,\psi\,\mathrm{V}(r\theta)] & \mathrm{C}\,\psi\,\mathrm{S}(r\theta) & rx \\ ? & -\mathrm{S}(r\phi)[-\mathrm{S}\,\psi\,\mathrm{C}\,\psi\,\mathrm{V}(r\theta)] + \mathrm{C}(r\phi)[\mathrm{C}^2\,\psi\,\mathrm{V}(r\theta) + \mathrm{C}(r\theta)] & \mathrm{S}\,\psi\,\mathrm{S}(r\theta) & ry \\ ? & -\mathrm{S}(r\phi)[-\mathrm{C}\,\psi\,\mathrm{S}(r\theta)] + \mathrm{C}(r\phi)[-\mathrm{S}\,\psi\,\mathrm{S}(r\theta)] & \mathrm{C}(r\theta) & rz \\ 0 & 0 & 0 & 1 \end{bmatrix} \tag{5.69}$$

Motion in joint coordinates separates kinematics from dynamics. It requires transformations between coordinate systems based only on kinematic considerations and not at servo rate as in the Cartesian motion system. By relating the rate of transformation between Cartesian coordinates and joint coordinates to changes in configuration, instead of to changes in acceleration, a significant reduction in computing power can be achieved.

5.11 References

Grossman, D. D. & Taylor, R. H. "Interactive Generation of Object Models with a Manipulator," *IEEE Trans. on Systems, Man, and Cybernetics* **SMC-8**, 9 (Sept 1978), 667–679.

Paul, R. P. Modeling, Trajectory Calculation and Servoing of a Computer Controlled Arm, Stanford Artificial Intelligence Laboratory, Stanford University, AIM 177, 1972.

Paul, R. P. "Manipulator Cartesian Path Control," *IEEE Trans. on Systems, Man, and Cybernetics* **SMC-9**, 11 (Nov. 1979), 702–711.

Takase, K., Paul, R., Berg, E. "A Structured Approach to Robot Programming and Teaching," *IEEE Trans. on Systems, Man, and Cybernetics* **SMC-11**, 4 (Apr. 1981), 274–289.

CHAPTER 6

DYNAMICS

6.1 Introduction

We have now completed our study of kinematics and the specification of manipulator tasks. In this chapter we will study the dynamics of manipulators for the purpose of control. Manipulators represent a complicated dynamic system and if we are to analyze their dynamics we must take a very systematic approach to solving the problem. We will make use of Lagrangian mechanics as this method allows us to obtain the dynamics equations for very complicated systems in the simplest manner possible. (If the reader is unfamiliar with Lagrangian mechanics she or he should read one of the excellent references on the subject, such as the text by [Symon], before proceeding.) We are interested in obtaining a symbolic solution to the manipulator dynamics as this provides insight into the control problem. (For a survey of numerical solutions to the dynamic problem see [Hollerbach].)

We will first give a simple example of Lagrangian mechanics: we will obtain the dynamics equations for a simple two degree of freedom manipulator. This will give us insight into manipulator dynamics. We will then develop the Lagrangian for manipulators in general, obtaining the dynamics equations. The dynamics equations relate forces and torques to positions, velocities, and accelerations; they are usually solved in order to obtain the equations of motion of the manipulator. That is, given forces and torques as input, these equations specify resulting motion of the system. In our case it is not necessary to solve the equations, as we have already specified the motion of the manipulator and simply wish to know what forces and torques we must apply in order to control it. The dynamics equations give us this information, which is fortunate, as it is very difficult merely to obtain the dynamics equations for a system as complicated as a manipulator, let alone to solve them. These equations, representing six coupled, non-linear, differential equations, are in fact impossible to solve in all but the most trivial cases. When we obtain the dynamics equations in matrix form, we will simplify them in order to obtain the necessary information for control. As will be seen in the next chapter, we are particularly interested in obtaining an approximation to the effective inertias of each of the joints and the inertial coupling between them. In other words, we require to know the relationship between torque and acceleration at a joint, and the relationship between torque at one joint and accelerations at other joints. If the coupling inertias are small with regard to the effective joint inertias, then we can treat the manipulator as a series of independent mechanical systems.

We also need to determine the torques to be applied at the joints of the manipulator in order to overcome the effects of gravity. We will disregard the velocity dependent torques for a number of reasons: they are typically small compared to other system torques, there are too many of them to compute, and they are too complicated to solve for symbolically. Furthermore, they are important only when the manipulator is moving at high speed, at which time positional accuracy is usually of little importance.

We will obtain the full and complete dynamics equations and then simplify them, based on significance analysis and dynamic reasoning. The full equations are very complex, as they contain many thousands of terms, but simplification is rapid and quite easy to perform. The resulting equations are simple, can be computed at servo rate, and provide insight into the system to be controlled. The simplified manipulator state equations are more useful than numeric techniques which, although they calculate the exact torques as functions of positions, velocities, and accelerations, provide no insight into the system.

6.2 Lagrangian Mechanics — A Simple Example

The Lagrangian L is defined as the difference between the kinetic energy K and the potential energy P of the system

$$L = K - P \tag{6.1}$$

The kinetic and potential energy of the system may be expressed in any convenient coordinate system that will simplify the problem. It is not necessary to use Cartesian coordinates.

The dynamics equations, in terms of the coordinates used to express the kinetic and potential energy, are obtained as

$$F_i = \frac{d}{dt}\frac{\partial L}{\partial \dot{q}_i} - \frac{\partial L}{\partial q_i} \tag{6.2}$$

where q_i are the coordinates in which the kinetic and potential energy are expressed, $\dot{q}_i$ is the corresponding velocity, and F_i the corresponding force or torque. F_i is either a force or a torque, depending upon whether q_i is a linear or an angular coordinate. These forces, torques, and coordinates are referred to as generalized forces, torques, and coordinates.

To clarify the problem, let us proceed immediately to an example. Consider the two link manipulator shown in Figure 6.1. The mass of both links, m_1 and m_2,

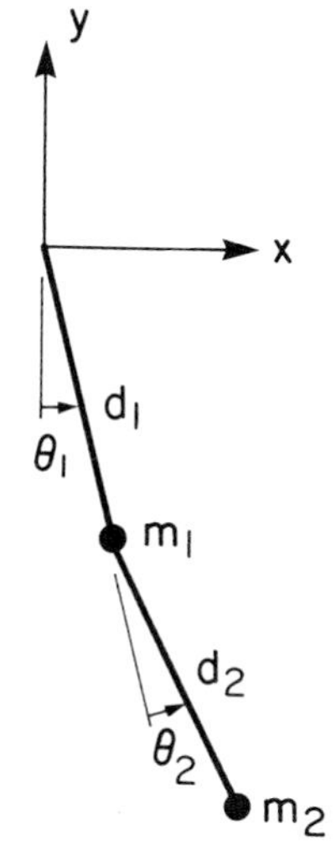

Figure 6.1. A Two Link Manipulator

is represented by point masses at the end of the links. The links are of length d_1 and d_2, respectively. The manipulator hangs straight down in a gravity field of acceleration g. The generalized coordinates are chosen as θ_1 and θ_2, as shown in the figure.

6.2.1 The Kinetic and Potential Energy

We first compute the kinetic energy. To do we this we need expressions for the velocity squared of the masses as $K = \frac{1}{2}mv^2$. The kinetic energy of mass m_1 can be written directly as

$$K_1 = \frac{1}{2}m_1 d_1^2 \dot{\theta}_1^2 \tag{6.3}$$

The potential energy is related to the vertical height of the mass expressed by the y coordinate and may be written directly as

$$P_1 = -m_1 g d_1 \cos(\theta_1) \tag{6.4}$$

In the case of the second mass we will first write expressions for the Cartesian position coordinates and then differentiate them in order to obtain the velocity

$$x_2 = d_1 \sin(\theta_1) + d_2 \sin(\theta_1 + \theta_2) \tag{6.5}$$

$$y_2 = -d_1 \cos(\theta_1) - d_2 \cos(\theta_1 + \theta_2) \tag{6.6}$$

The Cartesian components of velocity are then

$$\dot{x}_2 = d_1 \cos(\theta_1)\, \dot{\theta}_1 + d_2 \cos(\theta_1 + \theta_2)(\dot{\theta}_1 + \dot{\theta}_2) \tag{6.7}$$

$$\dot{y}_2 = d_1 \sin(\theta_1)\, \dot{\theta}_1 + d_2 \sin(\theta_1 + \theta_2)(\dot{\theta}_1 + \dot{\theta}_2) \tag{6.8}$$

The magnitude of the velocity squared is then

$$\begin{aligned} v_2^2 = & d_1^2\dot{\theta}_1^2 + d_2^2(\dot{\theta}_1^2 + 2\dot{\theta}_1\dot{\theta}_2 + \dot{\theta}_2^2) \\ & + 2d_1d_2\cos(\theta_1)\cos(\theta_1+\theta_2)(\dot{\theta}_1^2 + \dot{\theta}_1\dot{\theta}_2) \\ & + 2d_1d_2\sin(\theta_1)\sin(\theta_1+\theta_2)(\dot{\theta}_1^2 + \dot{\theta}_1\dot{\theta}_2) \\ = & d_1^2\dot{\theta}_1^2 + d_2^2(\dot{\theta}_1^2 + 2\dot{\theta}_1\dot{\theta}_2 + \dot{\theta}_2^2) + 2d_1d_2\cos(\theta_2)(\dot{\theta}_1^2 + \dot{\theta}_1\dot{\theta}_2) \end{aligned} \tag{6.9}$$

and the kinetic energy is

$$K_2 = \frac{1}{2}m_2d_1^2\dot{\theta}_1^2 + \frac{1}{2}m_2d_2^2(\dot{\theta}_1^2 + 2\dot{\theta}_1\dot{\theta}_2 + \dot{\theta}_2^2) + m_2d_1d_2\cos(\theta_2)(\dot{\theta}_1^2 + \dot{\theta}_1\dot{\theta}_2) \tag{6.10}$$

The height of the mass is expressed by Equation 6.6, and the potential energy is then

$$P_2 = -m_2gd_1\cos(\theta_1) - m_2gd_2\cos(\theta_1+\theta_2) \tag{6.11}$$

6.2.2 The Lagrangian

The Lagrangian $L = K - P$ is then obtained from Equations 6.3, 6.4, 6.10, and 6.11

$$\begin{aligned} L = & \frac{1}{2}(m_1+m_2)d_1^2\dot{\theta}_1^2 + \frac{1}{2}m_2d_2^2(\dot{\theta}_1^2 + 2\dot{\theta}_1\dot{\theta}_2 + \dot{\theta}_2^2) \\ & + m_2d_1d_2\cos(\theta_2)(\dot{\theta}_1^2 + \dot{\theta}_1\dot{\theta}_2) \\ & + (m_1+m_2)gd_1\cos(\theta_1) + m_2gd_2\cos(\theta_1+\theta_2) \end{aligned} \tag{6.12}$$

6.2.3 The Dynamics Equations

In order to obtain the dynamics equations we now differentiate the Lagrangian L according to Equation 6.2,

$$\begin{aligned} \frac{\partial L}{\partial \dot{\theta}_1} = & (m_1+m_2)d_1^2\dot{\theta}_1 + m_2d_2^2\dot{\theta}_1 + m_2d_2^2\dot{\theta}_2 \\ & + 2m_2d_1d_2\cos(\theta_2)\dot{\theta}_1 + m_2d_1d_2\cos(\theta_2)\dot{\theta}_2 \end{aligned} \tag{6.13}$$

$$\begin{aligned} \frac{d}{dt}\frac{\partial L}{\partial \dot{\theta}_1} = & [(m_1+m_2)d_1^2 + m_2d_2^2 + 2m_2d_1d_2\cos(\theta_2)]\ddot{\theta}_1 \\ & + [m_2d_2^2 + m_2d_1d_2\cos(\theta_2)]\ddot{\theta}_2 \\ & - 2m_2d_1d_2\sin(\theta_2)\dot{\theta}_1\dot{\theta}_2 - m_2d_1d_2\sin(\theta_2)\dot{\theta}_2^2 \end{aligned} \tag{6.14}$$

$$\frac{\partial L}{\partial \theta_1} = -(m_1+m_2)gd_1\sin(\theta_1) - m_2gd_2\sin(\theta_1+\theta_2) \tag{6.15}$$

Combining Equations 6.14 and 6.15 according to Equation 6.2 we obtain the torque at joint 1 as

$$\begin{aligned} T_1 = {} & [(m_1 + m_2)d_1^2 + m_2 d_2^2 + 2m_2 d_1 d_2 \cos(\theta_2)]\ddot{\theta}_1 \\ & + [m_2 d_2^2 + m_2 d_1 d_2 \cos(\theta_2)]\ddot{\theta}_2 \\ & - 2m_2 d_1 d_2 \sin(\theta_2)\dot{\theta}_1\dot{\theta}_2 - m_2 d_1 d_2 \sin(\theta_2)\dot{\theta}_2^2 \\ & + (m_1 + m_2) g d_1 \sin(\theta_1) + m_2 g d_2 \sin(\theta_1 + \theta_2) \end{aligned} \tag{6.16}$$

We now proceed to obtain the equation for the torque at joint 2 by performing the differentiation of the Lagrangian with respect to $\dot{\theta}_2$ and θ_2

$$\frac{\partial L}{\partial \dot{\theta}_2} = m_2 d_2^2 \dot{\theta}_1 + m_2 d_2^2 \dot{\theta}_2 + m_2 d_1 d_2 \cos(\theta_2)\dot{\theta}_1 \tag{6.17}$$

$$\frac{d}{dt}\frac{\partial L}{\partial \dot{\theta}_2} = m_2 d_2^2 \ddot{\theta}_1 + m_2 d_2^2 \ddot{\theta}_2 + m_2 d_1 d_2 \cos(\theta_2)\ddot{\theta}_1 - m_2 d_1 d_2 \sin(\theta_2)\dot{\theta}_1\dot{\theta}_2 \tag{6.18}$$

$$\frac{\partial L}{\partial \theta_2} = -m_2 d_1 d_2 \sin(\theta_2)\dot{\theta}_1\dot{\theta}_2 - m_2 g d_2 \sin(\theta_1 + \theta_2) \tag{6.19}$$

The torque is then

$$\begin{aligned} T_2 = {} & [m_2 d_2^2 + m_2 d_1 d_2 \cos(\theta_2)]\ddot{\theta}_1 + m_2 d_2^2 \ddot{\theta}_2 \\ & - 2m_2 d_1 d_2 \sin(\theta_2)\dot{\theta}_1\dot{\theta}_2 - m_2 d_1 d_2 \sin(\theta_2)\dot{\theta}_1^2 \\ & + m_2 g d_2 \sin(\theta_1 + \theta_2) \end{aligned} \tag{6.20}$$

Let us rewrite Equations 6.16 and 6.20 in the form

$$\begin{aligned} T_1 . = {} & D_{11}\ddot{\theta}_1 + D_{12}\ddot{\theta}_2 \\ & + D_{111}\dot{\theta}_1^2 + D_{122}\dot{\theta}_2^2 \\ & + D_{112}\dot{\theta}_1\dot{\theta}_2 + D_{121}\dot{\theta}_2\dot{\theta}_1 \\ & + D_1 \end{aligned} \tag{6.21}$$

$$\begin{aligned} T_2 = {} & D_{12}\ddot{\theta}_1 + D_{22}\ddot{\theta}_2 \\ & + D_{211}\dot{\theta}_1^2 + D_{222}\dot{\theta}_2^2 \\ & + D_{212}\dot{\theta}_1\dot{\theta}_2 + D_{221}\dot{\theta}_2\dot{\theta}_1 \\ & + D_2 \end{aligned} \tag{6.22}$$

In these equations, a coefficient of the form D_{ii} is known as the effective inertia at joint i, as an acceleration at joint i causes a torque at joint i equal to $D_{ii}\ddot{\theta}_i$.

A coefficient of the form D_{ij} is known as the coupling inertia between joints i and j, as an acceleration at joint i or j causes a torque at joint j or i equal to $D_{ij}\ddot{\theta}_i$ or $D_{ij}\ddot{\theta}_j$, respectively. A term of the form $D_{ijj}\dot{\theta}_j^2$ is the centripetal force acting at joint i due to a velocity at joint j. A combination of terms of the form $D_{ijk}\dot{\theta}_j\dot{\theta}_k + D_{ikj}\dot{\theta}_k\dot{\theta}_j$ is known as the Coriolis force acting at joint i due to velocities at joints j and k. Finally, a term of the form D_i represents the gravity forces at joint i. By comparing Equations 6.16 and 6.20 with 6.21 and 6.22, respectively, we obtain values for the coefficients as:
effective inertias

$$D_{11} = [(m_1 + m_2)d_1^2 + m_2 d_2^2 + 2m_2 d_1 d_2 \cos(\theta_2)] \tag{6.23}$$

$$D_{22} = m_2 d_2^2 \tag{6.24}$$

coupling inertia

$$D_{12} = m_2 d_2^2 + m_2 d_1 d_2 \cos(\theta_2) \tag{6.25}$$

centripetal acceleration coefficients

$$D_{111} = 0 \tag{6.26}$$

$$D_{122} = -m_2 d_1 d_2 \sin(\theta_2) \tag{6.27}$$

$$D_{211} = -m_2 d_1 d_2 \sin(\theta_2) \tag{6.28}$$

$$D_{222} = 0 \tag{6.29}$$

Coriolis acceleration coefficients

$$D_{112} = D_{121} = -m_2 d_1 d_2 \sin(\theta_2) \tag{6.30}$$

$$D_{212} = D_{221} = -m_2 d_1 d_2 \sin(\theta_2) \tag{6.31}$$

and gravity terms

$$D_1 = (m_1 + m_2)g d_1 \sin(\theta_1) + m_2 g d_2 \sin(\theta_1 + \theta_2) \tag{6.32}$$

$$D_2 = m_2 g d_2 \sin(\theta_1 + \theta_2) \tag{6.33}$$

Let us assign some numbers to our example and evaluate Equations 6.21 and 6.22 for the manipulator at rest in a gravity free environment under two conditions: joint 2 locked ($\ddot{\theta}_2 = 0$), and joint 2 free ($T_2 = 0$). Under the first condition, Equations 6.21 and 6.22 reduce to

$$T_1 = D_{11}\ddot{\theta}_1 \tag{6.34}$$

$$T_2 = D_{12}\ddot{\theta}_1 \tag{6.35}$$

Under the second condition $T_2 = 0$, we may solve Equation 6.22 for $\ddot{\theta}_2$ and substitute this into Equation 6.21 for $\ddot{\theta}_2$ to obtain T_1

$$T_2 = 0 = D_{12}\ddot{\theta}_1 + D_{22}\ddot{\theta}_2$$

Then

$$\ddot{\theta}_2 = -\frac{D_{12}}{D_{22}}\ddot{\theta}_1$$

and substituting for $\ddot{\theta}_2$ in Equation 6.21 we obtain

$$T_1 = [D_{11} - \frac{D_{12}^2}{D_{22}}]\ddot{\theta}_1 \tag{6.36}$$

We will pick $d_1 = d_2 = 1$ and $m_1 = 2$. We will evaluate the coefficients for three values of m_2: 1, 4, and 100 representing respectively an unloaded manipulator, a loaded manipulator, and a loaded manipulator in outer space, where gravity loading is absent, allowing much greater loads. Based on the coefficients and Equations 6.34 and 6.36, we will calculate the inertia at joint 1 corresponding to the locked case I_l and the free case I_f

Table 6.1 $m_1 = 2, m_2 = 1, d_1 = 1, d_2 = 1$

θ_2	$\cos\theta_2$	D_{11}	D_{12}	D_{22}	I_l	I_f
0°	1	6	2	1	6	2
90°	0	4	1	1	4	3
180°	−1	2	0	1	2	2
270°	0	4	1	1	4	3

Table 6.2 $m_1 = 2, m_2 = 4, d_1 = 1, d_2 = 1$

θ_2	$\cos\theta_2$	D_{11}	D_{12}	D_{22}	I_l	I_f
0°	1	18	8	4	18	2
90°	0	10	4	4	10	6
180°	−1	2	0	4	2	2
270°	0	10	4	4	10	6

Table 6.3 $m_1 = 2, m_2 = 100, d_1 = 1, d_2 = 1$

θ_2	$\cos\theta_2$	D_{11}	D_{12}	D_{22}	I_l	I_f
0°	1	402	200	100	402	2
90°	0	202	100	100	202	102
180°	−1	2	0	100	2	2
270°	0	202	100	100	202	102

The right hand two columns of the above tables are the effective inertias seen at joint 1. In the case of the unloaded manipulator, as shown in Table 6.1, 3:1 variations in inertia are experienced due to variation in θ_2 and dependent upon whether joint 2 is locked or free. The loaded manipulator, described in Table 6.2, exhibits 9:1 variations in inertia due to variations in θ_2, and up to 3:1 variations from no load to full load. In the case of the manipulator in outer space with a load of 100, the inertia variations are 201:1! These inertia variations will have a major impact on the control of the manipulator.

6.3 The Manipulator Dynamics Equation

We will now derive the dynamics equation for any manipulator described by a set of A transformations [Uicker] [Kahn] [Paul72]. We will perform this derivation in five steps. We first compute the velocity of any point in any link and next compute the kinetic energy. We then develop the potential energy, form the Lagrangian, and differentiate it to obtain the dynamics equations.

6.3.1 The Velocity of a Point on the Manipulator

Given a point ${}^i\mathbf{r}$ described with respect to link i, its position in base coordinates is

$$\mathbf{r} = \mathbf{T}_i\, {}^i\mathbf{r} \tag{6.37}$$

Its velocity then is

$$\frac{d\mathbf{r}}{dt} = \left(\sum_{j=1}^{i} \frac{\partial \mathbf{T}_i}{\partial q_j} \dot{q}_j \right) {}^i\mathbf{r} \tag{6.38}$$

The velocity squared is

$$\left(\frac{d\mathbf{r}}{dt}\right)^2 = \mathbf{r} \cdot \mathbf{r}$$

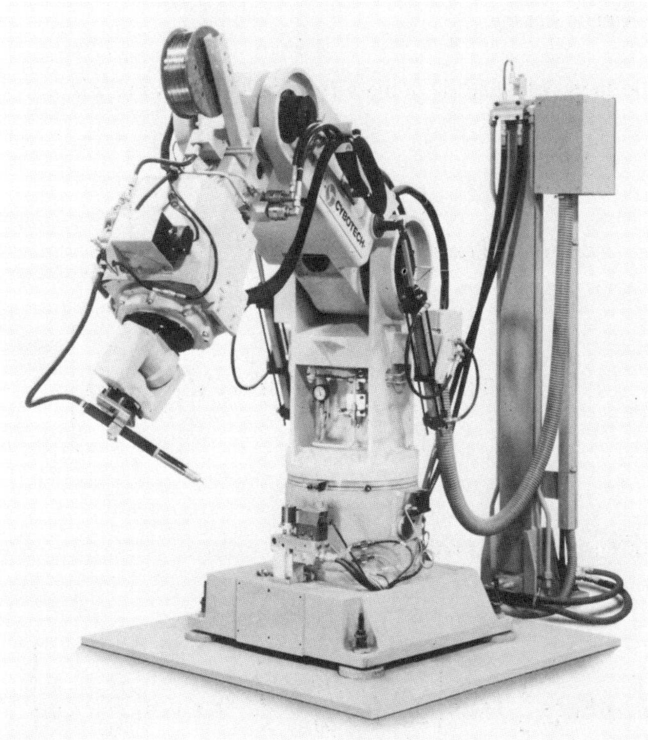

Figure 6.2. The Cybotech Vertical 80 Robot (Courtesy of Cybotech)

or, in matrix form

$$\left(\frac{d\mathbf{r}}{dt}\right)^2 = \mathrm{Trace}(\mathbf{r}\,\mathbf{r}^T) \tag{6.39}$$

Substituting from Equation 6.38 we obtain

$$\begin{aligned}\left(\frac{d\mathbf{r}}{dt}\right)^2 &= \mathrm{Trace}\left[\sum_{j=1}^{i} \frac{\partial \mathbf{T}_i}{\partial q_j} \dot{q}_j \, {}^i\mathbf{r} \sum_{k=1}^{i} \left(\frac{\partial \mathbf{T}_i}{\partial q_k} \dot{q}_k \, {}^i\mathbf{r}\right)^T\right] \\ &= \mathrm{Trace}\left[\sum_{j=1}^{i} \sum_{k=1}^{i} \frac{\partial \mathbf{T}_i}{\partial q_j} {}^i\mathbf{r} \, {}^i\mathbf{r}^T \frac{\partial \mathbf{T}_i}{\partial q_k}^T \dot{q}_j \dot{q}_k\right]\end{aligned} \tag{6.40}$$

6.3.2 The Kinetic Energy

The kinetic energy of a particle of mass dm located on link i at ${}^i\mathbf{r}$ is

$$dK_i = \frac{1}{2}\,\text{Trace}\left[\sum_{j=1}^{i}\sum_{k=1}^{i}\frac{\partial \mathrm{T}_i}{\partial q_j}{}^i\mathrm{r}\,{}^i\mathrm{r}^T\frac{\partial \mathrm{T}_i}{\partial q_k}^T\dot{q}_j\dot{q}_k\right]dm$$
$$= \frac{1}{2}\,\text{Trace}\left[\sum_{j=1}^{i}\sum_{k=1}^{i}\frac{\partial \mathrm{T}_i}{\partial q_j}({}^i\mathrm{r}\,dm\,{}^i\mathrm{r}^T)\frac{\partial \mathrm{T}_i}{\partial q_k}^T\dot{q}_j\dot{q}_k\right] \tag{6.41}$$

The kinetic energy of link i is then

$$K_i = \int_{link_i} dK_i = \frac{1}{2}\,\text{Trace}\left[\sum_{j=1}^{i}\sum_{k=1}^{i}\frac{\partial \mathrm{T}_i}{\partial q_j}\left(\int_{link_i}{}^i\mathrm{r}\,{}^i\mathrm{r}^T dm\right)\frac{\partial \mathrm{T}_i}{\partial q_k}^T\dot{q}_j\dot{q}_k\right] \tag{6.42}$$

The integral in Equation 6.42 is known as the pseudo inertia matrix J_i and is given by

$$J_i = \int_{link_i}{}^i\mathrm{r}\,{}^i\mathrm{r}^T dm =$$
$$\begin{bmatrix} \int_{link_i}{}^ix^2dm & \int_{link_i}{}^ix\,{}^iydm & \int_{link_i}{}^ix\,{}^izdm & \int_{link_i}{}^ixdm \\ \int_{link_i}{}^ix\,{}^iydm & \int_{link_i}{}^iy^2dm & \int_{link_i}{}^iy\,{}^izdm & \int_{link_i}{}^iydm \\ \int_{link_i}{}^ix\,{}^izdm & \int_{link_i}{}^iy\,{}^izdm & \int_{link_i}{}^iz^2dm & \int_{link_i}{}^izdm \\ \int_{link_i}{}^ixdm & \int_{link_i}{}^iydm & \int_{link_i}{}^izdm & \int_{link_i}dm \end{bmatrix} \tag{6.43}$$

Recalling that the moments of inertia, cross products of inertia, and first moments of a body are defined as

$$I_{xx} = \int (y^2 + z^2) dm$$

$$I_{yy} = \int (x^2 + z^2) dm$$

$$I_{zz} = \int (x^2 + y^2) dm$$

$$I_{xy} = \int xy\, dm$$

$$I_{xz} = \int xz\, dm$$

$$I_{yz} = \int yz\, dm$$

$$m\bar{x} = \int x\, dm$$

$$m\bar{y} = \int y\, dm$$

$$m\bar{z} = \int z\, dm$$

and that

$$\begin{aligned}\int x^2 dm &= -\frac{1}{2}\int (y^2 + z^2) dm + \frac{1}{2}\int (x^2 + z^2) dm + \frac{1}{2}\int (x^2 + y^2) dm \\ &= (-I_{xx} + I_{yy} + I_{zz})/2 \end{aligned} \tag{6.44}$$

$$\begin{aligned}\int y^2 dm &= +\frac{1}{2}\int (y^2 + z^2) dm - \frac{1}{2}\int (x^2 + z^2) dm + \frac{1}{2}\int (x^2 + y^2) dm \\ &= (+I_{xx} - I_{yy} + I_{zz})/2 \end{aligned} \tag{6.45}$$

$$\begin{aligned}\int z^2 dm &= +\frac{1}{2}\int (y^2 + z^2) dm + \frac{1}{2}\int (x^2 + z^2) dm - \frac{1}{2}\int (x^2 + y^2) dm \\ &= (+I_{xx} + I_{yy} - I_{zz})/2 \end{aligned} \tag{6.46}$$

then J_i can be expressed as

$$J_i = \begin{bmatrix} \frac{-I_{ixx}+I_{iyy}+I_{izz}}{2} & I_{ixy} & I_{ixz} & m_i\bar{x}_i \\ I_{ixy} & \frac{I_{ixx}-I_{iyy}+I_{izz}}{2} & I_{iyz} & m_i\bar{y}_i \\ I_{ixz} & I_{iyz} & \frac{I_{ixx}+I_{iyy}-I_{izz}}{2} & m_i\bar{z}_i \\ m_i\bar{x}_i & m_i\bar{y}_i & m_i\bar{z}_i & m_i \end{bmatrix} \tag{6.47}$$

The total kinetic energy of the manipulator is then

$$K = \sum_{i=1}^{6} K_i = \frac{1}{2}\sum_{i=1}^{6} \mathrm{Trace}\left[\sum_{j=1}^{i}\sum_{k=1}^{i} \frac{\partial \mathrm{T}_i}{\partial q_j} J_i \frac{\partial \mathrm{T}_i}{\partial q_k}^T \dot{q}_j \dot{q}_k\right] \tag{6.48}$$

This equation represents the kinetic energy of the manipulator structure. There is, however, another important contribution to the kinetic energy, that of the actuators at the joints. We can represent this by an actuator inertia, referred to the joint velocity, as

$$Kactuator_i = \frac{1}{2} Ia_i \dot{q}_i^2$$

In the case of a prismatic joint, Ia becomes an equivalent mass.

Exchanging the Trace and sum operations and adding in the contribution from the actuators, we obtain finally

$$K = \frac{1}{2} \sum_{i=1}^{6} \sum_{j=1}^{i} \sum_{k=1}^{i} \text{Trace}\left(\frac{\partial \mathrm{T}_i}{\partial q_j} J_i \frac{\partial \mathrm{T}_i}{\partial q_k}^T \right) \dot{q}_j \dot{q}_k + \frac{1}{2} \sum_{1=1}^{6} Ia_i \dot{q}_i^2 \qquad (6.49)$$

6.3.3 The Potential Energy

The potential energy of an object of mass m at a height h above some zero reference elevation in a gravity field g is

$$P = mgh \qquad (6.50).$$

If the acceleration due to gravity is expressed by a vector $\mathbf{g}$, and the position of the center of mass of the object by a vector $\bar{\mathbf{r}}$, then Equation 6.50 becomes

$$P = -m\mathbf{g} \cdot \bar{\mathbf{r}} \qquad (6.51).$$

For example, a mass m located at $\bar{\mathbf{r}} = 10\mathbf{i} + 20\mathbf{j} + 30\mathbf{k}$ in a gravity field $\mathbf{g} = 0\mathbf{i} + 0\mathbf{j} - 32.2\mathbf{k}$ has a potential energy $966 n.m.$.

The potential energy of a link whose center of mass is described by a vector $\mathbf{r}_i$ with respect to link i coordinate frame T_i is then

$$P_i = -m_i \mathbf{g}^T \mathrm{T}_i {}^i\bar{\mathbf{r}}_i \qquad (6.52)$$

where

$$\mathbf{g} = \begin{bmatrix} g_x \\ g_y \\ g_z \\ 0 \end{bmatrix} \qquad (6.53)$$

and the total potential energy of the manipulator is

$$P = -\sum_{i=1}^{6} m_i \mathbf{g}^T \mathrm{T}_i {}^i\bar{\mathbf{r}}_i \qquad (6.54)$$

6.3.4 The Lagrangian

Forming the Lagrangian $L = K - P$ we obtain from Equations 6.49 and 6.54

$$L = \frac{1}{2}\sum_{i=1}^{6}\sum_{j=1}^{i}\sum_{k=1}^{i} \text{Trace}\left(\frac{\partial \mathbf{T}_i}{\partial q_j} J_i \frac{\partial \mathbf{T}_i}{\partial q_k}^T\right)\dot{q}_j\dot{q}_k + \frac{1}{2}\sum_{1=1}^{6} Ia_i\dot{q}_i^2 + \sum_{i=1}^{6} m_i \mathbf{g}^T \mathbf{T}_i {}^i\bar{\mathbf{r}}_i \tag{6.55}$$

We now obtain the dynamics equations by applying the Euler Lagrange equation

$$F_i = \frac{d}{dt}\frac{\partial L}{\partial \dot{q}_i} - \frac{\partial L}{\partial q_i} \tag{6.56}$$

6.3.5 The Dynamics Equations

Performing the first differentiation we obtain

$$\frac{\partial L}{\partial \dot{q}_p} = \frac{1}{2}\sum_{i=1}^{6}\sum_{k=1}^{i} \text{Trace}\left(\frac{\partial \mathbf{T}_i}{\partial q_p} J_i \frac{\partial \mathbf{T}_i}{\partial q_k}^T\right)\dot{q}_k$$
$$+ \frac{1}{2}\sum_{i=1}^{6}\sum_{j=1}^{i} \text{Trace}\left(\frac{\partial \mathbf{T}_i}{\partial q_j} J_i \frac{\partial \mathbf{T}_i}{\partial q_p}^T\right)\dot{q}_j + Ia_p\dot{q}_p \tag{6.57}$$

Changing the dummy index j to k in the second term and exchanging the derivatives in the first term as

$$\text{Trace}\left(\frac{\partial \mathbf{T}_i}{\partial q_j} J_i \frac{\partial \mathbf{T}_i}{\partial q_k}^T\right) = \text{Trace}\left(\frac{\partial \mathbf{T}_i}{\partial q_j} J_i \frac{\partial \mathbf{T}_i}{\partial q_k}^T\right)^T = \text{Trace}\left(\frac{\partial \mathbf{T}_i}{\partial q_k} J_i \frac{\partial \mathbf{T}_i}{\partial q_j}^T\right)$$

we obtain

$$\frac{\partial L}{\partial \dot{q}_p} = \sum_{i=1}^{6}\sum_{k=1}^{i} \text{Trace}\left(\frac{\partial \mathbf{T}_i}{\partial q_k} J_i \frac{\partial \mathbf{T}_i}{\partial q_p}^T\right)\dot{q}_k + Ia_p\dot{q}_p \tag{6.58}$$.

As

$$\frac{\partial \mathbf{T}_i}{\partial q_p} = 0 \qquad \text{for } p > i$$

we obtain finally

$$\frac{\partial L}{\partial \dot{q}_p} = \sum_{i=p}^{6}\sum_{k=1}^{i} \text{Trace}\left(\frac{\partial \mathbf{T}_i}{\partial q_k} J_i \frac{\partial \mathbf{T}_i}{\partial q_p}^T\right)\dot{q}_k + Ia_p\dot{q}_p \tag{6.59}$$

We now differentiate Equation 6.58 with respect to time

$$\frac{d}{dt}\frac{\partial L}{\partial \dot{q}_p} = \sum_{i=p}^{6}\sum_{k=1}^{i} \mathrm{Trace}\left(\frac{\partial \mathrm{T}_i}{\partial q_k} J_i \frac{\partial \mathrm{T}_i}{\partial q_p}^T\right)\ddot{q}_k \qquad + Ia_p\ddot{q}_p$$

$$+ \sum_{i=p}^{6}\sum_{k=1}^{i}\sum_{m=1}^{i} \mathrm{Trace}\left(\frac{\partial^2 \mathrm{T}_i}{\partial q_k \partial q_m} J_i \frac{\partial \mathrm{T}_i}{\partial q_p}^T\right)\dot{q}_k\dot{q}_m \tag{6.60}$$

$$+ \sum_{i=p}^{6}\sum_{k=1}^{i}\sum_{m=1}^{i} \mathrm{Trace}\left(\frac{\partial^2 \mathrm{T}_i}{\partial q_p \partial q_m} J_i \frac{\partial \mathrm{T}_i}{\partial q_k}^T\right)\dot{q}_k\dot{q}_m$$

The last term of the Euler Lagrange equation is

$$\frac{\partial L}{\partial q_p} = \frac{1}{2}\sum_{i=p}^{6}\sum_{j=1}^{i}\sum_{k=1}^{i} \mathrm{Trace}\left(\frac{\partial^2 \mathrm{T}_i}{\partial q_j \partial q_p} J_i \frac{\partial \mathrm{T}_i}{\partial q_k}^T\right)\dot{q}_j\dot{q}_k$$

$$+ \frac{1}{2}\sum_{i=p}^{6}\sum_{j=1}^{i}\sum_{k=1}^{i} \mathrm{Trace}\left(\frac{\partial^2 \mathrm{T}_i}{\partial q_k \partial q_p} J_i \frac{\partial \mathrm{T}_i}{\partial q_j}^T\right)\dot{q}_j\dot{q}_k \tag{6.61}$$

$$+ \sum_{i=p}^{6} m_i \mathbf{g}^T \frac{\partial \mathrm{T}_i}{\partial q_p} {}^i\bar{\mathbf{r}}_i$$

Interchanging the dummy indices of summation j and k in the second term of Equation 6.61 and then combining this term with the first, we obtain

$$\frac{\partial L}{\partial q_p} = \sum_{i=p}^{6}\sum_{j=1}^{i}\sum_{k=1}^{i} \mathrm{Trace}\left(\frac{\partial^2 \mathrm{T}_i}{\partial q_p \partial q_j} J_i \frac{\partial \mathrm{T}_i}{\partial q_k}^T\right)\dot{q}_j\dot{q}_k$$

$$+ \sum_{i=p}^{6} m_i \mathbf{g}^T \frac{\partial \mathrm{T}_i}{\partial q_p} {}^i\bar{\mathbf{r}}_i \tag{6.62}$$

Combining Equations 6.60 and 6.62 according to Equation 6.56, and further interchanging the dummy indices of summation in Equation 6.62 from j to m, such that the first term of Equation 6.62 cancels the third term of Equation 6.60, we obtain

$$\frac{d}{dt}\frac{\partial L}{\partial \dot{q}_p} - \frac{\partial L}{\partial q_p} = \sum_{i=p}^{6}\sum_{k=1}^{i} \mathrm{Trace}\left(\frac{\partial \mathrm{T}_i}{\partial q_k} J_i \frac{\partial \mathrm{T}_i}{\partial q_p}^T\right)\ddot{q}_k \qquad + Ia_p\ddot{q}_p$$

$$+ \sum_{i=p}^{6}\sum_{k=1}^{i}\sum_{m=1}^{i} \mathrm{Trace}\left(\frac{\partial^2 \mathrm{T}_i}{\partial q_k \partial q_m} J_i \frac{\partial \mathrm{T}_i}{\partial q_p}^T\right)\dot{q}_k\dot{q}_m \tag{6.63}$$

$$- \sum_{i=p}^{6} m_i \mathbf{g}^T \frac{\partial \mathrm{T}_i}{\partial q_p} {}^i\bar{\mathbf{r}}_i$$

Finally, exchanging dummy summation indices p and i for i and j we obtain the dynamics equation

$$F_i = \sum_{j=i}^{6}\sum_{k=1}^{j} \mathrm{Trace}\left(\frac{\partial \mathrm{T}_j}{\partial q_k} J_j \frac{\partial \mathrm{T}_j}{\partial q_i}^T\right)\ddot{q}_k \qquad + Ia_i\ddot{q}_i$$

$$+ \sum_{j=i}^{6}\sum_{k=1}^{j}\sum_{m=1}^{j} \mathrm{Trace}\left(\frac{\partial^2 \mathrm{T}_j}{\partial q_k \partial q_m} J_j \frac{\partial \mathrm{T}_j}{\partial q_i}^T\right)\dot{q}_k\dot{q}_m \tag{6.64}$$

$$- \sum_{j=i}^{6} m_j \mathbf{g}^T \frac{\partial \mathrm{T}_j}{\partial q_i} {}^j\bar{\mathbf{r}}_j$$

These equations are independent of the order of summation, so we may rewrite Equation 6.64 as

$$F_i = \sum_{j=1}^{6} D_{ij}\ddot{q}_j + Ia_i\ddot{q}_i + \sum_{j=1}^{6}\sum_{k=1}^{6} D_{ijk}\dot{q}_j\dot{q}_k + D_i \tag{6.65}$$

where

$$D_{ij} = \sum_{p=\max i,j}^{6} \operatorname{Trace}\left(\frac{\partial \mathrm{T}_p}{\partial q_j} J_p \frac{\partial \mathrm{T}_p}{\partial q_i}^T\right) \tag{6.66}$$

$$D_{ijk} = \sum_{p=\max i,j,k}^{6} \operatorname{Trace}\left(\frac{\partial^2 \mathrm{T}_p}{\partial q_j \partial q_k} J_p \frac{\partial \mathrm{T}_p}{\partial q_i}^T\right) \tag{6.67}$$

$$D_i = \sum_{p=i}^{6} -m_p \mathrm{g}^T \frac{\partial \mathrm{T}_p}{\partial q_i} {}^p\bar{\mathrm{r}}_p \tag{6.68}$$

These equations are now in the same form as the equations obtained in Subsection 6.2.3, where terms of the form D_{ii} represent the effective inertia at joint i. Terms of the form D_{ij} represent coupling inertia between joints i and j. Terms of the form D_{ijj} represent centripetal forces at joint i due to velocity at joint j. Terms of the form D_{ijk} represent Coriolis forces at joint i due to velocities at joints j and k. Finally, terms of the form D_i represent the gravity loading at joint i. The inertial terms and the gravity terms are particularly important in manipulator control as they affect the servo stability and positioning accuracy. The centripetal and Coriolis forces are important only when the manipulator is moving at high speed, at which time the errors they introduce are small. The actuator inertias Ia_i are frequently of large relative magnitude and have the effect of decreasing the structural dependence of the effective inertias and of decreasing the relative importance of the coupling inertia terms.

6.3.6 The Simplification of the Inertial Terms D_{ij}

We will now simplify the terms D_{ij} and then D_i. In Chapter 4 we developed the partial derivatives in the following form

$$\frac{\partial \mathrm{T}_6}{\partial q_i} = \mathrm{T}_6 \, {}^{T_6}\Delta_i \tag{6.69}$$

as shown in Equation 4.57.

We may generalize this to

$$\frac{\partial \mathrm{T}_p}{\partial q_i} = \mathrm{T}_p \, {}^{T_p}\Delta_i \tag{6.70}$$

where

$${}^{T_p}\Delta_i = (\mathrm{A}_i \mathrm{A}_{i+1} \ldots \mathrm{A}_p)^{-1} \, {}^{i-1}\Delta_i \, (\mathrm{A}_i \mathrm{A}_{i+1} \ldots \mathrm{A}_p) \tag{6.71}$$

the differential coordinate transform is

$$(\mathrm{A}_i \mathrm{A}_{i+1} \ldots \mathrm{A}_p) = {}^{i-1}\mathrm{T}_p \tag{6.72}$$

If the joint is revolute, the differential translation and rotation vectors are obtained from Equations 4.62 and 4.63

$$\begin{aligned}
{}^{p}\mathbf{d}_{i_x} &= -{}^{i-1}n_{p_x}{}^{i-1}p_{p_y} + {}^{i-1}n_{p_y}{}^{i-1}p_{p_x} \\
{}^{p}\mathbf{d}_{i_y} &= -{}^{i-1}o_{p_x}{}^{i-1}p_{p_y} + {}^{i-1}o_{p_y}{}^{i-1}p_{p_x} \\
{}^{p}\mathbf{d}_{i_z} &= -{}^{i-1}a_{p_x}{}^{i-1}p_{p_y} + {}^{i-1}a_{p_y}{}^{i-1}p_{p_x}
\end{aligned} \tag{6.73}$$

$${}^{p}\delta_i = {}^{i-1}n_{p_z}\mathbf{i} + {}^{i-1}o_{p_z}\mathbf{j} + {}^{i-1}a_{p_z}\mathbf{k} \tag{6.74}$$

where we have abbreviated

$${}^{T_p}d_i \text{ to } {}^{p}d_i$$
$$\text{and } {}^{T_{i-1}}n_p \text{ to } {}^{i-1}n_p \text{ etc.}$$

If the joint is prismatic, the vectors are obtained from Equations 4.64 and 4.65

$${}^{p}\mathbf{d}_i = {}^{i-1}n_{p_z}\mathbf{i} + {}^{i-1}o_{p_z}\mathbf{j} + {}^{i-1}a_{p_z}\mathbf{k} \tag{6.75}$$

$${}^{p}\delta_i = 0\mathbf{i} + 0\mathbf{j} + 0\mathbf{k} \tag{6.76}$$

If we substitute from Equation 6.69 into Equation 6.66, we obtain

$$D_{ij} = \sum_{p=\max i,j}^{6} \operatorname{Trace}\left(\mathrm{T}_p{}^{p}\Delta_j J_p{}^{p}\Delta_i^T \mathrm{T}_p^T\right) \tag{6.77}$$

and on expanding the middle three terms

$$D_{ij} = \sum_{p=\max i,j}^{6} \operatorname{Trace}\left(\mathrm{T}_p \begin{bmatrix} 0 & -{}^{p}\delta_{j_z} & {}^{p}\delta_{j_y} & {}^{p}d_{j_x} \\ {}^{p}\delta_{j_z} & 0 & -{}^{p}\delta_{j_x} & {}^{p}d_{j_y} \\ -{}^{p}\delta_{j_y} & {}^{p}\delta_{j_x} & 0 & {}^{p}d_{j_z} \\ 0 & 0 & 0 & 0 \end{bmatrix} \right.$$
$$\times \begin{bmatrix} \frac{-I_{xx}+I_{yy}+I_{zz}}{2} & I_{xy} & I_{xz} & m_i\bar{x}_i \\ I_{xy} & \frac{I_{xx}-I_{yy}+I_{zz}}{2} & I_{yz} & m_i\bar{y}_i \\ I_{xz} & I_{yz} & \frac{I_{xx}+I_{yy}-I_{zz}}{2} & m_i\bar{z}_i \\ m_i\bar{x}_i & m_i\bar{y}_i & m_i\bar{z}_i & m_i \end{bmatrix}$$
$$\left. \times \begin{bmatrix} 0 & {}^{p}\delta_{i_z} & -{}^{p}\delta_{i_y} & 0 \\ -{}^{p}\delta_{i_z} & 0 & {}^{p}\delta_{i_x} & 0 \\ {}^{p}\delta_{i_y} & -{}^{p}\delta_{i_x} & 0 & 0 \\ {}^{p}d_{i_x} & {}^{p}d_{i_y} & {}^{p}d_{i_z} & 0 \end{bmatrix} \mathrm{T}_p^T \right) \tag{6.78}$$

When we multiply the middle three matrices together we obtain a matrix whose bottom row and right hand column are all zeros. Premultiplying by $\mathbf{T}_p$ and postmultiplying by its transpose makes use of only the rotation part of the transformation. The trace of a matrix is invariant under such an operation. Therefore we need only the trace of the inner three terms of the above expression, which on simplification becomes in vector form

$$D_{ij} = \sum_{p=\max i,j}^{6} m_p \left[{}^p\delta_i^T \mathbf{K}_p {}^p\delta_j + {}^p\mathbf{d}_i \cdot {}^p\mathbf{d}_j + {}^p\bar{\mathbf{r}}_p \cdot ({}^p\mathbf{d}_i \times {}^p\delta_j + {}^p\mathbf{d}_j \times {}^p\delta_i) \right] \tag{6.79}$$

where

$$\mathbf{K}_p = \begin{bmatrix} k^2_{pxx} & -k^2_{pxy} & -k^2_{pxz} \\ -k^2_{pxy} & k^2_{pyy} & -k^2_{pxz} \\ -k^2_{pxz} & -k^2_{pxy} & k^2_{pzz} \end{bmatrix}$$

and

$$\begin{aligned} m_p k^2_{pxx} &= I_{pxx} \\ m_p k^2_{pyy} &= I_{pyy} \\ m_p k^2_{pzz} &= I_{pzz} \\ m_p k^2_{pxy} &= I_{pxy} \\ m_p k^2_{pyz} &= I_{pyz} \\ m_p k^2_{pxz} &= I_{pxz} \end{aligned} \tag{6.80}$$

If we assume that the off-diagonal inertia terms are zero in Equation 6.80, a normal assumption, then Equation 6.79 simplifies further to

$$\begin{aligned} D_{ij} = \sum_{p=\max i,j}^{6} m_p \Big\{ & \left[{}^p\delta_{i_x} k^2_{pxx} {}^p\delta_{j_x} + {}^p\delta_{i_y} k^2_{pyy} {}^p\delta_{j_y} + {}^p\delta_{i_z} k^2_{pzz} {}^p\delta_{j_z} \right] \\ & + \left[{}^p\mathbf{d}_i \cdot {}^p\mathbf{d}_j \right] \\ & + \left[{}^p\bar{\mathbf{r}}_p \cdot ({}^p\mathbf{d}_i \times {}^p\delta_j + {}^p\mathbf{d}_j \times {}^p\delta_i) \right] \Big\} \end{aligned} \tag{6.81}$$

Each element of the sum of D_{ij} consists of three groups of terms. The first group of terms, ${}^p\delta_{i_x} k^2_{pxx} \ldots$, represents the effect of the distribution of the mass on link p. The second group of terms represents the separation of the mass p by the effective moment arm ${}^p\mathbf{d}_i \cdot {}^p\mathbf{d}_j$. The last group of terms is due to the fact that the center of mass of link p is not at the coordinate frame origin of link p. When the mass centers of the links are widely separated, the second group of terms dominates, and it is possible to ignore the first and last groups of terms.

6.3.7 The Simplification of the Inertial Terms D_{ii}

When i equals j in Equation 6.81 further simplifications are possible and we obtain

$$D_{ii} = \sum_{p=i}^{6} m_p \Big\{ \Big[{}^p\delta_{i_x}^2 k_{pxx}^2 + {}^p\delta_{i_y}^2 k_{pyy}^2 + {}^p\delta_{i_z}^2 k_{pzz}^2 \Big] + [{}^p\mathbf{d}_i \cdot {}^p\mathbf{d}_i] + [2\,{}^p\bar{\mathbf{r}}_p \cdot ({}^p\mathbf{d}_i \times {}^p\delta_i)] \Big\} \tag{6.82}$$

If the joint is revolute, we may substitute from Equation 6.73 and 6.74 into the above equation to obtain

$$D_{ii} = \sum_{p=i}^{6} m_p \Big\{ \Big[n_{p_x}^2 k_{pxx}^2 + o_{p_z}^2 k_{pyy}^2 + a_{p_z}^2 k_{pzz}^2 \Big] + \Big[\bar{\mathbf{p}}_p \cdot \bar{\mathbf{p}}_p \Big] + \Big[2\,{}^p\bar{\mathbf{r}}_p \cdot (\bar{\mathbf{p}}_p \cdot \mathbf{n}_p)\mathbf{i}\, (\bar{\mathbf{p}}_p \cdot \mathbf{o}_p)\mathbf{j}\, (\bar{\mathbf{p}}_p \cdot \mathbf{a}_p)\mathbf{k} \Big] \Big\} \tag{6.83}$$

where $\mathbf{n}_p$, $\mathbf{o}_p$, $\mathbf{a}_p$, and $\mathbf{p}_p$ are the column vectors of ${}^{(i-1)}\mathbf{T}_p$ and

$$\bar{\mathbf{p}} = p_x\mathbf{i} + p_y\mathbf{j} + 0\mathbf{k} \tag{6.84}$$

We may identify the following correspondences between terms of Equations 6.81 and 6.83

$$\Big[{}^p\delta_{i_x}^2 k_{pxx}^2 + {}^p\delta_{i_y}^2 k_{pyy}^2 + {}^p\delta_{i_z}^2 k_{pzz}^2 \Big] = \Big[n_{p_x}^2 k_{pxx}^2 + o_{p_z}^2 k_{pyy}^2 + a_{p_z}^2 k_{pzz}^2 \Big] \tag{6.85}$$

$$[{}^p\mathbf{d}_i \cdot {}^p\mathbf{d}_i] = \Big[\bar{\mathbf{p}}_p \cdot \bar{\mathbf{p}}_p \Big] \tag{6.86}$$

$$({}^p\mathbf{d}_i \times {}^p\delta_i) = (\bar{\mathbf{p}}_p \cdot \mathbf{n}_p)\mathbf{i} + (\bar{\mathbf{p}}_p \cdot \mathbf{o}_p)\mathbf{j} + (\bar{\mathbf{p}}_p \cdot \mathbf{a}_p)\mathbf{k} \tag{6.87}$$

As in Equation 6.81, each element of the sum of D_{ii} is composed of three groups of terms. The first group of terms represents the effect of the distribution of the mass of link p, the second group represents the separation of the mass of link p from the axis of joint i, and is equivalent to the parallel axis theorem, and the last group of terms again represents the fact that the mass center of link p is not coincident with the origin of coordinates of link p. We will see shortly that it is frequently possible to ignore all terms except the second group representing the separation of the mass centers.

If the joint is prismatic ${}^p\delta_i = 0$ and ${}^p\mathbf{d}_i \cdot {}^p\mathbf{d}_i = 1$, thus

$$D_{ii} = \sum_{p=i}^{6} m_p \tag{6.88}$$

6.3.8 The Simplification of the Gravity Terms D_i

Substituting from Equation 6.69 into Equation 6.68, we obtain

$$D_i = \sum_{p=i}^{6} -m_p \mathbf{g}^T \mathbf{T}_p {}^p\Delta_i {}^p\bar{\mathbf{r}}_p \tag{6.89}$$

Splitting up $\mathbf{T}_p$ into $\mathbf{T}_{i-1} {}^{i-1}\mathbf{T}_p$ and postmultiplying Δ by ${}^{i-1}\mathbf{T}_p{}^{-1} {}^{i-1}\mathbf{T}_p$ we obtain

$$D_i = \sum_{p=i}^{6} -m_p \mathbf{g}^T \mathbf{T}_{i-1} {}^{i-1}\mathbf{T}_p {}^p\Delta_i {}^{i-1}\mathbf{T}_p{}^{-1} {}^{i-1}\mathbf{T}_p {}^p\bar{\mathbf{r}}_p \tag{6.90}$$

and as

$$\begin{aligned} {}^{i-1}\Delta_i &= {}^{i-1}\mathbf{T}_p {}^p\Delta_i {}^{i-1}\mathbf{T}_p{}^{-1} \\ {}^i\bar{r}_p &= {}^i\mathbf{T}_p {}^p\bar{\mathbf{r}}_p \end{aligned} \tag{6.91}$$

we obtain further

$$D_i = -\mathbf{g}^T \mathbf{T}_{i-1} {}^{i-1}\Delta_i \sum_{p=i}^{6} m_p {}^{i-1}\bar{\mathbf{r}}_p \tag{6.92}$$

Defining

$${}^{i-1}\mathbf{g} = -\mathbf{g}^T \mathbf{T}_{i-1} {}^{i-1}\Delta_i \tag{6.93}$$

and multiplying out the transform expressions, we obtain

$${}^{i-1}\mathbf{g} = -\begin{bmatrix} g_x & g_y & g_z & 0 \end{bmatrix} \begin{bmatrix} n_x & o_x & a_x & p_x \\ n_y & o_y & a_y & p_y \\ n_z & o_z & a_z & p_z \\ 0 & 0 & 0 & 1 \end{bmatrix} \begin{bmatrix} 0 & -\delta_z & \delta_y & d_x \\ \delta_z & 0 & -\delta_x & d_y \\ -\delta_y & \delta_x & 0 & d_z \\ 0 & 0 & 0 & 0 \end{bmatrix} \tag{6.94}$$

Table 6.4 Link Parameters for the Two Link Manipulator

Link	Variable	α	a	d	$\cos\alpha$	$\sin\alpha$
1	θ_1	$0°$	d_1	0	1	0
2	θ_2	$0°$	d_2	0	1	0

In the case of a revolute joint i, ${}^{i-1}\Delta_i$ correponds to a rotation about the z axis and the expression simplifies to

$$
{}^{i-1}\mathbf{g} = -\begin{bmatrix} g_x & g_y & g_z & 0 \end{bmatrix} \begin{bmatrix} n_x & o_x & a_x & p_x \\ n_y & o_y & a_y & p_y \\ n_z & o_z & a_z & p_z \\ 0 & 0 & 0 & 1 \end{bmatrix} \begin{bmatrix} 0 & -1 & 0 & 0 \\ 1 & 0 & 0 & 0 \\ 0 & 0 & 0 & 0 \\ 0 & 0 & 0 & 0 \end{bmatrix} \tag{6.95}
$$
$$
= \begin{bmatrix} -\mathbf{g}\cdot\mathbf{o} & \mathbf{g}\cdot\mathbf{n} & 0 & 0 \end{bmatrix}
$$

In the case of a prismatic joint, ${}^{i-1}\Delta_i$ corresponds to a translation along the z axis and

$$
{}^{i-1}\mathbf{g} = -\begin{bmatrix} g_x & g_y & g_z & 0 \end{bmatrix} \begin{bmatrix} n_x & o_x & a_x & p_x \\ n_y & o_y & a_y & p_y \\ n_z & o_z & a_z & p_z \\ 0 & 0 & 0 & 1 \end{bmatrix} \begin{bmatrix} 0 & 0 & 0 & 0 \\ 0 & 0 & 0 & 0 \\ 0 & 0 & 0 & 1 \\ 0 & 0 & 0 & 0 \end{bmatrix} \tag{6.96}
$$
$$
= \begin{bmatrix} 0 & 0 & 0 & -\mathbf{g}\cdot\mathbf{a} \end{bmatrix}
$$

Thus we may write D_i as

$$
D_i = {}^{i-1}\mathbf{g} \sum_{p=i}^{6} m_p \, {}^{i-1}\bar{\mathbf{r}}_p \tag{6.97}
$$

Example 6.1

Compute the effective inertia and coupling inertia terms and the gravity terms for the two link manipulator described in Figure 6.1.

Solution:

We must first assign coordinate frames to the manipulator and compute the A and T matrices. This is done in Figure 6.3.

The A and T matrices are as follows

$$
\mathrm{A}_1 = {}^0\mathrm{T}_1 = \begin{bmatrix} \mathrm{C}_1 & -\mathrm{S}_1 & 0 & d_1\mathrm{C}_1 \\ \mathrm{S}_1 & \mathrm{C}_1 & 0 & d_1\mathrm{S}_1 \\ 0 & 0 & 1 & 0 \\ 0 & 0 & 0 & 1 \end{bmatrix} \tag{6.98}
$$

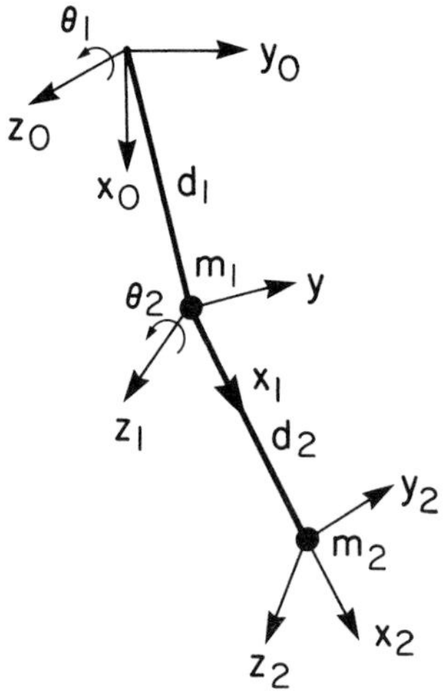

Figure 6.3. A Two Link Manipulator with Coordinate Frames

$$A_2 = {}^1T_2 = \begin{bmatrix} C_2 & -S_2 & 0 & d_2 C_2 \\ S_2 & C_2 & 0 & d_2 S_2 \\ 0 & 0 & 1 & 0 \\ 0 & 0 & 0 & 1 \end{bmatrix} \tag{6.99}$$

$${}^0T_2 = \begin{bmatrix} C_{12} & -S_{12} & 0 & d_1 C_1 + d_2 C_{12} \\ S_{12} & C_{12} & 0 & d_1 S_1 + d_2 S_{12} \\ 0 & 0 & 1 & 0 \\ 0 & 0 & 0 & 1 \end{bmatrix} \tag{6.100}$$

As both joints are revolute, we compute **d** and δ by Equations 6.73 and 6.74

based on ${}^1T_2$ $\quad {}^2\mathbf{d}_2 = 0\mathbf{i} + d_2\mathbf{j} + 0\mathbf{k} \quad {}^2\delta_2 = 0\mathbf{i} + 0\mathbf{j} + 1\mathbf{k}$ (6.101)

based on ${}^0T_2$ $\quad {}^2\mathbf{d}_1 = S_2 d_1 \mathbf{i} + (C_2 d_1 + d_2)\mathbf{j} + 0\mathbf{k} \quad {}^2\delta_1 = 0\mathbf{i} + 0\mathbf{j} + 1\mathbf{k}$ (6.102)

based on ${}^0T_1$ $\quad {}^1\mathbf{d}_1 = 0\mathbf{i} + d_1\mathbf{j} + 0\mathbf{k} \quad {}^1\delta_1 = 0\mathbf{i} + 0\mathbf{j} + 1\mathbf{k}$ (6.103)

For this simple manipulator all the moments of inertia are zero as are ${}^1\bar{\mathbf{r}}_1$ and ${}^2\bar{\mathbf{r}}_2$. Thus we have immediately from Equation 6.83

$$\begin{aligned} D_{11} &= m_1 p_{1_x}^2 + p_{1_y}^2 \qquad + m_2 p_{2_x}^2 + p_{2_y}^2 \\ &= m_1 d_1^2 \qquad + m_2(d_1^2 + d_2^2 + 2\,C_2\, d_1 d_2) \end{aligned} \tag{6.104}$$

$$D_{22} = m_2 {}^1p_{2_x}^2 + {}^1p_{2_y}^2 \\ = m_2 d_2^2 \tag{6.105}$$

We obtain D_{12} from Equation 6.81

$$D_{12} = m_2({}^2\mathbf{d}_1 \cdot {}^2\mathbf{d}_2) = m_2(\mathrm{C}_2\, d_1 d_2 + d_2^2) \tag{6.106}$$

In order to compute the gravity terms, we first compute ${}^1\mathbf{g}$ and ${}^2\mathbf{g}$ according to Equation 6.95 as

$$\mathbf{g} = [g \quad 0 \quad 0 \quad 0] \tag{6.107}$$

$${}^0\mathbf{g} = [0 \quad g \quad 0 \quad 0] \tag{6.108}$$

$${}^1\mathbf{g} = [g\,\mathrm{S}_1 \quad g\,\mathrm{C}_1 \quad 0 \quad 0] \tag{6.109}$$

and then the various mass center vectors ${}^i\bar{\mathbf{r}}_p$

$${}^2\bar{\mathbf{r}}_2 = \begin{bmatrix} 0 \\ 0 \\ 0 \\ 1 \end{bmatrix} \quad {}^1\bar{\mathbf{r}}_2 = \begin{bmatrix} \mathrm{C}_2\, d_2 \\ \mathrm{S}_2\, d_2 \\ 0 \\ 1 \end{bmatrix} \quad {}^0\bar{\mathbf{r}}_2 = \begin{bmatrix} \mathrm{C}_1\, d_1 + \mathrm{C}_{12}\, d_2 \\ \mathrm{S}_1\, d_2\, \mathrm{S}_{12}\, d_2 \\ 0 \\ 1 \end{bmatrix}$$

$${}^1\bar{\mathbf{r}}_1 = \begin{bmatrix} 0 \\ 0 \\ 0 \\ 1 \end{bmatrix} \quad {}^0\bar{\mathbf{r}}_1 = \begin{bmatrix} \mathrm{C}_1\, d_1 \\ \mathrm{S}_1\, d_1 \\ 0 \\ 1 \end{bmatrix}$$

The gravity terms are then given by Equation 6.97

$$D_1 = m_1 g\, \mathrm{S}_1\, d_1 + m_2 g(\mathrm{S}_1\, d_1 + \mathrm{S}_{12}\, d_2) \tag{6.110}$$

$$D_2 = m_2 g d_2(\mathrm{S}_1\, \mathrm{C}_2 + \mathrm{C}_1\, \mathrm{S}_2) \tag{6.111}$$

These results check with those obtained in Equations 6.23 – 6.33.

6.4 The Dynamics of the Stanford Manipulator

We will now look at the dynamics of the Stanford manipulator [Scheinman] and compute the effective inertias and gravity loading terms. This work was first performed by Bejczy and we make extensive use of his excellent report [Bejczy]. This manipulator has the following dynamic constants:

Table 6.5 Link Mass and First Moments for the Stanford Manipulator

Link	Mass kg.	$\bar{x}$ cm.	$\bar{y}$ cm.	$\bar{z}$ cm.
1	9.29	0	1.75	—11.05
2	5.01	0	—10.54	0
3	4.25	0	0	—64.47
4	1.08	0	0.92	—0.54
5	0.63	0	0	5.66
6	0.51	0	0	15.54

Table 6.6 Actuator and Link Inertias for the Stanford Manipulator

Link	Ia	mk^2_{xx} kg. m.^{2}	mk^2_{yy} kg. m.^{2}	mk^2_{zz} kg. m.^{2}
1	0.953 kg. m.^{2}	0.276	0.255	0.071
2	2.193 kg. m.^{2}	0.108	0.018	0.100
3	0.782 kg.	2.51	2.51	0.006
4	0.106 kg. m.^{2}	0.002	0.001	0.001
5	0.097 kg. m.^{2}	0.003	0.003	0.0004
6	0.020 kg. m.^{2}	0.013	0.013	0.0003

The coordinate frame for link 6 is located at the intersection of joints 4, 5, and 6. There is a $25cm$ extension to the end effector in the z direction. We will assume that the center of mass of any load the manipulator carries is located at the end effector. In order to account for any load the manipulator is carrying we will combine the mass of link 6 with that of the load, recomputing the mass, moments of inertia and center of gravity of the link. Thus m_6, $^6\mathrm{r}$, k_{6xx}, k_{6yy}, and k_{6zz} will be the constants for both the link and the load. In computing the dynamics for the manipulator we will start at link 6 and work back towards the base.

6.4.1 The Effective Inertias

In order to compute D_{66} we will need $^5\mathrm{T}_6$, $^6\mathrm{d}_6$, and $^6\delta_6$. These have already been computed in Equation 2.49 and 4.84.

$$^5\mathrm{T}_6 = \begin{bmatrix} \mathrm{C}_6 & -\mathrm{S}_6 & 0 & 0 \\ \mathrm{S}_6 & \mathrm{C}_6 & 0 & 0 \\ 0 & 0 & 1 & 0 \\ 0 & 0 & 0 & 1 \end{bmatrix} \qquad {}^6\mathrm{d}_6 = \begin{bmatrix} 0 \\ 0 \\ 0 \\ 1 \end{bmatrix} \qquad {}^6\delta_6 = \begin{bmatrix} 0 \\ 0 \\ 1 \\ 0 \end{bmatrix}$$

D_{66} is given by Equation 6.83

$$D_{66} = m_6 k^2_{6zz}$$

or

$$D_{66} = b_{60}^{L}$$

where the constant b_{60}^{L} is given by

$$b_{60}^{L} = m_6 k_{6zz}^2$$

the superscript L indicates that this constant term is load dependent.

In order to compute D_{55} we will need ${}^4T_6$, obtained previously (see Equation 2.50) by premultiplying ${}^5T_6$ by A_5, and ${}^4T_5$, which is A_5 (see Equation 2.47). From these transformations we will obtain ${}^6d_5$, ${}^6\delta_5$, ${}^5d_5$, and ${}^5\delta_5$

$${}^4T_6 = \begin{bmatrix} C_5C_6 & -C_5S_6 & S_5 & 0 \\ S_5C_6 & -S_5S_6 & -C_5 & 0 \\ S_6 & C_6 & 0 & 0 \\ 0 & 0 & 0 & 1 \end{bmatrix} \quad {}^6d_5 = \begin{bmatrix} 0 \\ 0 \\ 0 \\ 1 \end{bmatrix} \quad {}^6\delta_5 = \begin{bmatrix} S_6 \\ C_6 \\ 0 \\ 0 \end{bmatrix}$$

$${}^4T_5 = \begin{bmatrix} C_5 & 0 & S_5 & 0 \\ S_5 & 0 & -C_5 & 0 \\ 0 & 1 & 0 & 0 \\ 0 & 0 & 0 & 1 \end{bmatrix} \quad {}^5d_5 = \begin{bmatrix} 0 \\ 0 \\ 0 \\ 1 \end{bmatrix} \quad {}^5\delta_5 = \begin{bmatrix} 0 \\ 1 \\ 0 \\ 0 \end{bmatrix}$$

The joint has the following effective inertia

$$\begin{aligned} D_{55} = & m_5 k_{5yy}^2 \\ & + m_6\left(S_6^2 k_{6xx}^2 + C_6^2 k_{6yy}^2\right) \end{aligned}$$

In the Stanford manipulator $k_{6xx} \approx k_{6yy} \gg k_{6zz}$, so that D_{55} may be approximated quite well by

$$D_{55} \approx b_{50}^{L}$$

where

$$b_{50}^{L} = m_5 k_{5yy}^2 + m_6 k_{6xx}^2$$

Moving now to link 4, we will need ${}^3T_6$, ${}^3T_5$, and ${}^3T_4$. These are obtainable by premultiplying the transformations obtained for the previous link by A_4, and of course $A_4 = {}^3T_4$. From each of these transformations we will obtain the appropriate differential translation and rotation vectors.

$${}^3T_6 = \begin{bmatrix} C_4C_5C_6 - S_4S_6 & -C_4C_5S_6 - S_4C_6 & C_4S_5 & 0 \\ S_4C_5C_6 + C_4S_6 & -S_4C_5S_6 + C_4C_6 & S_4S_5 & 0 \\ -S_5C_6 & S_5S_6 & C_5 & 0 \\ 0 & 0 & 0 & 1 \end{bmatrix}$$

$$^6\mathrm{d}_4 = \begin{bmatrix} 0 \\ 0 \\ 0 \\ 1 \end{bmatrix} \qquad ^6\delta_4 = \begin{bmatrix} S_5 C_6 \\ S_5 S_6 \\ C_5 \\ 0 \end{bmatrix}$$

$$^3\mathrm{T}_5 = \begin{bmatrix} C_4 C_5 & -S_4 & C_4 S_5 & 0 \\ S_4 C_5 & C_4 & S_4 S_5 & 0 \\ -S_5 & 0 & C_5 & 0 \\ 0 & 0 & 0 & 1 \end{bmatrix} \qquad ^5\mathrm{d}_4 = \begin{bmatrix} 0 \\ 0 \\ 0 \\ 1 \end{bmatrix} \qquad ^5\delta_4 = \begin{bmatrix} -S_5 \\ 0 \\ C_5 \\ 0 \end{bmatrix}$$

$$^3\mathrm{T}_4 = \begin{bmatrix} C_4 & 0 & -S_4 & 0 \\ S_4 & 0 & C_4 & 0 \\ 0 & -1 & 0 & 0 \\ 0 & 0 & 0 & 1 \end{bmatrix} \qquad ^4\mathrm{D}_4 = \begin{bmatrix} 0 \\ 0 \\ 0 \\ 1 \end{bmatrix} \qquad ^4\delta_4 = \begin{bmatrix} 0 \\ -1 \\ 0 \\ 0 \end{bmatrix}$$

Thus

$$\begin{aligned} D_{44} &= m_4 k_{4yy}^2 \\ &\quad + m_5\left(S_5^2 k_{5xx}^2 + C_5^2 k_{5zz}^2\right) \\ &\quad + m_6\left(S_5^2 C_6^2 k_{6xx}^2 + S_5^2 S_6^2 k_{6yy}^2 + C_5^2 k_{6zz}^2\right) \end{aligned}$$

In this equation $k_{6xx} \approx k_{6yy} \gg k_{6zz}$; the m_5 dependent terms are very small compared to the constant terms and thus may be ignored. We may thus approximate D_{44} by

$$D_{44} \approx b_{40} + b_{60}^L S_5^2$$

where

$$b_{40} = m_4 k_{4yy}^2$$

Moving now to link 3, we will need $^2\mathrm{T}_6$, $^2\mathrm{T}_5$, $^2\mathrm{T}_4$, and $^2\mathrm{T}_3$. These are obtainable,as before, by premultiplying the transformations obtained for the previous link by A_3, and of course $\mathrm{A}_3 = {}^2\mathrm{T}_3$. As joint 3 of the Stanford manipulator is prismatic, we will use Equations 6.75 and 6.76 in order to obtain the differential and rotation vectors

$$^2\mathrm{T}_6 = \begin{bmatrix} C_4 C_5 C_6 - S_4 S_6 & -C_4 C_5 S_6 - S_4 C_6 & C_4 S_5 & 0 \\ S_4 C_5 C_6 + C_4 S_6 & -S_4 C_5 S_6 + C_4 C_6 & S_4 S_5 & 0 \\ -S_5 C_6 & S_5 S_6 & C_5 & d_3 \\ 0 & 0 & 0 & 1 \end{bmatrix}$$

$$^6\mathrm{d}_3 = \begin{bmatrix} S_5 C_6 \\ S_5 S_6 \\ C_5 \\ 1 \end{bmatrix} \qquad ^6\delta_3 = \begin{bmatrix} 0 \\ 0 \\ 0 \\ 0 \end{bmatrix}$$

$$^2T_5 = \begin{bmatrix} C_4C_5 & -S_4 & C_4S_5 & 0 \\ S_4C_5 & C_4 & S_4S_5 & 0 \\ -S_5 & 0 & C_5 & d_3 \\ 0 & 0 & 0 & 1 \end{bmatrix} \qquad {}^5\mathbf{d}_3 = \begin{bmatrix} -S_5 \\ 0 \\ C_5 \\ 1 \end{bmatrix} \qquad {}^5\delta_3 = \begin{bmatrix} 0 \\ 0 \\ 0 \\ 0 \end{bmatrix}$$

$$^2T_4 = \begin{bmatrix} C_4 & 0 & -S_4 & 0 \\ S_4 & 0 & C_4 & 0 \\ 0 & -1 & 0 & d_3 \\ 0 & 0 & 0 & 1 \end{bmatrix} \qquad {}^4\mathbf{d}_3 = \begin{bmatrix} 0 \\ -1 \\ 0 \\ 1 \end{bmatrix} \qquad {}^4\delta_3 = \begin{bmatrix} 0 \\ 0 \\ 0 \\ 0 \end{bmatrix}$$

$$^2T_3 = \begin{bmatrix} 1 & 0 & 0 & 0 \\ 0 & 1 & 0 & 0 \\ 0 & 0 & 1 & d_3 \\ 0 & 0 & 0 & 1 \end{bmatrix} \qquad {}^3\mathbf{d}_3 = \begin{bmatrix} 0 \\ 0 \\ 1 \\ 1 \end{bmatrix} \qquad {}^3\delta_3 = \begin{bmatrix} 0 \\ 0 \\ 0 \\ 0 \end{bmatrix}$$

The effective inertia of this joint is given simply by Equation 6.88. It is

$$D_{33} = m_3 + m_4 + m_5 + m_6$$

and may be represented by

$$D_{33} = b^L_{30}$$

where

$$b^L_{30} = m_3 + m_4 + m_5 + m_6$$

We now move to link 2, premultiplying all the T transformations by A_2 and obtaining the differential translation and rotation vectors as before

$$^1T_6 = \begin{bmatrix} C_2(C_4C_5C_6 - S_4S_6) - S_2S_5C_6 & -C_2(C_4C_5S_6 + S_4C_6) + S_2S_5S_6 & C_2C_4S_5 + S_2C_5 & S_2d_3 \\ S_2(C_4C_5C_6 - S_4S_6) + C_2S_5C_6 & -S_2(C_4C_5S_6 + S_4C_6) - C_2S_5S_6 & S_2C_4S_5 - C_2C_5 & -C_2d_3 \\ S_4C_5C_6 + C_4S_6 & -S_4C_5S_6 + C_4C_6 & S_4S_5 & d_2 \\ 0 & 0 & 0 & 1 \end{bmatrix}$$

$$^6\mathbf{d}_2 = \begin{bmatrix} d_3(C_4C_5C_6 - S_4S_6) \\ -d_3(C_4C_5S_6 + S_4C_6) \\ d_3C_4S_5 \\ 1 \end{bmatrix} \qquad {}^6\delta_2 = \begin{bmatrix} S_4C_5C_6 + C_4S_6 \\ -S_4C_5S_6 + C_4C_6 \\ S_4S_5 \\ 0 \end{bmatrix}$$

$$ {}^{6}\mathbf{d}_2 \times {}^{6}\delta_2 = -d_3\,S_5\,C_6\,\mathbf{i} + d_3\,S_5\,S_6\,\mathbf{j} + d_3\,C_5\,\mathbf{k} $$

$$ {}^{1}T_5 = \begin{bmatrix} C_2C_4C_5 - S_2S_5 & -C_2S_4 & C_2C_4S_5 + S_2C_5 & S_2d_3 \\ S_2C_4C_5 + C_2S_5 & -S_2S_4 & S_2C_4S_5 - C_2C_5 & -C_2d_3 \\ S_4C_5 & C_4 & S_4S_5 & d_2 \\ 0 & 0 & 0 & 1 \end{bmatrix} $$

$$ {}^{5}\mathbf{d}_2 = \begin{bmatrix} d_3C_4C_5 \\ -d_3S_4 \\ d_3C_4S_5 \\ 1 \end{bmatrix} \qquad {}^{5}\delta_2 = \begin{bmatrix} S_4C_5 \\ C_4 \\ S_4S_5 \\ 0 \end{bmatrix} $$

$$ {}^{5}\mathbf{d}_2 \times {}^{5}\delta_2 = -d_3\,S_5\,\mathbf{i} + 0\mathbf{j} + d_3\,C_5\,\mathbf{k} $$

$$ {}^{1}T_4 = \begin{bmatrix} C_2C_4 & -S_2 & -C_2S_4 & S_2d_3 \\ S_2C_4 & C_2 & -S_2S_4 & -C_2d_3 \\ S_4 & 0 & C_4 & d_2 \\ 0 & 0 & 0 & 1 \end{bmatrix} $$

$$ {}^{4}\mathbf{d}_2 = \begin{bmatrix} d_3C_4 \\ 0 \\ -d_3S_4 \\ 1 \end{bmatrix} \qquad {}^{4}\delta_2 = \begin{bmatrix} S_4 \\ 0 \\ C_4 \\ 0 \end{bmatrix} $$

$$ {}^{4}\mathbf{d}_2 \times {}^{4}\delta_2 = 0\mathbf{i} - d_3\mathbf{j}\ 0\mathbf{k} $$

$$ {}^{1}T_3 = \begin{bmatrix} C_2 & 0 & S_2 & S_2d_3 \\ S_2 & 0 & -C_2 & -C_2d_3 \\ 0 & 1 & 0 & d_2 \\ 0 & 0 & 0 & 1 \end{bmatrix} \qquad {}^{3}\mathbf{d}_2 = \begin{bmatrix} d_3 \\ 0 \\ 0 \\ 1 \end{bmatrix} \qquad {}^{3}\delta_2 = \begin{bmatrix} 0 \\ 1 \\ 0 \\ 0 \end{bmatrix} $$

$$ {}^{3}\mathbf{d}_2 \times {}^{3}\delta_2 = 0\mathbf{i} + 0\mathbf{j} + d_3\mathbf{k} $$

$$ {}^{1}T_2 = \begin{bmatrix} C_2 & 0 & S_2 & 0 \\ S_2 & 0 & -C_2 & 0 \\ 0 & 1 & 0 & d_2 \\ 0 & 0 & 0 & 1 \end{bmatrix} \qquad {}^{2}\mathbf{d}_2 = \begin{bmatrix} 0 \\ 0 \\ 0 \\ 1 \end{bmatrix} \qquad {}^{2}\delta_2 = \begin{bmatrix} 0 \\ 1 \\ 0 \\ 0 \end{bmatrix} $$

Using the above equations and Equation 6.83, we obtain D_{22} as

$$\begin{aligned}
D_{22} =& m_2 k_{2yy}^2 \\
&+ m_3\left[k_{3yy}^2 + d_3^2 + 2\bar{z}_3 d_3\right] \\
&+ m_4\left[\mathrm{S}_4^2 k_{4xx}^2 + \mathrm{C}_4^2 k_{4zz}^2 + d_3^2 - 2\bar{y}_4 d_3\right] \\
&+ m_5\Big[\mathrm{S}_4^2\,\mathrm{C}_5^2\,k_{5xx}^2 + \mathrm{C}_4^2 k_{5yy}^2 + \mathrm{S}_4^2\,\mathrm{S}_5^2\,k_{5zz}^2 + d_3^2 \\
&\quad + 2\bar{z}_5 d_3\,\mathrm{C}_5\Big] \\
&+ m_6\Big[(\mathrm{S}_4\,\mathrm{C}_5\,\mathrm{C}_6 + \mathrm{C}_4\,\mathrm{S}_6)^2 k_{6xx}^2 + (-\,\mathrm{S}_4\,\mathrm{C}_5\,\mathrm{S}_6 + \mathrm{C}_4\,\mathrm{C}_6)^2 k_{6yy}^2 \\
&\quad + \mathrm{S}_4^2\,\mathrm{S}_5^2\,k_{6zz}^2 + d_3^2 + 2\bar{z}_6 d_3\,\mathrm{C}_5\Big]
\end{aligned}$$

In the above equation the contribution to the effective inertia of joint 2 by links 4, 5, and 6 is due almost entirely to the separation of the mass centers, a function of d_3^2, and the effect of the mass distribution on the links can be ignored. The equation can then be simplified to

$$D_{22} \approx b_{20} + b_{21} d_3 + b_{30}^L d_3^2 + b_{22}^L d_3\,\mathrm{C}_5$$

where

$$\begin{aligned}
b_{20} &= m_2 k_{2yy}^2 + m_3 k_{3yy}^2 \\
b_{21} &\approx 2 m_3 \bar{z}_3 \\
b_{22}^L &= 2[m_5 \bar{z}_5 + m_6 \bar{z}_6]
\end{aligned}$$

We will now tackle joint 1. As before, we premultiply all the T transformations by A_1 and obtain the differential vectors and their cross products

$$^0\mathrm{T}_6 = \begin{bmatrix} n_x & o_x & a_x & p_x \\ n_y & o_y & a_y & p_y \\ n_z & o_z & a_z & p_z \\ 0 & 0 & 0 & 1 \end{bmatrix}$$

where

$$
\begin{aligned}
n_x &= C_1[C_2(C_4 C_5 C_6 - S_4 S_6) - S_2 S_5 C_6] - S_1(S_4 C_5 C_6 + C_4 S_6) \\
n_y &= S_1[C_2(C_4 C_5 C_6 - S_4 S_6) - S_2 S_5 C_6] + C_1(S_4 C_5 C_6 + C_4 S_6) \\
n_z &= - S_2(C_4 C_5 C_6 - S_4 S_6) - C_2 S_5 C_6 \\
o_x &= C_1[- C_2(C_4 C_5 S_6 + S_4 C_6) + S_2 S_5 S_6] - S_1(- S_4 C_5 S_6 + C_4 C_6) \\
o_y &= S_1[- C_2(C_4 C_5 S_6 + S_4 C_6) + S_2 S_5 S_6] + C_1(- S_4 C_5 S_6 + C_4 C_6) \\
o_z &= S_2(C_4 C_5 S_6 + S_4 C_6) + C_2 S_5 S_6 \\
a_x &= C_1(C_2 C_4 S_5 + S_2 C_5) - S_1 S_4 S_5 \\
a_y &= S_1(C_2 C_4 S_5 + S_2 C_5) + C_1 S_4 S_5 \\
a_z &= - S_2 C_4 S_5 + C_2 C_5 \\
p_x &= C_1 S_2 d_3 - S_1 d_2 \\
p_y &= S_1 S_2 d_3 + C_1 d_2 \\
p_z &= C_2 d_3
\end{aligned}
$$

$$
{}^6\mathbf{d}_1 = \begin{bmatrix} S_2 d_3(S_4 C_5 C_6 + C_4 S_6) - d_2[C_2(C_4 C_5 C_6 - S_4 S_6) - S_2 S_5 C_6] \\ S_2 d_3(- S_4 C_5 S_6 + C_4 C_6) + d_2[C_2(C_4 C_5 S_6 + S_4 C_6) - S_2 S_5 S_6] \\ S_2 d_3(S_4 S_5) - d_2[C_2 C_4 S_5 + S_2 C_5] \\ 1 \end{bmatrix}
$$

$$
{}^6\delta_1 = \begin{bmatrix} - S_2(C_4 C_5 C_6 - S_4 S_6) - C_2 S_5 C_6 \\ S_2(C_4 C_5 S_6 + S_4 C_6) + C_2 S_5 S_6 \\ - S_2 C_4 S_5 + C_2 C_5 \\ 0 \end{bmatrix}
$$

We need compute only the z component of the cross product, as ${}^6\bar{r}_{6_z}$ is the only significant component of ${}^6\bar{r}_6$

$$
({}^6\mathbf{d}_1 \times {}^6\delta_1)_z = S_2 d_3(C_2 C_4 S_5 + S_2 C_5) + d_2 S_4 S_5
$$

$$
{}^0T_5 = \begin{bmatrix} C_1(C_2 C_4 C_5 - S_2 S_5) - S_1 S_4 C_5 & - C_1 C_2 S_4 - S_1 C_4 & C_1(C_2 C_4 S_5 + S_2 C_5) - S_1 S_4 S_5 & C_1 S_2 d_3 - S_1 d_2 \\ S_1(C_2 C_4 C_5 - S_2 S_5) + C_1 S_4 C_5 & - S_1 C_2 S_4 + C_1 C_4 & S_1(C_2 C_4 S_5 + S_2 C_5) + C_1 S_4 S_5 & S_1 S_2 d_3 + C_1 d_2 \\ - S_2 C_4 C_5 - C_2 S_5 & S_2 S_4 & - S_2 C_4 S_5 + C_2 C_5 & C_2 d_3 \\ 0 & 0 & 0 & 1 \end{bmatrix}
$$

$$
{}^5\mathbf{d}_1 = \begin{bmatrix} S_2 d_3(C_2 C_4 C_5 - S_2 S_5) - d_2 S_4 C_5 \\ S_2 d_3(-C_2 S_4) - d_2 C_4 \\ S_2 d_3(C_2 C_4 S_5 + S_2 C_5) - d_2 S_4 S_5 \\ 1 \end{bmatrix}
$$

$$
{}^5\delta_1 = \begin{bmatrix} -S_2 C_4 C_5 - C_2 S_5 \\ S_2 S_4 \\ -S_2 C_4 S_5 + C_2 C_5 \\ 0 \end{bmatrix}
$$

Again we need compute only the z component of the cross product, as ${}^5\bar{r}_{5_z}$ is the only significant component of ${}^5\bar{r}_5$

$$
({}^5\mathbf{d}_1 \times {}^5\delta_1)_z = S_2 d_3(C_2 C_4 S_5 + S_2 C_5) + d_2 S_4 S_5
$$

$$
{}^0T_4 =
$$

$$
\begin{bmatrix} C_1 C_2 C_4 - S_1 S_4 & -C_1 S_2 & -C_1 C_2 S_4 - S_1 C_4 & C_1 S_2 d_3 - S_1 d_2 \\ S_1 C_2 C_4 + C_1 S_4 & -S_1 S_2 & -S_1 C_2 S_4 + C_1 C_4 & S_1 S_2 d_3 + C_1 d_2 \\ -S_2 C_4 & -C_2 & S_2 S_4 & C_2 d_3 \\ 0 & 0 & 0 & 1 \end{bmatrix}
$$

$$
{}^4\mathbf{d}_1 = \begin{bmatrix} S_2 d_3 S_4 - d_2 C_2 C_4 \\ S_2 d_2 \\ S_2 d_3 C_4 + d_2 C_2 S_4 \\ 1 \end{bmatrix} \qquad {}^4\delta_1 = \begin{bmatrix} -S_2 C_4 \\ -C_2 \\ S_2 S_4 \\ 0 \end{bmatrix}
$$

As ${}^4\bar{r}_4$ is small there is no need to compute ${}^4\mathbf{d}_1 \times {}^4\delta_1$

$$
{}^0T_3 = \begin{bmatrix} C_1 C_2 & -S_1 & C_1 S_2 & C_1 S_2 d_3 - S_1 d_2 \\ S_1 C_2 & C_1 & S_1 S_2 & S_1 S_2 d_3 + C_1 d_2 \\ -S_2 & 0 & C_2 & C_2 d_3 \\ 0 & 0 & 0 & 1 \end{bmatrix}
$$

$$
{}^3\mathbf{d}_1 = \begin{bmatrix} -C_2 d_2 \\ S_2 d_3 \\ -S_2 d_2 \\ 1 \end{bmatrix} \qquad {}^3\delta_1 = \begin{bmatrix} -S_2 \\ 0 \\ C_2 \\ 0 \end{bmatrix}
$$

$$
{}^3\mathbf{d}_1 \times {}^3\delta_1 = S_2 C_2 d_3 \mathbf{i} + d_2 \mathbf{j} + S_2^2 d_3 \mathbf{k}
$$

$$
{}^0\mathbf{T}_2 = \begin{bmatrix} C_1 C_2 & -S_1 & C_1 S_2 & -S_1 d_2 \\ S_1 C_2 & C_1 & S_1 S_2 & C_1 d_2 \\ -S_2 & 0 & C_2 & 0 \\ 0 & 0 & 0 & 1 \end{bmatrix}
$$

$$
{}^2\mathbf{d}_1 = \begin{bmatrix} -C_2 d_2 \\ 0 \\ -S_2 d_2 \\ 1 \end{bmatrix} \qquad {}^2\delta_1 = \begin{bmatrix} -S_2 \\ 0 \\ C_2 \\ 0 \end{bmatrix}
$$

$$
{}^2\mathbf{d}_1 \times {}^2\delta_2 = 0\mathbf{i} + d_2\mathbf{j} + 0\mathbf{k}
$$

$$
{}^0\mathbf{T}_1 = \begin{bmatrix} C_1 & 0 & -S_1 & 0 \\ S_1 & 0 & C_1 & 0 \\ 0 & -1 & 0 & 0 \\ 0 & 0 & 0 & 1 \end{bmatrix} \qquad {}^1\mathbf{d}_1 = \begin{bmatrix} 0 \\ 0 \\ 0 \\ 1 \end{bmatrix} \qquad {}^1\delta_1 = \begin{bmatrix} 0 \\ -1 \\ 0 \\ 0 \end{bmatrix}
$$

$$
{}^1\mathbf{d}_1 \times {}^1\delta_1 = 0\mathbf{i} + 0\mathbf{j} + 0\mathbf{k}
$$

When we compute D_{11} we will ignore the distributed mass effects of links 4, 5, and 6, obtaining

$$
\begin{aligned}
D_{11} \approx\; & m_1 k_{1yy}^2 \\
& + m_2\left[S_2^2 k_{2xx}^2 + C_2^2 k_{2zz}^2 + d_2^2 + 2\bar{y}_2 d_2\right] \\
& + m_3\left[S_2^2 k_{3xx}^2 + C_2^2 k_{3zz}^2 + S_2^2 d_3^2 + d_2^2 + 2\bar{z}_3 S_2^2 d_3\right] \\
& + m_4\left[S_2^2 d_3^2 + d_2^2\right] \\
& + m_5\left[S_2^2 d_3^2 + d_2^2 + 2\bar{z}_5[S_2 d_3(S_2 C_5 + C_2 C_4 S_5) + d_2 S_4 S_5]\right] \\
& + m_6\left[S_2^2 d_3^2 + d_2^2 + 2\bar{z}_6[S_2 d_3(S_2 C_5 + C_2 C_4 S_5) + d_2 S_4 S_5]\right]
\end{aligned}
$$

In order to simplify the above equation, we observe that as $k_{2xx} \approx k_{2zz}$ we can replace $S_2^2 k_{2xx}^2 + C_2^2 k_{2zz}^2$ with k_{2xx}. As k_{3zz} is very small it can be ignored. Ignoring a few small terms, we obtain

$$
D_{11} \approx b_{10}^L + b_{11} S_2^2 + b_{21}^L S_2^2 d_3 + b_{30} S_2^2 d_3^2 + b_{22}^L S_2^2 d_3 C_5
$$

where

$$
\begin{aligned}
b_{10}^L &= m_1 k_{1yy}^2 + m_2 k_{2xx}^2 + m_2 2\bar{y}_2 d_2 + d_2^2[m_2 + m_3 + m_4 + m_5 + m_6] \\
b_{11} &= m_3 k_{3xx}^2
\end{aligned}
$$

The constants b_{ij} can either be calculated or, better yet, measured, using the manipulator. Of course, some initial idea of the magnitudes of the constants is necessary in order to simplify the equations, but a number of measurements will provide more accurate results and save a great deal of detail accounting.

6.4.2 Coupling Inertias of the Stanford Manipulator

There is inertial coupling between the first three joints of the Stanford manipulator due to the concentration of mass at the end of link 3. In calculating these terms we will ignore the mass distribution effects and further consider that all the mass is concentrated at the end of link 3. That is, we will redefine m_3 to be M given by

$$M = m_3 + m_4 + m_5 + m_6$$

The coupling is given by Equation 6.81, and we will approximate the result by using only the second term in the equation. Thus

$$\begin{aligned} D_{12} &\approx M({}^3\mathbf{d}_1 \cdot {}^3\mathbf{d}_2) \\ &\approx -M\,C_2\,d_2 d_3 \end{aligned}$$

$$\begin{aligned} D_{13} &\approx M({}^3\mathbf{d}_1 \cdot {}^3\mathbf{d}_3) \\ &\approx -M\,S_2\,d_2 \end{aligned}$$

$$\begin{aligned} D_{23} &\approx M({}^3\mathbf{d}_2 \cdot {}^3\mathbf{d}_3) \\ &\approx 0 \end{aligned}$$

While there is coupling between the outer three joints and the first three, the actuator inertias of these joints dominates any coupling effects.

6.4.3 Gravity Loading Terms for the Stanford Manipulator

If the manipulator is standing upright then the gravity vector is

$$\mathbf{g} = [0 \quad 0 \quad -g \quad 0]$$

We first compute ${}^0\mathbf{g}$ through ${}^5\mathbf{g}$ using Equation 6.95 for all the joints except the prismatic joint, ${}^2\mathbf{g}$, for which we use Equation 6.96

$$\begin{aligned} {}^0\mathbf{g} &= [0 \quad 0 \quad 0 \quad 0] \\ {}^1\mathbf{g} &= [-g \quad 0 \quad 0 \quad 0] \\ {}^2\mathbf{g} &= [0 \quad 0 \quad 0 \quad g\,C_2] \\ {}^3\mathbf{g} &= [0 \quad -g\,S_2 \quad 0 \quad 0] \\ {}^4\mathbf{g} &= [-g\,C_2 \quad g\,S_2\,C_4 \quad 0 \quad 0] \\ {}^5\mathbf{g} &= [g\,S_2\,S_4 \quad g(S_2\,C_4\,C_5 + C_2\,S_5) \quad 0 \quad 0] \end{aligned}$$

As ${}^0\mathbf{g} = 0$ there will be no gravity loading on joint 1, since the joint axis is vertical.

We next compute ${}^i\bar{r}_p$ where

$$ {}^i\bar{r}_p = {}^{i-1}\mathrm{T}_p{}^p\bar{r}_p $$

The data necessary to specify ${}^p\bar{r}_p$ is contained in Table 6.5. As ${}^0\mathrm{g} = 0$ there will be no need to compute ${}^0\bar{\mathrm{r}}_p$ for any p.

Starting with link 6

$$ {}^6\bar{\mathrm{r}}_6 = \begin{bmatrix} 0 \\ 0 \\ \bar{z}_6 \\ 1 \end{bmatrix} \quad {}^5\bar{\mathrm{r}}_6 = \begin{bmatrix} 0 \\ 0 \\ \bar{z}_6 \\ 1 \end{bmatrix} \quad {}^4\bar{\mathrm{r}}_6 = \begin{bmatrix} \mathrm{S}_5\bar{z}_6 \\ -\mathrm{C}_5\bar{z}_6 \\ 0 \\ 1 \end{bmatrix} \quad {}^3\bar{\mathrm{r}}_6 = \begin{bmatrix} \mathrm{C}_4\mathrm{S}_5\bar{z}_6 \\ \mathrm{S}_4\mathrm{S}_5\bar{z}_6 \\ \mathrm{C}_5\bar{z}_6 \\ 1 \end{bmatrix} $$

$$ {}^2\bar{\mathrm{r}}_6 = \begin{bmatrix} \mathrm{C}_4\mathrm{S}_5\bar{z}_6 \\ \mathrm{S}_4\mathrm{S}_5\bar{z}_6 \\ \mathrm{C}_5\bar{z}_6 + d_3 \\ 1 \end{bmatrix} \quad {}^1\bar{\mathrm{r}}_6 = \begin{bmatrix} (\mathrm{C}_2\mathrm{C}_4\mathrm{S}_5 + \mathrm{S}_2\mathrm{C}_5)\bar{z}_6 + \mathrm{S}_2 d_3 \\ (\mathrm{S}_2\mathrm{C}_4\mathrm{S}_5 - \mathrm{C}_2\mathrm{C}_5)\bar{z}_6 - \mathrm{C}_2 d_3 \\ \mathrm{S}_4\mathrm{S}_5\bar{z}_6 + d_2 \\ 1 \end{bmatrix} $$

Link 5

$$ {}^5\bar{\mathrm{r}}_5 = \begin{bmatrix} 0 \\ 0 \\ \bar{z}_5 \\ 1 \end{bmatrix} \quad {}^4\bar{\mathrm{r}}_5 = \begin{bmatrix} \mathrm{S}_5\bar{z}_5 \\ \mathrm{C}_5\bar{z}_5 \\ 0 \\ 1 \end{bmatrix} \quad {}^3\bar{\mathrm{r}}_5 = \begin{bmatrix} \mathrm{C}_4\mathrm{S}_5\bar{z}_5 \\ \mathrm{S}_4\mathrm{S}_5\bar{z}_5 \\ \mathrm{C}_5\bar{z}_5 \\ 1 \end{bmatrix} $$

$$ {}^2\bar{\mathrm{r}}_5 = \begin{bmatrix} \mathrm{C}_4\mathrm{S}_5\bar{z}_5 \\ \mathrm{S}_4\mathrm{S}_5\bar{z}_5 \\ \mathrm{C}_r\bar{z}_5 + d_3 \\ 1 \end{bmatrix} \quad {}^1\bar{\mathrm{r}}_5 = \begin{bmatrix} (\mathrm{C}_2\mathrm{C}_4\mathrm{S}_5 + \mathrm{S}_2\mathrm{C}_5)\bar{z}_5 + \mathrm{S}_2 d_3 \\ (\mathrm{S}_2\mathrm{C}_4\mathrm{S}_5 - \mathrm{C}_2\mathrm{C}_5)\bar{z}_5 - \mathrm{C}_2 d_3 \\ \mathrm{S}_4\mathrm{S}_5\bar{z}_5 + d_2 \\ 1 \end{bmatrix} $$

Link 4

$$ {}^4\bar{\mathrm{r}}_4 = \begin{bmatrix} 0 \\ \bar{y}_4 \\ \bar{z}_4 \\ 1 \end{bmatrix} \quad {}^3\bar{\mathrm{r}}_4 = \begin{bmatrix} -\mathrm{S}_4\bar{z}_4 \\ \mathrm{C}_4\bar{z}_4 \\ -\bar{y}_4 \\ 1 \end{bmatrix} \quad {}^2\bar{\mathrm{r}}_4 = \begin{bmatrix} -\mathrm{S}_4\bar{z}_4 \\ \mathrm{C}_4\bar{z}_4 \\ -\bar{y}_4 + d_3 \\ 1 \end{bmatrix} \approx \begin{bmatrix} -\mathrm{S}_4\bar{z}_4 \\ \mathrm{C}_4\bar{z}_4 \\ d_3 \\ 1 \end{bmatrix} $$

$$ {}^1\bar{\mathrm{r}}_4 = \begin{bmatrix} -\mathrm{S}_2\bar{y}_4 - \mathrm{C}_2\mathrm{S}_4\bar{z}_4 + \mathrm{S}_2 d_3 \\ \mathrm{C}_2\bar{y}_4 - \mathrm{S}_2\mathrm{S}_4\bar{z}_4 - \mathrm{C}_2 d_3 \\ \mathrm{C}_4\bar{z}_4 + d_2 \\ 1 \end{bmatrix} \approx \begin{bmatrix} \mathrm{S}_2 d_3 \\ -\mathrm{C}_2 d_3 \\ d_2 \\ 1 \end{bmatrix} $$

Link 3

$$
{}^3\bar{\mathbf{r}}_3 = \begin{bmatrix} 0 \\ 0 \\ \bar{z}_3 \\ 1 \end{bmatrix} \qquad {}^2\bar{\mathbf{r}}_3 = \begin{bmatrix} 0 \\ 0 \\ \bar{z}_3 + d_3 \\ 1 \end{bmatrix} \qquad {}^1\bar{\mathbf{r}}_3 = \begin{bmatrix} S_2(\bar{z}_3 + d_3) \\ -C_2(\bar{z}_3 + d_3) \\ d_2 \\ 1 \end{bmatrix}
$$

Link 2

$$
{}^2\bar{\mathbf{r}}_2 = \begin{bmatrix} 0 \\ \bar{y}_2 \\ 0 \\ 1 \end{bmatrix} \qquad {}^1\bar{\mathbf{r}}_2 = \begin{bmatrix} 0 \\ 0 \\ \bar{y}_2 + d_2 \\ 1 \end{bmatrix}
$$

Link 1 makes no contribution to the gravity loading.
We are now ready to use Equation 6.97 to compute the gravity loading terms

$$
\begin{aligned} D_6 &= {}^5\mathbf{g} m_6 {}^5\bar{\mathbf{r}}_6 \\ &= 0 \end{aligned}
$$

$$
\begin{aligned} D_5 &= {}^4\mathbf{g}\left[m_5 {}^4\bar{\mathbf{r}}_5 + m_6 {}^4\bar{\mathbf{r}}_6 \right] \\ &= g[m_5(-C_2 S_5 + S_2 C_4 C_5)\bar{z}_5 + m_6(-C_2 S_5 + S_2 C_4 C_5)\bar{z}_6] \\ &= c_{50}(-C_2 S_5 + S_2 C_4 C_5) \end{aligned}
$$

where

$$
c_{50} = g(m_5\bar{z}_5 + m_6\bar{z}_6) = g\frac{b_{22}^L}{2}
$$

$$
\begin{aligned} D_4 &= {}^3\mathbf{g}\left[m_4 {}^3\bar{\mathbf{r}}_4 + m_5 {}^3\bar{\mathbf{r}}_5 + m_6 {}^3\bar{\mathbf{r}}_6 \right] \\ &= g\, S_2\, [m_4 C_4 \bar{z}_4 + m_5 S_4 S_5 \bar{z}_5 + m_6 S_4 S_5 \bar{z}_6] \\ &\approx c_{40} S_2 S_4 S_5 \end{aligned}
$$

where

$$
c_{40} = c_{50}
$$

$$
\begin{aligned} D_3 &= g\, C_2\, [m_3 + m_4 + m_5 + m_6] \\ &= c_{30}^L \end{aligned}
$$

where

$$
c_{30}^L = g b_{30}^L
$$

$$
\begin{aligned}
D_2 = & - gm_3[\mathrm{S}_2(\bar{z}_3 + d_3)] \\
& - gm_4[\mathrm{S}_2\, d_3] \\
& - gm_5[(\mathrm{C}_2\,\mathrm{C}_4\,\mathrm{S}_5 + \mathrm{S}_2\,\mathrm{C}_5)\bar{z}_5 + \mathrm{S}_2\, d_3] \\
& - gm_6[(\mathrm{C}_2\,\mathrm{C}_4\,\mathrm{S}_5 + \mathrm{S}_2\,\mathrm{C}_5)\bar{z}_6 + \mathrm{S}_2\, d_3] \\
\approx & c_{20}\,\mathrm{S}_2 + c_{21}\,\mathrm{S}_2\, d_3 + c_{22}(\mathrm{C}_2\,\mathrm{C}_4\,\mathrm{S}_5 + \mathrm{S}_2\,\mathrm{C}_5)
\end{aligned}
$$

where

$$
\begin{aligned}
c_{20} &= - gm_3\bar{z}_3 = -g\frac{b_{21}}{2} \\
c_{21} &= - g[m_3 + m_4 + m_5 + m_6] = c^L_{30} \\
c_{22} &= - g[m_5\bar{z}_5 + m_6\bar{z}_6] = -g\frac{b_{22}}{2}
\end{aligned}
$$

6.5 Summary

In this chapter we obtained the dynamics equation for any manipulator given the generalized forces in terms of the joint positions, velocities, and accelerations

$$
F_i = \sum_{j=1}^{6} D_{ij}\ddot{q}_j + Ia_i\ddot{q} + \sum_{j=1}^{6}\sum_{k=1}^{6} D_{ijk}\dot{q}_j\dot{q}_k + D_i \tag{6.65}
$$

where

$$
D_{ij} = \sum_{p=\max i,j}^{6} \mathrm{Trace}\left(\frac{\partial \mathrm{T}_p}{\partial q_j} J_p \frac{\partial \mathrm{T}_p}{\partial q_i}^T\right) \tag{6.66}
$$

$$
D_{ijk} = \sum_{p=\max i,j,k}^{6} \mathrm{Trace}\left(\frac{\partial^2 \mathrm{T}_p}{\partial q_j \partial q_k} J_p \frac{\partial \mathrm{T}_p}{\partial q_i}^T\right) \tag{6.67}
$$

$$
D_i = \sum_{p=i}^{6} -m_p \mathbf{g}^T \frac{\partial \mathrm{T}_p}{\partial q_i} {}^p\bar{\mathbf{r}}_p \tag{6.68}
$$

We then proceeded to simplify some of the terms in the above equation

$$
\begin{aligned}
D_{ij} = \sum_{p=\max i,j}^{6} m_p \Big\{ & \left[{}^p\delta_{i_x} k^2_{pxx}\, {}^p\delta_{j_x} + {}^p\delta_{i_y} k^2_{pyy}\, {}^p\delta_{j_y} + {}^p\delta_{i_z} k^2_{pzz}\, {}^p\delta_{j_z}\right] \\
& + \left[{}^p\mathbf{d}_i \cdot {}^p\mathbf{d}_j\right] \\
& + \left[{}^p\bar{\mathbf{r}}_p \cdot ({}^p\mathbf{d}_i \times {}^p\delta_j + {}^p\mathbf{d}_j \times {}^p\delta_i)\right]\Big\}
\end{aligned} \tag{6.81}
$$

$$D_{ii} = \sum_{p=i}^{6} m_p \Big\{ \Big[n_{p_x}^2 k_{pxx}^2 + o_{p_z}^2 k_{pyy}^2 + a_{p_z}^2 k_{pzz}^2 \Big] + \Big[\bar{\mathbf{p}}_p \cdot \bar{\mathbf{p}}_p \Big] + \Big[2\,{}^p\bar{\mathbf{r}}_p \cdot (\bar{\mathbf{p}}_p \cdot \mathbf{n}_p)\mathbf{i} + (\bar{\mathbf{p}}_p \cdot \mathbf{o}_p)\mathbf{j} + (\bar{\mathbf{p}}_p \cdot \mathbf{a}_p)\mathbf{k} \Big] \Big\} \tag{6.83}$$

where $\mathbf{n}_p$, $\mathbf{o}_p$, $\mathbf{a}_p$, and $\mathbf{p}_p$ are the column vectors of ${}^{(i-1)}\mathbf{T}_p$ and

$$\bar{\mathbf{p}} = p_x\mathbf{i} + p_y\mathbf{j} + 0\mathbf{k} \tag{6.84}$$

$$D_i = {}^{i-1}\mathbf{g} \sum_{p=i}^{6} m_p\,{}^{i-1}\bar{\mathbf{r}}_p \tag{6.97}$$

A rather lengthy example was then given to develop the actual symbolic expressions for the above terms for the Stanford manipulator.

The effective inertias were found to be

$$D_{11} \approx b_{10}^L + b_{11}\,\mathrm{S}_2^2 + b_{21}^L\,\mathrm{S}_2^2\,d_3 + b_{30}\,\mathrm{S}_2^2\,d_3^2 + b_{22}^L\,\mathrm{S}_2^2\,d_3\,\mathrm{C}_5$$

$$D_{22} \approx b_{20} + b_{21}d_3 + b_{30}^L d_3^2 + b_{22}^L d_3\,\mathrm{C}_5$$

$$D_{33} = b_{30}^L$$

$$D_{44} \approx b_{40} + b_{60}^L\,\mathrm{S}_5^2$$

$$D_{55} \approx b_{50}^L$$

$$D_{66} = b_{60}^L$$

The gravity loading terms were found to be

$$D_2 \approx c_{20}\,\mathrm{S}_2 + c_{30}^L\,\mathrm{S}_2\,d_3 + c_{22}(\mathrm{C}_2\,\mathrm{C}_4\,\mathrm{S}_5 + \mathrm{S}_2\,\mathrm{C}_5)$$

$$D_3 = c_{30}^L$$

$$D_4 \approx c_{50}\,\mathrm{S}_2\,\mathrm{S}_4\,\mathrm{S}_5$$

$$D_5 = c_{50}(-\,\mathrm{C}_2\,\mathrm{S}_5 + \mathrm{S}_2\,\mathrm{C}_4\,\mathrm{C}_5)$$

where

$$\begin{aligned}
c_{50} &= g\frac{b_{22}^L}{2} \\
c_{30}^L &= g b_{30}^L \\
c_{20} &= -\,g\frac{b_{21}}{2} \\
c_{22} &= -\,g\frac{b_{22}}{2} \\
b_{60}^L &= m_6 k_{6zz}^2 \\
b_{50}^L &= m_5 k_{5yy}^2 + m_6 k_{6xx}^2 \\
b_{40} &= m_4 k_{4yy}^2 \\
b_{30}^L &= m_3 + m_4 + m_5 + m_6 \\
b_{20} &= m_2 k_{2yy}^2 + m_3 k_{3yy}^2 \\
b_{21} &\approx 2 m_3 \bar{z}_3 \\
b_{22}^L &= 2[m_5 \bar{z}_5 + m_6 \bar{z}_6] \\
b_{10}^L &= m_1 k_{1yy}^2 + m_2 k_{2xx}^2 + m_2 2 \overline{y}_2 d_2 \\
&\qquad + d_2^2[m_2 + m_3 + m_4 + m_5 + m_6] \\
b_{11} &= m_3 k_{3xx}^2
\end{aligned}$$

6.6 References

Bejczy, A. K. Robot Arm Dynamics and Control, NASA - JPL Technical Memorandum, 33-669, Feb. 1974.

Hollerbach, J. M. "A Recursive Lagrangian Formulation of Manipulator Dynamics and a Comparative Study of Dynamics Formulation," *IEEE Trans. on Systems, Man, and Cybernetics* **SMC-10**, 11 (Nov. 1980), 730–736.

Kahn, M. & Roth, B "The Near-Minimum-Time Control of Open Loop Kinematic Chains," *Trans ASME, Series G* **93** (1971), 164–172.

Paul, R. P. Modeling, Trajectory Calculation and Servoing of a Computer Controlled Arm, Stanford Artificial Intelligence Laboratory, Stanford University, AIM 177, 1972.

Scheinman, V. D. Design of a Computer Manipulator, Stanford Artificial Intelligence Laboratory, Stanford University, AIM 92, 1969.

Symon, K. R. *Mechanics*, Addison-Wesley, New York, 1961.

Uicker, J. J. Jr. "Dynamic Force Analysis of Spatial Linkages," *Mechanisms Conference*, 1966.

CHAPTER 7

CONTROL

7.1 Introduction

We have thus far developed methods of describing the position and orientation of objects, including the manipulator, by means of homogeneous transformations. We have also studied the kinematics of manipulators, relating manipulator joint coordinates and rates to Cartesian end effector coordinates and rates. We have developed the concept of a trajectory, describing a desired motion of a manipulator as an array of time-based functions defining the joint angles, rates, and accelerations. In the previous chapter we formulated the dynamics equations and simplified some of their terms, notably the effective joint inertias and gravity loading terms. We will now consider the control of manipulators so that the specified position trajectory motion can be achieved. This will be a very general treatment, as the actual control of any manipulator is governed by many second order effects which must be tackled on a joint by joint basis. The intent is to identify the major problems and outline possible solutions [Paul72]. There have been many other suggested approaches to manipulator control and the interested reader is referred to [Albus75a] [Albus75b] [Horn] [Raibert] [Luh80a] [Luh80b] and [Orin]. The methods outlined in this chapter are close to industrial practice.

7.2 Control of a Single Link Manipulator

We will begin our study by considering a very simple single link manipulator. The link has mass, a moment of inertia about the joint axis, and structural stiffness resulting in some structural resonant frequency, $\omega_{structural}$. If a load is added to the end of the link, we increase the effective link mass and moment of inertia. The effect of increasing the link mass is to decrease the natural structural frequency $\omega_{structural}$ by the square root of the relative increase in inertia, to a first approximation. For a well designed manipulator, a no-load to full-load variation of inertia of 10:1 can be expected. Thus if the structural resonant frequency ω_0 is measured at some value of inertia J_0, then the structural frequency at some other value of inertia J is given by

Table 7.1 Actuator and Effective Link Inertias for the Stanford Manipulator

$Link_i$	Ia_i	J_{ii}no load, min	J_{ii}no load, max	J_{ii}full load,max
1	0.953	1.417	6.176	9.57
2	2.193	3.59	6.95	10.3
3	0.782	7.257	7.257	9.057
4	0.106	0.108	0.123	0.234
5	0.097	0.114	0.114	0.225
6	0.040	0.04	0.04	0.04

$$\omega_{structural} = \omega_0\sqrt{\frac{J_0}{J}} \tag{7.1}$$

The link of our simple manipulator is driven by an actuator through a gear reduction of ratio a; in other words, the link velocity is $1/a$ times the actuator velocity. In the case when direct drive is used, $a = 1$. The actuator inertia reflected through the gear reduction is increased by a^2.

Employing the notation from the previous chapter we may write the effective link inertia J_{ii} as

$$J_{ii} = D_{ii} + Ia_i \tag{7.2}$$

where D_{ii} is the effective link inertia, excluding the actuator inertia, and Ia_i is the actuator inertia increased by a^2. Note that the actuator inertia, which is constant, tends to mask any variations in D_{ii}, the structural component of J_{ii}. Referring to [Bejczy] and [Roderick] once again, values of J_{ii} are calculated for three cases (see Table 7.1).

Actuators are generally either hydraulic or electric, and both types are characterized by an actuator gain km and a viscous damping factor F. Both types of actuators introduce considerable Coulomb friction. Coulomb friction is independent of velocity and always tends to oppose the motion. Ignoring Coulomb friction, we can model the actuator as

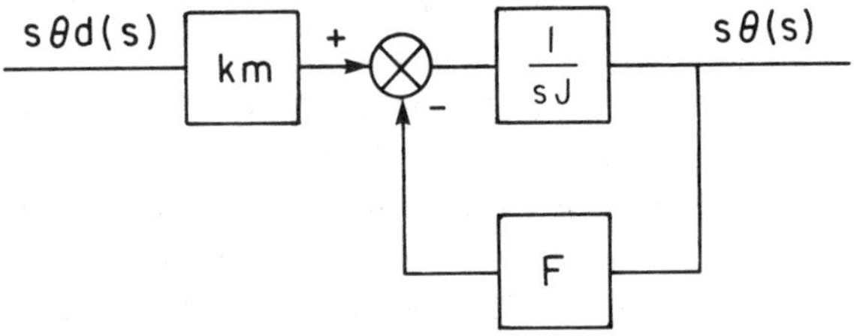

The input is the desired joint velocity $\dot{\theta}_d$ or, in terms of its Laplace transformation, $s\theta_d$. The input multiplied by the actuator gain, less the viscous damping term $Fs\theta$, produces a torque which is applied to the link represented by $1/sJ$. The output is the actual joint velocity $s\theta(s)$.

This block diagram is of standard form

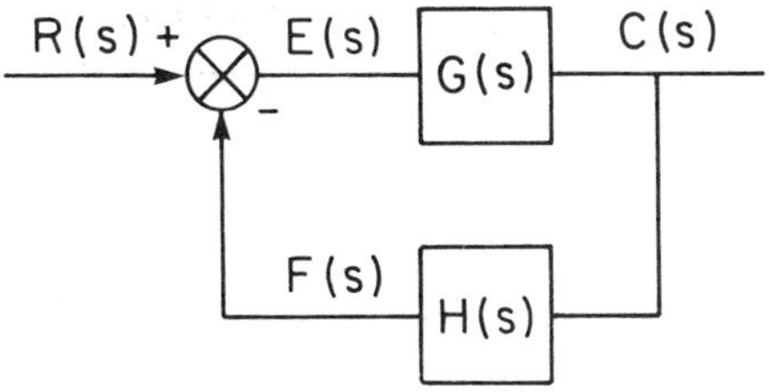

which reduces to

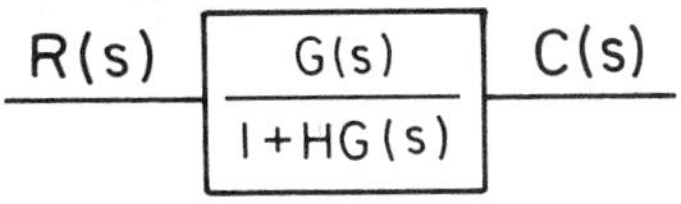

and thus the actuator and link transfer function becomes

$$\frac{s\theta(s)}{s\theta_d(s)} = \frac{km}{sJ + F} \tag{7.3}$$

We will increase the natural damping of the actuator by providing rate feedback from a tachometer generator or by some other means. The block diagram then becomes

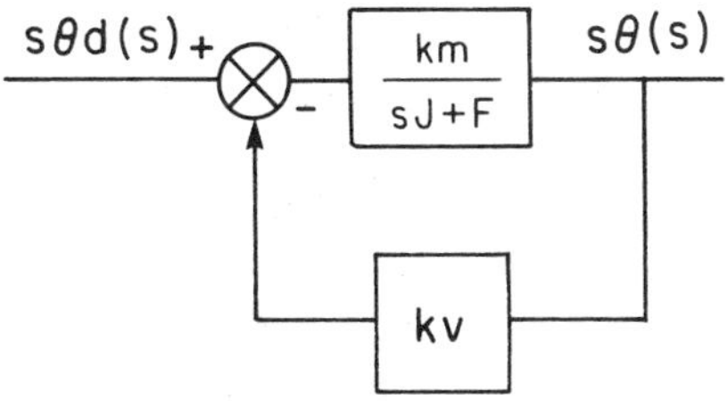

and the transfer function of the link and actuator, including rate feedback, becomes

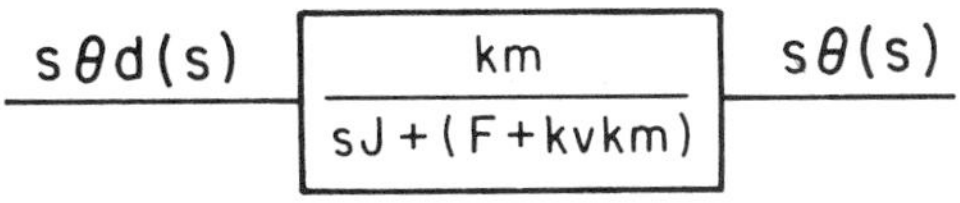

If we now provide position feedback around the system we have

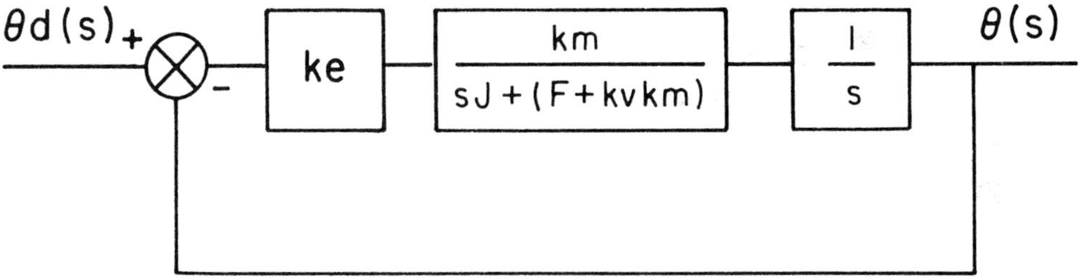

and the transfer function becomes

$$\frac{\theta(s)}{\theta_d(s)} = \frac{kekm}{s^2 J + s(F + kvkm) + kekm} \tag{7.4}$$

This is a second order system of the form

$$\frac{1}{s^2 + 2\varsigma\omega s + \omega^2}$$

where ω corresponds to the characteristic frequency of the system and ς is the damping factor. An underdamped system with $\varsigma < 1$ has fast response, and many servo systems achieve fast response employing ς in the range $0.3 < \varsigma < 0.7$. An underdamped system response to a step function input is characterized by a sinusoidal response superimposed on top of an exponential, and overshoots the final position. Such behavior is of no use in manipulator control as motions must never overshoot the desired set point. Consider a joint, controlling the height of an object, which is commanded to lower the object down to a surface. An overshoot would cause the object to be driven into the surface. For non-oscillatory behavior we require $\varsigma > 1$. The system is critically damped when $\varsigma = 1$, resulting in the fastest non oscillatory response. Thus from Equation 7.4 we have

$$\omega = \sqrt{\frac{kekm}{J}}$$
$$\varsigma = \frac{F + kvkm}{2\sqrt{Jkekm}} \tag{7.5}$$

For critical damping $\varsigma = 1$ and thus

$$F + kvkm = 2\sqrt{Jkekm} \tag{7.6}$$

We have, however, ignored the link structure, which we have characterized by a resonant frequency $\omega_{structural}$ approximated by Equation 7.1. If we are to prevent exciting structural oscillations and ensure system stability, including the link, we must limit ω to $0.5\omega_{structural}$. Substituting from Equations 7.1 and 7.5

Table 7.2 Structural Frequency Position Gain Limitations

Link	f_0	J_0	$\overline{kekm}$
1	4	5	790
2	6	5	1780
3	20	7	27600
4	15	0.1	220
5	15	0.1	220
6	20	0.04	1580

we obtain

$$\begin{aligned} \sqrt{\frac{kekm}{J}} &< 0.5\omega_0\sqrt{\frac{J_0}{J}} \\ kekm &< 0.25(2\pi f_0)^2 J_0 \\ kekm &< \pi^2 f_0^2 J_0 \end{aligned} \tag{7.7}$$

The maximum value of $kekm$ indicated by $\overline{kekm}$ is then

$$\overline{kekm} = \pi^2 f_0^2 J_0 \tag{7.8}$$

For example, in the case of the Stanford manipulator [Scheinman], we take an educated guess at the link structural frequencies and, using midrange values of J from Table 7.1, we calculate actual maximum values of $\overline{kekm}$.

Thus it would appear that a fixed position servo gain and variable velocity servo gain are appropriate to servo a manipulator link of variable inertia. The position feedback gain ke is limited by Equation 7.8 and is given by

$$ke < \frac{\pi^2 f_0^2 J_0}{km} \tag{7.9}$$

The velocity feedback gain is selected to provide critical damping, given by Equation 7.6, and must vary as the square root of the inertia

$$F + kvkm = 2\sqrt{Jkekm} \tag{7.10}$$

If a gain kv_0 is selected to provide critical damping with inertia J_0

$$kv_0 km + F = 2\sqrt{J_0 kekm} \tag{7.11}$$

we can then obtain the correct gain kv for any value of inertia by

$$\begin{aligned} kv &= \left((kv_0 km + F)\sqrt{\frac{J}{J_0}} - F\right)\frac{1}{km} \\ &= \left(G\sqrt{J} - F\right)\frac{1}{km} \end{aligned} \tag{7.12}$$

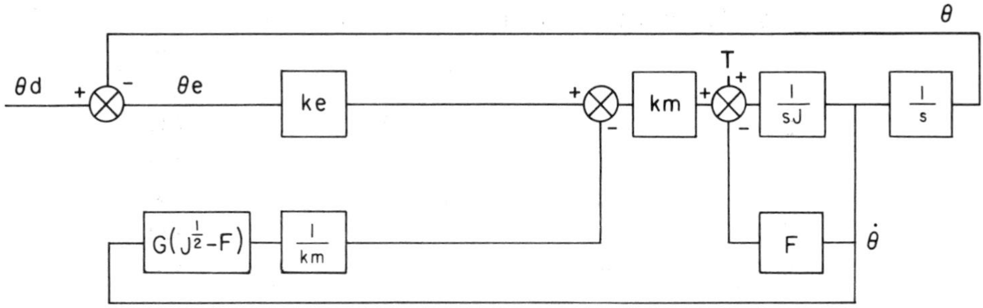

Figure 7.1. System Block Diagram

where

$$G = \frac{kv_0 km + F}{\sqrt{J_0}} \tag{7.13}$$

If we do not know the effective joint inertia J then kv must be determined by the maximum possible value of inertia, and the resulting overdamped response accepted in the case that the actual inertia is less than the maximum. Such a system has constant time response to a step change in position input, independent of the load inertia, with the response changing from overdamped to critically damped as the maximum inertia is reached. If the inertia were known, critically damped response could be maintained for all values of inertia, resulting in faster response when the inertia is less than maximum.

7.3 Steady State Servo Errors

Equation 7.9 establishes an upper bound on *ke*, the position feedback gain. In order to establish a minimum bound we must obtain the steady state errors. These errors correspond to disturbing torques T, which we will add into the servo system after the actuator and gear reduction. The disturbing torque T corresponds to a combination of the following torques: error in determining the load, external forces, Coulomb friction, and gravity loading.

The system block diagram is shown in Figure 7.1 with the disturbing torque T added in.

The error $E(s)$ for this system, defined as $E(s) = \theta_o(s) - \theta_d(s)$, is given by

$$E(s) = \frac{-s[sJ + (F + kvkm)]\theta_d(s)}{s^2J + (F + kvkm)s + kekm} + \frac{T}{s^2J + (F + kvkm)s + kekm} \tag{7.14}$$

Table 7.3 Stanford Manipulator Deflection for a Force of 1 newton

Link	r m.	$\overline{kekm}$	dx mm.
1	0.54	790	0.37
2	0.50	1780	0.14
3		27600	0.04
4	0.25	220	0.28
5	0.25	220	0.28
6	0.25	1580	0.04

The steady state error of the system θ_e is given by

$$\theta_e = \lim_{s \to 0} sE(s) \tag{7.15}$$

The error corresponding to a step input torque T/s is thus obtained from Equation 7.14 as

$$\theta_e = \frac{T}{kekm} \tag{7.16}$$

This equation may be solved for $kekm$ in terms of the servo stiffness T/θ_e

$$kekm = \frac{T}{\theta_e} \tag{7.17}$$

Thus the third column of Table 7.3 represents the maximum servo stiffness for each joint of the Stanford manipulator, in newton meters per radian for the revolute joints, and in newtons per meter for the prismatic joint. In order to calculate the stiffness of the manipulator, consider a 1 newton load applied to its end when each of the joints has the effective lever arm r shown in Table 7.3. The deflection dx in mm. is shown in the right hand column of Table 7.3. In the case of joint 6, which has no lever arm r, we have simply used the same lever arm as joint 5.

We will next examine the error torque due to Coulomb friction. This is a frictional effect which must be overcome before a joint will begin to move; it is characterized loosely by a joint torque T_{static}. Once the joint is in motion, the torque drops to a value $T_{dynamic}$ which opposes the motion. Measured values of Coulomb friction $T_{dynamic}$ for the Stanford manipulator are given in Table 7.4. The repeatability of the servo can be defined in terms of the Coulomb friction as that position error dx which causes a servo torque response equal to $T_{dynamic}$. Assuming that the manipulator has the same values of r used to compute load deflection, we compute the repeatability dx for the Stanford manipulator in Table 7.4.

Table 7.4 Servo Repeatability Based on Coulomb Friction

Link	r m.	$\overline{kekm}$	$T_{dynamic}$ n.m.	dx mm.
1	0.54	790	1.91	1.31
2	0.50	1780	3.18	0.89
3		27600	12.0	0.43
4	0.25	220	0.565	0.64
5	0.25	220	0.635	0.72
6	0.25	1580	0.424	0.07

Table 7.5 Deflection Based on Gravity Loading

Link	r m.	$\overline{kekm}$	Tg n.m.	dx mm.
1	0.54	790	0	0
2	0.50	1780	69.3	19.47
3		27600	81.73	2.96
4	0.25	220	5.54	6.30
5	0.25	220	5.54	6.30
6	0.25	1580	0	0

The repeatability values given in Table 7.4 are quite poor. They may be somewhat reduced when the joint is in motion by applying an additional feedforward torque T_{ff} to the joint equal to

$$T_{ff}(s) = \begin{cases} \frac{T_{dynamic}}{s} & \text{if } \dot{\theta} > 0 \\ \frac{-T_{dynamic}}{s} & \text{if } \dot{\theta} < 0 \end{cases} \tag{7.18}$$

and an impulse when the joint is stationary

$$T_{ff}(s) = \begin{cases} T_{static} & \text{if } \theta_e > 0 \\ -T_{static} & \text{if } \theta_e < 0 \end{cases} \tag{7.19}$$

The final steady state error we will consider is that due to gravity loading. We obtain values of Tg, the gravity loading at maximum load, from Bejczy. Based on $\overline{kekm}$ and the effective lever arm r we have been considering, we calculate the deflection at the end of the manipulator. Values for the Stanford manipulator are shown in Table 7.5

The deflections due to gravity loading are excessive, but present no problem as we have already calculated the gravity torques D_i. For any joint for which gravity loading is a problem, we can provide an additional feedforward torque to the joint motors equal to the calculated gravity loading torque. This is shown in the modified servo block diagram in Figure 7.2.

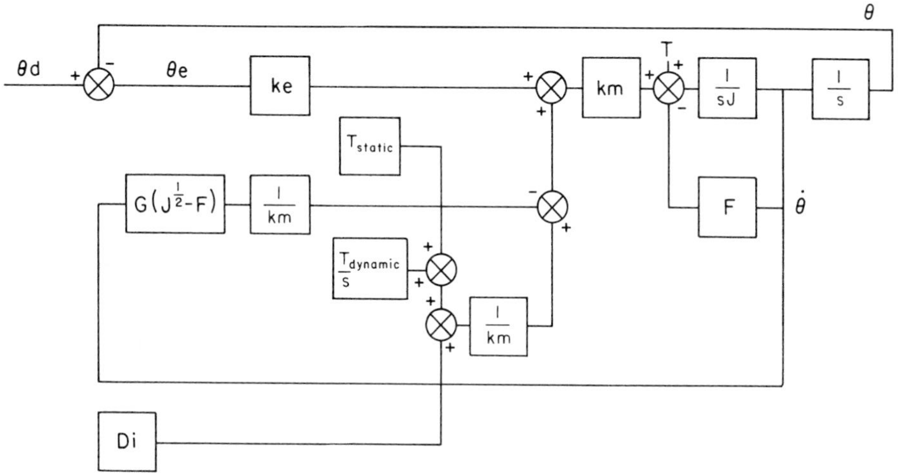

Figure 7.2. Joint Servo with Coulomb Friction and Gravity Compensation

If the joints are compensated for gravity loading and Coulomb friction then any steady state error of the system can be converted into equivalent steady state error torques due to unknown loading or external forces

$$T = kekm\theta_e \tag{7.20}$$

7.4 Steady State Velocity Errors

When the set point represents a constant velocity, errors are introduced into the servo system. This type of error is important if the manipulator is to be used in a moving coordinate system, such as working on a conveyor. The Laplace transform of a constant velocity v_c is v_c/s^2. Substituting this for $\theta_d(s)$ in Equation 7.14 and taking the limit (see Equation 7.15), we obtain the steady state error as

$$\theta_e = \frac{kvkm + F}{kekm} v_c \tag{7.21}$$

Assuming critical damping, substituting from Equation 7.6, and then using Equations 7.10 and 7.1 to simplify the result, we obtain

$$\theta_e = \frac{2}{\pi f_0} v_c \tag{7.22}$$

Assuming a conveyor speed of $10cm.sec.^{-1}$ with the manipulator situated $0.5m.$ from the conveyor, the corresponding $v_c = 0.2sec.^{-1}$. Tracking errors are shown in Table 7.6

Table 7.6 Tracking Errors for the Stanford Manipulator

Link	f_0	r	dx $mm.$
1	4	.54	17.19
2	6	.50	10.61
3	20		3.18
4	15	0.25	2.12
5	15	0.25	2.12
6	20		

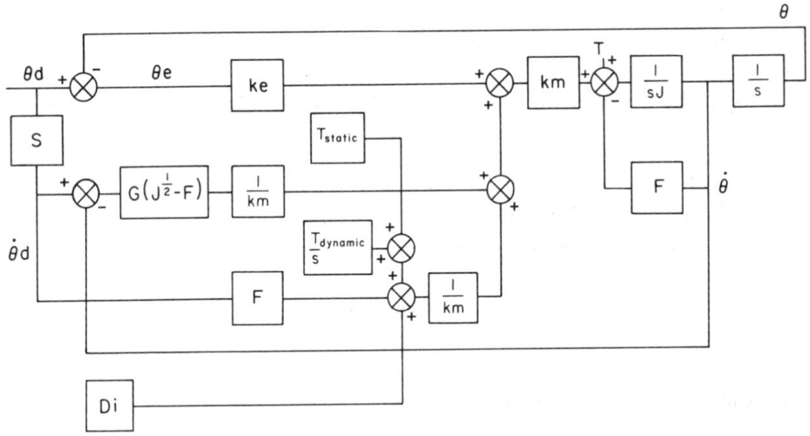

Figure 7.3. Joint Servo with Velocity Compensation

These tracking errors are excessive, but can be reduced to zero by providing further feedforward based on the desired velocity. Two terms are added to the servo block diagram, one to overcome the effects of F, and one to overcome the effects of the damping term kv. The results of this compensation are shown in Figure 7.3

7.5 Acceleration Errors

Before we look at position errors caused by joint acceleration, we will develop a very simple motion model. This model will correspond to the application of positive acceleration a for half the motion time and $-a$ for the second half of the motion. The resultant maximum velocity v is $at/2$ where T is the total time of the motion. The change in position $\Delta\theta$ is $at^2/4$. The trajectory is shown in Figure 7.4.

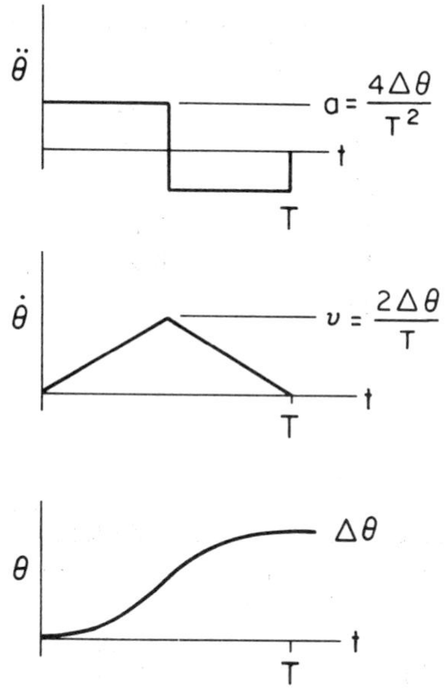

Figure 7.4. Motion Trajectory

Solving for v and a in terms of t and $\Delta\theta$ we obtain

$$\begin{aligned} v &= \frac{2\Delta\theta}{t} \\ a &= \frac{4\Delta\theta}{t^2} \end{aligned} \tag{7.23}$$

Let us consider a fairly high speed motion, say $\Delta\theta = 2 radians$ in a time of $1 second$.This would correspond to $v = 4$ and $a = 8$. Assuming that velocity feedforward is employed to eliminate any velocity dependent errors, the steady state errors caused by constant acceleration a, correspond to an input $\theta_d(s) = a/s^3$. Using this as input and taking the limit (see Equation 7.15), we obtain

$$\begin{aligned} \theta_e &= \frac{-J}{kekm} a \\ &= \frac{a}{\pi^2 f_0^2} \end{aligned} \tag{7.24}$$

Values for θ_e for the acceleration 8 are shown in Table 7.7

While these errors are unimportant when the manipulator is moving at high speed ($2m.sec.^{-1}$ in this case), they are important at the beginning and end of the motion. It is possible to compensate for these errors by adding another feed-forward term, $Js^2\theta_d$, shown in Figure 7.5. If the effective joint inertia is unknown,

Table 7.7 Acceleration Errors for the Stanford Manipulator

Link	f_0	r	$dx\ mm.$
1	4	.54	27.36
2	6	.50	11.26
3	20		2.03
4	15	0.25	0.90
5	15	0.25	0.90
6	20		

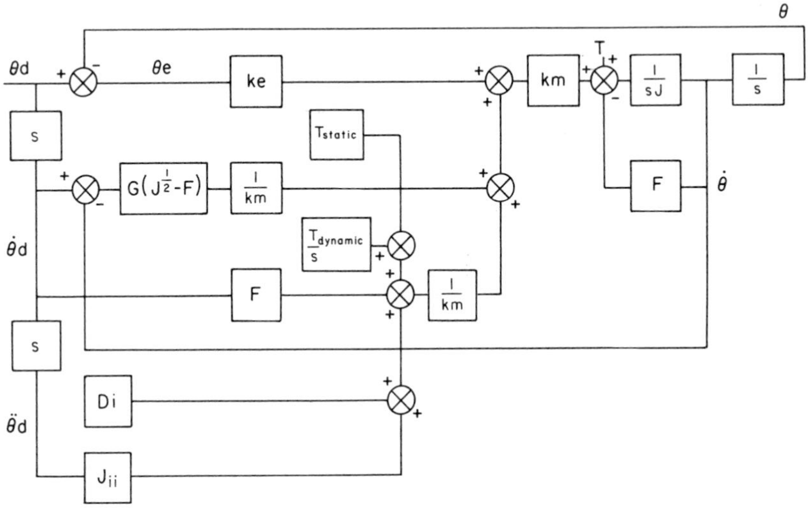

Figure 7.5. Servo with Acceleration Compensation

then the minimum value of J can be used to provide some compensation. Use of the maximum value of J would result in an overshooting motion if the joint inertia were less than maximum.

The transfer function for the servo, shown in Figure 7.5, is simply

$$E(s) = \frac{T}{s^2 J + (F + kvkm)s + kekm} \tag{7.25}$$

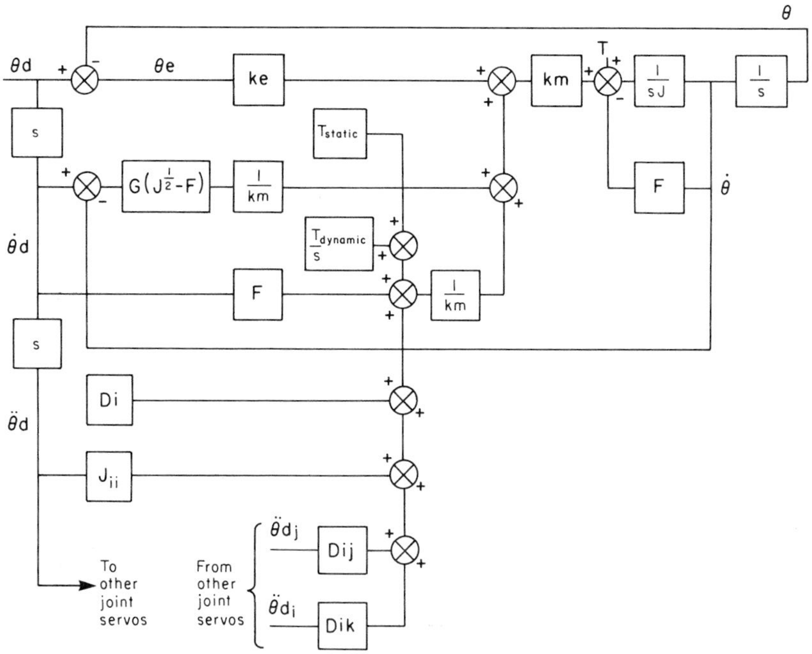

Figure 7.6. Servo with Joint Coupling

7.6 Control of a Multiple Link Manipulator

Thus far we have been considering the control of a single link of a manipulator. In effect, we have been considering controlling a single link of a manipulator when all the other links are locked solid. What happens when we free them up? We have three effects to consider: inertial coupling, centripetal forces, and Coriolis forces.

The relationship between acceleration and torque at a joint

$$F_i = J_{ii}\ddot{q}_i = (D_{ii} + Ia_i)\ddot{q}_i \tag{7.26}$$

assumes that torques

$$F_j = D_{ji}\ddot{q}_i \tag{7.27}$$

are applied simultaneously at all j other joints. This may be done in one of three ways: by calculating the torque by Equation 7.27 and applying it, by applying a brake at the joint, or by an active servo at the joint. Any method may be used at any joint. If the coupling is appreciable, $D_{ji} \approx J_{ii}$. D_{ji} can then be evaluated and simplified using Equation 6.81 and an additional feedforward term added to the appropriate joint servo (see Figure 7.6).

For example, the coupling between joints 1, 2, and 3 was calculated in Chapter 6 to be

$$\begin{aligned} D_{12} &= - b^L_{30}\, C_2\, d_2 d_3 \\ D_{13} &= - b^L_{30}\, S_2\, d_2 \end{aligned} \tag{7.28}$$

Feedforward would be added to the joint 1 servo as

$$T_{ff} = -D_{12}\ddot{\theta}_2 - D_{13}\ddot{d}_3 \tag{7.29}$$

To joint 2 we would add

$$T_{ff} = -D_{12}\ddot{\theta}_1 \tag{7.30}$$

and to joint 3 we would add

$$T_{ff} = -D_{13}\ddot{\theta}_1 \tag{7.31}$$

Normally, we can rely on the active servos at each of the joints to provide the torques. Care must be taken if the characteristic frequencies of both servos are similar, as coupling between joints can occur. For example, there is little need to provide compensation between joints 1 and 3.

The remaining torques to be considered are those due to centripetal and Coriolis forces. These torques occur only at high speed and do not affect servo stability. They do, however, cause position errors. How large are they? A simple manipulator is shown in Figure 7.7 moving according to the motion trajectory shown in Figure 7.4. The manipulator consists of two links of length r and a single mass m located at its end. A motion to change θ_1 by $\Delta\theta_1$ results in the following torques

$$T_1 = mr^2\ddot{\theta}_1 \qquad T_2 = mr\dot{\theta}_1 r \tag{7.32}$$

T_1 is an inertial torque and T_2 is a centripetal torque. Substituting from Equation 7.23 we obtain

$$T_1 = \frac{4mr^2\Delta\theta}{T^2} \qquad T_2 = \frac{4mr^2\Delta\theta}{T^2}\Delta\theta \tag{7.33}$$

It can be seen that inertial torques will dominate in this form of trajectory for changes in position of less than 1 radian, and that the centripetal torques are related linearly to the inertial torques by

$$T_{centripetal} = T_{inertial}\Delta\theta \tag{7.34}$$

If we were to evaluate these torques for a change $\Delta\theta = 2radians$ as we did when we were considering the acceleration errors (see Table 7.7), we would find that in the middle of the motion, when the manipulator is moving at $2m.sec.^{-1}$, Joint 2 would have an error of $2cm.$ and joint 3 would have an error of $4mm.$. Joint 1 is unaffected by these forces. Unless positional accuracy is important at high speed, errors resulting from centripetal and Coriolis forces may be ignored.

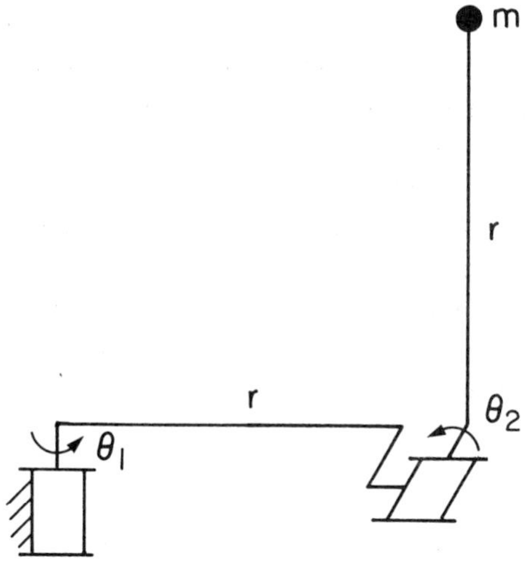

Figure 7.7. Another Two Link Manipulator

7.7 Calculation of Servo Parameters

In the previous chapter, methods were given for obtaining the equations for the effective joint inertias, coupling inertias, and gravity loads. The equations for the Stanford manipulator were given in the summary of Chapter 6. In evaluating these equations it is necessary to know the manipulator's load and its moments of inertia. This information is not always available. Consider the case of a manipulator picking up pieces of ore. In the next chapter we will show that it is relatively simple to measure the mass of an unknown load, but difficult to measure the moments of inertia. It is the inner joints of the manipulator which are most affected by variations in load as these joints have the lowest frequency response. This is important, as these joints have a major effect on positioning accuracy of the manipulator. The effective inertia calculation for these joints is, fortunately, based only on the load mass, as the load inertia is too far removed from the joint to have any major effect. Maximum values of inertia can be used for the outer joints and the resulting overdamped response tolerated, as these joints have high frequency response and do not limit the motion time of the manipulator.

7.8 Sample Data Servo Rate

The servo system shown in Figure 7.6 is quite complicated and many of the apparent constant gains, such as J_{ii}, are the result of numeric calculations. We have a choice of implementing the servo as a sampled data system, as an analog device, or as a combination of both. Any analog components, including any final power amplifier, must have bandwidths greater than the link structural frequency by a factor of at least 15 if they are not to introduce additional phase shifts in the servo loop [Roderick]. This wide bandwidth can present a problem in the case of a hydraulic servo valve. Those parts of the servo loop implemented as a sampled data system should have a sampling rate of at least 15 times the link structural frequency based on similar considerations. Thus, in the case of the Stanford manipulator, a sampled data system would have a sample rate of 300 hz. or a sample period of 3.3 m. sec. This is very little time in which to perform all the calculations necessary to servo a joint, let alone six joints.

7.9 Torque Servo

When performing such operations as assembly it is important that the manipulator be able to exert forces as well as control position. This is made possible by changing the position servo to a joint torque servo [Wu]. Strain gauges are located at the joint output shaft and provide an electrical signal proportional to the output torque of the joint. The gauges are located after the motor and gear reduction, if any, as this is the chief source of friction in the system. The strain gauges measure the strain in a short section of the joint output shaft of reduced section such that the stress in the section due to joint torque produces a maximum signal. The stress section is characterized by a spring constant ks, that is, the joint torque Te is related to the strain $d\theta$ by

$$Te = ks\, d\theta \tag{7.35}$$

The torque servo is shown in Figure 7.8 and is of the form of a position servo with strain $d\theta$ as the error signal. This error is immediately converted to a torque signal by a gain of ks, the spring constant in Equation 7.35. This error signal is then amplified by the torque gain kt, which functions as a position error gain. Rate damping is employed, as in the case of the position servo. The only other major difference in the servos is that, as the joint is connected to the actuator directly, there is a feedforward term from the joint torque to the motor. In the case of the torque servo, we will assume that the end of the joint is fixed and cannot move, so that the inertia of the system is only that of the motor and gear reduction referred to the output shaft, $J = Ia_i$.

By redrawing the servo loop as in Figure 7.9, we can obtain the loop gain directly as

$$H(s)G(s) = \frac{ks(1 + kt\, kv\, km)}{s(sJ + F + kvkm)} \tag{7.36}$$

The characteristic equation is given by

$$s^2J + s(F + kvkm) + ks(1 + kt\, kv\, km) = 0 \tag{7.37}$$

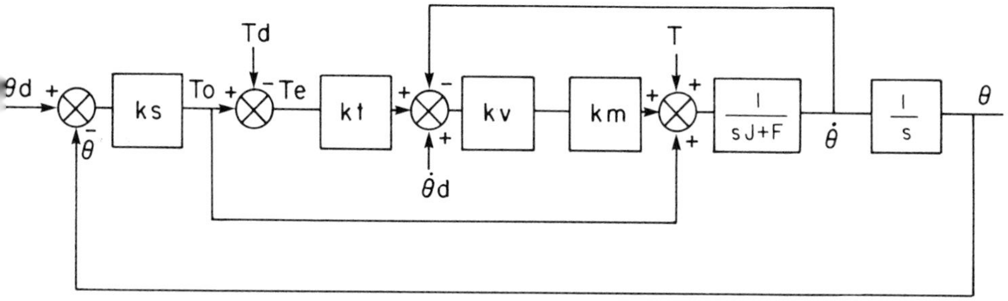

Figure 7.8. Torque Servo

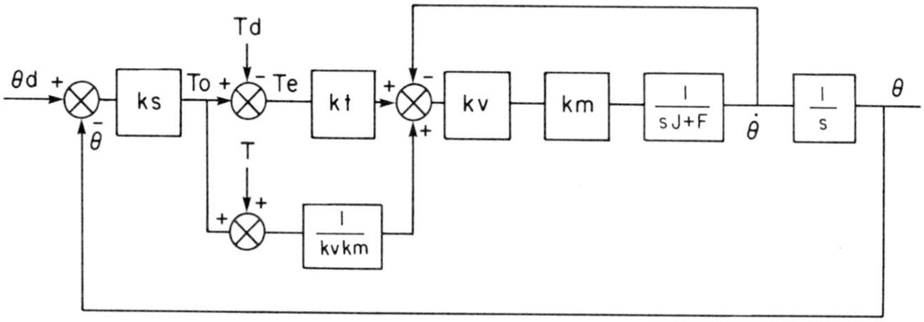

Figure 7.9. Equivalent Torque Servo Diagram

from which we obtain the characteristic frequency ω and damping factor ς as

$$\omega = \sqrt{\frac{ks}{J}(1 + kt\,kv\,km)} \tag{7.38}$$

$$\varsigma = \frac{kvkm}{\sqrt{4Jks(1 + kt\,kv\,km)}} \tag{7.39}$$

The characteristic frequency of this system is much higher than that of the manipulator as the stress section provides the principal compliance of the link. The spring constant ks is chosen to provide the link structural frequency at around 10kz when combined with the link inertia D_{ii}. As $D_{ii} \approx 10Ia_i$ for the inner joints, the characteristic frequency given by Equation 7.38 is at least three times that of the link structural frequency. The term $kt\,kv\,km \approx 10$, and thus the characteristic frequency of the torque servo is approximately ten times the position servo characteristic frequency. While it is not necessary to provide critical damping for the torque servo, the damping cannot be too low, and thus fairly high values of rate feedback must be used. The input torque T represents system friction, and the steady state torque error Te is readily obtained for a step input friction torque T/s as

$$Te = \frac{T}{(1 + kt\,kv\,km)} \tag{7.40}$$

The torque gain kt can thus be used to reduce the effects of friction. The torque Td represents a desired torque preload, and the steady state transfer function between input and output To for a step input is given by

$$To = \frac{Td}{(1 + \frac{1}{kt\,kv\,km})} \tag{7.41}$$

With the servo bandwidth at about 100hz., servo components of 1k hz. minimum bandwidth would seem appropriate for the servo loop. This is much greater bandwidth than is required by the position servo system and analog components would seem appropriate.

7.10 Summary

A multi-link manipulator may be considered as a series of independent servo systems which are only weakly coupled. The coupling effects are reduced by the actuator inertia and by ensuring that the outer joints have greater servo bandwidth than the inner joints. The coupling inertia terms can, however, be computed fairly readily and the joints made independent by appropriate feedforward between joints. The inertial coupling should be taken into account to compensate for the nominal trajectory acceleration. While the servo systems can be considered as independent, they are characterized by variable effective inertia and loading effects. It is very important to calculate the effective inertia as this affects the response time of the manipulator and the acceleration compensation.

The feedback gains, and hence the servo bandwidth, are determined by friction and gravity loading effects. It is important to compensate for these effects in order to reduce the gain and servo bandwidth as far as possible. This compensation results in reduced structural stiffness requirements for the manipulator, lower energy inputs, and faster speed.

Centripetal and Coriolis forces only come into play when the manipulator is moving at high speed, at which time their effects are minimal, as the position tolerance of manipulators is normally quite large at high speed. These effects do not lead to servo instability but simply cause position and velocity errors.

In order to compensate for gravity loading and to calculate the effective inertia of the joints, the mass and moments of any load the manipulator is carrying must be known. We shall see in the next chapter that we can actually measure any unknown load that the manipulator is carrying.

7.11 References

Albus, J. S. "A New Approach to Manipulator Controls: The Cerebellar Model Articulation Controller (CMAC)," *Transactions ASME, Journal of Dynamic Systems, Measurement, and Control* 97 (Sept. 1975), 220–227.

Albus, J. S. "Data Storage in the Cerebellar Model Articulation Controller," *Transactions ASME, Journal of Dynamic Systems, Measurement, and Control* 97 (Sept. 1975), 228–233.

Bejczy, A. K. Robot Arm Dynamics and Control, NASA - JPL Technical Memorandum, 33-669, Feb. 1974.

Horn, B. K. P. & Raibert, M. H. "Configuration Space Control," *The Industrial Robot* (June 1978), 69-73.

Luh, J., Walker, M., Paul, R. "Resolved Acceleration Control of Mechanical Manipulation," *IEEE Trans. on Automatic Control* AC-25, 3 (June 1980), 468–474.

Luh,J., Walker, M., Paul, R. "On-Line Computational Scheme for Mechanical Manipulation," *Trans. ASME, Journal of Dynamic Systems, Measurement, and Control* 102, 2 (June 1980), 69-71.

Orin, D. E., McGhee, R. B., Vukobratovic, M., et al. "Kinematic and Kinetic Analysis of Open-Chain Linkages utilizing Newton-Euler Methods," *Math. Biosc.* 43 (1979), 107-130.

Paul, R. P. Modeling, Trajectory Calculation and Servoing of a Computer Controlled Arm, Stanford Artificial Intelligence Laboratory, Stanford University, AIM 177, 1972.

Raibert, M. H. Motor Control and Learning by the State Space Model, TR-439, Sept. 1977.

Roderick, M. D. The Discrete Control of a Manipulator, Stanford Artificial Intelligence Laboratory, Stanford University, AIM 287, Aug 1976.

Scheinman, V. D. Design of a Computer Manipulator, Stanford Artificial Intelligence Laboratory, Stanford University, AIM 92, 1969.

Wu, C-H. & Paul, R. P. "Manipulator Compliance Based on Joint Torque Control," *19th. IEEE Conference on Decision and Control*, Dec. 1980, 88–94.

CHAPTER 8

STATIC FORCES

8.1 Introduction

In this chapter we will develop methods for representing static forces and moments and for transforming them between coordinate frames. We will also develop the relationship between manipulator static joint torques and forces, and between static forces and moments in coordinate frames bearing a fixed relationship to the manipulator. This will enable us to treat such problems as finding those forces at a force measuring sensor located at the end of the manipulator which are equivalent to forces at some point on an object that the manipulator is holding. We will also consider the problem of determining the mass of an object being carried by the manipulator.

8.2 The Representation of Forces and Moments

Forces and moments are vector quantities and are described with respect to some defining coordinate frame. We will denote forces by a vector **f** and we will precede the vector by a superscript to denote the defining coordinate frame. The force is assumed to act at the origin of the defining coordinate frame. Moments will be denoted by a vector **m**, also preceded by a superscript, to indicate any defining coordinate frame other than base coordinates. The effect of a moment acting on some object is independent of its point of application, so that only its defining coordinate frame is of importance. We will also have occasion to refer to both force and moment together, which we will denote by **F** where

$$\mathbf{F} = \begin{bmatrix} f_x \\ f_y \\ f_z \\ m_x \\ m_y \\ m_z \end{bmatrix} \tag{8.1}$$

Thus a force $\mathbf{f} = 10\mathbf{i} + 0\mathbf{j} - 150\mathbf{k}$ and moment $\mathbf{m} = 0\mathbf{i} - 100\mathbf{j} + 0\mathbf{k}$ could also be represented by

$$\mathbf{F} = [10 \quad 0 \quad -150 \quad 0 \quad -100 \quad 0]^{\mathrm{T}}$$

8.3 Transformation of Forces Between Coordinate Frames

In this section we will develop a method for transforming static forces and moments between coordinate frames. That is, given a force and moment acting at the origin of some coordinate frame attached to a fixed object, what is an equivalent force and moment acting at, and described with respect to, some other coordinate frame also attached rigidly to the object? By an equivalent force and moment we mean one that will have the same external effect on the object.

We will use the method of virtual work to solve this problem. That is, we will consider a force and moment F applied to an object, which causes a differential imaginary displacement, known as a virtual displacement, D, performing virtual work δW. The displacement is small in the limit and does not change the energy of the system. Thus the virtual work performed by a number of forces acting on the object must be zero.

The virtual work resulting from the application of a force F is then

$$\delta W = \mathbf{F}^{\mathrm{T}}\,\mathbf{D} \tag{8.2}$$

where D is the differential motion vector representing the virtual displacement

$$\mathbf{D} = [d_x \quad d_y \quad d_z \quad \delta_x \quad \delta_y \quad \delta_z]^{\mathrm{T}} \tag{8.3}$$

and F is the force vector

$$\mathbf{F}^{\mathrm{T}} = [f_x \quad f_y \quad f_z \quad m_x \quad m_y \quad m_z] \tag{8.4}$$

If this same displacement were caused by another force and moment acting at some different point on the object, described by a coordinate frame C, then the same virtual work would result, or

$$\delta W = \mathbf{F}^{\mathrm{T}}\,\mathbf{D} = {}^{C}\mathbf{F}^{\mathrm{T}}\,{}^{C}\mathbf{D} \tag{8.5}$$

and

$$\mathbf{F}^{\mathrm{T}}\,\mathbf{D} = {}^{C}\mathbf{F}^{\mathrm{T}}\,{}^{C}\mathbf{D} \tag{8.6}$$

The virtual displacement ${}^{C}\mathbf{D}$ in coordinate frame C is equivalent to the virtual displacement D in reference coordinates, and thus from Chapter 4 Equation 4.44 we have

$$\begin{bmatrix} {}^{C}\mathrm{d}_x \\ {}^{C}\mathrm{d}_y \\ {}^{C}\mathrm{d}_z \\ {}^{C}\delta_x \\ {}^{C}\delta_y \\ {}^{C}\delta_z \end{bmatrix} = \begin{bmatrix} n_x & n_y & n_z & (\mathbf{p}\times\mathbf{n})_x & (\mathbf{p}\times\mathbf{n})_y & (\mathbf{p}\times\mathbf{n})_z \\ o_x & o_y & o_z & (\mathbf{p}\times\mathbf{o})_x & (\mathbf{p}\times\mathbf{o})_y & (\mathbf{p}\times\mathbf{o})_z \\ a_x & a_y & a_z & (\mathbf{p}\times\mathbf{a})_x & (\mathbf{p}\times\mathbf{a})_y & (\mathbf{p}\times\mathbf{a})_z \\ 0 & 0 & 0 & n_x & n_y & n_z \\ 0 & 0 & 0 & o_x & o_y & o_z \\ 0 & 0 & 0 & a_x & a_y & a_z \end{bmatrix} \begin{bmatrix} \mathrm{d}_x \\ \mathrm{d}_y \\ \mathrm{d}_z \\ \delta_x \\ \delta_y \\ \delta_z \end{bmatrix} \tag{8.7}$$

or

$$^{C}\mathbf{D} = \mathbf{J}\,\mathbf{D} \tag{8.8}$$

and we obtain

$$\mathbf{F}^{\mathrm{T}}\,\mathbf{D} = {}^{C}\mathbf{F}^{\mathrm{T}}\,\mathbf{J}\,\mathbf{D} \tag{8.9}$$

This relationship must hold for any virtual displacement D and thus we may write

$$\mathbf{F}^{\mathrm{T}} = {}^{C}\mathbf{F}^{\mathrm{T}}\,\mathbf{J} \tag{8.10}$$

or

$$\mathbf{F} = \mathbf{J}^{\mathrm{T}}\,{}^{C}\mathbf{F} \tag{8.11}$$

That is

$$\begin{bmatrix} f_x \\ f_y \\ f_z \\ m_x \\ m_y \\ m_z \end{bmatrix} = \begin{bmatrix} n_x & o_x & a_x & 0 & 0 & 0 \\ n_y & o_y & a_y & 0 & 0 & 0 \\ n_z & o_z & a_z & 0 & 0 & 0 \\ (\mathbf{p}\times\mathbf{n})_x & (\mathbf{p}\times\mathbf{o})_x & (\mathbf{p}\times\mathbf{a})_x & n_x & o_x & a_x \\ (\mathbf{p}\times\mathbf{n})_y & (\mathbf{p}\times\mathbf{o})_y & (\mathbf{p}\times\mathbf{a})_y & n_y & o_y & a_y \\ (\mathbf{p}\times\mathbf{n})_z & (\mathbf{p}\times\mathbf{o})_z & (\mathbf{p}\times\mathbf{a})_z & n_z & o_z & a_z \end{bmatrix} \begin{bmatrix} {}^{C}f_x \\ {}^{C}f_y \\ {}^{C}f_z \\ {}^{C}m_x \\ {}^{C}m_y \\ {}^{C}m_z \end{bmatrix} \tag{8.12}$$

This relationship may be inverted to obtain

$$\begin{bmatrix} {}^{C}f_x \\ {}^{C}f_y \\ {}^{C}f_z \\ {}^{C}m_x \\ {}^{C}m_y \\ {}^{C}m_z \end{bmatrix} = \begin{bmatrix} n_x & n_y & n_z & 0 & 0 & 0 \\ o_x & o_y & o_z & 0 & 0 & 0 \\ a_x & a_y & a_z & 0 & 0 & 0 \\ (\mathbf{p}\times\mathbf{n})_x & (\mathbf{p}\times\mathbf{n})_y & (\mathbf{p}\times\mathbf{n})_z & n_x & n_y & n_z \\ (\mathbf{p}\times\mathbf{o})_x & (\mathbf{p}\times\mathbf{o})_y & (\mathbf{p}\times\mathbf{o})_z & o_x & o_y & o_z \\ (\mathbf{p}\times\mathbf{a})_x & (\mathbf{p}\times\mathbf{a})_y & (\mathbf{p}\times\mathbf{a})_z & a_x & a_y & a_z \end{bmatrix} \begin{bmatrix} f_x \\ f_y \\ f_z \\ m_x \\ m_y \\ m_z \end{bmatrix} \tag{8.13}$$

Finally, by exchanging the first and last three rows of the right and left hand sides we obtain

$$\begin{bmatrix} {}^{C}m_x \\ {}^{C}m_y \\ {}^{C}m_z \\ {}^{C}f_x \\ {}^{C}f_y \\ {}^{C}f_z \end{bmatrix} = \begin{bmatrix} n_x & n_y & n_z & (\mathbf{p}\times\mathbf{n})_x & (\mathbf{p}\times\mathbf{n})_y & (\mathbf{p}\times\mathbf{n})_z \\ o_x & o_y & o_z & (\mathbf{p}\times\mathbf{o})_x & (\mathbf{p}\times\mathbf{o})_y & (\mathbf{p}\times\mathbf{o})_z \\ a_x & a_y & a_z & (\mathbf{p}\times\mathbf{a})_x & (\mathbf{p}\times\mathbf{a})_y & (\mathbf{p}\times\mathbf{a})_z \\ 0 & 0 & 0 & n_x & n_y & n_z \\ 0 & 0 & 0 & o_x & o_y & o_z \\ 0 & 0 & 0 & a_x & a_y & a_z \end{bmatrix} \begin{bmatrix} m_x \\ m_y \\ m_z \\ f_x \\ f_y \\ f_z \end{bmatrix} \tag{8.14}$$

The first matrix on the right hand side of Equation 8.14 is the same as the first matrix on the right hand side of Equation 8.7, the Jacobian, and thus moments and forces between coordinate frames transform in the same manner as differential translations and rotations. In analogy with Equations 4.44, 4.45 and 4.46 we may therefore write

$$\begin{aligned} {}^{C}\mathbf{m}_x &= \mathbf{n} \cdot ((\mathbf{f} \times \mathbf{p}) + \mathbf{m}) \\ {}^{C}\mathbf{m}_y &= \mathbf{o} \cdot ((\mathbf{f} \times \mathbf{p}) + \mathbf{m}) \\ {}^{C}\mathbf{m}_z &= \mathbf{a} \cdot ((\mathbf{f} \times \mathbf{p}) + \mathbf{m}) \end{aligned} \tag{8.15}$$

$$\begin{aligned} {}^{C}\mathbf{f}_x &= \mathbf{n} \cdot \mathbf{f} \\ {}^{C}\mathbf{f}_y &= \mathbf{o} \cdot \mathbf{f} \\ {}^{C}\mathbf{f}_z &= \mathbf{a} \cdot \mathbf{f} \end{aligned} \tag{8.16}$$

where once again **n**, **o**, **a**, and **p** are the columns of the differential coordinate transformation defined in Chapter 4, Section 4.5. Moments transform in the same manner as differential translations. Forces transform in the same manner as differential rotations.

Example 8.1

Given the following coordinate frame **A**

$$A = \begin{bmatrix} 0 & 0 & 1 & 10 \\ 1 & 0 & 0 & 5 \\ 0 & 1 & 0 & 0 \\ 0 & 0 & 0 & 1 \end{bmatrix}$$

and the following force and moment applied in the base coordinate frame

$$\begin{aligned} \mathbf{f} &= 10\mathbf{i} + 0\mathbf{j} + 0\mathbf{k} \\ \mathbf{m} &= 0\mathbf{i} + 100\mathbf{j} + 0\mathbf{k} \end{aligned}$$

what is the equivalent force and moment in coordinate frame **A**?

Solution:

With

$$\begin{aligned} \mathbf{n} &= 0\mathbf{i} + 1\mathbf{j} + 0\mathbf{k}; \\ \mathbf{o} &= 0\mathbf{i} + 0\mathbf{j} + 1\mathbf{k}; \\ \mathbf{a} &= 1\mathbf{i} + 0\mathbf{j} + 0\mathbf{k}; \\ \mathbf{p} &= 10\mathbf{i} + 5\mathbf{j} + 0\mathbf{k}. \end{aligned}$$

we first form **f** × **p**

$$\begin{aligned} \mathbf{f} \times \mathbf{p} &= \begin{vmatrix} \mathbf{i} & \mathbf{j} & \mathbf{k} \\ 10 & 0 & 0 \\ 10 & 5 & 0 \end{vmatrix} \\ &= 0\mathbf{i} + 0\mathbf{j} + 50\mathbf{k} \end{aligned}$$

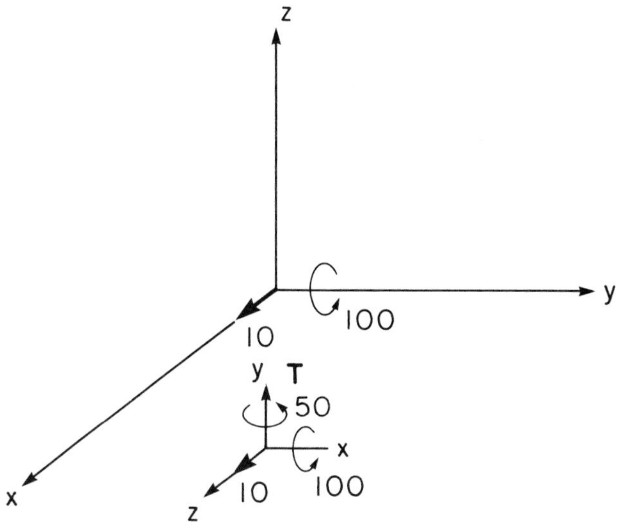

Figure 8.1. Equivalent Force and Moment for Example 8.1

then add **m** to it

$$\mathbf{f} \times \mathbf{p} + \mathbf{m} = 0\mathbf{i} + 100\mathbf{j} + 50\mathbf{k}$$

We now use Equations 8.15 and 8.16 to evaluate ${}^A\mathbf{m}$ and ${}^A\mathbf{f}$

$$ {}^A\mathbf{m} = 100\mathbf{i} + 50\mathbf{j} + 0\mathbf{k}; $$
$$ {}^A\mathbf{f} = 0\mathbf{i} + 0\mathbf{j} + 10\mathbf{k}. $$

The equivalent force and moment are shown in Figure 8.1.

To relate forces and moments between coordinate frames in a transform equation, we identify the differential coordinate transformation in the same manner as we did for differential displacements. The differential coordinate transformation is the transform expression defined by the path from the head of the link representing the transform in which the force is given to the head of the transform link in which an equivalent force is desired.

Example 8.2

A manipulator and end effector are positioned by $\mathbf{Z}\,\mathbf{T}_6\,\mathbf{E}$ to insert a screw into a hole described by $\mathbf{O}\,\mathbf{H}$, as shown in Figure 8.2

$$\mathbf{Z}\,\mathbf{T}_6\,\mathbf{E} = \mathbf{O}\,\mathbf{H}$$

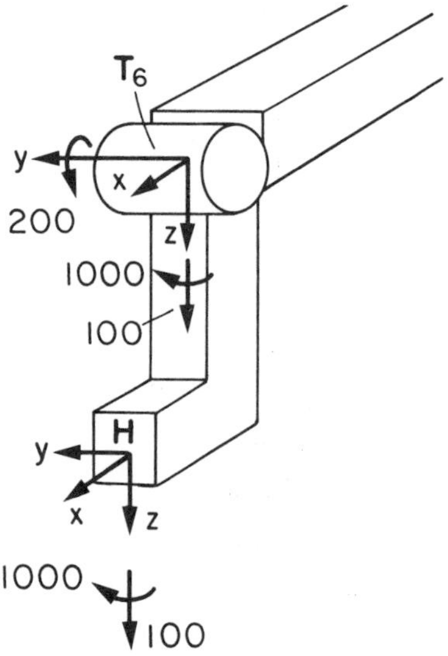

Figure 8.2. Transforming Forces Between Coordinate Frames

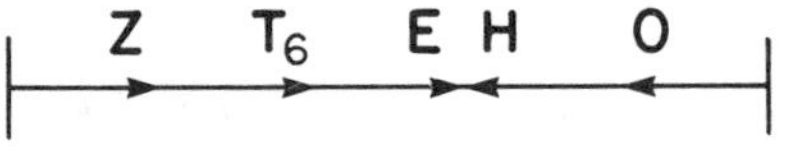

Figure 8.3. Transform Graph for Example 8.2

The end effector is described by

$$E = \begin{bmatrix} 1 & 0 & 0 & 2 \\ 0 & 1 & 0 & 0 \\ 0 & 0 & 1 & 10 \\ 0 & 0 & 0 & 1 \end{bmatrix}$$

The manipulator is to exert a force of $\mathbf{f} = 0\mathbf{i} + 0\mathbf{j} + 100\mathbf{k}$ and moment of $\mathbf{m} = 0\mathbf{i} + 0\mathbf{j} + 1000\mathbf{k}$ in hole coordinates H. What is the equivalent force and moment in frame T_6?

Solution:

From the transform graph shown in Figure 8.3 we obtain the differential coordinate transformation as E^{-1}

$$E^{-1} = \begin{bmatrix} 1 & 0 & 0 & -2 \\ 0 & 1 & 0 & 0 \\ 0 & 0 & 1 & -10 \\ 0 & 0 & 0 & 1 \end{bmatrix}$$

$\mathbf{p}$ is then $-2\mathbf{i} + 0\mathbf{j} - 10\mathbf{k}$ and

$$\mathbf{f} \times \mathbf{p} = \begin{vmatrix} \mathbf{i} & \mathbf{j} & \mathbf{k} \\ 0 & 0 & 100 \\ -2 & 0 & -10 \end{vmatrix}$$
$$= 0\mathbf{i} - 200\mathbf{j} + 0\mathbf{k}$$
$$\mathbf{f} \times \mathbf{p} + \mathbf{m} = 0\mathbf{i} - 200\mathbf{j} + 1000\mathbf{k}$$

and finally from Equations 8.15 and 8.16 we obtain

$$^{T_6}\mathbf{m} = 0\mathbf{i} - 200\mathbf{j} + 1000\mathbf{k}$$
$$^{T_6}\mathbf{f} = 0\mathbf{i} + 0\mathbf{j} + 100\mathbf{k}$$

or

$$^{T_6}\mathbf{F} = [0 \quad 0 \quad 100 \quad 0 \quad -200 \quad 1000]^{\mathrm{T}}$$

8.4 Forces, Moments, and Equivalent Joint Torques

We now have the capability to transform forces and moments between coordinate frames. In this section we will solve the problem of relating forces and moments applied in coordinate frame T_6 to equivalent joint torques and forces. We will again use the method of virtual work, equating the virtual work performed by a force and moment applied in coordinate frame T_6 to the virtual work performed at the joints [Whitney72] [Shimano]. That is

$$\delta W = {}^{T_6}\mathbf{F}^{\mathrm{T}}\, {}^{T_6}\mathbf{D} = \tau^{\mathrm{T}}\, \mathbf{Q} \tag{8.17}$$

where τ is a column vector of generalized joint forces, of torques in the case of revolute joints, and of forces in the case of prismatic joints. $\mathbf{Q}$ is a column vector of virtual joint displacements, with rotations $\delta\theta$ in the case of revolute joints, and translations δd in the case of prismatic joints. Thus, for the Stanford manipulator, the virtual work performed by virtual joint motions is given by

$$\delta W = [T_1 \quad T_2 \quad F_3 \quad T_4 \quad T_5 \quad T_6] \begin{bmatrix} \delta\theta_1 \\ \delta\theta_2 \\ \delta d_3 \\ \delta\theta_4 \\ \delta\theta_5 \\ \delta\theta_6 \end{bmatrix} \tag{8.18}$$

where T_i is the joint torque and F_3 is the force acting at prismatic joint 3. Returning to Equation 8.17, if the manipulator is in equilibrium then the virtual work performed is zero and

$$^{T_6}\mathbf{F}^{\mathrm{T}}\ ^{T_6}\mathbf{D} = \tau^{\mathrm{T}}\mathbf{Q} \tag{8.19}$$

Substituting from Equation 4.66 for ^{T_6}D we obtain

$$^{T_6}\mathbf{F}^{\mathrm{T}}\,\mathbf{J}\,\mathbf{Q} = \tau^{\mathrm{T}}\mathbf{Q} \tag{8.20}$$

This equation is independent of the virtual displacement **Q** and thus

$$^{T_6}\mathbf{F}^{\mathrm{T}}\,\mathbf{J} = \tau^{\mathrm{T}}$$

or

$$\tau = \mathbf{J}^{\mathrm{T}}\ ^{T_6}\mathbf{F} \tag{8.21}$$

which is an important relationship. That is, given an applied force and moment in frame T_6, Equation 8.21 gives us the torques and forces which must be applied at the manipulator joints in order to maintain equilibrium. If the manipulator is also free to move in the direction of the applied force and moment, then the joint torques and forces specified by Equation 8.21 will result in the application of the specified force and moment. Notice further that Equation 8.21 holds for a manipulator of any number of degrees of freedom.

Example 8.3

The Stanford manipulator is in the state given in Example 4.4

$$\mathrm{T}_6 = \begin{bmatrix} 0 & 1 & 0 & 20 \\ 1 & 0 & 0 & 6.0 \\ 0 & 0 & -1 & 0 \\ 0 & 0 & 0 & 1 \end{bmatrix}$$

which corresponds to the following joint coordinates whose sines and cosines are given in Table 8.1

Table 8.1 Manipulator State

Coordinate	Value	Sine	Cosine
θ_1	0°	0	1
θ_2	90°	1	0
d_3	20in.		
θ_4	0°	0	1
θ_5	90°	1	0
θ_6	90°	1	0

The Jacobian is given by

$$\frac{\partial T_6}{\partial q_i} = \begin{bmatrix} 20.0 & 0.0 & 0.0 & 0.0 & 0.0 & 0.0 \\ -6.0 & 0.0 & 1.0 & 0.0 & 0.0 & 0.0 \\ 0.0 & 20.0 & 0.0 & 0.0 & 0.0 & 0.0 \\ 0.0 & 1.0 & 0.0 & 0.0 & 1.0 & 0.0 \\ 0.0 & 0.0 & 0.0 & 1.0 & 0.0 & 0.0 \\ -1.0 & 0.0 & 0.0 & 0.0 & 0.0 & 1.0 \end{bmatrix}$$

Compute the joint torques and forces necessary to exert the force and moment obtained in Example 8.2.

$${}^{T_6}\mathrm{F} = [0 \quad 0 \quad 100 \quad 0 \quad -200 \quad 1000]^{\mathrm{T}}$$

Solution:
The joint torques are then given by Equation 8.21

$$\begin{bmatrix} T_1 \\ T_2 \\ F_3 \\ T_4 \\ T_5 \\ T_6 \end{bmatrix} = \begin{bmatrix} 20 & -6 & 0 & 0 & 0 & -1 \\ 0 & 0 & 20 & 1 & 0 & 0 \\ 0 & 1 & 0 & 0 & 0 & 0 \\ 0 & 0 & 0 & 0 & 1 & 0 \\ 0 & 0 & 0 & 1 & 0 & 0 \\ 0 & 0 & 0 & 0 & 0 & 1 \end{bmatrix} \begin{bmatrix} 0 \\ 0 \\ 100 \\ 0 \\ -200 \\ 1000 \end{bmatrix}$$

$$\begin{bmatrix} T_1 \\ T_2 \\ F_3 \\ T_4 \\ T_5 \\ T_6 \end{bmatrix} = \begin{bmatrix} -1000 \\ 2000 \\ 0 \\ -200 \\ 0 \\ 1000 \end{bmatrix}$$

8.5 Mass Determination of Load by Joint Torques

If the manipulator is to move an unknown load, we proceed as follows. We assume the worst case load and set the velocity gains high to prevent an under-damped response, then command the manipulator to move so as to lift the load at constant velocity. As soon as all joints are in motion the error torques and forces are given by Equation 7.20. These error torques may then be related to the load mass as follows [Paul72]. Assume that the manipulator is positioned with respect to base coordinates by a transform **Z** and that the unknown load is held at its center of mass by an end effector described by ${}^{T_6}\mathrm{E}$. The position of the load is

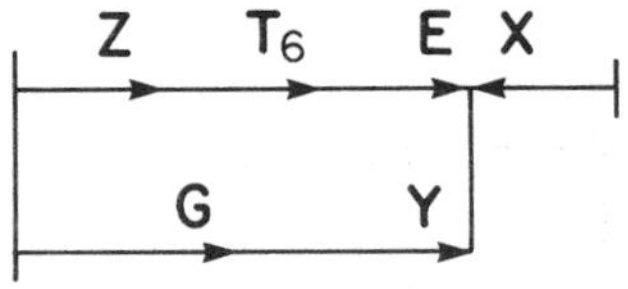

Figure 8.4. Mass Determination by Means of Joint Torques Transform Graph

then given by **X** as

$$\mathbf{X} = \mathbf{Z}\,\mathbf{T}_6\,\mathbf{E} \tag{8.22}$$

A 1 kg. load located at the end effector will exert a force

$$^{G}\mathrm{F} = [0 \quad 0 \quad -g \quad 0 \quad 0 \quad 0] \tag{8.23}$$

in a coordinate frame **G** where

$$\mathbf{G} = \begin{bmatrix} 1 & 0 & 0 & ^{X}p_x \\ 0 & 1 & 0 & ^{X}p_y \\ 0 & 0 & 1 & ^{X}p_z \\ 0 & 0 & 0 & 1 \end{bmatrix} \tag{8.24}$$

The frame **G** is thus aligned with the base coordinate frame but located at the center of mass of the load. We further define a transformation **Y** which relates **G** to **X** by

$$\mathbf{G}\,\mathbf{Y} = \mathbf{X} \tag{8.25}$$

as shown in Figure 8.4.
Y is then given by

$$\mathbf{Y} = \mathbf{G}^{-1}\mathbf{X}$$

$$\mathbf{Y} = \begin{bmatrix} ^{X}\mathbf{n}_x & ^{X}\mathbf{o}_x & ^{X}\mathbf{a}_x & 0 \\ ^{X}\mathbf{n}_y & ^{X}\mathbf{o}_y & ^{X}\mathbf{a}_y & 0 \\ ^{X}\mathbf{n}_z & ^{X}\mathbf{o}_z & ^{X}\mathbf{a}_z & 0 \\ 0 & 0 & 0 & 1 \end{bmatrix} \tag{8.26}$$

The differential transformation which relates $^{G}\mathrm{F}$ to $^{T_6}\mathrm{F}$ is similarly obtained from Figure 8.4 as YE^{-1}. The force at T_6 for a 1 kg. load is thus obtained from Equations 8.15 and 8.16 using YE^{-1} as the differential coordinate transformation. The equivalent joint torques τ are then obtained from Equation 8.21. The mass m can be obtained by an inner product between τ and the error torques T, obtained from Equation 7.20, and normalized with respect to τ.

$$m = \frac{\tau^{\mathrm{T}}\mathrm{T}}{\tau^{\mathrm{T}}\tau} \tag{8.27}$$

As soon as the mass of the load is determined, the mass of link 6 is updated and the dynamics recalculated to compensate for the load mass. Notice that there is no need to stop the manipulator, as these calculations are simple to perform.

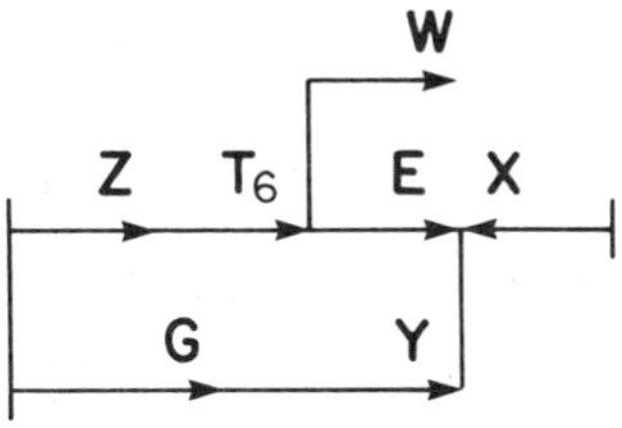

Figure 8.5. Mass Determination by Means of a Wrist Force Sensor

Example 8.4

The manipulator is positioned as in Examples 8.2 and 8.3 by

$$Z\,T_6\,E = X$$

where

$$Z = \begin{bmatrix} 0 & -1 & 0 & 20 \\ 1 & 0 & 0 & 15 \\ 0 & 0 & 1 & 15 \\ 0 & 0 & 0 & 1 \end{bmatrix} \qquad T_6 = \begin{bmatrix} 0 & 1 & 0 & 20 \\ 1 & 0 & 0 & 6 \\ 0 & 0 & -1 & 0 \\ 0 & 0 & 0 & 1 \end{bmatrix} \qquad E = \begin{bmatrix} 1 & 0 & 0 & 2 \\ 0 & 1 & 0 & 0 \\ 0 & 0 & 1 & 10 \\ 0 & 0 & 0 & 1 \end{bmatrix}$$

When a load has just been lifted, the error torques and forces at the joints are

$$\tau = [17 \quad 53 \quad 2 \quad -5 \quad 5 \quad 2]^T$$

What is the mass of the load?
Solution:

$$Y = \begin{bmatrix} -1 & 0 & 0 & 0 \\ 0 & 1 & 0 & 0 \\ 0 & 0 & -1 & 0 \\ 0 & 0 & 0 & 1 \end{bmatrix}$$

$$YE^{-1} = \begin{bmatrix} -1 & 0 & 0 & -2 \\ 0 & 1 & 0 & 0 \\ 0 & 0 & -1 & -10 \\ 0 & 0 & 0 & 1 \end{bmatrix}$$

$${}^{G}F = [0 \quad 0 \quad -9.81 \quad 0 \quad 0 \quad 0]^T$$

$$\mathbf{f} \times \mathbf{p} + \mathbf{m} = 0\mathbf{i} + 19.62\mathbf{j} + 0\mathbf{k}$$

$$^{T_6}\mathrm{F} = [0 \quad 0 \quad 9.81 \quad 0 \quad 19.62 \quad 0]^{\mathrm{T}}$$

The Jacobian transpose is given in Example 8.2 and thus τ is given by

$$\tau = \begin{bmatrix} 20 & -6 & 0 & 0 & 0 & -1 \\ 0 & 0 & 20 & 1 & 0 & 0 \\ 0 & 1 & 0 & 0 & 0 & 0 \\ 0 & 0 & 0 & 0 & 1 & 0 \\ 0 & 0 & 0 & 1 & 0 & 0 \\ 0 & 0 & 0 & 0 & 0 & 1 \end{bmatrix} \begin{bmatrix} 0 \\ 0 \\ 9.81 \\ 0 \\ 19.62 \\ 0 \end{bmatrix}$$

$$\tau = [0 \quad 196.2 \quad 0 \quad 19.62 \quad 0 \quad 0]^{\mathrm{T}}$$

and, finally, m is given by Equation 8.27 as

$$m = 0.26 \text{ kg.}$$

8.6 Mass Determination by Wrist Force Sensor

If a wrist force sensor, located with respect to T_6 by a transformation $^{T_6}\mathbf{W}$, measures all six forces and torques $^{W}\mathrm{F}$, then the mass of an unknown load can also be determined. Figure 8.5 shows the the transformation graph from which we obtain the relationship between forces in frame **G** and frame **W** by the differential transform expression $\mathrm{YE}^{-1}\mathrm{W}$. We proceed, as in the case of the mass determination, by means of the joint torques, and we find the equivalent forces in frame **W** due to a 1 kg. load $^{W}\mathbf{F}_g$. After the manipulator has lifted the unknown load, we observe the forces at the wrist force sensor $^{W}\mathbf{F}_o$ to determine the mass by the following normalized inner product

$$m = \frac{{}^{W}\mathbf{F}_g^{\mathrm{T}}\,{}^{W}\mathbf{F}_o}{{}^{W}\mathbf{F}_g^{\mathrm{T}}\,{}^{W}\mathbf{F}_g} \tag{8.28}$$

8.7 Summary

Two important results were obtained in this chapter. The transformation of forces and torques between coordinate frames where

$$\begin{aligned} {}^{C}\mathrm{m}_x &= \mathbf{n} \cdot ((\mathbf{f} \times \mathbf{p}) + \mathbf{m}) \\ {}^{C}\mathrm{m}_y &= \mathbf{o} \cdot ((\mathbf{f} \times \mathbf{p}) + \mathbf{m}) \\ {}^{C}\mathrm{m}_z &= \mathbf{a} \cdot ((\mathbf{f} \times \mathbf{p}) + \mathbf{m}) \end{aligned} \tag{8.15}$$

$$
\begin{aligned}
{}^{C}\mathbf{f}_x &= \mathbf{n} \cdot \mathbf{f} \\
{}^{C}\mathbf{f}_y &= \mathbf{o} \cdot \mathbf{f} \\
{}^{C}\mathbf{f}_z &= \mathbf{a} \cdot \mathbf{f}
\end{aligned}
\tag{8.16}
$$

where once again **n**, **o**, **a**. and **p** are the columns of the differential coordinate transformation.It was shown that moments transform in the same manner as differential translations and that forces transform in the same manner as differential rotations.

The second important result related forces and torques in T_6 coordinates to manipulator joint torques

$$
\tau = \mathbf{J}^{\mathrm{T}}\, {}^{T_6}\mathbf{F} \tag{8.21}
$$

8.8 References

Paul, R. P. Modeling, Trajectory Calculation and Servoing of a Computer Controlled Arm, Stanford Artificial Intelligence Laboratory, Stanford University, AIM 177, 1972.

Shimano, B. E. The Kinematic Design and Force Control of Computer Controlled Manipulators, Stanford Artificial Intelligence Laboratory, Stanford University, AIM 313, 1978.

Whitney, D. E. "The Mathematics of Coordinated Control of Prosthetic Arms and Manipulators," *Trans. ASME, Journal of Dynamic Systems, Measurement, and Control* (Dec. 1972), 303–309.

CHAPTER 9

COMPLIANCE

9.1 Introduction

In this chapter we will consider the problem of interaction between objects and the manipulator. We have so far considered only the manipulator moving in free space. We must now examine the interface problem of acquiring objects and placing them on or into other objects [Bolles] [Goto72] [Inoue] [Mason] [Paul76] [Salisbury] [Shimano] [Whitney76]. Goertz summarizes the problem well: "The general-purpose manipulator may be used for moving objects, moving levers or knobs, assembling parts, and manipulating wrenches. In all these operations the manipulator must come into physical contact with the object before the desired force and moment can be made on it. A collision occurs when the manipulator makes this contact. General-purpose manipulation consists essentially of a series of collisions with unwanted forces, the application of wanted forces, and the application of desired motions. The collision forces should be low, and any other unwanted forces should also be small." [Goertz]

Let us first define a coordinate frame in which to describe the motion and forces of interaction, and then consider the problem of detecting contact or collisions. We will then consider a more active role for the manipulator, in which it exerts forces or torques and complies with external constraints. As there is much information to be gained during the above interactions, a method of recording the positional information will be developed. We will conclude the chapter with some subproblems related to assembly.

9.2 Compliant Motion Coordinate Frame

In order to describe interface problems which occur when the manipulator is acquiring objects or mating them, we need to describe motions and forces. We will thus require some coordinate frame in which to specify forces and motions. Whitney was the first to recognize this need, and he developed a set of coordinates relative to the end effector [Whitney69]. These coordinates are lift, sweep, and reach, corresponding to motions along the end effector's x, y, and z axes, respectively; and turn, tilt, and twist, corresponding to small rotations about the x, y, and z axes, respectively. While these are appropriate coordinates in which to express the motion of the manipulator when acquiring objects, they are inappropriate to describe the mating of parts when one part is held by the manipulator. In this case, we need to express motion in a coordinate frame attached to the mating surface of the carried part. We also need to describe forces, and while "reach" adequately describes the movement of the manipulator in the z direction in which the end effector is pointing, it does not adequately describe a force applied in the same direction. We will therefore rely on describing motion and forces in terms of the principal axes, x, y, and z, of some coordinate frame.

Let us define this coordinate frame. In the case of an unloaded manipulator, it is the end effector coordinate frame. In the case of a manipulator carrying an object, it is some coordinate frame attached to the object in such a manner as to simplify the description of the task. In Chapter 5, Section 5.5, we defined a transformation expression TOOL such that every manipulator position could be described in the form

$$\mathrm{T_6\ TOOL = COORD\ POS} \tag{9.1}$$

It is in the $\mathrm{T_6}$ TOOL coordinate frame that we will specify all compliance, motions of accommodation, forces, etc. Reviewing the pin insertion task described in Chapter 5, we see that the TOOL is defined first as

```
TOOL:=E;
```

and then, when the pin has been picked up, as

```
TOOL  :=  E  -  PG
```

In the first case, motions are naturally expressed in terms of the end effector coordinate frame as in [Whitney]. After the pin is picked up, we express any compliances in terms of the coordinate frame located at the tip of the pin $\mathrm{E\ PG^{-1}}$

9.3 Stopping on Force

We will first consider the case of a planned collision with the environment, which we call stopping on force. Consider the following simple pick and place task. An object is located at PICK and is to be moved to PLACE via an approach position DP which is defined relative to the object. The object is to be grasped at GRIP, which is defined with respect to the object. The manipulator approaches the object via a position APP. The manipulator is defined in terms of a calibration transformation Z and end effector E. The program might be

```
TOOL := E;                  Attach tool
COORD := -Z + PICK;         Coord wrt object
MOVE APP;                   Approach
MOVE GRIP;                  Move to grasping position
GRASP;
TOOL := E - GRIP;           Tool now object
MOVE DP;                    Departure position for object
COORD := -Z + PLACE;        Coord wrt place position
MOVE DP;                    Approach place position
MOVE ORG;                   Move to origin of coord frame
RELEASE;
TOOL := E;                  Move now wrt end effector
MOVE APP;                   and depart
```

A major problem occurs in this program at the MOVE ORG statement. When this statement has been executed, the manipulator is holding the object at the place where it is to be released. As we expect that the object is to be supported at this position, we will be in of one two states: either the object is above the supporting surface and is currently not supported, so that if released it will drop; or the object has already been pushed into the surface, or is currently being pushed into the surface as the manipulator attempts to move to the specified position. If the object is released in this latter state, the energy of deformation will probably cause the object to move when released. Similarly, in the former state, if the object is dropped, it will also move as it falls. Clearly, the object cannot be dropped if we hope to have any control over its final position. Neither can we limit the deformation energy by controlling the position tolerance, as a decrease in position tolerance is normally accompanied by an increase in positional stiffness. Furthermore, the position of the support surface may be only approximately known. The solution to this problem is to define the termination of the MOVE ORG statement, not by a positional constraint, but by a force constraint. We do this by defining a termination clause UNTIL <condition> such that the motion will be made to and through the position indicated until some terminating condition is met, at which time a zero acceleration time transition will occur to the next path segment. These termination conditions will be specified in the tool coordinate frame. In the example we have been considering, the tool coordinate is the coordinate frame located in the object. Let us assume that the z axis of this frame is pointing up in the vertical direction and that the object weighs 1kg. We may then specify a stopping condition of a force of 10n. in the $-z$ direction. That is, the manipulator should stop the current path segment when it is exerting a force in addition to any gravity compensation of 10n. in the downward or $-z$ direction. The program statement becomes

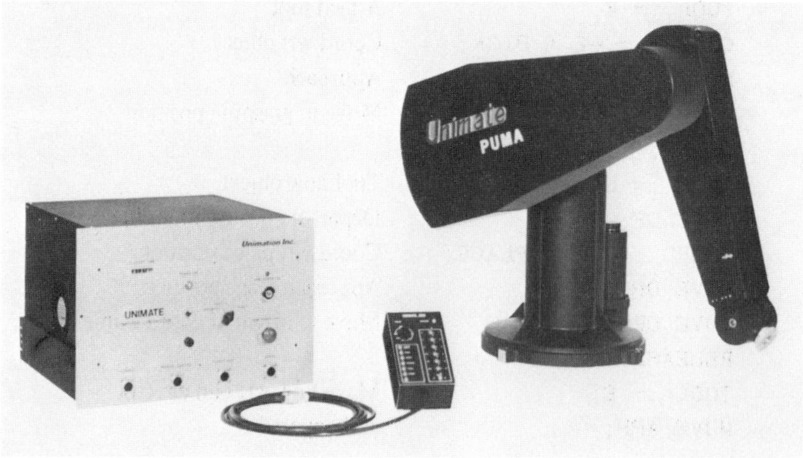

Figure 9.1. The Unimate PUMA Robot (Courtesy of Unimation Inc.)

```
MOVE ORG
UNTIL FORCE ( Z<=-10);
```

This clause is implemented in much the same manner as the mass of an unknown object is determined. The stopping force or torque is transformed into frame T_6 employing the methods outlined in Section 8.3, and the equivalent joint torques are then determined, using the methods described in Section 8.4. In the case we are considering, the differential coordinate transformation is **GRIP E**$^{-1}$, which is the inverse of the current TOOL transform expression. The transpose of the Jacobian for the current position is used to find the equivalent joint torques. Armed with this information, the error joint torques (see Equation 7.20) are compared to the equivalent stopping torque while the motion to ORG is being executed. The motion terminates when the following condition is met

$$\frac{\tau^{T}\mathrm{T}}{\tau^{T}\tau} > 1 \tag{9.2}$$

where T is the column matrix representing the error torques and τ is the column matrix representing the stopping torque. An equivalent condition can, of course, also be specified for a wrist sensor.

9.4 Exerting Forces

In this section we will consider a very similar problem, that of causing the manipulator to exert forces on some object. If the end effector is set rigidly, so that it is impossible for it to move, then it is possible to exert any force or torque. In order to exert a given force, we calculate the reaction forces at the manipulator joints and then drive the joints at those torques. While these are the necessary reaction torques to be applied at the joints, the specified force will only be exerted if the manipulator is potentially capable of motion in the direction of the exerted force. This can be determined by evaluating the determinant of the Jacobian; if it is zero, the manipulator is degenerate and motion is impossible along or around some axis. The reaction torques to be exerted at the joints are simply determined by first transforming the specified force and torque from the tool coordinate frame to T_6 (using the inverse of the TOOL transform expression as the differential coordinate transformation) and then into the joint torques. These torques plus the gravity loading torques are then exerted at the joints in place of the torques calculated by the position feedback servo loop.

The situation of the end effector of the manipulator being set rigidly is, of course, rare. Usually the manipulator is free to move in some directions but constrained to move in others. In this case, it is important to align the axes of the tool coordinate frame with the directions of free and constrained motion. The end effector of the manipulator has only six degrees of freedom, three of them translational, and three rotational. For each of the six degrees of freedom we may specify either a force or a position. In order to ensure that our specifications are consistent, we will specify them along or about the axes of the tool coordinate frame; checking for consistency then becomes a simple problem.

Let us look at some examples of partially constrained motion. Sliding an object over a surface has five unconstrained degrees of freedom as motion is constrained in the direction normal to the surface. We will assume that the object does not constrain the end effector orientation. In this case, one of the axes of the tool coordinate frame should be in the direction of the surface normal. Another example is the task of inserting a pin into a hole. Here, the pin is free to translate along, and rotate about, the hole axis. Assuming that the pin does not constrain the end effector orientation, this task has four degrees of freedom, and one of the axes of the compliant coordinate frame should be aligned with the hole axis. If the pin constrains the orientation of the end effector, then the task has only two degrees of freedom, namely, translation along the hole axis and rotation about it. If the pin were a screw partially inserted, then the task would have only one degree of freedom, that of rotation about the hole axis.

Let us consider as an example of force exertion the task of sliding the object, which has been successfully located at `ORG`, along the surface to a location `SLIDE`. To do this we will need to exert a force downward along the $-z$ direction of, say, 5n. while the motion takes place. We will specify this force by a condition clause `WITH <condition>` as follows

```
WITH FORCE ( Z=-5)
MOVE SLIDE
```

How is this to be performed? We can certainly calculate the equivalent joint torques τ to exert the force, and these joint torques and forces should be added to any gravity compensating forces while the motion is being made. However, as we are using a position servo, the addition of these forces will cause only a slight offset in end effector position; no force will be actively exerted. There have been many approaches to solving this problem but we will present only one, perhaps the simplest.

We will match one manipulator joint to each specified force or torque to provide for the necessary compliance [Inoue71] [Paul72] [Shimano]. These joints will then be torque-servoed instead of position-servoed. In order to match the joints to the forces or torques, we first determine the equivalent joint torques necessary to exert the force, τ_i. We must also make sure that the selected joints will provide for motion in the specified direction. For example, the Stanford manipulator with the axis of joint six aligned with the vertical axis will react to any torque exerted about this axis. Joint one will react equally, as its axis is also aligned with the vertical axis. To exert a torque about the vertical axis requires that the manipulator be able to rotate about this axis, a motion which can be made by joint six in this case, but not by joint one. Thus we must also examine the possibility of motion in the compliant direction. We employ the inverse Jacobian (Section 4.7) to calculate the differential change in joint coordinates, dq_i, for a unit motion in the direction specified for the force or moment to be exerted. For each joint of the manipulator we will then calculate the virtual work necessary to make a unit motion by each joint

$$W_i = dq_i \tau_i \tag{9.3}$$

The virtual works are then normalized with respect to the effective joint inertia to obtain a figure of merit m_i.

$$m_i = \frac{dq_i \tau_i}{J_i} \tag{9.4}$$

Notice that we are calculating six figures of merit in Equation 9.4, one for each joint. The joint which has the largest figure of merit m is then selected as the joint to provide the necessary compliance to exert the required force or torque. This joint can react to the specified force and can provide for motion in the direction of the force. During execution of the path segment for which a force is to be exerted, the selected joint is torque-servoed in place of position-servoed. The gravity torques have been augmented by the necessary torques to exert the compliant force, and a joint which has a component of motion in the specified direction has been selected to be free to move. Thus the manipulator will indeed exert the specified force. As the manipulator moves, its kinematic configuration changes; the matching of joints to degrees of freedom must be reevaluated periodically and the joint torques recalculated.

Example 9.1

Let us look at the compliant move to `SLIDE`. The force is 5n. in the $-z$ direction of the object. We will assume that the manipulator is positioned as in Example 8.3 with

$$\mathrm{T}_6 = \begin{bmatrix} 0 & 1 & 0 & 20 \\ 1 & 0 & 0 & 6.0 \\ 0 & 0 & -1 & 0 \\ 0 & 0 & 0 & 1 \end{bmatrix}$$

and the Jacobian is

$$\frac{\partial \mathrm{T}_6}{\partial q_i} = \begin{bmatrix} 20.0 & 0.0 & 0.0 & 0.0 & 0.0 & 0.0 \\ -6.0 & 0.0 & 1.0 & 0.0 & 0.0 & 0.0 \\ 0.0 & 20.0 & 0.0 & 0.0 & 0.0 & 0.0 \\ 0.0 & 1.0 & 0.0 & 0.0 & 1.0 & 0.0 \\ 0.0 & 0.0 & 0.0 & 1.0 & 0.0 & 0.0 \\ -1.0 & 0.0 & 0.0 & 0.0 & 0.0 & 1.0 \end{bmatrix}$$

The equivalent force in frame T_6 is

$$^{T_6}\mathrm{F} = [0 \quad 0 \quad 5 \quad 0 \quad 0 \quad 0]$$

and the equivalent joint torques are

$$\tau = [0 \quad 100 \quad 0 \quad 0 \quad 0 \quad 0]$$

indicating, as we would expect, that joint two is to exert the downward force. These equivalent joint torques are then added to the gravity loading torques. The differential change in joint coordinates for a unit change in the z direction is

$$dq = [0 \quad 0.02 \quad 0 \quad 0 \quad -0.02 \quad 0]$$

and the figures of merit given by Equation 9.4, using an effective inertia of 5.0 for joint 2, are

$$m = [0 \quad 0.4 \quad 0 \quad 0 \quad 0 \quad 0]$$

clearly indicating that joint two should be selected to provide the compliance in this case.

9.4.1 Complying with External Constraints

The situation frequently occurs in which we must comply with an external constraint and exert no force or moment at all. Consider the situation when inserting a pin into a hole. The manipulator is required to comply in two directions normal to the hole axis. We might write the program statement

```
WITH FORCE ( X=0, Y=0 )
MOVE IN;
```

assuming that the x and y directions of the tool coordinate frame are normal to the hole axis. We must now match two joints to the two degrees of freedom. We select one joint to match the first degree of freedom and then, from the remaining joints, match a second joint to provide for the second degree of freedom. Each additional joint selected to provide for a degree of freedom is chosen from among the remaining joints. We cannot use one joint to provide for more than one degree of freedom. We also check that we are not asked to provide for a degree of freedom twice. For example

```
WITH FORCE ( X=0, X=0 )
MOVE IN;
```

would match two joints to provide for a degree of freedom in the same direction. This checking process is very simple, as compliant forces and torques must be specified along the principal axes of only one coordinate frame. In a similar manner, if a stopping condition is included in a motion, then a force cannot also be specified in that direction. The following statements would stop the pin insertion when a resistance of 10n. was encountered in the $-z$ direction while providing compliance in the x and y directions

```
WITH FORCE ( X=0, Y=0 )
MOVE IN;
UNTIL FORCE ( Z<=-10 )
```

The following statement makes no sense

```
WITH FORCE ( X=0, Y=0 )
MOVE IN;
UNTIL FORCE ( X=10 )
```

When we attempt to match joints as outlined in this section, we run into a snag if the required force is zero, as the figure of merit m_i is then zero for all joints. In order to select a joint in this case, we must assume a unit force in the direction specified and calculate the equivalent joint torques based on the unit force or torque. We do not augment the gravity loading torques in this case.

9.4.2 Compensating for Compliant Motion

The method we have developed is correct provided none of the complying joints is actually required to move in response to the force it is exerting. If the joints are required to move, a problem exists in that joint motion is not entirely along the direction of compliant motion. For example, in moving the object to `SLIDE`, as described above, we selected joint two to provide the compliance. While this joint certainly controls motion in the specified z direction, it also causes rotations about the y axis, and translations in the x direction as the joint starts to rotate in order to comply in the z direction. These effects can be quite severe, and may cause as much unwanted motion in another direction as is provided in accordance with a specified compliance. It is important to note that these effects cannot cause the manipulator to jam. Where the unwanted motion is against a motion constraint, then this direction of motion should also have been specified as compliant, and thus some other joint will be free to move to prevent jamming. The problem occurs with the non-compliant degrees of freedom when the manipulator deviates from the specified position. In the case discussed above, compliant motion in z causes an unwanted translation in x and an unwanted rotation about y. These unwanted effects can be compensated for in the following manner. During all compliant moves, the manipulator set point equation, Equation 5.31, should be modified to include a transform **COMPLY**, representing the changes in coordinates due to accommodation to the external constraints.

$$\mathrm{T_6\,TOOL = COORD\,COMPLY\,POS} \tag{9.5}$$

As the manipulator moves, errors in joint coordinates are computed by the joint servos for position-servoed joints and also for torque-servoed joints. We would expect the errors to be small in the case of position-servoed joints, but quite large in the case of the torque-servoed joints. These joint position errors are transformed into Cartesian position errors in frame $\mathrm{T_6}$, using the Jacobian

$$\begin{bmatrix} {}^{T_6}\mathbf{d}_x \\ {}^{T_6}\mathbf{d}_y \\ {}^{T_6}\mathbf{d}_z \\ {}^{T_6}\delta_x \\ {}^{T_6}\delta_y \\ {}^{T_6}\delta_z x \end{bmatrix} = \begin{bmatrix} {}^{T_6}\mathbf{d}_{1_x} & {}^{T_6}\mathbf{d}_{2_x} & {}^{T_6}\mathbf{d}_{3_x} & {}^{T_6}\mathbf{d}_{4_x} & {}^{T_6}\mathbf{d}_{5_x} & {}^{T_6}\mathbf{d}_{6_x} \\ {}^{T_6}\mathbf{d}_{1_y} & {}^{T_6}\mathbf{d}_{2_y} & {}^{T_6}\mathbf{d}_{3_y} & {}^{T_6}\mathbf{d}_{4_y} & {}^{T_6}\mathbf{d}_{5_y} & {}^{T_6}\mathbf{d}_{6_y} \\ {}^{T_6}\mathbf{d}_{1_z} & {}^{T_6}\mathbf{d}_{2_z} & {}^{T_6}\mathbf{d}_{3_z} & {}^{T_6}\mathbf{d}_{4_z} & {}^{T_6}\mathbf{d}_{5_z} & {}^{T_6}\mathbf{d}_{6_z} \\ {}^{T_6}\delta_{1_x} & {}^{T_6}\delta_{2_x} & {}^{T_6}\delta_{3_x} & {}^{T_6}\delta_{4_x} & {}^{T_6}\delta_{5_x} & {}^{T_6}\delta_{6_x} \\ {}^{T_6}\delta_{1_y} & {}^{T_6}\delta_{2_y} & {}^{T_6}\delta_{3_y} & {}^{T_6}\delta_{4_y} & {}^{T_6}\delta_{5_y} & {}^{T_6}\delta_{6_y} \\ {}^{T_6}\delta_{1_z} & {}^{T_6}\delta_{2_z} & {}^{T_6}\delta_{3_z} & {}^{T_6}\delta_{4_z} & {}^{T_6}\delta_{5_z} & {}^{T_6}\delta_{6_z} \end{bmatrix} \begin{bmatrix} dq_1 \\ dq_2 \\ dq_3 \\ dq_4 \\ dq_5 \\ dq_6 \end{bmatrix} \tag{9.6}$$

The differential translation and rotation vectors ${}^{T_6}\mathbf{d}$ and ${}^{T_6}\delta$ are then transformed into the constraint coordinate frame using the inverse of the TOOL transformation expression to obtain ${}^{TOOL}\mathbf{d}$ and ${}^{TOOL}\delta$. Elements of these two vectors which do not correspond to compliant directions of translation or rotation are set to zero. They represent the unwanted motion coupled into the non-complying directions of motion due to the non-orthogonality of the joint axes and the compliant coordinate frame. The modified differential translation and rotation vectors are transformed into the **COMPLY** coordinate frame by $\mathbf{POS}^{-1}$ and are then used to construct a differential change transformation $^{COMPLY}\Delta$ (see Section 4.3) to modify **COMPLY** as follows

$$\text{COMPLY} \leftarrow \text{COMPLY}(\text{I} + {}^{COMPLY}\Delta) \tag{9.7}$$

This has the effect of changing the effective **COORD** transformation along the compliant directions, but not along the position-controlled directions. The next time that the joint coordinates are obtained using the solution

$$\text{J}_D = \text{solve}(\text{COORD COMPLY POS TOOL}^{-1}) \tag{9.8}$$

the undesired components of motion will be eliminated. In the example we have been discussing, where joint two provides a compliance in the z direction, the unwanted motion in x and y, caused by the rotation of joint two, will be eliminated the next time a solution is obtained.

9.5 Updating the World Model

The **COMPLY** transform is also used during a stop-on-force termination clause. If a motion segment is terminated by an `UNTIL FORCE` clause, the **COMPLY** transform is modified to cause the motion to extend a distance specified in the `UNTIL` clause. When the motion stops, the **COMPLY** transform is again modified to account for the position in which the manipulator actually stopped. In the example we were considering, the placement of the block

```
MOVE ORG
UNTIL FORCE ( Z<=-10);
```

We will now change the statement to include the distance modifier

```
MOVE ORG
UNTIL FORCE ( Z<=-10) DISTANCE=0.5;
```

This has the effect of changing **COMPLY** to cause an additional motion of magnitude `DISTANCE` in the direction of the specified stopping force or torque. When the motion stops due to the force limit, **COMPLY** is changed in the direction of the stopping force to reflect the current position of the manipulator. Furthermore, unless the manipulator stops within the specified distance, the control program will assume an error has occurred.

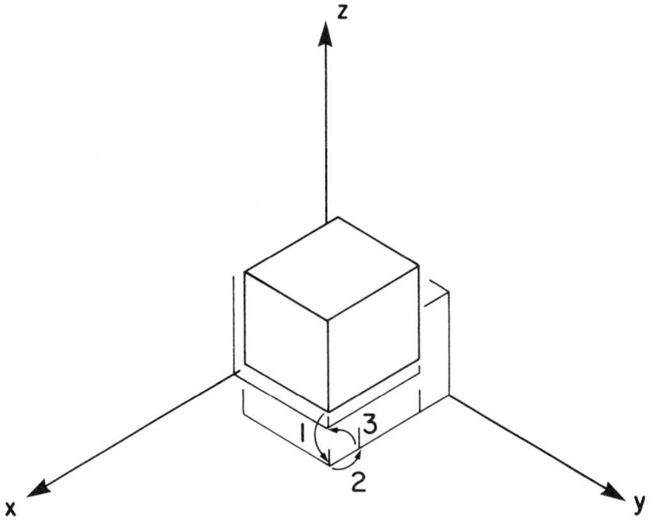

Figure 9.2. Block in a Corner Task

The **COMPLY** transform is not changed between path segments but accumulates motions of accommodation. This is made use of in the following program. This program segment locates a block into a corner by first placing it on the horizontal xy plane, then sliding it towards the xz plane, and finally moving it into the corner by sliding it along the xz and xy planes simultaneously (see Figure 9.1). The **COMPLY** transform accounts for the displacements from planned positions, first the z component, then the y component, and finally the x component.

```
TOOL ::= E - BLOCK;                   end effector holding block
COORD ::= BOX;                        corner of box
MOVE CORNERXY
    UNTIL (FORCE Z<=-10)
    DISTANCE=0.5;                     set block down
WITH (FORCE Z=-10)
    MOVE CORNERX
        UNTIL (FORCE Y<=-10)
        DISTANCE=0.5;                 move against x face
WITH (FORCE Y=-10, Z=-10)
    MOVE CORNER
        UNTIL (FORCE X<=-10)
        DISTANCE=0.5;                 and into corner
```

While it is useful to have the **COMPLY** transform keeping track of all the motions of accommodation, these changes need to be transferred to some other coordinate transformation and **COMPLY** reset to an identity transform. This is done whenever a new COORD is specified or by the use of the UPDATE statement which resets **COMPLY** to an identity transformation. However, UPDATE can also have as an argument any one of the transforms in the most recent manipulator position equation, with the exception of T_6. This has the effect of transforming the differential changes represented by **COMPLY** into the coordinate frame specified and then changing that transform differentially. In other words, the manipulator position equation is solved for the specified transform in terms of the current position, allowing only those changes specified by compliances in previous move statements. The block in the corner program segment might then terminate with an UPDATE BOX; statement

```
TOOL ::= E - BLOCK;                     end effector holding block
COORD ::= BOX;                          corner of box
MOVE CORNERXY
    UNTIL (FORCE Z<=-10)
    DISTANCE=0.5;                       set block down
WITH (FORCE Z=-10)
    MOVE CORNERX
        UNTIL (FORCE Y<=-10)
        DISTANCE=0.5;                   move against x face
WITH (FORCE Y=-10, Z=-10)
    MOVE CORNER
        UNTIL (FORCE X<=-10)
        DISTANCE=0.5;                   and into corner
UPDATE BOX;                             save the position of the box
```

This is very useful as any future MOVE CORNER; statement would return the manipulator with the block into the exact corner position we went to such lengths to find. The transform **BOX** has been updated to account for the exact position of the corner.

9.6 Motion Until Free

Another terminating condition of a trajectory path segment occurs when a constrained coordinate becomes free. Consider the task of pulling a pin out of a hole. While the pin is in the hole, it is constrained in both rotation about and translation along axes normal to the hole axis. As the pin moves out of the hole, it becomes totally unconstrained, and a transition to a new path segment should occur in which the pin is position-controlled in all six degrees of freedom. Such a transition can be observed by providing a small force preload in some constrained direction and then monitoring the change in position along that coordinate, dx, dy, dz, or monitoring the change in rotation, rx, ry, rz. For example

```
WITH FORCE ( X=10, Y=0 )
WITH TORQUE ( X=0, Y=0 )
   MOVE OUT
      UNTIL ( DX>=0.1 ) DISTANCE=0.2;
UPDATE;
```

9.6.1 Wobble

In some types of assembly no feedback is obtainable. Consider the case of mounting a ball bearing on a shaft. The shaft is of reduced diameter up to the point at which the ball bearing is to be mounted. At this point the diameter is increased in a step manner to a sliding fit with the ball bearing. The ball bearing is assembled by sliding it along the shaft, complying as necessary, until it runs into the step in the shaft. At this time it stops, and there is no feedback available to indicate in which direction to move the bearing in order to move it over the step. We now add a perturbing sinusoidal motion in x, y, and z of some specified excursion to the end effector while the manipulator is commanded to move forward. When the random perturbation of the end effector causes the ball bearing and the step in the shaft to line up, then forward motion occurs and the assembly progresses. Thus we might write

```
WITH FORCE ( X=0, Y=0 )
WITH WOBBLE (0.1)
   MOVE ALONG;
```

9.7 Summary

In this chapter we have introduced the concept of compliance in assembly. We have shown that many motions are properly terminated by force conditions and that, in all cases, the information obtained during interactions with the environment should be saved and used in updating the structural task model.

9.8 References

Bolles, R. & Paul, R. P. The Use of Sensory Feedback in a Programmable Assembly System, The Stanford Artificial Intelligence Laboratory, Stanford University, AIM-220, Oct. 1973.

Goertz, R. C. "Manipulators Used for Handling Radioactive Materials," *Human Factors in Technology* , Chapter 27, edited by E. M. Bennett, McGraw-Hill, 1963.

Goto, T., Takeyasu, K., Inoyama, T., et al. "Compact Packaging by Robot with Tactile Sense," *Proc. 2nd. International Symposium on Industrial Robots*, May 1972, 149–159.

Inoue, H. "Computer Controlled Bilateral Manipulator," *Bulletin of the Japanese Society of Mechanical Engineers* **14**, 69 (1971), 199–207.

Inoue, H. Force Feedback in Precise Assembly Tasks, Massachusetts Institute of Technology, Artificial Intelligence Laboratory Report, TR-308, Aug 1974.

Mason, M. T. Compliance and Force Control for Computer Controlled Manipulation, Massachusetts Institute of Technology, Artificial Intelligence Laboratory Report, TR-515, April 1979.

Paul, R. P. Modeling, Trajectory Calculation and Servoing of a Computer Controlled Arm, Stanford Artificial Intelligence Laboratory, Stanford University, AIM 177, 1972.

Paul, R. P., & Shimano, B. E. "Compliance and Control," *The 1976 Joint Automatic Control Conference*, 1976, 694–699.

Salisbury, K. J. "Active Stiffness Control of a Manipulator in Cartesian Coordinates," *19th. IEEE Conference on Decision and Control*, Dec. 1980.

Shimano, B. E. The Kinematic Design and Force Control of Computer Controlled Manipulators, Stanford Artificial Intelligence Laboratory, Stanford University, AIM 313, 1978.

Whitney, D. E. "Resolved Motion Rate Control of Manipulators and Human Prostheses," *IEEE Trans. on Man-Machine Systems* **MMS-10** (1969), 47–53.

Whitney, D. E. "Force Feedback Control of Manipulator Fine Motions," *The 1976 Joint Automatic Control Conference*, 1976, 694–699.

CHAPTER 10

PROGRAMMING

10.1 Introduction

In this final chapter we will try to bring together all that we have learned in the previous chapters by developing a robot manipulator programming system. Robot manipulator programming systems and languages have historically been standalone systems, concentrating on manipulator control and tending to ignore data manipulation. One of the first manipulator programming languages, WAVE [Paul72] [Paul77a], and its later high level language version, AL [Finkel], were overwhelmed by the vast amount of computation related to manipulator control, and therefore employed a planning phase, during which the program was simulated and all the necessary computations stored in modifiable form in an execution file. This led to enormous complications when the execution varied significantly from the planned execution, or when branching was involved, necessitating the simulation of all possible branches. The VAL system, and a Cartesian motion system developed at SRI International, eliminated the need to simulate the entire program first, and interpreted the program on a line-by-line basis. All of these systems were based on standalone languages, involving scanners, parsers, symbol tables, etc. In this chapter we will take a different approach, and describe how to embed the necessary data structures and motion primitives into a general purpose, high level computer language. We will make use of the PASCAL language here, but many other languages would serve as well. It is assumed that the reader is familiar with the PASCAL language, and if she or he is not, then one of the excellent references [Jensen] should be read before proceeding further in this chapter.

We will first describe data structures to define transformations and transform expressions. We will then show how our data representation can be used to solve the transform equations. Motion primitives will then be introduced which correspond to joint motion, Cartesian motion, and a new form of functional motion. Program execution will be considered in terms of a co-processor structure: one processor for the program and one for the manipulator. A synchronization structure will be developed to coordinate the two processors. These processors may, of course, be implemented in one physical processor or in a multi-processor configuration. While the program appearance is a little clumsy, as it will be implemented in terms of dynamic data structures and procedure calls, this approach reveals the essential structure of the problem and will provide the input to those wishing to develop new languages or to modify the syntax of existing languages to incorporate manipulation in a more elegant manner.

10.2 Declarations and Data Structures

We will begin this section by describing two new data types: vectors and transforms. A vector presents no real challenge and is represented simply as

```
type vector = record x,y,z:real end;
```

A transform is then defined as four vectors

```
type transform = record n,o,a,p:vector end;
```

If we declare two transforms by

```
var T1,T2:transform;
```

then the following are valid assignment statements:

```
T1:= T2;
T1.n:= T2.a;
with T2 do
    T1.n.x:= o.y * a.z - o.z * a.y;
```

Transforms also have inverses, which we will store in another record and link together

```
type transpointer = ↑transform;
    transform = record n,o,a,p:vector;
        inverse: transpointer;
        valid: boolean;
        inversep: boolean
end;
```

The field `inverse` is a pointer to another record of type transform. In the case where the transform or its inverse is changed, the inverse of the modified transform is marked invalid by setting `valid false`. Finally, a field `inversep` informs the lost-in-a-data-structure user if the transform she or he has found is a defined transform or its inverse. For the case of a defining transform, and not an inverse, we will wish to store some additional information if the transform is defined by a function

```
type transform = record n,o,a,p:vector;
    inverse: transpointer;
    valid: boolean;
    case inversep: boolean of
        false: (fn: functionname);
        true: ( )
end;{transform}
```

The scalar type `functionname` is a list of all transform functions. For each function included in `functionname` a function must be declared. These functions are called with only one argument, a pointer to the functionally defined transform. If additional arguments are necessary, they must be passed as global variables. For example, the drive function $D(r)$ defined in Equation 5.69, which provides for straight line motion between points, might be defined in terms of global variables `rx, ry, rz, rtheta, rphi,` and `psi` as

```
function drive ( ptr:transpointer);
  var sinrtheta,cosrtheta,verrtheta:real
    sinpsi,cospsi,sinrphi,cosrphi:real;
  begin{drive}
    sinrtheta:=sin(rtheta);
    cosrtheta:=cos(rtheta);
    verrtheta:=1 - cosrtheta;
    sinpsi:=sin(psi); cospsi:=cos(psi);
    sinrphi:=sin(rphi); cosrphi:= cos(rphi);
    with ptr↑do begin
      with p  do begin
        x:=rx; y:=ry; z:=rz end ;
      with a  do begin
        x:=cospsi * sinrtheta;
        y:=sinpsi * sinrtheta;
        z:=cosrtheta end ;
      with o  do begin
        x:=-sinrphi * (sqr(sinpsi) + cosrtheta)
          -cosrphi * (sinpsi * cospsi * verrtheta);

          etc.

      cross(n,o,a) end ;
  end ;{drive}
```

This function is associated with a scalar value dfn and is called by the following function

```
procedure evalfn ( p:transpointer )
  begin {evalfn}     case p↑.fn of
    none: begin
      error("undefined transform");
      halt
    end ;
    dfn: drive(p);
    conv: conveyorfn(p);
    rotatez: rotatez(p);
      etc.
    end ;
  end ;{evalfn}
```

In order to access a transform, we will define a function evaltrans as follows

```
procedure evaltran ( tptr:transpointer )
  var ptr: transpointer;
  begin
    if not tptr↑.valid{if valid all done}
    then begin
      if tptr↑.inversep
      then begin {we have the inverse}
        ptr:= tptr↑.inverse;
        if ptr↑.valid{is the inverse valid?}
        then begin
          invert(tptr,ptr);{then just invert it}
          tptr↑.valid:=true
        end
        else begin
          evalfn(ptr);{inverse functionally defined}
          invert(tptr,ptr)
        end end
      else evalfn(tptr){transform functionally defined}
    end
  end ;{evaltran}
```

10.2.1 Transform Equation Data Structure

We are now ready to represent the transform equations defining a manipulator task. We will do this in two stages. Initially, we will represent the left hand side of an equation, then the right hand side, and finally we will link them together to represent the equation. We will represent each term of a transform equation by a term record which links the transform into the equation.

```
type termpointer = ↑term;
  term = record
    nxt,inv:termpointer;
    trans:transpointer
  end;{term}
```

The first (right most) element of either the left or right hand side of the equation is formed by the function atom

```
function atom (t:transpointer):termpointer;
  var tptr,invptr:termpointer;
  begin {atom}
    new(tptr); new(invptr);
    with tptr↑do begin
      nxt:=NIL; inv:=invptr; trans:=t end ;
    with invptr↑do begin
      inv:=tptr; trans:=t↑.inverse end ;
    atom:=tptr
  end ;{atom}
```

Additional elements of the equation (reading right to left) are added to the front of the data structure by the function cons

```
function cons (t:transpointer; l:termpointer):termpointer;
  var tptr,invptr:termpointer;
  begin {cons}
    new(tptr); new(invptr);
    with tptr↑do begin
      inv:=invptr; trans:=t;
      nxt:=l end ;
    with invptr↑do begin
      inv:=tptr; trans:=t↑.inverse end ;
    l↑.inv↑.nxt:=invptr;
    cons:=tptr
  end ;{cons}
```

In order to construct the data structure corresponding to p1 of the task described in Section 5.3

$$\texttt{p1}: Z\,T_6\,E = P\,PA$$

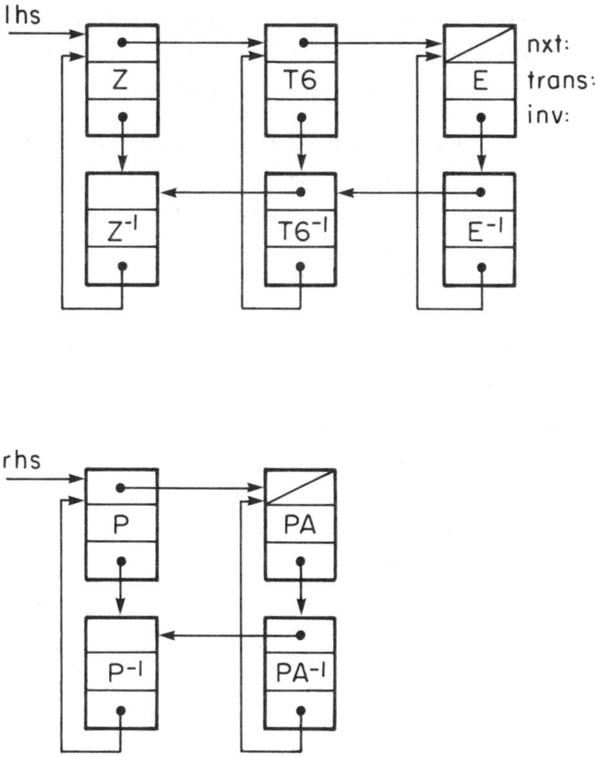

Figure 10.1. Transform Equation Data Structure

we would first define a series of functions which could be used to create data structure lists corresponding to equations which contain $2, 3, \ldots, n$ transformations: `list2, list3,..., listn`, respectively. For example

```
function list3 (a,b,c:transpointer):termpointer;
  begin {list3}
    list3:=cons(a,cons(b,atom(c)))
  end ;{list3}
```

and then execute the following calls

```
var z,t6,e,p,pa:transpointer;
  lhs,rhs:termpointer;

lhs:=list3(z,t6,e);
rhs:=list2(p,pa);
```

The resulting data structure is shown in Figure 10.1.

The full transform equation is represented by forming two circular data structures to represent the closed link chain in both directions (see Figure 10.2). This is accomplished by a position function `makeposition`, which returns a position record. This record points to the equation data structure in terms of T_6, and to the right hand most transform of TOOL (see Equation 5.31). Information relating to the manipulator configuration might also be stored in this record, thus defining `position` as follows

```
type positionpointer = ↑position;
  position = record
    t6ptr,tolptr:termpointer;
    righty,flip:boolean
  end
```

```
function makeposition (lhs,rhs:termpointer;
    tcp:transpointer; right,fl:boolean):positionpointer;
  var p:positionpointer;
    p1,p2:termpointer;
  begin {makeposition}
    lhs↑.inv↑.nxt:=rhs;{link the heads together}
    rhs↑.inv↑.nxt:=lhs;
    p1:=lhs;{find the end of the lhs and rhs}
    while p1↑.nxt <> NIL do p1:=p1↑.nxt;
    p2:=rhs;
    while p2↑.nxt <> NIL do p2:=p2↑.nxt;
    p1↑.nxt:=p2↑.inv;{link the ends together}
    p2↑.nxt:=p1↑.inv;
    p1:=lhs;{find t6}
    while p1↑.trans <> t6 do p1:=p1↑.nxt;
    p2:=rhs;{find tcp}
    while (p2↑.nxt↑.trans <> tcp)
      and (p2↑.nxt↑.inv↑.trans <> tcp) do p2:=p2↑.nxt;
    new(p);{create header}
    with p↑do begin
      t6ptr:=p1;
      tolptr:=p2;
      righty:=right; flip:=fl end;
    makeposition:=p
  end;{makeposition}
```

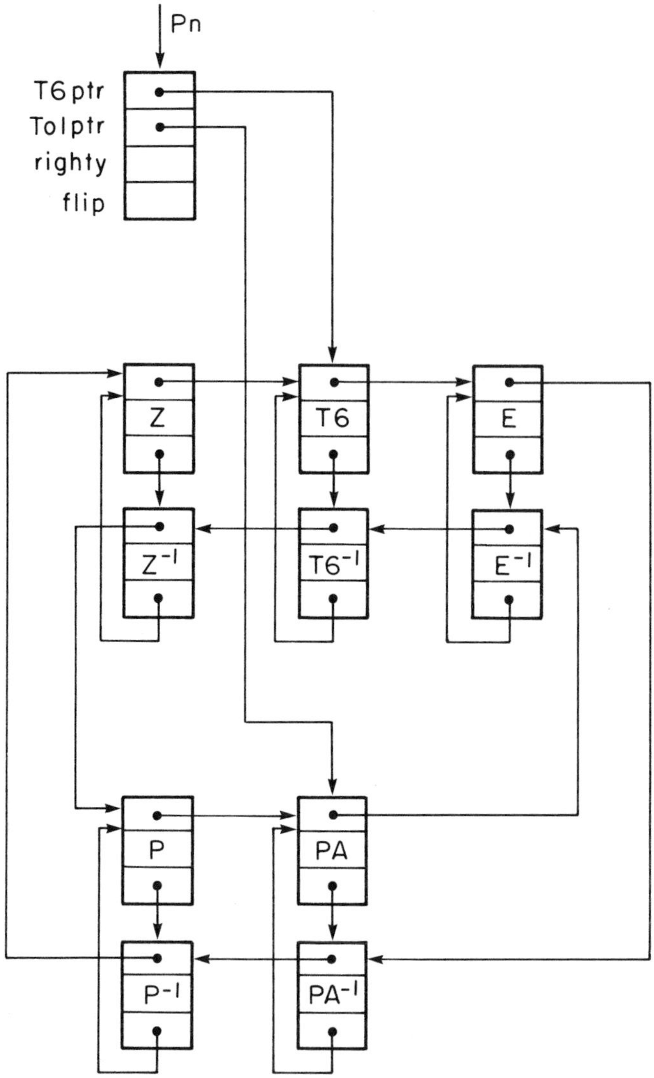

Figure 10.2. Complete Transform Equation Data Structure

10.2.2 Solving Transform Data Structure Equations

We have two uses for the transform equation data structure we have defined. One is to solve for T_6, and the other is to obtain the differential coordinate transformation expressions. In each case, we will return the result in an array of transform pointers together with a value indicating the number of pointers in the array

```
type solvelist = array [1..n] of transpointer;
  ntrans = [0..n];
```

We will first define a procedure `solvet6` to obtain the solution for T_6.

```
procedure solvet6 (var sl:solvelist; var n:ntrans;
  pp:positionpointer);
  var p:termpointer;
  begin {solvet6}
    p:=pp↑.t6ptr↑.inv↑.nxt;{the tail of t6}
    n:=0;
    while p↑.inv↑.trans <> t6 do begin
      n:=n + 1
      sl[n]:=p↑.trans;
      p:=p↑.nxt end
  end ;{solvet6}
```

For example, the solution for T_6, given the transform equation represented in Figure 10.2, is

```
solvet6(sl,n,p1);
```

and would result in

```
n=4
sl[1]=-z
sl[2]=p
sl[3]=pa
sl[4]=-e
```

10.2.3 Obtaining the Differential Coordinate Transform Expression

We will now define a procedure which uses the transform data structure in order to obtain the differential coordinate transformation. The differential coordinate transformation expression defined in Chapter 4 corresponds to the transform expression needed to relate differential changes between coordinate frames. It is found by tracing the path from the head of the transform in which the change occurred to the head of the transform in which the equivalent change is required (see Section 4.5). There are always two equivalent solutions for the differential coordinate transformation. We obtain one by traversing the transform graph from the transform in which the change occurred to the transform in which the change is desired, from left to right. We obtain the other transform expression by traversing the transform graph from right to left. The procedure which we will define first obtains the forward path and then the backward path, returning whichever path is the shorter.

```
procedure solvediff (var sl:solvelist; var n:ntrans;
  f,t:transpointer; pp:positionpointer);
  {the result is returned in sl and its length in n
  the differential relationship desired is from f to t
  in equation pp}
  var sb,sf:solvelist;{the backward and forward solns}
    nb,nf:ntrans;{the length of the solutions}
    p,pf,pb:termpointer;
    last:transpointer;
  begin{solvediff}
    p:=pp↑.t6ptr;{find t6 in equation}
    {find from}
    while (p↑.trans↑<> f)
      and (p↑.inv↑.trans↑<> f) do p:=p↑.nxt;
    {set up forward and backward search pointers}
    if p↑.trans = f
      then begin pf:=p↑.nxt; pb:=p↑.inv end
      else begin pf:=p↑.inv↑.nxt; pb:=p end;
    {find the forward solution}
    nf:=0; last:=f;
    while (pf↑.inv↑.trans↑<> t) and (last <> t) do begin
      nf:=nf + 1;
      last:=pf↑.trans;
      sf[nf]:=last;
      pf:=pf↑.nxt end;
    {now find the backsolution}
    nb:=0; last:=f;
    while (pb↑.inv↑.trans↑<> t) and (last <> t)
      and nb < nf do begin
      nb:=nb + 1;
      last:=pb↑.trans↑;
      sb[nb]:=last;
      pb:=pb↑.nxt end;
    {now return shortest result}
    if nf <= nb
      then begin sl:=sf; n:=nf end
      else begin sl:=sb; n:=nb end
  end;{solvediff}
```

For example, in the transform equation represented in Figure 10.2

```
solvediff(sl,n,t6,p,p1);
```

would return

```
n=2
sl[1]=e
sl[2]=-pa
```

10.3 Embedding Manipulator Motion into PASCAL

We are now in a position to define all of the manipulator positions in a task and to solve the resulting transform equations for all the information necessary to execute the task. How is this to be done? We will define a motion procedure `move` with two arguments: a position equation and a mode record. The position equation describes the next position to which the manipulator is to be moved (C in Chapter 5). The mode record describes how the manipulator is to be moved and is defined partially as follows

```
type modepointer=↑mode;
  mode = record
  typeofmotion:(joint,cartesian);
    {joint motion or Cartesian}
  tacc,tsegment:integer;
    {acceleration time and segment time}
  mass:real;{mass of load}
  end ;
```

Times are specified in milliseconds. The procedure `move` is aware of the minimum possible acceleration and segment times and will use these if smaller times are specified. Thus times of 0 inform `move` to compute the times.

Let us define the positions and modes for the task we described in Chapter 5

```
p1:=makeposition(list3(z,t6,e),
    list3(conv,p,pa),e,true,true);
with m1↑do begin{set up mode}
  typeofmotion:=joint;
  tacc:=0; tsegment:= 0; mass:=0 end ;
p2:=makeposition(list3(z,t6,e),
    list3(conv,p,pg),e,true,true);
m2↑:=m1↑; with m2↑do typeofmotion:=cartesian;
```

```
p3:=makeposition(list3(z,t6,e),
   list4(conv,p,pd,pg),pg,true,true);
m3↑:=m2↑; with m3↑do begin
  tsegment:=500; mass:=10 end;
p4:=makeposition(list3(z,t6,e),
   list4(h,ht,pha,pg),pg,true,false);
m4↑:=m3↑; with m4↑do begin
  typeofmotion:=joint; tsegment:=0 end;
{notice that during this joint move, flip changes}
p5:=makeposition(list3(z,t6,e),
   list4(h,ht,pch,pg),pg,true,false);
m5↑:=m4↑; with m5↑do begin
  typeofmotion:=cartesian; tsegment:=1000 end;
p6:=makeposition(list3(z,t6,e),
   list4(h,ht,pac,pg),pg,true,false);
m6↑:=m5↑; with m6↑do tsegment:=0;
p7:=makeposition(list3(z,t6,e),
   list3(h,ht,pn),pg,true,false);
m7↑:=m6↑; with m7↑do tsegment:=500;
p8:=makeposition(list3(z,t6,e),
   list4(h,ht,pn,pa),e,true,false);
m8↑:=m2↑{an unloaded move}
```

The program then becomes:

```
for i:=1,2 do begin
  read(camera, pc);{Read in position of pin}
  matrixmultiply(p,cam,pc);{Set p}
  move(p1,m1);{approach pin}
  move(p2,m2);{over pin}
  close;
  move(p3,m3);{departure position}
  ht↑:=hr[i]↑;{Temp position of hole}
  move(p4,m4);{Hole approach}
  move(p5,m5);{Contact hole}
  move(p6,m6);{Stand up}
  move(p7,m7);{Insert pin}
  open(10);
  move(p8,m8){Depart from pin}
end
```

10.4 Software Organization

The procedure `move` communicates with another process which, driven by a real time interrupt, actually runs the manipulator. The `move` procedure simply passes to the interrupt process two pointers defining the position and mode (more will be said about the interrupt process below). If, at the time of the call, the manipulator is already in motion, then program execution waits until the segment time $t = T - t_{acc}$ (see Chapter 5). At this time, **A** and **B** are evaluated and the transition to the new position commences without the manipulator stopping. Program execution then continues. If the manipulator reaches the transition point without the program entering a move wait state, then the manipulator is brought to rest at the position currently represented by **C**. Note that the manipulator always has the ability to stop in t_{acc}, which is the time remaining in the current segment. The manipulator is brought to rest by repeating **C** as the next set point and transitioning to it.

Sometimes it is necessary to bring the manipulator to rest, as is the case at positions `p2` and `p7`, when the object is grasped and released. This is accomplished by a procedure `movewait`, which holds program execution until the manipulator is brought to rest at its current final position. Thus our program should be changed to read

```
for i:=1,2 do begin
  read(camera, pc);{Read in position of pin}
  matrixmultiply(p,cam,pc);{Set p}
  move(p1,m1);{approach pin}
  move(p2,m2);{over pin}
  movewait;
  close;
  move(p3,m3);{departure position}
  ht↑:=hr[i]↑;{Temp position of hole}
  move(p4,m4);{Hole approach}
  move(p5,m5);{Contact hole}
  move(p6,m6);{Stand up}
  move(p7,m7);{Insert pin}
  movewait;
  open(10);
  move(p8,m8){Depart from pin}
end
```

The camera and end effector are also asynchronous processes and we will define some procedures by which to communicate requests for image processing

```
camerafindpin;
{scan for a pin and record conveyor position}
```

and for the communication of results

```
readcamera(p:transpointer; conveyorposition:integer);
   {set the transform pointed to by transpointer equal
    to the image transformation at the time the
    image was processed.
    set conveyorposition to the position of the
    conveyor when the image was processed}
```

If no image has been found then `readcamera` will hold program execution until a valid image is processed. Finally, we define the next procedure to hold program execution while the end effector is operating

```
operatewait;
   {wait until end effector operation finishes}
```

Armed with these new procedures, we can rewrite the program in terms of three processes: the manipulator process, the end effector process, and the camera process

```
camerafindpin;{find first pin};
for i:=1,2 do begin
  ht↑:=hr[i]↑;{Temp position of hole}
  readcamera(pc,sc);{wait here until pin found}
  matrixmultiply(p,cam,pc);{Set p}
  move(p1,m1);{approach pin}
  move(p2,m2);{over pin}
  movewait;
  close;
  operatewait;{wait until grasped}
  move(p3,m3);{departure position}
  move(p4,m4);{Hole approach}
  camerafindpin;{start looking for next pin}
  move(p5,m5);{Contact hole}
  move(p6,m6);{Stand up}
  move(p7,m7);{Insert pin}
  movewait;
  open(10);{no need to wait here}
  move(p8,m8){Depart from pin}
end
```

10.5 Specifying Compliance

We will specify the compliance of the manipulator in terms of a servo mode for each of the six Cartesian coordinates. The servo mode is itself a record, which is defined as follows

```
type servomode = record
  case servo: (position,force,stopforce,goforce) of
  position: (tolerance:real);
    {the position tolerance if the manipulator
    is to stop}
  force: (value:real);
    {the force to be exerted in a compliance mode}
  stopforce: (limit,distance:real);
    {monitor the force along this axis and change to
    a force command when the force condition is met
    terminate the current motion when this condition
    is met or distance is exceeded}
  goforce: (value,limit,distance:real)
    {exert this force until position error in this
    direction exceeds limit or the motion exceeds
    distance, then change to a position servo mode.
    Terminate the current motion when this condition
    is met}
end ;{servomode}
```

The manipulator process is aware of the minimum values of tolerance, force, stopping force, and goforce displacement. If these are specified as zero, then the minimum values are employed instead. Mode is redefined to be

```
type mode = record
  typeofmotion: (joint,cartesian);
  tacc,tsegment: integer;
  mass: real;{mass of load}
  dx,dy,dz,rx,ry,rz: servomode
    {dx,dy, and dz refer to translations or forces
    along the principal axes of the TOOL frame.
    rx,ry,and rz refer to rotations or torques about
    the axes}
  end ;
```

We must also specify the right hand most transform in **COORD** so that the compliance transform **COMPLY** may be included in the data structure. This is done by modifying the `position` record and function `makeposition` to include an additional argument `comptr`, a pointer to the right hand most transform of COORD (see Section 9.4.2) The modification is

```
type positionpointer = ↑position;
  position = record
    t6ptr,tolptr,comptr:termpointer;
    righty,flip:boolean
  end
```

```
function makeposition (lhs,rhs:termpointer;
   tcp,comptr:transpointer; right,fl:boolean):
   positionpointer;
```

The modified data structure is shown in Figure 10.3. The task modes of our example will be redefined as

```
p1:=makeposition(list3(z,t6,e),
   list3(conv,p,pa),e,p,true,true);

        etc.

with m1↑do begin {set up mode}
  typeofmotion:=joint;
  tacc:=0; tsegment:= 0; mass:=0;
  with dx do begin servo:=position; tolerance:=0 end ;
  with dy do begin servo:=position; tolerance:=0 end ;
  with dz do begin servo:=position; tolerance:=0 end ;
  with rx do begin servo:=position; tolerance:=0 end ;
  with ry do begin servo:=position; tolerance:=0 end ;
  with rz do begin servo:=position; tolerance:=0 end ;
end ;
m2↑:=m1↑; with m2↑do typeofmotion:=cartesian;
m3↑:=m2↑; with m3↑do begin
  tsegment:=500; mass:=10 end ;
m4↑:=m3↑; with m4↑do  begin
  typeofmotion:=joint; tsegment:=0 end ;
m5↑:=m4↑; with m5↑do begin
  typeofmotion:=cartesian; tsegment:=1000;
  with dx do begin servo:=stopforce; limit:=10;
    distance:=5 end ;
end ;
```

```
m6↑:=m5↑; with m6↑do begin
  tsegment:=0;
  with dx do begin servo:=force; value:=10 end ;
  with dy do begin servo:=force; value:=0 end ;
  with dz do begin servo:=force; value:=2 end
end ;
m7↑:=m6↑; with m7↑do begin
  tsegment:=500;
  with dx do begin servo:=force; value:=0 end ;
  with dz do begin servo:=stopforce; limit:=50;
    distance:= 5 end ;
  with rx do begin servo:=force; value:=0 end ;
  with ry do begin servo:=force; value:=0 end
end ;
m8↑:=m2↑{an unloaded move}
```

In order to provide for updating the world model (see Section 9.5), we add two additional fields to the mode record: a boolean indicating that an update is to occur at the end of the current motion, and a pointer to the transform which is to be changed. The appropriate differential coordinate transformation expression is obtained from the current position data structure by procedure **solvediff**.

```
type mode = record
  typeofmotion:(joint,cartesian);
  tacc,tsegment:integer;
  mass:real;{mass of load}
  dx,dy,dz,rx,ry,rz:servomode;
  update:boolean;{update at end of motion?}
  utrans:transpointer{which transform}
end ;{mode}
```

We will change m1 and m7 as follows

```
with m1↑do begin {set up mode}
  typeofmotion:=joint;
  tacc:=0; tsegment:= 0; mass:=0;
  with dx do begin servo:=position; tolerance:=0 end ;
  with dy do begin servo:=position; tolerance:=0 end ;
  with dz do begin servo:=position; tolerance:=0 end ;
  with rx do begin servo:=position; tolerance:=0 end ;
  with ry do begin servo:=position; tolerance:=0 end ;
  with rz do begin servo:=position; tolerance:=0 end ;
  update:=false; utrans:=NIL end ;
```

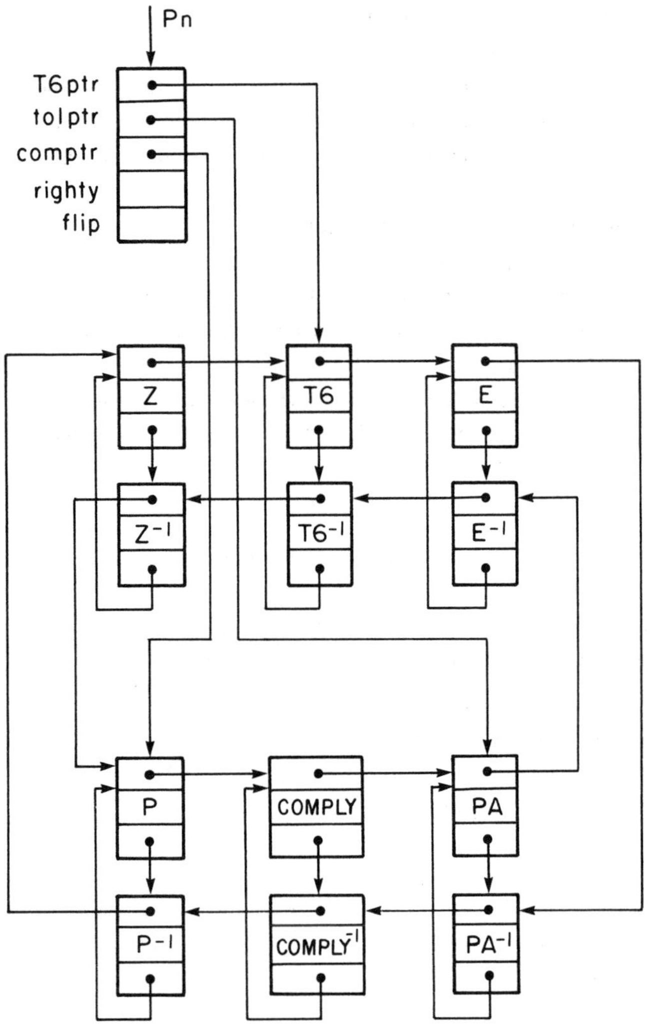

Figure 10.3. Data Structure Modified to Include **COMPLY**

```
    etc.

m7↑:=m6↑; with m7↑do begin
  tsegment:=500;
  with dx do begin servo:=force; value:=0 end ;
  with dz do begin servo:=stopforce; limit:=50;
    distance:= 5 end ;
  with rx do begin servo:=force; value:=0 end ;
  with ry do begin servo:=force; value:=0 end ;
  update:=true; utrans:=h
end ;
```

And the program becomes

```
camerafindpin;{find first pin};
for i:=1,2 do begin
  ht↑:=hr[i]↑;{Temp position of hole}

    etc.

  move(p7,m7);{Insert pin and update h}
  movewait;
  open(10);{no need to wait here}
  move(p8,m8){Depart from pin}
end
```

10.6 The Move Process

The move process is interrupt driven at joint servo sample rate: when running in Cartesian mode, the process is required to solve the current position transform equation for T_6, obtain the joint coordinates, and servo the manipulator every sample period. This amount of computation is beyond the capabilities of most computers; generally a set point is evaluated only every nth. sample period and intermediate values are obtained by linear interpolation. This affects the response time of the manipulator to changes in the set point, but in many applications this does not present a problem. At interrupt level, then, we will assume that joint coordinates are obtained by interpolation, the current state of the manipulator observed, and a servo calculation performed in order to drive the manipulator. Joints selected for compliance are driven at the required torque level. Any stop-force condition is also monitored in case the motion is to be terminated.

Every nth. sample period, the set point must be recalculated by evaluating the transform equation and obtaining the joint coordinates. As this process will probably take more than one sample period to perform, the processor interrupt priority is lowered to allow for the continuation of the servo process while the next set point is obtained. In other words, this process will be interrupted again before it completes itself. After lowering the processor priority, an interlock is set in case the set point is not obtained before the call for the subsequent set point evaluation is made. In this case the manipulator must be stopped, as the data used to obtain intermediate set points by interpolation is no longer valid. After a set point has been obtained, the interlock is cleared and the data is made available to the joint interpolator when needed. After the interpolator takes the data, work on obtaining the next set point commences.

As the manipulator moves, its configuration changes, and a number of other computations must be made. The effective joint inertias, the gravity loads, and the velocity feedback gain must be calculated. If the manipulator is in a complying mode, then joints must also be matched to degrees of freedom, and the joint torques which correspond to the specified Cartesian forces must be calculated. These computations are made after a solution has been obtained. Before the interrupt process dismisses, it checks the change in manipulator configuration. If the configuration has changed sufficiently to warrant recomputing the dynamics and compliances, then the processor priority is once again lowered, the set point interlock cleared, and a dynamics interlock set. The dynamics and compliance calculations are then performed. When they are completed, the state of the manipulator is updated, and the interrupt dismissed.

As the dynamics and compliance calculations are performed at a low priority and are themselves very time consuming, considerable time can elapse from the start of a path segment until the necessary servo modes can be determined. This problem is partially solved by maintaining constant servo modes between path segments. That is, at the end of one path segment, the servo modes are maintained unchanged into the next path segment, by which time the processor will have had sufficient time to perform the necessary calculations. If it is important that the manipulator move off in the new mode immediately, it can always be stopped between segments. The only exception to this rule is in the case of `stopforce` and `goforce` modes, which are immediately changed into a force and a position mode, respectively, as soon as they have triggered.

If joint mode is specified, then the manipulator set point is evaluated once for the end of the motion and again for the end of the motion at the time estimated to reach the setpoint. In the case of a Cartesian motion, the set point is repeatedly evaluated. This is done by inserting the functionally defined transformation $\mathbf{D}(r)$ into the position transform data structure immediately to the right of the transform to which `tolptr` is pointing. The transform to which `tolptr` is pointing

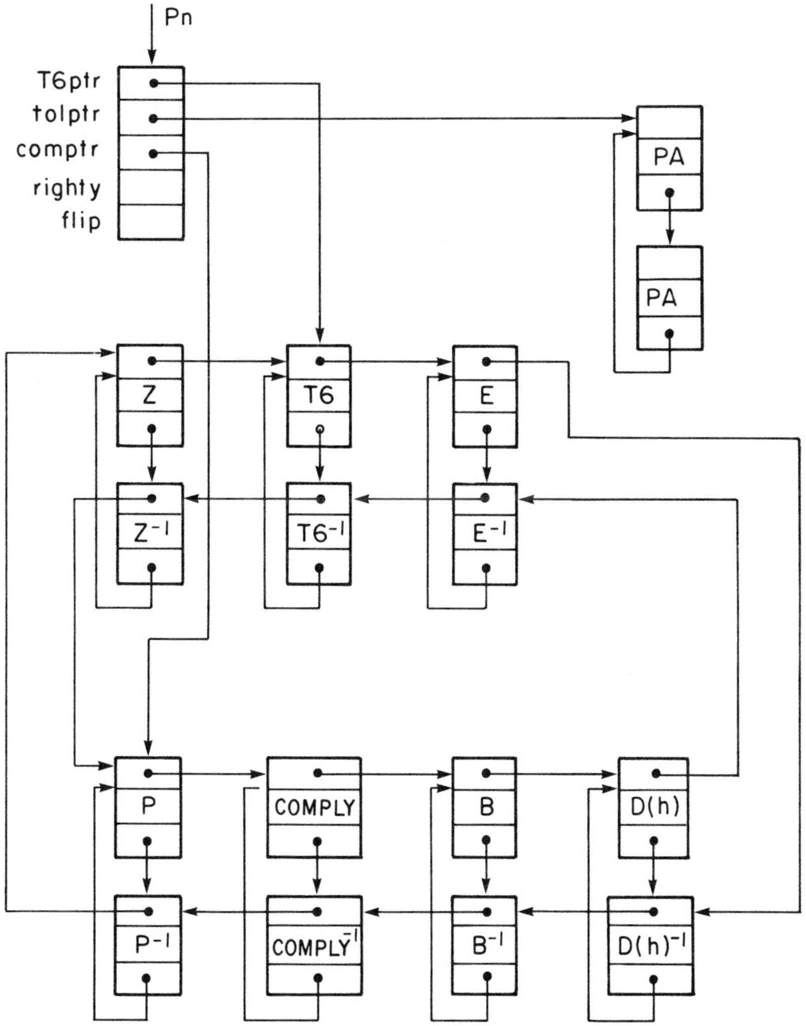

Figure 10.4. A Cartesian Move Data Structure

is replaced by **B** (see Section 5.9.2) for the duration of the move. The modified data structure is shown in Figure 10.4.

Once the move segment is completed, **D**(r) is removed, and **B** is replaced by the original transform to which `tolptr` was pointing.

Should the manipulator be stopped, either by failing to obtain a move statement before the manipulator reaches the transition point or by encountering a `movewait` statement which brings the manipulator to rest, it enters the Cartesian mode and servos to the current position. This mode transition has important properties, as we will show in the next section.

10.7 Functionally Defined Motion

Whenever it is waiting for a `move` statement, the manipulator enters the Cartesian servo mode and continues to evaluate the current transform expression set point. This feature enables us to provide functionally defined motions. For example, we might wish to describe a circle with the end effector or trace out some curve defined by a polynomial. But before we discuss functionally defined motions we first need to discuss time variables.

There are two global time variables available. One, `segmenttime`, is defined by the motion generator and is reset to $-t_{acc}$ at the beginning of a transition and continuously updated until the end of a segment is reached, at which time its value is T and remains unchanged until a new segment starts. If a normal transition occurs, then `segmenttime` does not, of course, reach T, as the transition occurs at $T - t_{acc}$. `segmenttime` is a read only variable and may not appear on the left hand side of an assignment statement. The other time variable, `time`, simply increments at a millisecond rate. It is, however, assignable, so it may be reset to zero at any time. After it is assigned it simply continues to increment at a millisecond rate.

We could make use of `segmenttime` to release an object in the middle of a motion segment. For example

```
m1↑.tsegment:=2000;
move(p1,m1);
while segmenttime < 1000 do ;
open(10);
```

We will now employ the Cartesian servo mode and the `time` variable to illustrate a functionally defined motion. Consider the crank shown in Figure 10.4. The transform equation describing the manipulator holding the crank handle is

$$\mathbf{Z\,T_6\,E = PIVOT\;ROTPZ\;CRANK\;ROTMZ\;G}$$

where **ROTPZ** is a function transform representing a positive rotation about the z axis of `theta` degrees. **ROTMZ** is another function transform, representing a negative rotation about the z axis of `theta` degrees. The following program will move the manipulator to the crank handle and then turn the crank around twice

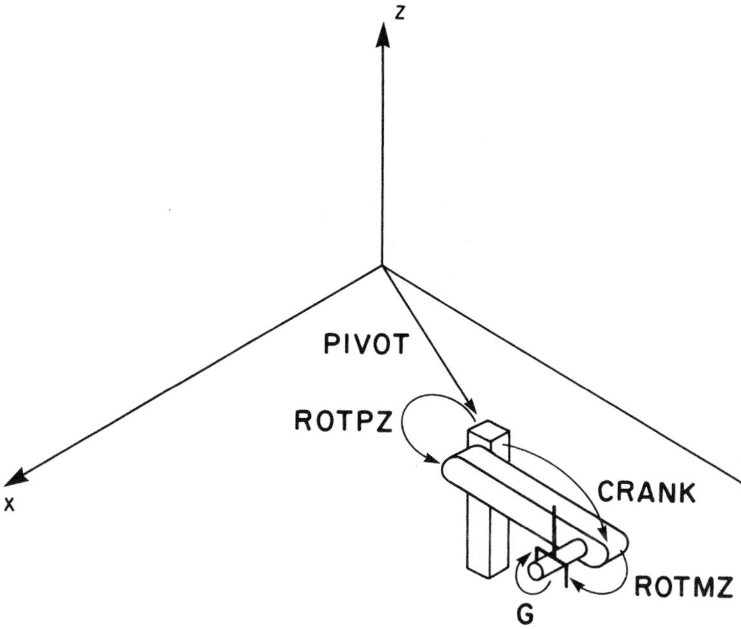

Figure 10.5. Crank Turning Example

```
p1:=makeposition(list3(z,t6,e),
  list5(pivot,rotpz,crank,rotmz,g),
  rotmz,pivot,true,true);
theta:=0;

    etc.

move(p1,m0);{move to the crank handle}
movewait;{and stay there}
close;
time:=0;
{reset time}
while time<5000 do theta:=720 * (time / 5000);
```

The manipulator moves to the crank handle and grasps it. The **while** statement takes five seconds to execute, and the manipulator remains in Cartesian servo mode, evaluating the transform equation which is functionally dependent on `theta`. This causes the crank to be rotated twice.

We have, however, ignored compliance in the above example. Let us assume that `m0` is a regular joint servo move. Examination of the `makeposition`

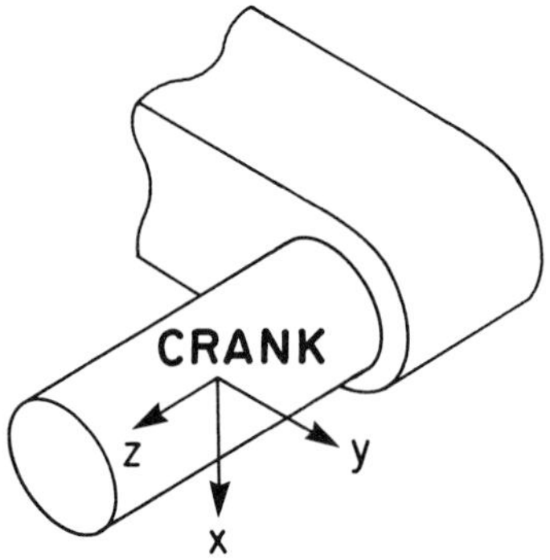

Figure 10.6. Crank Handle Coordinates

statement reveals that the TOOL is defined over the handle rotation and is thus attached to the end of the crank and moves with it. Let us assume that the y axis of the **CRANK** coordinate frame is pointing radially out from the pivot and that the z axis is along the pivot axis (see Figure 10.5). We will define a new mode record `m1` as

```
m1↑:=m0↑;  with m1↑do begin
  typeofmotion:=cartesian;
  with dy  do begin servo:=force;  value:=0  end ;
  with dz  do begin servo:=force;  value:=0  end
end
```

and then change the program to include another `move` statement whose function is to change the compliance mode

```
move(p1,m0);{move to the crank handle}
movewait;{and stay there}
close;
move(p1,m1);{change servo mode to provide compliance}
time:=0;
{reset time}
while time<5000 do theta:=720 * (time / 5000);
```

10.7.1 End Effector Integration

The end effector we have been considering is a simple parallel jaw hand with two touch sensors located on the inside of each finger tip. The opening of the hand is controlled by a variable `opening` whose value is the current hand opening.

Assigning a value to it causes the hand to be servoed to the specified value: it is the hand opening servo set point. The touch sensors are integrated into the program by means of two external boolean variables

```
left,right:boolean;
```

If either touch sensor is in contact, then the corresponding boolean variable is true.

We are now in a position to define the `open` and `close` procedures.

```
procedure open (gap:real);
  var t1:integer;{local time variable}
    intlopen:real;{initial hand opening}
  begin {open}
    t1:=time;
    intlopen:=opening;
    while opening < gap do
      opening:=intlopen + 0.004 * (time-t1)
  end ;{open}
```

which was simple. Now, for `close`

```
procedure close;
  var t1:integer;{local time variable}
    intlopen:real;{initial hand opening}
  begin {close}
    movewait;{wait for manipulator to stop}
    t1:=time;
    intlopen:=opening;
    while not (left or right) do
      opening:= intlopen - 0.001 * (time-t1);
    {now squeeze it}
    opening:= opening-0.1
  end ;{close}
```

Finally, we might define a procedure `center` which centers the end effector over an object by closing the hand until one of the touch sensors makes contact. At that time, the end effector is translated in the TOOL y direction so as to maintain, fixed in space, the finger which has made contact, while the hand continues to close. When the other finger makes contact, the object is squeezed as in `close`.

```
procedure center;
  var t1:integer;{local time variable}
    intlopen:real;{initial hand opening}
    py:real;{the initial tool.p.y value}
  begin {center}
    movewait;{wait for manipulator to stop}
    t1:=time;
    intlopen:=opening;
    while not (left or right) do
      opening:= intlopen - 0.001 * (time-t1);
    t1:=time;
    intlopen:=opening;
    py:=tool.p.y;
    if left
      then while not right do begin
        tool.p.y:= py + 0.0005 * (time-t1);
        opening:= intlopen - 0.001 * (time-t1) end
      else while not left do begin
        tool.p.y:= py - 0.0005 * (time-t1);
        opening:= intlopen - 0.001 * (time-t1) end
    opening:=opening - 0.1
  end ;{center}
```

10.8 Summary

In this final chapter we have tried to bring together in one place all the preceding material. We have done this by showing how to represent transforms and transform equations in a high level computer language. Manipulator control was then dealt with as two interacting processes. The arguments to the motion process are a data structure, representing the kinematics of the position, and a record, representing the dynamics and compliance of the required motion. The development is sketchy and is not a description of an actual system, but it is based on many systems and partial systems. One reason that a system such as we have described does not exist is that the computational requirements are very high. As computers become faster and cheaper, and with the advent of multi-microprocessor systems, such an approach will become feasible. The system we have described above integrates efficient joint motion, Cartesian motion, and functionally defined motion into a common frame of reference. Furthermore, the end effector is integrated into the manipulator system such that functions like `center` can be written directly in the language.

10.9 References

Finkel, R. et al. "An Overview of AL, A Programming Language for Automation," *Fourth International Joint Conference on Artificial Intelligence* , Tbilisi, Georgia, USSR, 1975, 758–765.

Jensen, K. & Wirth, N. *PASCAL User Manual and Report* , Springer-Verlag, 1974.

Paul, R. P. Modeling, Trajectory Calculation and Servoing of a Computer Controlled Arm, Stanford Artificial Intelligence Laboratory, Stanford University, AIM 177, 1972.

Paul, R. P. "WAVE: A Model-Based Language for Manipulator Control," *The Industrial Robot* 4, 1 (March 1977), 10–17.

INDEX

A, *see* Matrix
Abbreviations for sine and cosine, 56
Actuator gain km, 198
AL, 245
Ambiguity, quadrant, 82
Angle θ_n, the, 51
Arc tangent, 67, 82
Assembly, 4
Atan2, 67
`atom`, **function**, 249
Axis of rotation, 29

Bandwidth, 214
Boundary conditions, *see* Conditions

C_i, 56
C_{ij}, 56
`camerafindpin`, 258
Cartesian
  coordinates, 3
  servo mode, 266–267
`center`, **procedure**, 269–270
Cincinnati Milacron, 5
  T3 robot, 97
Circular data structure, 251
`close`, **procedure**, 269
Compliance, 130, 231, 268
  direction of, 4
  effects of, 130
  specifying, 259
  tool frame, 233, 235
COMPLY, 239–242, 259
Complying with external constraints, 231, 238
Conditions
  boundary, 135
  initial, 138
`cons`, **function**, 249
Contact, detecting, 231
Continuity of position, velocity, and acceleration, 134, 138
Control
  manipulators, of, 197, 270
    multiple link, 209
  position servo, 4
CONV, 130
Conveyor
  moving, 5, 130
  position, 130
  tracking, 130
    accuracy, 152
COORD, 129, 132
Coordinate frames, *see* Frames
Coordinates
  camera, 128
  Cartesian, *see* Cartesian coordinates
  moving, 5, 134, 205
  object's, 119
Co-processor, 245
Cosine relationship, 80
Crank, turning, 4, 266
Cross product, 11
Cybotech robot, 165

Cyl(z, a, r), 49–50
Cylindrical coordinates, 47

D(r), 141–142, 247, 264
${}^T\mathbf{d}$, 94–95, 117
${}^T\delta$, 94–95, 117
${}^{T_6}\mathbf{d}$, 103, 117
${}^{T_6}\delta$, 103, 117
Δ, 87–88
ΔB, 135
ΔC, 135
Δ_i, 102
${}^T\Delta$, 94, 117
${}^{T_6}\Delta$, 102
Damped
  critically, 200
  over, 202
  under, 200
Damping
  factor ς, 200
  natural, 199
  rate, *see* Velocity
  viscous, 198
Degeneracy, 69, 77, 83, 137, 139
Degrees of freedom, *see* Freedom
Denavit, J., 1
Derivative, 85
Devol, G., 2
Differential
  change graph, 98
  changes between coordinate frames, 92
  changes in position and orientation, 85
  coordinate transformation, *see* Transformation
  equivalence of rotations, 88
  motion vector **D**, 91
  relationships, 4, 85
    in transform expressions, 97
  rotation vector δ, 90
  transformation, *see* Transformation
  translation and rotation, 86
  translation vector **d**, 90
Digital servo loops, 2
Distance d_n, the, 51
Docking tasks, 131
Dot product, 11
Drive function D(h), *see* D(h)
`drive`, **function**, 247
Dynamics, 157
  equations, 4, 157, 160

Elbow manipulator, *see* Manipulator
Encoder, digital, 5
End effector, 2, 37, 268
Equations
  kinematic, 41
    solving, 65
  transformation, *see* Transformations
Equivalent
  angle of rotation, *see* Rotation
  force and moment, *see* Force
Ernst, H. A., 2
Euler(ϕ, θ, ψ), 45, 50
  solution, 65
Euler angles, 43
  equivalent, 70
`evalfn`, **procedure**, 248
`evaltran`, **procedure**, 248

${}^C\mathbf{f}$, 220
Feedback
  rate, *see* Velocity
Feedforward, 204–207
Focal
  length, 35
  point, 36

Force
centripetal, 162, 172, 210
Coriolis, 162, 172, 210
equivalent, 218
joint torque, 223–234, 236
feedback, 4
generalized F_i, 158
gravity, 162
representation of, 217
static, 217
stopping on, 232
Forces
exerting, 231, 234
reaction, 235
transformation of, 218
Frames
coordinate, 9, 19, 22, 37
defining, 10
reference, 20–21
successive, relationship between, 53
transformation, 21
Freedom, degrees of, 4
Frequency, characteristic, 200, 210, 213
Friction, Coulomb, 198
functionname, 247

Gear reduction, 198
Goertz, R. C., 1, 231
`goforce`, 264
Gravity
effects of, 158
loading, 172, 189, 204, 214

h, 135–136
Hand, 42, 268
Homogeneous coordinate transformation, *see* Transformation
Homogeneous transformation, *see* Transformation

Image distance, 36
Inertia
actuator, 168, 172
calculation of, 211
coupling, 157, 162, 172, 189
effective, 157, 161–162, 172, 264
Interlock, 264
Interpolation, 152
Interrupt
dismissed, 264
driven, 263
level, 263
`inverse`, 246
Inverse, *see* Transformation

Jacobian, 103, 234, 239
inverse, 109, 117
manipulator, 101, 117
transpose of, 234
Jamming, 239
Joint
acceleration, 206
complying, 239, 263
coordinates, 3, 41
unique value, 77
equivalent, *see* Force
error torques, 234
motion trajectories, 4
output torque, 212
rates, unbounded, 139
revolute, 51
selected for compliance, 263
servo sample rate, 263

k, components of, 31
Kinetic energy K, 158–160

Lagrangian L, 158, 160
Lagrangian mechanics, *see* Mechanics Lagrangian

Laplace transformation, 198
Language, manipulator programming, 5, 245
Left to right, 39
Length, the, 51
Lens, 35
Link
  head of the, 38
  of the graph, 38
  parameters, 55
  tail of the, 38
  zero, 50
Linkages, mechanical, 41
`termpointer`, 249
Links
  manipulator, of the, 41
  series of, 41
`list3`, **function**, 250
Look ahead, 136

M.I.T.
  Lincoln Laboratory, 2
  Radiation Laboratory, 2
Machine tools, numerically controlled, *see* Numerically controlled machine tools
`makeposition`, **function**, 251
Manipulation, robot, 9
Manipulator, 41
  base of, 50
  elbow, kinematic equations, 59
    solution of, 78
  general purpose, 1
  serial link, 50
  single link, 197
  six link, 41
  structural description, 121–122
  transform graph, 102
  two degree of freedom, 157
Mass
  determination of
    by joint torques, 225
    by wrist force sensor, 228
  distribution of, 174
  recomputation of, 180
  separation of, 174
  unknown load, calculation of, 211
Matrix
  A, 41, 53
    specification of, 50
  column, 11
  equality, 73
  identity, 13
  product, 13
    noncommutative, 18
  row, 12
  T, 41, 55
  $^{n-1}T_6$, 55
Mechanics, Lagrangian, 4, 157
  simple example of, 158
^{C}m, 220
`mode`, 255, 259, 261, 268
Moments, representation of, 217
Motion
  between positions
    Cartesian, 139, 245, 264, 270
    joint, 137, 245, 270
  compliant frame, 231
  control, 119
    in Cartesian coordinates, 119, 139
      computation necessary, 139
      disadvantages, 139
    in joint coordinates, 119, 137
  equations of, 157
  functionally defined, 139, 245, 266, 270
  until free, 242
  unwanted, 239
Motions of accommodation, 4, 85
  accumulation of, 241

Move process, 263
`move`, **procedure**. 255, 257, 268
`movewait`, **procedure**, 257

Normal
  common, 51
  distance, a_n, 50
  outward pointing, 12
N.C. machine tool, 1
N.C. milling machine, 2
Numerically controlled, *see* N.C.

Objects, 22
`open`, **procedure**, 269
`opening`, 268–269
`operatewait`, 258
Orientation, specification of, 42
Overshoot, 151

Parallel
  axes, 51
  joints, 83
PASCAL, 5, 245
  embedding manipulator motion in, 255
Perspective
  image, 35
  see Transformation
Pieper, D. L., 3
Pitch, 45
Planes, 9,12
POS, 129, 231
Position
  servo control, *see* Control, position servo
  specification of, 47
Position and orientation, 3, 22
`positionpointer`, 251
Postmultiply, 21
Potential energy P, 158–160, 168
Premultiply, 21
Prismatic joint, 51
Program, 129–131
Programming, manipulator aspects of, 5

q, 135–136
$\dot{q}$, 135–136
$\ddot{q}$, 135–136

READ, 128
`readcamera`, 258
Real time interrupt, 257
Repeatability, 203
Resonant frequency, structural, 151, 197
Restrictions on **o** and **a**, 43
Right to left, 39
Roberts, L. G., 2
Robot
  industrial, 2
    computer controlled, 5
Roll, 45
Roll, pitch, and yaw, 45
Rot($\mathbf{k}, \theta$), 28, 50
Rot(x, δ_x), 89
Rot(y, δ_y), 89
Rot(z, δ_z), 89
Rot(x, θ), 15
Rot(y, θ), 15
Rot(z, θ), 15
Rotation
  equivalent angle of, 29
  equivalent axis of,
Rotations
  about a fixed axis, 140
  combination of, 16, 34
RPY(ϕ, θ, ψ), 47, 50
  solution of, 70

SRI International, 245
S_i, 56

S_{ij}, 56
Scale, 35
factor, 10, 20
Scaling *see* Transformation
`segmenttime`, 266
Servo
force, 4
mode, 259, 266
sampled data, 211
set point, 264, 269
steady state errors, 202–203
acceleration, 206
velocity, 205
stiffness, 203
system, 2
torque, 212, 236
`servomode`, 259
Software organization, 257
Solution evaluation period, 151
`solvediff`, **procedure**, 254, 261
`solvelist`, 253
`solvet6`, **procedure**, 253
Sph(α, β, r), 50
solution of, 72
Spherical coordinates, 49
`stopforce`, 264
Straight lines, 139
Stanford
Manipulator, 29, 151–152, 201, 203–204, 212
A matrices, 57
products of, 58
dynamics of, 179
Jacobian, 103
solution to, 109
kinematic equations, 56
solution of, 73
University, 3–4
Stretching, *see* Transformation
Structural task description, *see* Task
Subscript, 10
Superscript, 10–11
Swept, space volume, 140
Synchronization, 245

dT, 86, 116
dT_6, 102
T matrix, *see* Matrix
T_6, 132
specification of, 50
τ, 224
Task description, 119
structural, 4, 119
Teleoperator, 1–2
telecheric, see teleoperator
`time`, 266
Time, t, 133
acceleration, t_{acc}, 133
segment, T_i, 133
Tool, 53
TOOL, 129, 132
Torque gain kt, 212
Torques, velocity dependent, 158
Touch
feedback, 2
sensors, 268
Track the motion, 130–131
Trajectory segments
extremum points, 151
initial and final, 139
Trajectories, 4, 135
time coordinated, 119, 136
Transformation, 3, 9, 13, 39, 245, 270
A
differential of, 86
for the Stanford manipulator, 57
deforming, 34

differential, 85
coordinate, 99, 117, 220, 234, 253
differential translation and rotation Δ, 87
directed graph, 38
traverse the, 38
equations, 37, 122
data structure, 248
expressions, 245
functionally defined, 247
general rotation, 25
identity, 25
inverse, 25
perspective, 35
plane, 13
relative, 20
rotation, 15, 39
scaling, 34
stretching, 34
T, 41
translation, 13, 39
Transition, 135
beginning of, 135
between path segments, 144
symmetry of, 135
Trigonometry, 82
Twist α_n, the, 51

Underdamped system, 200
Unimate
2100G, 71
industrial robot, 2
PUMA Arm, 234
UNTIL, 233
update, 261
UPDATE, 242
Updating the world model, 240

VAL, 245
Vectors, 9–10, 246
a, 42
infinite, 11
n, 42
name of, 10
null, 11, 19
o, 42
p, 42
unit, 19
Velocity
feedback, 199, 212, 264
of a point on a manipulator, 164
Vers, *see* Versine
Versine, 28
Virtual work, 218, 236
Vision, 128
computer, 9

Water pump, 4
WAVE, 4, 245
Whitney, D. E., 231
WITH, 235
Wobble, 243

Yaw, 45

Zero
position, 53
time transition, 233
+, 128
—, 128
·, *see* Dot product
×, *see* Cross product